UNCTAD/DITE/3(Vol. IX)

United Nations Conference on Trade and Development
Division on Investment, Technology and Enterprise Development

International Investment Instruments: A Compendium

Volume IX

United Nations
New York and Geneva, 2002

Note

UNCTAD serves as the focal point within the United Nations Secretariat for all matters related to foreign direct investment and transnational corporations. In the past, the Programme on Transnational Corporations was carried out by the United Nations Centre on Transnational Corporations (1975-1992) and the Transnational Corporations and Management Division of the United Nations Department of Economic and Social Development (1992-1993). In 1993, the Programme was transferred to the United Nations Conference on Trade and Development. UNCTAD seeks to further the understanding of the nature of transnational corporations and their contribution to development and to create an enabling environment for international investment and enterprise development. UNCTAD's work is carried out through intergovernmental deliberations, technical assistance activities, seminars, workshops and conferences.

The term "country", as used in the boxes added by the UNCTAD secretariat at the beginning of the instruments reproduced in this volume, also refers, as appropriate, to territories or areas; the designations employed and the presentation of the material do not imply the expression of any opinion whatsoever on the part of the Secretariat of the United Nations concerning the legal status of any country, territory, city or area or of its authorities, or concerning the delimitation of its frontiers or boundaries. Moreover, the country or geographical terminology used in the boxes may occasionally depart from standard United Nations practice when this is made necessary by the nomenclature used at the time of negotiation, signature, ratification or accession of a given international instrument.

To preserve the integrity of the texts of the instruments reproduced in this volume, references to the sources of the instruments that are not contained in their original text are identified as "note added by the editor".

The texts of the instruments included in this volume are reproduced as they were written in one of their original languages or as an official translation thereof. When an obvious linguistic mistake has been found, the word "sic" has been added in brackets.

The materials contained in this volume have been reprinted with special permission of the relevant institutions. For those materials under copyright protection, all rights are reserved by the copyright holders.

It should be further noted that this collection of instruments has been prepared for documentation purposes only, and its contents do not engage the responsibility of UNCTAD.

UNCTAD/DITE/3 Vol. IX

UNITED NATIONS PUBLICATION

Sales No. E.02.II.D.16

ISBN 92-1-112565-0

PREFACE

International Investment Instruments: A Compendium contains a collection of international instruments relating to foreign direct investment (FDI) and transnational corporations (TNCs). The collection is presented in nine volumes. The first three volumes were published in 1996. *Volumes IV* and *V* were published in 2000 followed by *Volume VI* in 2001. *Volumes VII, VIII and IX* bring the collection up to date. Most of the instruments reproduced in these volumes were adopted in the 1990s, the rest were adopted between 2000 and 2002.

The collection has been prepared to make the texts of international investment instruments conveniently available to interested policy-makers, scholars and business executives. The need for such a collection has increased in recent years as bilateral, regional, interregional and multilateral instruments dealing with various aspects of FDI have proliferated, and as new investment instruments are being negotiated or discussed at all levels.

While by necessity selective, the present collection seeks to provide a faithful record of the evolution and present status of intergovernmental cooperation concerning FDI and TNCs. Although the emphasis of the collection is on relatively recent documents (the majority of the instruments reproduced date from after 1990), it was deemed useful to include important older instruments as well, with a view towards providing some indications of the historical development of international concerns over FDI in the decades since the end of the Second World War.

The core of this collection consists of legally binding international instruments, mainly multilateral conventions, regional agreements, and bilateral treaties that have entered into force. In addition, a number of "soft law" documents, such as guidelines, declarations and resolutions adopted by intergovernmental bodies, have been included since these instruments also play a role in the elaboration of an international framework for FDI. In an effort to enhance the understanding of the efforts behind the elaboration of this framework, certain draft instruments that never entered into force, or texts of instruments on which the negotiations were not concluded, are also included; prototypes of bilateral investment treaties are reproduced as well. Included also are a number of influential documents prepared by business, consumer and labour organizations, as well as by other non-governmental organizations. It is clear from the foregoing that no implications concerning the legal status or the legal effect of an instrument can be drawn from its inclusion in this collection.

In view of the great diversity of the instruments in this *Compendium* -- in terms of subject matter, approach, legal form and extent of participation of States -- the simplest possible method of presentation was deemed the most appropriate. Thus, the relevant instruments are distributed among the *nine volumes of the Compendium* as follows:

- *Volume I* is devoted to multilateral instruments, that is to say, multilateral conventions as well as resolutions and other documents issued by multilateral organizations.

- *Volume II* covers interregional and regional instruments, including agreements, resolutions and other texts from regional organizations with an inclusive geographical context.

- *Volume III* is divided into three annexes covering three types of instruments that differ in their context or their origin from those included in the first two volumes:

  - Annex A reproduces investment-related provisions in free trade and regional integration agreements. The specific function and, therefore, the effect of such provisions is largely determined by the economic integration process which they are intended to promote and in the context of which they operate.

  - Annex B (the only section that departs from the chronological pattern) offers the texts of prototype bilateral treaties for the promotion and protection of foreign investments (BITs) of several developed and developing countries, as well as a list of these treaties concluded up to July 1995. The bilateral character of these treaties differentiates them from the bulk of the instruments included in this *Compendium*. Over 900 such treaties had been adopted by July 1995.

  - Annex C supplies the texts of documents prepared by non-governmental organizations; these give an indication of the broader environment in which the instruments collected here are prepared.

- *Volume IV*, divided into two parts, covers additional multilateral (Part One) and regional instruments (Part Two) not covered in *Volumes I* and *II*, including, but not limited to, those adopted between 1996 and the end of 1999.

- *Volume V* is divided into four parts, as follows:

  - Part One reproduces investment-related provisions in a number of additional free trade and economic integration agreements not covered in *Volume III*.

  - Part Two includes for the first time investment-related provisions in association agreements as well as bilateral and interregional cooperation agreements. These are divided into three annexes. Annex A is devoted to agreements signed between the countries members of the European Free Trade Association (EFTA) and third countries. Annex B covers investment-related provisions in agreements signed between the countries members of the European Community (EC) and third countries as well as other regional groups. Annex C includes types of bilateral agreements related to investment that differ from those covered in other parts.

  - Part Three contains the texts of a number of additional prototype BITs of several developed and developing countries, as well as a list of these treaties concluded between July 1995 and the end of 1998, when the total number of BITs concluded since 1959 reached over 1,730.

- Part Four reproduces additional texts of recent documents prepared by non-governmental organizations.

- *Volume VI* is divided into the following six parts:

  - Part One contains an additional multilateral instrument.

  - Part Two covers additional interregional and regional instruments, including agreements, resolutions and other texts from regional organizations with an inclusive geographical context.

  - Part Three reproduces investment-related provisions in a number of additional free trade and economic integration agreements not covered in previous volumes.

  - Part Four includes investment-related provisions in association agreements as well as bilateral and interregional cooperation agreements not covered in previous volumes.

  - Part Five contains the texts of a number of additional prototype BITs of several developed and developing countries not covered in previous volumes.

  - Part Six includes for the first time prototype double taxation treaties (DTTs).

- *Volume VII* is divided into the following three parts:

  - Part One contains an additional multilateral instrument.

  - Part Two reproduces investment-related provisions in a number of additional free trade and cooperation agreements signed between countries members of the European Free Trade Association (EFTA) and countries members of the European Community (EC) with third countries not covered in previous volumes.

  - Part Three contains the texts of a number of additional prototype BITs not covered in previous volumes.

- *Volume VIII* is divided into the following three parts:

  - Part One covers additional interregional and regional instruments, including agreements and other texts from regional organizations with an inclusive geographical context.

- Part Two reproduces investment-related provisions in a number of additional free trade, economic integration and cooperation agreements not covered in previous volumes.

- Part Three contains the texts of a number of additional prototype BITs not covered in previous volumes.

- *Volume IX* is divided into the following three parts:

  - Part One covers additional interregional and regional instruments, including agreements and other texts from regional organizations with an inclusive geographical context.

  - Part Two reproduces investment-related provisions in a number of additional free trade, economic integration and cooperation agreements not covered in previous volumes.

  - Part Three contains the texts of a number of additional prototype BITs not covered in previous volumes.

Within each of these subdivisions, instruments are reproduced in chronological order, except for the sections dedicated to prototype instruments.

The multilateral and regional instruments covered are widely differing in scope and coverage. Some are designed to provide an overall, general framework for FDI and cover many, although rarely all, aspects of investment operations. Most instruments deal with particular aspects and issues concerning FDI. A significant number address core FDI issues, such as the promotion and protection of investment, investment liberalization, dispute settlement and insurance and guarantees. Others cover specific issues, of direct but not exclusive relevance to FDI and TNCs, such as transfer of technology, intellectual property, avoidance of double taxation, competition and the protection of consumers and the environment. A relatively small number of instruments of this last category has been reproduced, since each of these specific issues often constitutes an entire system of legal regulation of its own, whose proper coverage would require an extended exposition of many kinds of instruments and arrangements.[a]

The *Compendium* is meant to be a collection of instruments, not an anthology of relevant provisions. Indeed, to understand a particular instrument, it is normally necessary to take its entire text into consideration. An effort has been made, therefore, to reproduce complete instruments, even though, in a number of cases, reasons of space and relevance have dictated the inclusion of excerpts.

The UNCTAD secretariat has deliberately refrained from adding its own commentary to the texts reproduced in the *Compendium*. The only exception to this rule is the boxes added to each instrument. They provide some basic facts, such as its date of adoption and date of entry

---

[a] For a collection of instruments (or excerpts therefrom) dealing with transfer of technology, see UNCTAD, *Compendium of International Arrangements on Transfer of Technology: Selected Instruments* (Geneva: United Nations), United Nations publication, Sales No. E.01.II.D.28.

into force and, where appropriate, signatory countries. Also, a list of agreements containing investment-related provisions signed by the EFTA countries and by the EC countries with third countries or regional groups are reproduced in the *Compendium*. Moreover, to facilitate the identification of each instrument in the table of contents, additional information has been added, in brackets, next to each title, on the year of its signature and the name of the relevant institution involved.

Rubens Ricupero
Secretary-General of UNCTAD

Geneva, June 2002

ACKNOWLEDGEMENTS

Volume IX of the *Compendium* was prepared by Abraham Negash under the overall direction of Karl P. Sauvant. Comments were received from Americo Beviglia Zampetti. The cooperation of the relevant countries and organizations from which the relevant instruments originate is acknowledged with gratitude.

CONTENTS

VOLUME IX

PART ONE

INTERREGIONAL AND REGIONAL INSTRUMENTS

PART TWO

BILATERAL INSTRUMENTS

PART THREE

PROTOTYPE INSTRUMENTS

CONTENTS OF OTHER VOLUMES

VOLUME I
MULTILATERAL INSTRUMENTS

VOLUME II
REGIONAL INSTRUMENTS

REGIONAL INSTRUMENTS

VOLUME III

REGIONAL INTEGRATION, BILATERAL AND NON-GOVERNMENTAL INSTRUMENTS

ANNEX C. NON-GOVERNMENTAL INSTRUMENTS

VOLUME IV

MULTILATERAL AND REGIONAL INSTRUMENTS

PART ONE

MULTILATERAL INSTRUMENTS

PART TWO

REGIONAL INSTRUMENTS

VOLUME V

REGIONAL INTEGRATION, BILATERAL AND NON-GOVERNMENTAL INSTRUMENTS

PART ONE

INVESTMENT-RELATED PROVISIONS IN FREE TRADE AND ECONOMIC INTEGRATION AGREEMENTS

PART TWO

INVESTMENT-RELATED PROVISIONS IN ASSOCIATION AGREEMENTS, BILATERAL AND INTERREGIONAL COOPERATION AGREEMENTS

ANNEX A. **INVESTMENT-RELATED PROVISIONS IN FREE TRADE AGREEMENTS SIGNED BETWEEN THE COUNTRIES MEMBERS OF THE EUROPEAN FREE TRADE ASSOCIATION AND THIRD COUNTRIES AND LIST OF AGREEMENTS SIGNED (END-1999)**

ANNEX B. **INVESTMENT-RELATED PROVISIONS IN ASSOCIATION, PARTNERSHIP AND COOPERATION AGREEMENTS SIGNED BETWEEN THE COUNTRIES MEMBERS OF THE EUROPEAN COMMUNITY AND THIRD COUNTRIESAND LIST OF AGREEMENTS SIGNED (END-1999)**

ANNEX C. OTHER BILATERAL INVESTMENT-RELATED AGREEMENTS

PART THREE

PROTOTYPE BILATERAL INVESTMENT TREATIES AND LIST OF BILATERAL INVESTMENT TREATIES (MID-1995 — END-1998)

PART FOUR

NON-GOVERNMENTAL INSTRUMENTS

VOLUME VI

PART THREE

INVESTMENT-RELATED PROVISIONS IN FREE TRADE AND ECONOMIC INTEGRATION AGREEMENTS

PART FOUR

INVESTMENT-RELATED PROVISIONS IN ASSOCIATION AGREEMENTS, BILATERAL AND INTERREGIONAL COOPERATION AGREEMENTS

PART FIVE

PROTOTYPE BILATERAL INVESTMENT TREATIES

PART SIX

PROTOTYPE BILATERAL DOUBLE TAXATION TREATIES

VOLUME VII

PART ONE

MULTILATERAL INSTRUMENTS

PART TWO

BILATERAL INSTRUMENTS

PART THREE

PROTOTYPE INSTRUMENTS

VOLUME VIII

PART ONE

INTERREGIONAL AND REGIONAL INSTRUMENTS

PART TWO

BILATERAL INSTRUMENTS

PART THREE

PROTOTYPE INSTRUMENTS

PART ONE

INTERREGIONAL AND REGIONAL

INSTRUMENTS

AGREEMENT AMONG THE GOVERNMENTS OF THE MEMBER STATES OF THE CARIBBEAN COMMUNITY FOR THE AVOIDANCE OF DOUBLE TAXATION AND THE PREVENTION OF FISCAL EVASION WITH RESPECT TO TAXES ON INCOME, PROFITS OR GAINS AND CAPITAL GAINS AND FOR THE ENCOURAGEMENT OF REGIONAL TRADE AND INVESTMENT*

(THE CARIBBEAN COMMUNITY)

The Agreement Among the Governments of the Member States of the Caribbean Community for the Avoidance of Double Taxation and the Prevention of Fiscal Evasion With Respect to Taxes on Income, Profits or Gains and Capital Gains and for the Encouragement of Regional Trade and Investment was signed by the Member States of the Caribbean Community namely, Antigua and Barbuda, Bahamas, Barbados, Belize, Dominica, Grenada, Guyana, Jamaica, Montserrat, St. Kitts and Nevis, St. Lucia, Suriname, St. Vincent and the Grenadines and Trinidad and Tobago on 6 July 1994. It entered into force in November 1994.

The Governments of the Member States of the Caribbean Community desiring to conclude an Agreement for the avoidance of double taxation and the prevention of fiscal evasion with respect to taxes on income, profits or gains and capital gains and for the encouragement of Regional Trade and Investment:

Have agreed as follows:

SCOPE, TAXES AND DEFINITIONS

Article 1
Scope of Agreement

This agreement shall apply to any person who is a resident of Member State in respect of which it has entered into force in accordance with Article 28.

Article 2
Taxes covered

1.   This Agreement shall apply to taxes on income, profits or gains and capital gains arising in a Member State in respect of which the Agreement has entered into force in accordance with Article 28 and which are listed in Schedule 1.

---

*   *Source*: The Caibbean Community Secretariat (1994). "Agreement Among the Governments of the Member States of the Caribbean Community for the Avoidance of Double Taxation and the Prevention of Fiscal Evasion With Respect to Taxes on Income, Profits or Gains and Capital Gains and for the Encouragement of Regional Trade and Investment"; available on the Internet (www.caricom.org/doubletaxation.htm). [Note added by the editor.]

However, a Member State which introduces taxes on income, profits or gains and capital gains after the entry into force of this Agreement shall, by notification to the Secretariat, list in Schedule 1 those taxes which will be subject to this Agreement.

2.   This Agreement shall also apply to any identical or substantially similar taxes which are imposed by a Member State after the date of signature of this Agreement in addition to, or in place of, those referred to in paragraph 1 of this Article.

3.   The competent authorities of Member States shall notify all others of any substantial change in their laws relating to the taxes which are the subject of this Agreement, within three (30 months after such change.

Article 3
General Definitions

1.   In this Agreement unless the context otherwise requires -

(a)   the word "company" means a body corporate or any entity which is treated as a body corporate for tax purposes;

(b)   the term "competent authority" means the Minister responsible for Finance or his duly authorised representative;

(c)   the term "enterprise of a Member State" means an enterprise that is carried on by a resident of a Member State;

(d)   the term "international traffic" means any transportation by a ship or aircraft operated by an enterprise of a Member State, except when the ship or aircraft is operated solely between places in one country and includes traffic between places in one country in the course of a journey which extends over more than one country;

(e)   the term "Member State means one of the States listed in Schedule II and shall include the territorial waters of any such member State and any area outside such territorial waters over which the State has sovereign rights or jurisdiction in accordance with international law.

(f)   the word "national" means -

(i)   a citizen of a Member State; or

(ii)   a person who has a connection with that State of a kind which entitles that person to be regarded as belonging to or, if it be so expressed, as being a native, resident or belonger of the State for the purposes of such laws thereof relating to immigration as are for the time being in force; or

(iii)   a company or other legal person deriving its status as such from the laws in force in a Member State or constituted in the Member State in conformity with the law thereof that such State regards as belonging to it;

(g)   the word "person" includes an individual, a company and any other body of persons;

2.   In the application of this Agreement by a Member State any word or term not defined in this Agreement shall, unless the context otherwise requires, have the meaning which it has under the laws of that Member State relating to the taxes which are the subject of this Agreement.

Article 4
Residence

1.   For the purposes of this Agreement, the term "resident of a Member State" means any person who under the law of that State is liable to tax therein by reason of that person's domicile, residence, place of management or any other criterion of a similar nature.

2.   Where by reason of the provisions;of paragraph 1 of this Article an individual is a resident of more than one Member State, than the status of that individual shall be determined as follows:

(a)   he shall be deemed to be a resident of the Member State in which he has a permanent home available to him; if he has a permanent home available to him in more than one Member State, he shall be deemed to be a resident of the Member State with which his personal and economic relations are closest (thereinafter referred to as his "centre of vital interests");

(b)   if the Member State in which he has his centre of vital interests cannot be determined, or if he has no permanent home available to him in an Member State, he shall be deemed to be a resident of the Member State in which he has an habitual abode;

(c)   if he has an habitual abode in more than one Member State or in none of them, he shall be deemed to be a resident of the Member State of which he is a national;

(d)   if he is a national of more than one Member State or of none of them, the competent authorities of the Member States concerned shall determine the question by agreement.

3.   Where by reason of the provisions of paragraph 1 of this Article a person other than an individual would be a resident of more than one Member State, then such person shall, for the purposes of this Agreement, be deemed to be a resident of the Member State in which its place of effective management is situated.

TAXES ON INCOME

Article 5
Tax Jurisdiction

Irrespective of the nationality or State of residence of a person, income of whatever nature accruing to or derived by such person shall be taxable only by the Member State in which the income arises, except for the cases specified in this Agreement.

Article 6
Income from Immovable Property

1.   Income from immovable property shall be taxable only in the Member State in which such property is situated.

2.   The term "immovable property" shall be construed in accordance with the law of the Member State in which the property in question is situated. The term shall in any case include property accessory to immovable property, livestock and equipment used in agriculture or forestry, rights to which the provisions of general law respecting landed property apply, usufruct of immovable property and rights to variable or fixed payments as consideration for the working of, or the rights to work, mineral deposits, sources and other natural resources; but ships, boats and aircraft shall not be regarded as immovable property.

3.   The provisions of paragraph 1 of this Article, shall apply to income derived from the direct use, letting, or use in any other form of immovable property.

4.   The provisions of paragraphs 1 and 3 of this Article shall also apply to the income from immovable property of an enterprise and to income from immovable property used for the performance of professional services.

Article 7
Capital Gains

1.   Except as otherwise provided in this Article, gains derived from the alienation of real property situated in a Member State shall be taxed only in that State.

2.   For the purposes of this Article real property includes -

   (i)   immovable property referred to in Article 6;

   (ii)   shares or similar rights in a company, the assets of which consist wholly or principally of immovable property; and

   (iii)   an interest in a partnership trust or estate, the assets of which consist wholly or principally of immovable property.

3.   Gains derived by an enterprise of a Member State from the alienation of ships, aircraft, or containers operated in international traffic shall be taxable only in that Member State.

4.   Gains from the alienation of property other than property referred to in paragraphs 1 and 3 shall be taxable only in the Member State in which the gains arise.

Article 8
Business Profits

1.   Profits resulting from business activities shall be taxable only by the Member State wherein such business activities are undertaken.

2.	A business enterprise shall be regarded as undertaking activities in the territory of a Member State when it has in such Member State any of, but not limited to, the following:

(a)	an office, or place of business management;

(b)	a factory, plant, industrial workshop or assembly shop;

(c)	a construction project in progress;

(d)	a place or facility wherein natural resources are extracted or exploited, such as a mine, well, quarry, plantation or fishing boat;

(e)	an agency, or premises, for the purchase or sale of goods;

(f)	a depository, storage facility, warehouse or any similar establishment used for receiving, storing or delivering goods;

(g)	any other premises, office or facilities, the purposes of which are preparatory or auxiliary to the business activities of the enterprise;

(h)	an agent or representative.

3.	In determining the profits from a business activity there shall be allowed as deductions expenses which are incurred for the purposes of that activity in accordance with the laws of the Member State in which such activity is undertaken.

4.	Where an enterprise carries on business activities in more than one Member State, each State may tax profits from sources within its territory. If the activities are undertaken through representatives, or through the use of facilities such as those indicated in paragraph 1 of this Article, the profits earned shall be attributed to such representatives or facilities provided that such representatives or facilities are totally independent from the business enterprise.

5.	Where the business profits include items of income which are dealt with separately in other Articles of this Agreement, the provisions of those Articles shall, except as otherwise provided therein, supersede the provisions of this Article.

Article 9
Shipping and Air Transport

1.	Profits derived by an enterprise of a Member State from the operation of ships or aircraft in international traffic shall be taxable only in that Member State.

2.	Profits derived from the operation of ships or aircraft used principally to transport passengers or goods exclusively between places in a member State shall be taxed only in that State.

3.	The provisions of paragraph 1 of this Article shall also apply to profits derived by an enterprise of a Member State from the participation in a pool, a joint business or in an international operating agency;

4.   For the purposes of this Article, profits from the operation of ships or aircraft in international traffic include profits derived from the rental of ships or aircraft if operated in international traffic by the lessee.

5.   Profits of an enterprise of a Member State from the use, maintenance or rental of containers (including trailers, barges and related equipment for the transport of containers) shall be taxable only in that State to the extent that such containers are used for the transport of goods or merchandise in international traffic.

Article 10
Associated Enterprises

Where -

(a)   an enterprise of a Member State participates directly or indirectly in the management, control or capital of an enterprise of another Member State; or

(b)   the same persons participate, directly or indirectly in the management, control or capital of an enterprise of a Member State and an enterprise of another Member State;

and in either case conditions are made or imposed between the enterprises in their commercial or financial relations which differ from those which would be made between independent enterprises, then any profits which would but for those conditions have accrued to one of the enterprises, but, by reason of those conditions have not so accrued, may be included in the profits of that enterprise and taxed accordingly.

Article 11
Dividends

1.   Dividends paid by a company which is a resident of a Member State to a resident of another Member State shall be taxed only in the first-mentioned State.

2.   The rate of tax on the gross dividends shall be zero per cent.

3.   The provisions of paragraph 1 of this Article shall not affect the taxation of the company in respect of the profits out of which the dividends are paid.

4.   In this Article, the word "dividends" means income from shares, mining shares, founders' shares or other rights, not being preference shares or debt claims, participating in profits, as well as income from other corporate rights which is subjected to the same taxation treatment as income from shares by the laws of the State of which the company making the distribution is a resident.

5.   The rate of tax on gross dividends from preference shares shall not exceed the rate specified in Article 12.

Article 12
Interest

1.   Interest arising in a Member State and paid to a resident of another Member State shall be taxed only by the first mentioned State.

2.   The rate of tax shall not exceed fifteen per cent of the gross amount of the interest.

3.   Notwithstanding the provisions of paragraphs 1 and 2 of this Article, interest derived from sources within a Member State shall be exempt from tax in that Member State if it is beneficially owned by the Government of another Member State, or by an agency or other entity of that Government.

4.   For the purpose of this Article, interest shall be deemed to arise in the Member State where the payer is that State itself, a political subdivision, a local authority or a resident of that State. However, where the person paying the interest carries on business through an office, branch or agency in a Member State, and such interest is borne by that office, branch or agency, such interest shall be deemed to arise in the Member State in which the office, branch or agency is situated.

5.   Where, owing to a special relationship between the payer and the recipient of the interest or between both of them and some other person, the amount of the interest paid, having regard to the debt-claim in respect of which it is paid, exceeds the amount which would have been agreed upon by the payer and the recipient in the absence of such relationship, the provisions of this Article shall apply only to the last-mentioned amount. In that case, the excess part of the payment shall remain taxable according to the laws of the Member State in which the interest shall be deemed to arise.

6.   In this Article, the word "interest" means income from debt-claims of every kind, whether or not secured by mortgage and whether or not carrying a right to participate in the debtor's profits, and in particular, income from government securities and income from bonds or debentures, including premiums and prizes attaching to such securities, bonds or debentures. Penalty charges for late payment shall not be regarded as interest for the purpose of this Article.

7.   The word "interest" shall not include any item of income which is treated as a distribution by the tax laws of a Member State.

Article 13
Royalties

1.   Royalties arising in a Member State and paid to a resident of another Member State shall be taxed only in the first-mentioned State.

2.   The rate of tax shall not exceed fifteen per cent of the gross amount of the royalties.

3.   In this Article, the word "royalties" means payments of any kind received as consideration for the use of, or the right to use any copyright of literary, artistic or scientific work, including cinematograph films and films or tapes of radio or television broadcasting, any patent, trademark, design or model, plan, secret formula or process or other like property or rights, or for the use of or the right to use industrial, commercial or scientific plant or equipment,

or for information concerning industrial, commercial or scientific experience; but does not include royalties or other amounts paid in respect of the operations of mines or quarries or in respect of the extraction or removal of natural resources.

4.   Royalties shall be deemed to arise in a Member State in which the copyright, patent, trade mark, design, model, plan, secret formula, process or non-patented technical knowledge or other similar intangible property is used.

5.   Where, owing to a special relationship between the payer and the recipient of the royalties or between both of them and some other person, the amount of the royalties paid having regard to the use, right or information for which they are paid, exceeds the amount which would have been agreed upon by the payer and the recipient in the absence of such relationship the provisions of this Article shall apply only to the last-mentioned amount. In that case the excess part of the payment shall remain taxable according to the laws of the Member State in which the royalty is deemed to arise.

Article 14
Management Fees

1.   Management fees arising in a Member State and paid to a resident of another Member State shall be taxed only in the first mentioned State.

2.   The rate of tax shall not exceed fifteen per cent of the management fees.

3.   In this Article, the term "management fees" means payments of any kind to any person, for or in respect of the provision of industrial or commercial advice or for management or technical services or similar services or facilities, but does not include payments for professional services mentioned in Article 16.

4.   Management fees shall be deemed to arise in a member State when the payer is that Member State itself, a local authority or a resident of that Member State.

5.   Where owing to a special relationship between the payer and the recipient of the management fees or between both of them and some other person, the amount of the management fees paid, having regard to the advice or services for which they are paid, exceeds the amount which would have been agreed upon by the payer and recipient in the absence of such relationship, the provisions of this Article shall apply only to the last-mentioned amount. In that case the excess part of the payment shall remain taxable according to the laws of the Member State in which the management fees arise.

Article 15
Dependent Personal Services

1.   Subject to the provisions of Articles 17, 19, and 20, salaries, wages and other similar remuneration derived by a resident of a Member State in respect of an employment shall be taxed only in the Member State in which the employment is exercised.

2.   Notwithstanding the provisions of paragraph 1 of this Article, remuneration derived by a resident of a Member State in respect of an employment exercised in another Member State shall be taxed only in the first-mentioned State if:

(a)   the recipient is present in the other State for a period or periods not exceeding an aggregate 183 days in the tax year; and

(b)   the remuneration is paid by, or on behalf of, an employer who is not a resident of the other State; and

(c)   such remuneration is not deducted in arriving at the profits of a trade, business, profession or vocation which is carried on by the employer in the other Member State.

3.   Notwithstanding the preceding the provisions of this Article, remuneration derived in respect of an employment exercised aboard a ship or aircraft operating in international traffic shall be taxed only in the Member State in which the person operating the ship or aircraft is a resident.

Article 16
Independent Personal Services

1.   Income derived by an individual, who is a resident of a Member State engaged in rendering professional services of an independent character shall be taxable only by the Member State wherein such services are rendered.

2.   Where a resident of a Member State derives income from another Member State in respect of professional services or other independent activities of a similar character, such person shall be subject to tax in that other Member State but only in respect of such income as is attributable to the services or activities performed in that other Member State. In determining the income attributable to such services or activities there shall be allowed as a deduction such expenses wherever incurred as would be deductible in accordance with the laws of that other Member State.

3.   In this Article, the term "professional services" includes, but is not restricted to, independent scientific, technical, literary, artistic, educational and teaching activities as well as the independent activities of physicians, lawyers, engineers, architects, dentists and accountants.

Article 17
Directors' Fees

Directors' fees and similar payments derived by a resident of a Member State in his capacity as a member of the Board of Directors of a Company which is a resident of another Member State shall be taxed only in that Member State of which the payer is a resident.

Article 18
Entertainers and Athletes

1.   Notwithstanding anything contained in this Agreement, income derived by entertainers, including theatre, motion picture, radio or television artistes and musicians, and by athletes, from their personal activities as such shall be taxed only in the Member State in which those activities are performed.

2.   Where income in respect of personal activities of any entertainer or athlete as such accrues not to that entertainer or athlete himself but to another person, that income shall, notwithstanding anything contained in this Agreement, be taxed only in the Member State in which the activities of the entertainer or athlete are performed.

3.   The provisions of paragraphs 1 and 2 shall not apply to:

(a)   income derived from activities performed in a Member State by entertainers or athletes if the visit to that Member State is substantially supported by public funds of the other Member State, including any political subdivision, local authority or statutory body thereof;

(b)   a non-profit organisation no part of the income of which was payable to, or was otherwise available for the personal benefit of, any proprietor, member or shareholder thereof, or

(c)   an entertainer or athlete in respect of services provided to an organisation referred to in subparagraph (b).

Article 19
Pensions and Annuities

1.   Pensions, annuities, alimony and other periodic payment of a similar character paid by a resident of a Member State to an individual who is a resident of another Member State shall be taxable only by the State from which the payment of such income is liable to be made.

2.   Any pensions paid by a Member State or local authority or under any Social Security or National Insurance Scheme established under the laws of a Member State shall be taxable only in that Member State.

3.   In this Article, the word "pensions" means periodic payments mad after retirement or death in consideration for services rendered, or by way of compensation for injuries received in connection with past employment.

4.   In this Article, the word "annuities" means a stated sum paid periodically at stated times during life or during a specified or ascertainable period of time under an obligation to make payments in return for adequate and full consideration in money or money's worth.

5.   In this Article, the word "alimony" means periodic payments made pursuant to a decree of divorce or of separate maintenance or of separation.

Article 20
Government Service

1.

(a)   Remuneration other than pensions paid by a member State or local authority thereof to any individual in respect of services rendered to that Member State authority shall be taxable only in that Member State.

(b)   However such remuneration shall be taxable only in another Member State if the services are rendered in that other State and the individual is a resident of that State who -

    (i)   is a national of that State; or

    (ii)   did not become a resident of that State solely for the purpose of rendering the services.

2.   The provisions of this article shall not apply to payments in respect of services rendered in connection with any trade or business carried on by a Member State or local authority thereof.

Article 21
Students and Trainees

1.   An individual who is a resident of a Member State immediately before his visit to another Member State and who is temporarily present in that other Member State for the primary purpose of:

    (i)   studying in that other Member State at a University or other educational institution approved by the appropriate educational authority of that Member State;

    (ii)   securing training required to qualify him to practice a profession or a professional speciality; or

    (iii)   studying or doing research as a recipient of a grant, allowance, or award from a governmental, religious, charitable, scientific, literary or educational organisation, or as a participant in other sponsored programmes,

shall not be taxable in respect of;

    (a)   gifts from a broad for the purpose of his maintenance, education, study, research or training;

    (b)   the grant, allowance or award; and

    (c)   remuneration for employment in that other member State provided that the remuneration constitutes earnings reasonably necessary for the maintenance and education of such person.

2.   The benefits under paragraph 1 shall only extend for such period of time as may be reasonable or customarily required to effectuate the purpose of the visit.

GENERAL PROVISIONS

Article 22
Non-discrimination

1.   The nationals of a Member State shall not be subjected in any other Member State to any taxation or any requirement connected therewith which is other or more burdensome than the taxation and connected requirements to which the nationals of that other Member State in the same circumstances are or may be subjected.

2.   The provisions of this Article shall not be construed as obliging a Member State to grant to residents of another Member State those personal allowances, credits and reliefs for tax purposes which are by law available only to residents of the first-mentioned Member State.

3.   In this Article the term "taxation" means taxes which are the subject of this Agreement.

Article 23
Consultation

1.   Where a person who is a resident of a Member State considers that the actions of one or more of the Member States result or will result in taxation not in accordance with this Agreement, such persons may, notwithstanding the remedies provided by the laws of those States, present a case to the competent authority of the Member State of which he is a resident.

2.   The competent authority shall endeavour, if the objection appears to it to be justified and if it is not itself able to arrive at an appropriate solution, to resolve that case by agreement with the competent authority of the other Member State, with a view to the avoidance of taxation not in accordance with this Agreement.

3.   The competent authorities of the Member States shall endeavour to resolve by agreement any difficulties or doubts arising as to the interpretation or application of this Agreement. They may also consult together for the elimination of double taxation in cases not provided for in this Agreement.

4.   The competent authorities of the Member States may communicate directly with each other for the purpose of reaching an agreement in accordance with the provisions of the preceding paragraphs.

Article 24
Exchange of Information

1.   The competent authorities of the Member States shall exchange such information as is necessary for the carrying out of this Agreement and of the domestic laws of the Member States concerning taxes covered by this Agreement in so far as the taxation thereunder is in accordance with this Agreement. Any information so exchanged shall be treated as secret and shall only be disclosed to persons or authorities including Courts and other administrative bodies concerned with the assessment or collection of the taxes which are the subject of this Agreement. Such persons or authorities shall use the information only for such purposes and may disclose the information in public court proceedings or judicial decisions.

2.   In no case shall the provisions of paragraph 1 be construed so as to impose on one of the Member States the obligation:

(a)   to carry out administrative measures at variance with the laws or the administrative practice of that or/of the other Member States;

(b)   to supply particulars which are not obtainable under the laws or in the normal course oft he administration of that or of the other Member States;

(c)   to supply information which would disclose any trade, business, industrial, commercial or professional secret or trade process the disclosure of which would be contrary to public policy.

Article 25
Diplomats and Consular Officials

Nothing in this Agreement shall affect the fiscal privileges of members of diplomatic missions or consular posts under the general rules of international law or under the provisions of special agreements.

Article 26
Signature

This Agreement shall be open for signature by any Member State.

Article 27
Ratification

This Agreement and any amendments thereto shall be subject to ratification by the Member States in accordance with their respective constitutional procedures.

Instruments of ratification shall be deposited with the Caribbean Community Secretariat which shall transmit certified copies tot he Government of each Member State.

Article 28
Entry into force

1.   This Agreement shall enter into force on the deposit of the second instrument of ratification in accordance with Article 27 and shall thereupon take effect -

(a)   in respect of taxes withheld at the source, on amounts paid or credited to a person, on the first day of the calendar month next following the month of deposit of the second instrument of ratification;

(b)   in respect of other taxes, for the taxable years beginning on or after the first day of January next following the deposit of the second instrument of ratification.

2.   Where a State ratifies this Agreement after it has entered into force, the Agreement shall take effect in relation to that State -

(a)   in respect of the taxes mentioned in paragraph 1(a), on the first day of the calendar month next following the deposit of its instrument of ratification;

(b)   in respect of other taxes, for the taxable years beginning on or after the first day of January next following the deposit of its instrument of ratification.

Article 29
Accession

1.   A Member State of the Caribbean Community which is not listed in Schedule II to this Agreement may accede to this Agreement by depositing with the Caribbean Community Secretariat an instrument of accession which shall also specify the taxes to which this Agreement shall apply in respect of that Member State and references in this Agreement to a Member State shall, unless the context otherwise requires, include such an acceding Member State.

2.   The Caribbean Community shall transmit a certified copy of the instrument of accession to the Government of each Member State which is a party to this Agreement.

Article 30
Termination

1.   This Agreement shall remain in force indefinitely, but a Member State which is a party to this Agreement may on or before 30th June in any calendar year beginning after the expiration of a period of three years from the date of its entry into force, give to the other Member States, through diplomatic channels, written notice of termination.

2.   In such event this Agreement shall cease to have effect in relation to that Member State -

(a)   in respect of taxes withheld at source on amounts paid or credited to a person, from the first day of January next following the year in which the notice of termination is given;

(b)   in respect of other taxes, for the taxable years commencing on or after the first day of January next following the year in which the notice of termination is given.

SCHEDULE I
TAXES COVERED

The Taxes which are the subject of this Agreement are:

(a)   in Antigua and Barbuda

(i)   Income Tax
(ii)   Business Tax

(b)   in Belize

- Income Tax

(c)   in Dominica

- Income Tax

(d)   in Grenada

- Income Tax

(e)   in Guyana

    (i)   Income Tax
    (ii)   Corporation Tax
    (iii)   Capital Gains Tax

(f)   in Jamaica

    (i)   Income Tax
    (ii)   Transfer Tax in relation to Capital Gains

(g)   in Montserrat

- Income Tax

(h)   in St. Kitts and Nevis

- Income Tax

(i)   in Saint Lucia

- Income Tax

(j)   in St. Vincent and the Grenadines

- Income Tax

(k)   in Trinidad and Tobago

    (i)   Income Tax
    (ii)   Corporation Tax
    (iii)   Unemployment Levy
    (iv)   Health Surcharge
    (v)   Petroleum Profits Tax
    (vi)   Supplemental Petroleum Tax
    (vii)   Business Levy

*

DECISION 439: GENERAL FRAMEWORK OF PRINCIPLES AND RULES AND FOR LIBERALIZING THE TRADE IN SERVICES IN THE ANDEAN COMMUNITY *
[excerpts]

(ANDEAN COMMUNITY)

DECISION 439: General Framework of Principles and Rules and for Liberalizing the Trade in Services in the Andean Community was signed on 11 June 1998.

THE COMMISSION OF THE ANDEAN COMMUNITY,

HAVING SEEN:

Articles 3, paragraph f) of the part about Economic and Social Cooperation Programs and Actions, 11, 55, and 139 of the Cartagena Agreement, and Proposal 3/Amend. 1 of the General Secretariat;

WHEREAS:

The IX Andean Presidential Council, meeting in Sucre, Bolivia, expressed its intention to liberalize the trade in services within the subregion and, accordingly, instructed the Commission to approve a general framework of principles and rules for attaining that objective;

For its part, the X Andean Presidential Council, meeting in Guayaquil, Ecuador, reiterated the importance placed on free trade in services within the Andean Community. To that end, it instructed the Commission to adopt during the first half of 1998 the aforementioned general framework with regard to services which shall serve as the basis for the pertinent Decisions,in order for the Andean Community to have a market with freely circulating services by the year 2005 at the latest;

The progressive creation of an Andean Common Market in Services is a basic element for the consolidation of subregional integration;

It is essential to establish Community principles and rules for liberalizing the trade in services in order to strengthen and diversify the service production and distribution sectors in the Andean Community;

Services are an essential element of the trade in goods, transfer of technology and circulation, within the subregion, of capital and persons connected with the provision of services;

---

* *Source*: The Andean Community (1998). "Andean Community DECISION 439: General Framework of Principles and Rules and for Liberalizing the Trade in Services in the Andean Community", available on the Internet (http://www.sice.oas.org/trade/JUNAC/decisiones/dec439e.asp). [Note added by the editor.]

The Member Countries of the Andean Community need to improve their share of the international trade in services in order to secure an effective position in the global market;

The growing importance of services in the economic and social development of Member Countries and the linkage between those services and the new technologies are a determining element for the consolidation of the competitive advantages of subregional production;

Services account for a significant percentage of the Subregion's gross domestic product and contribute effectively to the creation of jobs;

There are services of subregional origin that have already been liberalized with favorable results for both the providers and users, thus helping to bolster the process of Andean integration;

The World Trade Organization's (WTO) General Agreement on the Trade in Services, particularly article V, and the other multilateral and plurilateral negotiations underway have created a favorable climate for liberalizing the trade in services within the subregion;

DECIDES:

To approve this

General Framework of Principles and Rules For Liberalizing the Trade in Services in the Andean Community

CHAPTER I
GENERAL PURPOSE

Article 1. The purpose of this General Framework is to establish a set of principles and rules for the progressive liberalization of the trade in services within the subregion, with a view to creating the Andean Common Market in Services by eliminating restrictive measures within the Andean Community.

In accordance with the terms and conditions of the commitments established under this General Framework, the Member Countries shall the strengthening and diversification of Andean services and shall promote harmonize their sectoral national policies in the areas that require it.

CHAPTER II
DEFINITIONS

Article 2. The following definitions shall apply for purposes of this General Framework:

Trade in services: The supply of a service of any sector, using any of the following modes:

- From the territory of a Member Country into the territory of another Member Country;
- In the territory of a Member Country to a consumer of another Member Country;
- Through the commercial presence of service supplier of a Member Country in the territory of another Member Country; and

- By natural persons from a Member Country into the territory of another Member Country.

Measure: Any provision, whether in the form of a law, decree, resolution, regulation, rule, procedure, decision, administrative standard, or in any other form, adopted or applied by Member Countries.

Measures adopted by Member Countries that affect the trade in services:

This shall cover measures referring to:

- The purchase, payment or use of a service;
- Access to such services as are offered to the general public by order of those Member Countries and the use of those services as a result of the provision of a service; or
- The presence, including the commercial presence of persons from one Member Country in the territory of another Member Country for the purpose of providing a service.

Commercial presence: Any kind of business or professional establishment in the territory of a Member Country for the purpose of providing a service through, for example:

- The establishment, acquisition or maintenance of a juridical person; or
- The creation or maintenance of a branch or of a representative office.

Services provided in the exercise of governmental authority: those which the government or public institutions of any Member Country provide under non commercial conditions or not in competition with one or several service providers, including the activities of a central bank or a monetary and exchange authority or any other public institution.

Supply of a service: This shall cover the production, distribution, marketing, sale and provision of a service.

CHAPTER III
SCOPE OF APPLICATION

Article 3. This General Framework shall apply to measures adopted by Member Countries that affect the trade in services in all of the service sectors and in the different modes of supply, including those provided by the central, regional or local public sector, as well as those furnished by institutions delegated to do so.

Article 4. This General Framework shall not be applicable to services provided in the exercise of governmental authority.

The procurement of services by government agencies or public institutions of Member Countries shall be subject to the principle of national treatment among Member Countries, pursuant to a Decision to be adopted no later than January 1st, 2002. In the event that the Decision in question fails to be adopted by that date, the Member Countries shall grant national treatment immediately.

This Regulatory Framework shall not be applicable to measures connected with air transportation services.

Article 5. Service sectors or sub-sectors that are governed by sectoral Decisions that exist on the date this Decision or its amendments enter into effect, shall be regulated by the rules and regulations of those Decisions. With respect to those sectors and sub-sectors, the provisions provided in this General Framework shall apply in a supplementary manner.

CHAPTER IV
PRINCIPLES AND COMMITMENTS

Article 6. Each Member Country shall grant services and service providers from the other Member Countries access to its market through any of the modes established in the definition of the trade in services of article 2, without prejudice to the provisions of article 14 of this General Framework.

Article 7. Each Member Country shall immediately and unconditionally grant the services and service providers from other Member Countries treatment that is no less favorable than that granted to services and providers of similar services from any other country, whether or not a member of the Andean Community.

Without prejudice to that established under the foregoing paragraph, any Member Country may confer or grant advantages to adjacent countries in order to facilitate the exchange of services that are produced and used locally, limited to contiguous border zones.

Article 8. Each Member Country shall grant the services and service providers from other Member Countries treatment that is no less favorable than that granted to its own services or providers of similar services, without prejudice to the provisions of article 14 of this General Framework.

Article 9. Each Member County shall promptly publish, and in any case no later than the date of its entry into force, all measures of general application that refer to or affect the operation of what has been established in this General Framework, including international agreements signed with third parties, and shall inform the General Secretariat of the Andean Community thereof. If it is not practicable to publish that information, it shall be made otherwise publicly available.

Such international agreements signed with third parties as may refer to or affect the operation of what has been established in this General Framework shall be notified to the General Secretariat of the Andean Community, which in turn shall inform the Member Countries thereof.

For purposes of the first paragraph, Member Countries shall not be required to provide confidential information, the disclosure of which would impede compliance with the domestic body of laws of each Member Country, run counter to the public interest or national security, or cause prejudice to the legitimate commercial interests of public or private enterprises.

Article 10. The Member Countries, as of the entry into force of this General Framework, bind themselves not to establish new measures that would increase the degree of nonconformity or fail to comply with the commitments contained in articles 6 and 8. This commitment shall cover all measures adopted by Member Countries that affect the trade in services supplied by the central, regional or local public sector and by institutions delegated to provide them.

Article 11. Without prejudice to what is provided under this General Framework, each Member Country may adopt or apply the necessary measures to:

- Protect public morals or to maintain the public order;
- Protect the human, animal and plant life and health, and conserve the environment;
- Protect essential national security interests;
- Guarantee the imposition or the equitable and effective collection of direct taxes with respect to services or service providers of other Member Countries, even if such measures are inconsistent with the national treatment obligation contained in article 8;
- Implement provisions for avoiding double taxation contained in international agreements signed by the Member Country, even if such measures are inconsistent with the obligation stipulated in Article 7 to provide most-favored-nation treatment; and
- Obtain the enforcement of laws and regulations concerning:

  - The prevention of deceptive and fraudulent practices or related to the effects of default on services contracts;
  - The protection of the privacy of individuals with regard to the processing and dissemination of personal data and the protection of the confidential nature of the records and accounts of individuals; and
  - Public safety.

The measures listed in this article shall not be applied in manner that is disproportionate to the objective sought, be aimed at protecting national services or service providers, be implemented in such a way that they constitute an unnecessary obstacle to subregional trade in services or a means of discrimination against Andean Community services or service providers in relation to the treatment granted to other countries, whether or not they are members of the Andean Community.

Article 12. Member Countries shall facilitate the free movement and temporary presence of natural or physical persons and of employees of service suppliers from other Member Countries with relation to activities performed within the scope of this General Framework, as agreed in that regard by the Andean Council of Ministers of Foreign Affairs.

Article 13. Each Member Country shall recognize the licenses, certifications, professional degrees and accreditations granted by another Member Country, for any service activity requiring such documents, in accordance with the criteria established by a Decision on the subject to be adopted by the Commission.

CHAPTER V
LIBERALIZATION PROCESS

Article 14. Notwithstanding that provided in the previous articles, the Commission of the Andean Community, by December 31, 1999 at the latest, shall through a Decision adopt an inventory of the measures maintained by each Member Country that are contrary to the principles contained in articles 6 and 8 of this General Framework.

Article 15. With the purpose of moving forward in the liberalization of the trade in services within the subregion, which will have a substantial sectoral coverage, the Member Countries shall gradually and progressively eliminate the measures contained in the inventory referred to in the previous article, through annual negotiations coordinated by the General Secretariat, whose results shall be expressed in Decisions to be adopted by the Commission of the Andean Community.

The Commission of the Andean Community, meeting as the Enlarged Commission, when pertinent, may adopt Decisions based on sectoral studies prepared by the General Secretariat, in order to further the liberalization or harmonize rules and regulations in services sectors or subsectors included in the inventory referred to in the previous article. The Commission may also, based on those studies, define the sectors which because of their characteristics and unique features, shall be subject to specific sectoral liberalization or harmonization.

The liberalization of trade in services within the subregion shall conclude by the year 2005 at the latest, through the elimination of the measures maintained by each Member Country. In any case, the sectors covered by Decisions issued in accordance with the stipulations of the previous paragraph, shall be regulated by those Decisions.

Article 16. Two or more Member Countries may hasten or deepen the liberalization of particular service sectors or sub-sectors. Such benefits as may result from that acceleration and deepening shall be extended, immediately and unconditionally, to the country having already liberalized that sector and, through negotiation, to the other Andean Community Member Countries.

Negotiations conducted in accordance with the stipulations of the foregoing paragraph shall be open to the participation of the other Member Countries. Member Countries that do not take part in the resulting agreements may through negotiation accede to them at any time. These initiatives, together with any such bilateral agreements as may result from them, shall be notified to the General Secretariat of the Andean Community, which shall inform the pertinent Community bodies and the rest of the Member Countries.

CHAPTER VI
TREATMENT OF COMPLEMENTARY ISSUES

Article 17. Until the Community rules on the subject have been approved, the Member Countries shall adopt such measures as may be necessary to prevent, avoid and sanction practices that distort competition in the trade in services in their own market, including those that are needed to ensure that service providers established in their territories that have dominant market positions, do not abuse those positions.

Article 18. Member Countries shall ensure that such promotional measures as they may apply to service activities do not distort competition within the subregional market and shall adopt Community rules regarding incentives for the trade in services.

Article 19. No Member Country shall impose restrictions on international payments and transfers for current and capital transactions connected with the fulfillment of commitments stemming from this General Framework, except pursuant to article 20 below and in keeping with the rights and obligations derived from the Articles of Agreement of the International Monetary Fund.

CHAPTER VII
BALANCE OF PAYMENTS SAFEGUARDS

Article 20. Notwithstanding the stipulations of this General Framework, such Member Country as may have adopted restrictive measures on trade in services with third countries in order to cope with the existence or threat of serious external financial or balance of payments problems, may extend those measures, with the prior authorization of the General Secretariat, to trade in services within the subregion.

When the situation foreseen in the previous paragraph calls for immediate measures, the Member Country may apply such corrective measures as it deems necessary and shall inform the General Secretariat of the Andean Community thereof within a period not to exceed 5 days.

Such corrective measures as may be applied pursuant to the foregoing paragraphs:

- may not discriminate among the Member Countries of the Andean Community;
- shall be progressively eliminated as the situation that called for them improves;
- shall not exceed what is necessary in order to cope with national circumstances;
- may give priority to the supply of such services which are more essential to their economic or development programs, but they shall not select or maintain such restrictions for the purpose of protecting a particular service sector;
- shall be compatible with the Articles of Agreement of the International Monetary Fund.

Article 21. On being notified of the measures adopted pursuant to the foregoing article, the General Secretariat of the Andean Community, with the technical assistance of specialized experts, whose designation and form of participation shall be governed by the General Secretariat's regulations, shall analyze the balance of payments situation of the Member Country affected. Its corresponding decision shall be handed down within a period of no more than 30 days.

In making its decision, the General Secretariat shall consider the following elements:

- The nature and extent of the external financial and balance of payments problems of the Member Country affected;
- The economic environment of the Member Country affected;
- The observations of the other Member Countries; and
- Other possible corrective measures which may be available.

In the event that, pursuant to the balance of payment safeguard regulated by this Chapter, a Member Country adopts measures that restrict the flow of capital, thereby affecting other Andean Community Member Countries, an affected country could request the General Secretariat's pronouncement. If once the General Secretariat has made its pronouncement, the Member Country having imposed the measure requests its review by the Andean Court of Justice, the measure imposed shall remain in effect until the Court hands down its judgment.

CHAPTER VIII
SPECIAL TREATMENT FOR THE BENEFIT OF BOLIVIA AND ECUADOR

Article 22. Preferential treatment for Bolivia and Ecuador shall be given consideration during such negotiations as are carried out in the context of this General Framework, with regard to deadlines and temporary exceptions for compliance with their obligations, in keeping with the provisions of the Cartagena Agreement.

CHAPTER IX
ORIGIN OF THE SERVICES

Article 23. The following shall be considered as services originating in the subregion, for purposes of enjoying the benefits stemming from this General Framework:

Those furnished by natural or physical persons with permanent residence in any of the Member Countries, in accordance with the respective national regulations;

Services provided by juridical persons incorporated, authorized or residing according to domestic law in any of the Member Countries, which effectively carry out substantial operations in the territory of any of those Countries, or by Andean Multinational Enterprises; and
In the case of the cross-border provision of services, such services that are produced and furnished directly from the territory of a Member Country by natural or physical persons or by juridical persons as stipulated in paragraphs 1 and 2 above.

Article 24. In the event that a Member Country harbors doubts about the origin of a service, it may initiate consultations with the Member Country involved. If doubts about the origin of the service have not been dispelled within a maximum period of thirty days, either of the parties involved may request the intervention of the General Secretariat of the Andean Community.

The General Secretariat shall undertake the corresponding investigation and shall render its finding within a period not to exceed thirty days, as of the date of reception of the request.

CHAPTER X
FINAL PROVISIONS

Article 25. The General Secretariat shall summon government experts from the Member Countries to advise and support it in carrying out the activities provided for in this General Framework.

Article 26. In order to ensure the consistency and clarity of the General Framework established by this Decision, the ideas, definitions and interpretive elements contained in the General Agreement on Trade in Services GATS) shall be applied to said General Framework, whenever pertinent.

Article 27. This Decision shall become effective on the date of its publication in the Official Gazette of the Agreement of Cartagena.

TRANSITORY PROVISIONS

First. Until the adoption of the Decision referred to in article 14 of this General Framework and, in any case, by January 1st, 2000 at the latest, the commitments set out in articles 6 and 8 shall be valid in accordance with the domestic laws in force in each Member Country.

Second. In order to comply with article 14 of this Decision, Member Countries shall initiate an exchange of information about the measures provided in their legislation that limit the application of the principles contained in articles 6 and 8. The General Secretariat of the Andean Community shall coordinate the exchange of information, preparation of the inventory and drafting of the proposed Decision.

Third. In order to contribute to the understanding and correct implementation of this Decision by the competent national authorities, the General Secretariat shall undertake a study of the scope of the criteria of origin established in article 23. The results of that study shall be reported to the Commission no later than six months after this Decision takes effect.

Fourth. During the two months after this Decision takes effect at the latest, the General Secretariat of the Andean Community shall prepare a draft Decision containing the rules that will regulate the liberalization of trade in financial services among Member Countries. That proposal shall consider the conditions for implementation of the principles, commitments and rules and regulations contained in this General Framework.

Fifth. No later than two months after this Decision takes effect, the Andean Committee of Telecommunications Authorities (CAATEL) shall be convened by the General Secretariat to draw up the draft Decisions on telecommunications that will contain the rules for regulating the liberalization of trade in those services among Member Countries. Those draft Decisions will consider the conditions for implementation of the principles, commitments and rules and regulations contained in this General Framework.

Sixth. Within six months after this Decision takes effect, the General Secretariat shall draw up a draft Community regime on the recognition of licenses, certifications, professional degrees and accreditations in any service activity that requires them.

*

PROTOCOL TO AMEND THE FRAMEWORK AGREEMENT ON THE ASEAN INVESTMENT AREA[*]

The Protocol to Amend the Framework Agreement on the ASEAN Investment Area was signed at Hanoi, Viet Nam, on 14 September 2001. The Framework Agreement on the ASEAN Investment Area (AIA), reproduced in volume IV of this *Compendium,* was signed on 7 June 1998 and entered into force on 21 June 1999. The States members to the ASEAN are: Brunei Darussalam, Cambodia, Indonesia, Lao People's Democratic Republic, Malaysia, Myanmar, Philippines, Singapore, Thailand and Viet Nam.

The Governments of Brunei Darussalam, the Kingdom of Cambodia, the Republic of Indonesia, the Lao People's Democratic Republic, Malaysia, the Union of Myanmar, the Republic of the Philippines, the Republic of Singapore, the Kingdom of Thailand, the Socialist Republic of Viet Nam, Member States of the Association of South-East Asian Nations ("ASEAN");

RECALLING the Framework Agreement on the ASEAN Investment Area (" AIA Agreement") signed on 7 October 1998 at Makati, Philippines, which aims to establish a competitive and dynamic ASEAN Investment Area through a more liberal and transparent investment environment that would contribute towards the free flow of investments;

NOTING WITH SATISFACTION that the ASEAN Investment Area now extends across all ten Southeast Asian countries with the accession of the Kingdom of Cambodia to the AIA Agreement on 30 April 1999;

DESIRING to expedite the implementation of the AIA Agreement pursuant to the agreement of the ASEAN Leaders in paragraph 8 of the Statement on Bold Measures adopted at the Sixth ASEAN Summit on 16 December 1998 in Hanoi, Viet Nam, and to widen and elaborate its coverage as agreed by the First AIA Council Meeting on 5 March 1999 in, Phuket, Thailand;

NOTING that Article 18 of the AIA Agreement provides for amendments to it;

HAVE AGREED AS FOLLOWS:

ARTICLE 1

Article 2 of the AIA Agreement shall be substituted with the following:

"1. This Agreement shall cover all direct investments other than:

(a)   portfolio investments; and

(b)   matters relating to investment covered by other ASEAN Agreements.

---

[*] *Source*: Association of South East Asian Nations (2001). "Protocol to Amend the Framework Agreement on the ASEAN Investment Area"; available on the Internet (http://www.aseansec.org). [Note added by the editor.]

2.   Without prejudice to the provisions of paragraph I, this Agreement shall also include direct investments in the following sectors and services incidental to such sectors:

   (a)   manufacturing;
   (b)   agriculture;
   (c)   fishery;
   (d)   forestry;
   (e)   mining and quarrying.

3.   This Agreement shall further cover direct investments in such other sectors and services incidental to such sectors as may be agreed upon by all Member States."

ARTICLE 2

Article 7 of the AIA Agreement shall be amended as follows:

a)   by including the sentence below as a. new paragraph 4:

"Notwithstanding the provisions of paragraph 3, the Temporary Exclusion List for the manufacturing sector shall be progressively phased out by all Member States by 2003 except the Kingdom of Cambodia, the Lao People's Democratic Republic and the Socialist Republic of Viet Nam which shall do so not later than 2010."

b)   by renumbering the existing paragraph 4 as paragraph 5.

ARTICLE 3

Article 8 of the AIA Agreement shall be amended as follows:

a)   by including the sentence below as a new paragraph 4:

"Member States shall notify the AIA Council of the future investment related agreements or arrangements which grant preferential treatment which they enter into, as and when any such agreements are concluded and come into force."

b)   by renumbering the existing paragraph 4 as paragraph 5.

ARTICLE 4

Paragraph 2 of Article 9 of the AIA Agreement shall be substituted with the following:

"Having regard to the late entry into ASEAN of the Socialist Republic of Viet Nam, the Lao People's Democratic Republic, the Union of Myanmar and the Kingdom of Cambodia, the provisions of paragraph 1 of this Article shall only apply to:

(a) the Socialist Republic of Viet Nam after a period of 3 years;

(b) the Kingdom of Cambodia, the Lao People's Democratic Republic and the Union of Myanmar after a period of 5 years;

from the date this Agreement comes into force."

ARTICLE 5

1.   This Protocol shall enter into force upon the deposit of instruments of ratification or acceptance by all signatory Governments with the Secretary-General of ASEAN which shall be done within six months after the date of signing of this Protocol.

2.   This Protocol shall be deposited with the Secretary-General of ASEAN, who shall promptly furnish a certified copy thereof to each Member State.

IN WITNESS WHEREOF, the undersigned being duly authorised by their respective Governments, have signed this Protocol to Amend the Framework Agreement on the ASEAN Investment Area.

*

TRATADO SOBRE INVERSION Y COMERCIO DE SERVICIOS ENTRE LAS REPÚBLICAS DE COSTA RICA, EL SALVADOR, GUATEMALA, HONDURAS Y NICARAGUA[*]

The Agreement on Investment and Trade in Services among the Republics of Costa Rica, El Salvador, Guatemala, Honduras and Nicaragua was signed on 24 March 2002.

PREÁMBULO

Los Gobiernos de las Repúblicas de Costa Rica, El Salvador, Guatemala, Honduras y Nicaragua, Decididos a:

Alcanzar un mejor equilibrio en sus relaciones comerciales;

Propiciar un mercado más extenso y seguro para las inversiones y el intercambio de servicios en sus territorios;

Elevar la competitividad del sector servicios, requisito *sine qua non* para la facilitación del comercio de mercancías y el flujo de capitales y tecnologías, contribuyendo de manera determinante a consolidar la competitividad sistemática de las Partes;

Establecer un ordenamiento jurídico con reglas claras, transparentes y de beneficio mutuo para la promoción y protección de las inversiones, así como para el comercio de servicios;

Respetar sus respectivos derechos y obligaciones derivados del Acuerdo de Marrakech por el que se establece la Organización Mundial del Comercio (Acuerdo sobre la OMC), así como otros instrumentos bilaterales y multilaterales de integración y cooperación;

Crear oportunidades de empleo y mejorar los niveles de vida de sus respectivos países; y

Fomentar la participación dinámica de los distintos agentes económicos, en particular del sector empresarial, en los esfuerzos orientados a profundizar sus relaciones económicas;

Suscriben el presente Tratado sobre Inversión y Comercio de Servicios

---

[*] *Source*: The Governments of Central America (2002). "Tratado Sobre Inversion y Comercio de Servicios entre las Repúblicas de Costa Rica, El Salvador, Guatemala, Honduras y Nicaragua", available on the Internet (http://www.comex.go.cr). [Note added by the editor.]

PARTE I - DISPOSICIONES INICIALES

CAPÍTULO 1

OBJETIVOS

Artículo 1.01 Objetivos

1.   El presente Tratado tiene como principales objetivos los siguientes:

a)   establecer un marco jurídico, para la liberalización del comercio de los servicios y para la inversión entre las Partes, en consistencia con el Tratado General de Integración Económica Centroamericana, el Acuerdo General sobre el Comercio de Servicios (AGCS) que forma parte del Acuerdo sobre la OMC, así como otros instrumentos bilaterales y multilaterales de integración y cooperación.

Dicho marco promoverá los intereses de las Partes, sobre la base de ventajas recíprocas y la consecución de un equilibrio global de derechos y obligaciones entre las Partes;

b)   estimular la expansión y diversificación del comercio de servicios y la inversión entre las Partes;

c)   facilitar la circulación de servicios entre las Partes;

d)   promover, proteger y aumentar sustancialmente las inversiones en cada Parte; y

e)   crear procedimientos eficaces para la aplicación y cumplimiento de este Tratado, para su administración conjunta y para la solución de controversias entre una Parte y un inversionista de otra Parte.

2   Las Partes interpretarán y aplicarán las disposiciones de este Tratado a la luz de los objetivos establecidos en el párrafo 1 y de conformidad con las normas aplicables del Derecho Internacional.

3.   Las Partes, con el objeto de alcanzar una mayor integración entre ellas, procurarán de conformidad con el Artículo 9.02, iniciar negociaciones para definir un programa de trabajos futuros relativos a la inversión y el comercio de los servicios.

Artículo 1.02 Observancia del Tratado

Cada Parte asegurará, de conformidad con sus normas constitucionales, el cumplimiento de las disposiciones de este Tratado en su respectivo territorio.

Artículo 1.03 Relación con otros tratados

1.   Las Partes confirman los derechos y obligaciones vigentes entre ellas conforme a los tratados de los que sean parte.

2.   En caso de incompatibilidad entre las disposiciones de los tratados a que se refiere el párrafo anterior y las disposiciones de este Tratado, estas últimas prevalecerán en la medida de la incompatibilidad.

Artículo 1.04 Sucesión de tratados

Toda referencia a otro tratado se entenderá hecha en los mismos términos a un tratado sucesor del cual sean parte las Partes.

CAPÍTULO 2

DEFINICIONES DE APLICACIÓN GENERAL

Artículo 2.01 Definiciones de aplicación general

Para efectos de este Tratado, salvo que se especifique otra cosa, se entenderá por:

Acuerdo sobre la OMC: el Acuerdo de Marrakech por el que se establece la Organización Mundial del Comercio, de fecha 15 de abril de 1994.

AGCS: el Acuerdo General sobre el Comercio de Servicios, que forman parte del Acuerdo sobre la OMC;

Comisión: la Comisión establecida de conformidad con el artículo 9.02;

Consejo: el Consejo de Ministros de Integración Económica creado por el Artículo 37 del Protocolo de Guatemala;

días: días naturales, calendario o corridos;

empresa: cualquier persona jurídica constituida u organizada conforme a la legislación aplicable de una Parte, tenga o no fines de lucro y sea propiedad privada o gubernamental, incluidas las fundaciones, sociedades, fideicomisos, participaciones, empresas de propietario único, coinversiones u otras asociaciones;

empresa de una Parte: una empresa constituida u organizada de conformidad con la legislación de una Parte y una sucursal de una empresa ubicada en el territorio de otra Parte que desempeñe actividades comerciales en el mismo;

empresa del Estado: una empresa propiedad de una Parte o bajo el control de la misma, mediante derechos de dominio;

existente: vigente a la fecha de entrada en vigor de este Tratado;

medida: cualquier ley, reglamento, regla, procedimiento, disposición o práctica, entre otros;

mercancías: cualquier material, materia, producto o parte;

nacional: una persona física o natural que tiene la nacionalidad de una Parte conforme a su legislación y los residentes permanentes, quienes gozarán de los beneficios, derechos y obligaciones que este Tratado otorga a los nacionales, únicamente en lo concerniente a la aplicación del Tratado;

Parte: todo Estado respecto del cual haya entrado en vigor este Tratado;

persona: un nacional o una empresa; y

territorio: el territorio de cada una de las Partes.

PARTE II

DISPOSICIONES RELATIVAS A INVERSIÓN, SERVICIOS Y ASUNTOS RELACIONADOS

CAPÍTULO 3

INVERSIÓN

Sección A - Inversión

Artículo 3.01 Definiciones

Para efectos de este Capítulo, se entenderá por:

CIADI: el Centro Internacional de Arreglo de Diferencias Relativas a Inversiones;

Convención Interamericana: la Convención Interamericana sobre Arbitraje Comercial Internacional, celebrada en Panamá el 30 de enero de 1975;

Convenio del CIADI: el Convenio sobre Arreglo de Diferencias Relativas a Inversiones entre Estados y Nacionales de otros Estados, celebrado en Washington, D.C., el 18 de marzo de 1965;

Convención de Nueva York: la Convención de las Naciones Unidas sobre el Reconocimiento y Ejecución de Sentencias Arbitrales Extranjeras, celebrada en Nueva York el 10 de junio de 1958;

demanda: la reclamación sometida por un inversionista contendiente contra una Parte, en los términos de la Sección B de este Capítulo, cuyo fundamento sea una presunta violación a las disposiciones contenidas en la Sección A de este Capítulo;

empresa: una "empresa", tal como se define en el Artículo 2.01, y la sucursal de una empresa;

inversión: toda clase de bienes o derechos de cualquier naturaleza, adquiridos o utilizados con el propósito de obtener un beneficio económico u otros fines empresariales, adquiridos con recursos transferidos o reinvertidos por un inversionista, y comprenderá:

a)	una empresa, acciones de una empresa, participaciones en el capital social de una empresa, que le permitan al propietario participar en los ingresos o en las utilidades de la misma.

Instrumentos de deuda de una empresa y préstamos a una empresa cuando:

    i)	la empresa es una filial del inversionista, o

    ii)	la fecha de vencimiento original del instrumento de deuda o el préstamo sea por lo menos de tres (3) años;

b)	una participación en una empresa que otorgue derecho al propietario para participar del haber social de esa empresa en una liquidación, siempre que éste no derive de un instrumento de deuda o un préstamo excluidos conforme al literal (a);

c)	bienes raíces u otra propiedad, tangibles o intangibles, incluidos los derechos en el ámbito de la propiedad intelectual, así como cualquier otro derecho real (tales como hipotecas, derechos de prenda, usufructo y derechos similares) adquiridos con la expectativa de, o utilizados con el propósito de, obtener un beneficio económico o para otros fines empresariales; y

d)	la participación o beneficio que resulte de destinar capital u otros recursos comprometidos para el desarrollo de una actividad económica en territorio de una Parte, entre otros, conforme a:.

    i)	contratos que involucran la presencia de la propiedad de un inversionista en territorio de la Parte, incluidos, las concesiones, los contratos de construcción y de llave en mano; o

    ii)	contratos donde la remuneración depende sustancialmente de la producción, ingresos o ganancias de una empresa;

pero inversión no significa,

1.	una obligación de pago de, ni el otorgamiento de un crédito a, el Estado o una empresa del Estado;

2.	reclamaciones pecuniarias derivadas exclusivamente de:

    i)	contratos comerciales para la venta de bienes o servicios por un nacional o empresa en territorio de una Parte a una empresa en territorio de la otra Parte; o

    ii)	el otorgamiento de crédito en relación con una transacción comercial, cuya fecha de vencimiento sea menor a tres (3) años, como el financiamiento al comercio; salvo un préstamo cubierto por las disposiciones de un préstamo a una empresa según se establece en el literal (a); o

3.	cualquier otra reclamación pecuniaria que no conlleve los tipos de interés dispuestos en los literales del (a) al (d);

inversión de un inversionista de una Parte: la inversión propiedad o bajo control directo o indirecto de un inversionista de una Parte en el territorio de otra Parte.

En caso de una empresa, una inversión es propiedad de un inversionista de una Parte si ese inversionista tiene la titularidad de más del 50% de su capital social.

Una inversión está bajo el control de un inversionista de una Parte si ese inversionista tiene la facultad de:

    i)   designar a la mayoría de sus directores o

    ii)   dirigir de cualquier modo sus operaciones;

inversionista de una Parte: una Parte o una empresa de la misma, un nacional o una empresa de esa Parte, que lleve a cabo los actos materiales tendientes a realizar una inversión o, en su caso, realice o haya realizado una inversión en el territorio de otra Parte. La intención de realizar una inversión podrá manifestarse, entre otras formas, mediante actos jurídicos tendientes a materializar la inversión, o estando en vías de comprometer los recursos económicos necesarios para realizarla;

inversionista de un país no Parte: un inversionista que no es inversionista de una Parte que pretende realizar, realiza o ha realizado una inversión;

inversionista contendiente: un inversionista que somete una demanda en los términos de la Sección B de este Capítulo;

Parte contendiente: la Parte contra la cual se somete una demanda en los términos de la Sección B de este Capítulo;

parte contendiente: el inversionista contendiente o la Parte contendiente;

partes contendientes: el inversionista contendiente y la Parte contendiente;.

Reglas de Arbitraje de la CNUDMI: las Reglas de Arbitraje de la Comisión de Naciones Unidas sobre Derecho Mercantil Internacional (CNUDMI), aprobadas por la Asamblea General de las Naciones Unidas el 15 de diciembre de 1976;

Secretario General: el Secretario General del CIADI;

transferencias: las remisiones y pagos internacionales;

tribunal: un tribunal arbitral establecido conforme al Artículo 3.22; y

tribunal de acumulación: un tribunal arbitral establecido conforme al Artículo 3.29.

Artículo 3.02 Ámbito de aplicación y extensión de las obligaciones

1.   Este Capítulo se aplica a las medidas que adopte o mantenga una Parte relativas a:

    a)   los inversionistas de otra Parte, en todo lo relativo a su inversión;

b)   las inversiones de inversionistas de otra Parte realizadas en territorio de la Parte; y

c)   en lo que respecta al Artículo 3.07, todas las inversiones en el territorio de la Parte.

2.   Este Capítulo no se aplica a:

a)   las actividades económicas reservadas a cada Parte, tal como se señala en el Anexo II;

b)   las medidas que adopte o mantenga una Parte en materia de servicios financieros;

c)   las medidas que adopte una Parte para restringir la participación de las inversiones de inversionistas de otra Parte en su territorio, por razones de seguridad nacional u orden público; y

d)   las controversias o demandas surgidas con anterioridad a la entrada en vigor de este Tratado, o relacionadas con hechos acaecidos con anterioridad a su vigencia, incluso si sus efectos permanecen aún después de ésta.

3.   Este Capítulo se aplica en todo el territorio de las Partes y en cualquier nivel de gobierno, a pesar de las medidas incompatibles que pudieran existir en sus respectivas legislaciones.

4.   Ninguna disposición de este Capítulo se interpretará en el sentido de impedir a una Parte prestar servicios o llevar a cabo funciones relacionadas con la ejecución de las leyes, servicios de readaptación social, pensión o seguro de desempleo o servicios de seguridad social, bienestar social, educación pública, salud y protección de la niñez.

Artículo 3.03 Nivel mínimo de trato

Cada Parte otorgará a los inversionistas de otra Parte y a sus inversiones, un trato acorde con el Derecho Internacional, incluido el trato justo y equitativo, así como protección y seguridad jurídica dentro de su territorio..

Artículo 3.04 Trato nacional

Cada Parte otorgará al inversionista de otra Parte y a la inversión de un inversionista de otra Parte, un trato no menos favorable que el que otorgue, en circunstancias similares, a sus propios inversionistas y a las inversiones de dichos inversionistas en lo referente al establecimiento, adquisición, expansión, administración, conducción, operación, venta u otra disposición de las inversiones.

Artículo 3.05 Trato de nación más favorecida

Cada Parte otorgará al inversionista de otra Parte y a la inversión de un inversionista de otra Parte, un trato no menos favorable que el que otorgue, en circunstancias similares, al inversionista y a la inversión de un inversionista de cualquier otra Parte o de un país no Parte, en lo referente al establecimiento, adquisición, expansión, administración, conducción, operación, venta u otra disposición de las inversiones.

Artículo 3.06 Trato en caso de pérdidas

Cada Parte otorgará al inversionista de otra Parte, respecto de las inversiones que sufran pérdidas en su territorio debidas a conflictos armados o contiendas civiles, caso fortuito o fuerza mayor, un trato no discriminatorio respecto de cualquier medida que adopte o mantenga en vinculación con esas pérdidas.

Artículo 3.07 Requisitos de desempeño

1.   Ninguna Parte podrá imponer u obligar al cumplimiento de los siguientes requisitos o compromisos, en relación con el establecimiento, adquisición, expansión, administración, conducción u operación de una inversión de un inversionista de una Parte en su territorio para:

   a)   exportar un determinado tipo, nivel o porcentaje de mercancías o servicios;

   b)   alcanzar un determinado grado o porcentaje de contenido nacional;

   c)   adquirir, utilizar u otorgar preferencia a mercancías producidas o a servicios prestados en su territorio, o adquirir mercancías de productores o servicios de prestadores de servicios en su territorio;

   d)   relacionar en cualquier forma el volumen o valor de las importaciones con el volumen o valor de las exportaciones, o con el monto de las entradas de divisas asociadas con dicha inversión;

   e)   restringir las ventas en su territorio de las mercancías o servicios que tal inversión produzca o preste, relacionando de cualquier manera dichas ventas al volumen o valor de sus exportaciones o a ganancias que generen en divisas;

   f)   transferir a una persona en su territorio, tecnología, proceso productivo u otro conocimiento reservado, salvo cuando el requisito se imponga por un tribunal judicial o administrativo o autoridad competente, para reparar una supuesta violación a las leyes en materia de competencia o para actuar de una manera que no sea incompatible con otras disposiciones de este Tratado; o

   g)   actuar como el proveedor exclusivo de las mercancías que produzca o servicios que preste para un mercado específico, regional o mundial.

   Este párrafo no se aplica a ningún otro requisito distinto a los señalados en el mismo.

2.   La medida que exija que una inversión emplee una tecnología para cumplir con requisitos de salud, ambiente o seguridad de aplicación general, no se considerará incompatible con el párrafo 1 literal f). Para brindar mayor certeza, los Artículos 3.04 y 3.05 se aplican a la citada medida.

3.   Ninguna Parte podrá condicionar la recepción de una ventaja o que se continúe recibiendo la misma, en relación con una inversión en su territorio por parte de un inversionista de una Parte, al cumplimiento de cualquiera de los siguientes requisitos:

a)   adquirir, utilizar u otorgar preferencia a mercancías producidas en su territorio o a comprar mercancías de productores en su territorio;

b)   alcanzar un determinado grado o porcentaje de contenido nacional;

c)   relacionar en cualquier forma el volumen o valor de las importaciones con el volumen o valor de las exportaciones, o con el monto de las entradas de divisas asociadas con dicha inversión; o

d)   restringir las ventas en su territorio de las mercancías o servicios que tal inversión produzca o preste, relacionando de cualquier manera dichas ventas al volumen o valor de sus exportaciones o a ganancias que generen en divisas.

Este párrafo no se aplica a ningún otro requisito distinto a los señalados en el mismo.

4.   Nada de lo dispuesto en el párrafo 3 se interpretará como impedimento para que una Parte, en su territorio, imponga en relación con una inversión de un inversionista de otra Parte, requisitos legalmente establecidos de: localización geográfica de unidades productivas, generación de empleo o capacitación de mano de obra, o realización de actividades en materia de investigación y desarrollo.

5.   Siempre que dichas medidas no se apliquen de manera arbitraria o injustificada, o no constituyan una restricción encubierta al comercio o inversión internacionales, nada de lo dispuesto en los párrafos 1(b) ó (c) ó 2(a) ó (b) se interpretará en el sentido de impedir a una Parte adoptar o mantener medidas, incluidas las de naturaleza ambiental, necesarias para:

a)   asegurar el cumplimiento de leyes y reglamentaciones que no sean incompatibles con las disposiciones de este Tratado;

b)   proteger la vida o salud humana, animal o vegetal; o

c)   la preservación de recursos naturales no renovables, vivos o no.

6.   En caso que, a juicio de una Parte, la imposición por otra Parte de cualquier otro requisito no previsto en el párrafo 1 afecte negativamente el flujo comercial o constituya una barrera significativa a la inversión, el asunto será considerado por el Comité de Inversión y Comercio Transfronterizo de Servicios, establecido en el Artículo 4.09.

7.   Si el Comité considera que el requisito en cuestión afecta negativamente el flujo comercial o constituye una barrera significativa a la inversión, recomendará a la Comisión las disposiciones necesarias para suprimir la práctica de que se trate. Las Partes considerarán estas disposiciones como incorporadas a este Tratado.

Artículo 3.08 Alta dirección empresarial y consejos de administración

1.   Ninguna Parte podrá exigir que una empresa de esa Parte, designe a individuos de alguna nacionalidad en particular para ocupar puestos de alta dirección..2. Una Parte podrá exigir que la mayoría de los miembros de los órganos de administración o de cualquier comité de tales órganos de una empresa de esa Parte que sea una inversión de un inversionista de otra Parte, sea

de una nacionalidad en particular, o sea residente en territorio de la Parte, siempre que el requisito no menoscabe significativamente la capacidad del inversionista para ejercer el control de su inversión.

Artículo 3.09 Reservas y excepciones

1.   Los Artículos 3.04, 3.05, 3.07 y 3.08 no se aplican a:

      a)   cualquier medida incompatible existente que mantenga una Parte, siempre que la misma forme parte de su lista del Anexo I (Medidas Incompatibles Existentes) o del Anexo II (Actividades Económicas Reservadas a cada Parte);

      b)   la continuación o pronta renovación de cualquier medida incompatible a que se refiere la literal a); ni

      c)   la reforma a cualquier medida incompatible a que se refiere la literal a), siempre que dicha reforma no disminuya el grado de compatibilidad de la medida, tal como estaba en vigor antes de la reforma, con los Artículos 3.04, 3.05, 3.07 y 3.08.

2.   El trato otorgado por una Parte de conformidad con el Artículo 3.05 no se aplica a los tratados o sectores estipulados en su lista del Anexo III (Excepciones al Trato de Nación Más Favorecida).

3.   Los Artículos 3.04, 3.05 y 3.08 no se aplican a:

      a)   las compras realizadas por una Parte o por una empresa del Estado; ni

      b)   subsidios o aportaciones, incluyendo los préstamos, garantías y seguros gubernamentales otorgados por una Parte o por una empresa del Estado, salvo por lo dispuesto en el Artículo 3.06.

4.   Con miras a lograr un nivel de liberalización progresivamente más elevado, las Partes se comprometen a realizar negociaciones futuras, por lo menos cada dos (2) años, en el seno del Consejo, tendientes a eliminar las restricciones remanentes inscritas de conformidad con el párrafo 1 de este Artículo.

Artículo 3.10 Transferencias

1.   Cada Parte permitirá que todas las transferencias relacionadas con la inversión de un inversionista de otra Parte en su territorio, se hagan libremente y sin demora. Dichas transferencias incluyen:

      a)   ganancias, dividendos, intereses, ganancias de capital, pagos por regalías, gastos de administración, asistencia técnica y otros cargos, ganancias en especie y otros montos derivados de la inversión;

      b)   productos derivados de la venta o liquidación, total o parcial, de la inversión;

c)   pagos realizados conforme a un contrato del que sea parte un inversionista o su inversión, incluidos pagos efectuados conforme a un convenio de préstamo;

d)   pagos derivados de indemnizaciones por concepto de expropiación; y.

e)   pagos que provengan de la aplicación de las disposiciones relativas al mecanismo de solución de controversias contenido en la Sección B de este Capítulo.

2.   Para efectos de este Capítulo, una transferencia se considera realizada sin demora cuando se ha efectuado dentro del plazo normalmente necesario para el cumplimiento de las formalidades de transferencia.

3.   Ninguna Parte podrá exigir a sus inversionistas que efectúen transferencias de sus ingresos, ganancias, o utilidades u otros montos derivados de, o atribuibles a, inversiones llevadas a cabo en territorio de otra Parte, ni los sancionará en caso que no realicen la transferencia.

4.   Cada Parte permitirá que las transferencias se realicen en divisas de libre convertibilidad al tipo de cambio vigente de mercado en la fecha de la transferencia.

5.   No obstante lo dispuesto en los párrafos 1 y 4, cada Parte podrá impedir la realización de transferencias, mediante la aplicación equitativa, no discriminatoria y de buena fe de medidas:

a)   para proteger los derechos de los acreedores;

b)   relativas a asegurar el cumplimiento de las leyes y reglamentos:

i)   para la emisión, transmisión y negociación de valores, futuros y derivados; o

ii)   relativos a reportes o registros de transferencias; o

c)   relacionadas con infracciones penales o resoluciones en procedimientos administrativos o judiciales.

6.   No obstante lo dispuesto en este Artículo, cada Parte podrá establecer controles temporales a las operaciones cambiarias, siempre y cuando la balanza de pagos de la Parte de que se trate, presente un serio desequilibrio o dificultades excepcionales o graves, e instrumente un programa de acuerdo con los criterios internacionalmente aceptados.

Artículo 3.11 Expropiación e indemnización

1.   Ninguna Parte podrá nacionalizar ni expropiar, directa o indirectamente, una inversión de un inversionista de una Parte en su territorio, ni adoptar medida alguna equivalente a la expropiación o nacionalización de esa inversión, salvo que sea:

a)   por causa de utilidad pública conforme a lo dispuesto en el Anexo 3.11;

b)   sobre bases no discriminatorias;

c) con apego al principio de legalidad; y

d) mediante indemnización conforme a los párrafos 2 al 4.

2.   La indemnización será equivalente al valor justo de mercado que tenga la inversión expropiada inmediatamente antes que la medida expropiatoria se haya llevado a cabo (fecha de expropiación), y no reflejará ningún cambio en el valor, debido a que la intención de expropiar se haya conocido con antelación a la fecha de expropiación. Los criterios de valuación incluirán el valor fiscal declarado de bienes tangibles, así como otros criterios que resulten apropiados para determinar el valor justo de mercado.

3.   El pago de la indemnización se hará sin demora y será completamente liquidable.

4.   La cantidad pagada no será inferior a la cantidad equivalente que por indemnización se hubiera pagado en una divisa de libre convertibilidad en el mercado financiero internacional, en la fecha de expropiación, y esta divisa se hubiese convertido a la cotización de mercado vigente en la fecha de valuación, más los intereses que hubiese generado a una tasa bancaria o comercial hasta la fecha del día del pago.

Artículo 3.12 Formalidades especiales y requisitos de información

1.   Nada de lo dispuesto en el Artículo 3.04 se interpretará en el sentido de impedir a una Parte adoptar o mantener una medida que prescriba formalidades especiales conexas al establecimiento de inversiones por inversionistas de otra Parte, tales como que las inversiones se constituyan conforme a la legislación de la Parte, siempre que dichas formalidades no menoscaben sustancialmente la protección otorgada por una Parte conforme a este Capítulo.

2.   No obstante lo dispuesto en los Artículos 3.04 y 3.05, cada Parte podrá exigir, en su territorio, a un inversionista de otra Parte, que proporcione información rutinaria, referente a su inversión, exclusivamente con fines de información o estadística. La Parte protegerá la información que sea confidencial, de cualquier divulgación que pudiera afectar negativamente la situación competitiva de la inversión o del inversionista.

Artículo 3.13 Relación con otros capítulos

En caso de incompatibilidad entre una disposición de este Capítulo y las disposiciones de otro Capítulo de este Tratado prevalecerán las disposiciones de este último, en la medida de la incompatibilidad.

Artículo 3.14 Denegación de beneficios

Una Parte, previa notificación y consulta con otra Parte, podrá denegar los beneficios de este Capítulo a un inversionista de esa Parte que sea una empresa de la misma y a las inversiones de tal inversionista, si inversionistas de un país no Parte son propietarios mayoritarios o controlan la empresa y ésta no tiene actividades empresariales sustanciales en el territorio de la Parte conforme a cuya ley está constituida u organizada.

Artículo 3.15 Aplicación extraterritorial de la legislación de una Parte

1.   Las Partes, en relación con las inversiones de sus inversionistas, constituidas y organizadas conforme a la legislación de otra Parte, no podrán ejercer jurisdicción ni adoptar medida alguna que tenga por efecto la aplicación extraterritorial de su legislación o la obstaculización del comercio entre las Partes, o entre una Parte y un país no Parte.

2.   Si alguna de las Partes incumpliere lo dispuesto por el párrafo 1, la Parte en donde la inversión se hubiere constituido podrá, a su discreción, adoptar las medidas y ejercitar las acciones que considere necesarias, a fin de dejar sin efecto la legislación o la medida que se trate y los obstáculos al comercio consecuencia de las mismas.

Artículo 3.16 Medidas relativas al ambiente

1.   Nada de lo dispuesto en este Capítulo se interpretará como impedimento para que una Parte adopte, mantenga o ponga en ejecución cualquier medida, compatible con este Capítulo, que considere apropiada para asegurar que las inversiones en su territorio observen la legislación en materia ambiental.

2.   Las Partes reconocen que es inadecuado fomentar la inversión por medio de un relajamiento de las medidas internas aplicables a la salud, seguridad o relativas al ambiente. En consecuencia, ninguna Parte deberá eliminar o comprometerse a eximir de la aplicación de esas medidas a la inversión de un inversionista, como medio para inducir el establecimiento, la adquisición, la expansión o conservación de la inversión en su territorio. Si una Parte estima que otra Parte ha fomentado una inversión de tal manera, podrá solicitar consultas con esa otra Parte.

Artículo 3.17 Promoción de inversiones e intercambio de información

1.   Con la intención de incrementar significativamente la participación recíproca de las inversiones, las Partes podrán promover y apoyar la elaboración de documentos de promoción de oportunidades de inversión y el diseño de mecanismos para su difusión. Así mismo, las Partes podrán crear, mantener y perfeccionar mecanismos financieros que hagan viable las inversiones de una Parte en el territorio de otra Parte.

2.   Las Partes darán a conocer información disponible sobre oportunidades de:

    a)   inversión en su territorio, que puedan ser desarrolladas por inversionistas de otra Parte;

    b)   alianzas estratégicas entre inversionistas de las Partes, mediante la investigación y conjugación de intereses y oportunidades de asociación; y

    c)   inversión en sectores económicos específicos que interesen a las Partes y a sus inversionistas, de acuerdo a la solicitud expresa que haga cualquier Parte.

3.   A fin de mantenerse informadas y actualizadas, las Partes se intercambiaran información respecto de:

    a)   la legislación que, directa o indirectamente, afecte a la inversión extranjera incluyendo, entre otros, regímenes cambiarios y de carácter fiscal;

b)   el comportamiento de la inversión extranjera en sus respectivos territorios; y

c)   las oportunidades de inversión a que se refiere el párrafo 2 de este Artículo, incluyendo la difusión de los instrumentos financieros disponibles que coadyuven al incremento de la inversión en el territorio de las Partes.

Sección B - Solución de Controversias entre una Parte y un inversionista de otra Parte

Artículo 3.18 Objetivo

Esta Sección establece un mecanismo para la solución de controversias de naturaleza jurídica en materia de inversión que se susciten, a partir de la entrada en vigor del presente Tratado, como consecuencia de la violación de una obligación establecida en la Sección A de este Capítulo y asegura, tanto el trato igual entre inversionistas de las Partes de acuerdo con el principio de reciprocidad, como el debido ejercicio de la garantía de audiencia y defensa dentro de un proceso legal ante un tribunal arbitral.

Artículo 3.19 Demanda del inversionista de una Parte, por cuenta propia o en representación de una empresa

1.   De conformidad con esta Sección, el inversionista de una Parte podrá, por cuenta propia o en representación de una empresa de otra Parte que sea de su propiedad o que esté bajo su control directo o indirecto, someter a arbitraje una demanda cuyo fundamento sea el que otra Parte o una empresa controlada directa o indirectamente por esa Parte, ha violado una obligación establecida en este Capítulo, siempre y cuando el inversionista o su inversión hayan sufrido pérdidas o daños en virtud de la violación o como consecuencia de ella.

2.   El inversionista no podrá presentar una demanda conforme a esta Sección, si han transcurrido más de tres (3) años a partir de la fecha en la cual tuvo conocimiento o debió haber tenido conocimiento de la presunta violación cometida a su inversión, así como de las pérdidas o daños sufridos.

3.   Cuando un inversionista presente una demanda en representación de una empresa que sea de su propiedad o que esté bajo su control directo o indirecto, o de manera paralela un inversionista que no tenga el control de una empresa presente una demanda por cuenta propia como consecuencia de los mismos actos que dieron lugar a la presentación de una demanda de acuerdo con este Artículo, y dos (2) o más demandas se sometan a arbitraje en los términos del Artículo 3.22, el tribunal de acumulación establecido de conformidad con el Artículo 3.29, examinará conjuntamente dichas demandas, salvo que ese tribunal determine que los intereses de una parte contendiente se verían perjudicados.

4.   Una inversión no podrá someter una demanda a arbitraje conforme a esta Sección.

Artículo 3.20 Solución de controversias mediante consultas y negociaciones

Las partes contendientes primero intentarán dirimir la controversia por vía de consulta o negociación.

Artículo 3.21 Notificación de la intención de someter la demanda a arbitraje

El inversionista contendiente notificará por escrito a la Parte contendiente su intención de someter una demanda a arbitraje, cuando menos noventa (90) días antes que se presente formalmente la demanda. La notificación señalará lo siguiente:

a) el nombre y domicilio del inversionista contendiente y, cuando la demanda se haya presentado en representación de una empresa, la denominación o razón social y el domicilio de la misma;

b) los hechos en que se funde la demanda;.

c) las disposiciones de este Capítulo presuntamente incumplidas y cualquier otra disposición aplicable; y

d) la reparación que se solicite y el monto aproximado de los daños reclamados en la moneda en que se haya realizado la inversión.

Artículo 3.22 Sometimiento de la demanda a arbitraje

1. Salvo lo dispuesto en el Anexo 3.22 y párrafo 3 del presente Artículo y siempre que hayan transcurrido seis (6) meses desde que tuvieron lugar los actos que motivan la demanda, un inversionista contendiente podrá someter la demanda a arbitraje de acuerdo con:

a) el Convenio del CIADI, siempre que tanto la Parte contendiente como la Parte del inversionista sean Estados Parte del mismo;

b) Las Reglas del Mecanismo Complementario del CIADI, cuando la Parte contendiente o la Parte del inversionista, pero no ambas, sea parte del Convenio del CIADI; o

c) las Reglas de Arbitraje de la CNUDMI.

2. Las reglas de arbitraje elegidas, regirán el arbitraje, salvo en la medida de lo modificado por esta Sección.

3. Una reclamación de un inversionista de una Parte:

a) por cuenta propia podrá someterse a arbitraje de conformidad con esta sección, siempre que tanto dicho inversionista como la empresa que sea una persona jurídica de su propiedad o que esté bajo su control directo o indirecto, no hayan sometido la misma reclamación ante un tribunal nacional competente de la Parte contendiente;

b) en representación de una empresa podrá someterse a arbitraje de conformidad con esta sección, siempre que tanto dicho inversionista como la empresa que sea una persona jurídica de su propiedad o que esté bajo su control directo o indirecto, no hayan sometido la misma reclamación ante un tribunal nacional competente de la Parte contendiente;

En consecuencia, una vez que el inversionista o la empresa hayan sometido la reclamación al tribunal nacional competente de la Parte contendiente, la elección de dicho procedimiento será única y definitiva, excluyendo la posibilidad de someter la reclamación a un procedimiento arbitral de conformidad con esta sección.

Artículo 3.23 Condiciones previas al sometimiento de una demanda al procedimiento arbitral

1.   El consentimiento de las partes contendientes al procedimiento de arbitraje conforme a este Capítulo se considerará como consentimiento a ese arbitraje con exclusión de cualquier otro mecanismo.

2.   Cada Parte podrá exigir el agotamiento previo de sus recursos administrativos como condición a su consentimiento al arbitraje conforme a este Capítulo. Sin embargo, si transcurridos seis (6) meses a partir del momento en que se interpusieron los recursos administrativos correspondientes, las autoridades administrativas no han emitido su resolución final, el inversionista podrá recurrir directamente al arbitraje, de conformidad con lo establecido en esta Sección.

3.   Un inversionista contendiente por cuenta propia podrá someter una demanda al procedimiento arbitral de conformidad con esta Sección, sólo si:

a)   consiente someterse a arbitraje en los términos de los procedimientos establecidos en esta Sección; y

b)   el inversionista y, cuando la demanda se refiera a pérdida o daño en una participación en una empresa de otra Parte que sea propiedad del inversionista o que esté bajo su control directo o indirecto, la empresa renuncian a su derecho a iniciar cualquier procedimiento ante un tribunal nacional competente conforme al derecho de la Parte contendiente u otros procedimientos de solución de controversias respecto a la medida de la Parte contendiente presuntamente violatoria de las disposiciones a las que se refiere el Artículo 3.19, salvo los procedimientos en que se solicite la aplicación de medidas precautorias de carácter suspensivo, declarativo o extraordinario, que no impliquen el pago de daños ante el tribunal nacional competente, conforme a la legislación de la Parte contendiente, tales como el agotamiento de los recursos administrativos ante las propias autoridades ejecutoras de la medida presuntamente violatoria, previstos en la legislación de la Parte contendiente.

4.   Un inversionista contendiente, en representación de una empresa, podrá someter una demanda al procedimiento arbitral de conformidad con esta Sección, sólo si tanto el inversionista como la empresa:

a)   consienten en someterse a arbitraje en los términos de los procedimientos establecidos en esta Sección; y

b)   renuncian a su derecho de iniciar cualquier procedimiento con respecto a la medida de la Parte contendiente que presuntamente sea una de las violaciones a las que se refiere el Artículo 3.19 ante cualquier tribunal nacional competente conforme a la legislación o derecho de una Parte u otros procedimientos de solución de controversias, salvo los procedimientos en que se solicite la aplicación de medidas precautorias de carácter suspensivo, declarativo o extraordinario, que no impliquen el pago de daños ante el tribunal nacional competente, conforme a la legislación o derecho de la Parte contendiente, tales como el agotamiento de los recursos administrativos ante las propias autoridades ejecutoras de la medida presuntamente violatoria, previstos en la legislación de la Parte contendiente.

5.   El consentimiento y la renuncia requeridos por este Artículo se manifestarán por escrito, se entregarán a la Parte contendiente y se incluirán en el sometimiento de la demanda a arbitraje.

6.   Sólo en el caso que la Parte contendiente haya privado al inversionista contendiente del control de una empresa:

   a)   no se requerirá la renuncia de la empresa conforme a las literales b) de los párrafos 3 ó 4; y

   b)   no será aplicable el párrafo 3 del Artículo 3.22.

Artículo 3.24 Consentimiento a arbitraje

1.   Cada Parte consiente en someter demandas a arbitraje con apego a los procedimientos y requisitos señalados en esta Sección.

2.   El sometimiento de una demanda a arbitraje por parte de un inversionista contendiente cumplirá con los requisitos señalados en:

   a)   el Capítulo II del Convenio del CIADI (Jurisdicción del Centro) y las Reglas del Mecanismo Complementario que exigen el consentimiento por escrito de las Partes;

   b)   el Artículo II de la Convención de Nueva York, que exige un acuerdo por escrito; o

   c)   el Artículo I de la Convención Interamericana, que requiere un acuerdo.

Artículo 3.25 Número de árbitros y método de nombramiento

Con excepción de lo dispuesto por el Artículo 3.29, y sin perjuicio que las partes contendientes acuerden algo distinto, el tribunal estará integrado por tres (3) árbitros. Cada una de las partes contendientes nombrará a un árbitro. El tercer árbitro, quien será el presidente del tribunal, será designado por las partes contendientes de común acuerdo pero no será nacional de una de las partes contendientes.

Artículo 3.26 Integración del tribunal en caso que una parte contendiente no designe árbitro o no se logre un acuerdo en la designación del presidente del tribunal

En caso que una parte contendiente no designe árbitro o no se logre un acuerdo en la designación del presidente del tribunal:

a)   el Secretario General nombrará a los árbitros en los procedimientos de arbitraje, de conformidad con esta Sección;

b)   cuando un tribunal, que no sea el establecido de conformidad con el Artículo 3.29, no se integre en un plazo de noventa (90) días a partir de la fecha en que la demanda se someta a arbitraje, el Secretario General, a petición de cualquiera de las partes contendientes, nombrará, a su discreción, al árbitro o árbitros no designados todavía, pero no al presidente del tribunal, quién será designado conforme a lo dispuesto en la literal c). En todo caso, la mayoría de los árbitros no podrá ser nacional de la Parte contendiente o nacional de la Parte del inversionista contendiente.; o

c)   el Secretario General designará al presidente del tribunal de entre los árbitros de la lista a que se refiere el Artículo 3.27, asegurándose que el presidente del tribunal no sea nacional de la Parte contendiente o nacional de la Parte del inversionista contendiente. En caso que no se encuentre en la lista un árbitro disponible para presidir el tribunal, el Secretario General designará, de la Lista de Árbitros del CIADI, al presidente del tribunal, siempre que sea de nacionalidad distinta a la de la Parte contendiente o a la de la Parte del inversionista contendiente.

Artículo 3.27 Lista de árbitros

A la fecha de entrada en vigor de este Tratado, las Partes establecerán y mantendrán una lista de árbitros como posibles presidentes del tribunal, o para nombrar los árbitros de un tribunal de acumulación, según el párrafo 4 del Artículo 3.29, que reúnan las mismas cualidades a que se refiere el Convenio del CIADI, las Reglas del Mecanismo Complementario del CIADI o las Reglas de Arbitraje de la CNUDMI y que cuenten con experiencia en Derecho Internacional y en asuntos en materia de inversiones. Para tal efecto, los miembros de la lista serán designados por consenso sin importar su nacionalidad y cada Parte propondrá hasta cinco (5) árbitros por un plazo de dos años, renovables si por consenso las Partes así lo acuerdan. En caso de muerte o renuncia de un miembro de la lista, las Partes de mutuo acuerdo designarán a otra persona que le reemplace en sus funciones para el resto del período para el que aquél fue nombrado.

Artículo 3.28 Consentimiento para la designación de árbitros

Para efectos del Artículo 39 del Convenio del CIADI y del Artículo 7 de la parte C de las Reglas del Mecanismo Complementario del CIADI, y sin perjuicio de objetar a un árbitro con fundamento en la literal c) del Artículo 3.26, o sobre base distinta a la de nacionalidad:

a)   la Parte contendiente acepta la designación de cada uno de los miembros de un tribunal establecido de conformidad con el Convenio del CIADI o con las Reglas del Mecanismo Complementario del CIADI; y

b)   un inversionista contendiente, sea por cuenta propia o en representación de una empresa, podrá someter una demanda a arbitraje o continuar el procedimiento conforme al Convenio del CIADI, o a las Reglas del Mecanismo Complementario del CIADI, únicamente a condición de que el inversionista contendiente y, en su caso, la empresa que representa, manifiesten su consentimiento por escrito sobre la designación de cada uno de los miembros del tribunal.

Artículo 3.29 Acumulación de procedimientos

1.   Un tribunal de acumulación establecido conforme a este Artículo se instalará con apego a las Reglas de Arbitraje de la CNUDMI y procederá de conformidad con lo establecido en dichas reglas, salvo lo que disponga esta Sección.

2.   Cuando un tribunal de acumulación determine que las demandas sometidas a arbitraje de acuerdo con el Artículo 3.22, plantean cuestiones de hecho y de derecho en común, el tribunal de acumulación, en interés de su resolución justa y eficiente, y habiendo escuchado a las partes contendientes, podrá asumir jurisdicción, dar trámite y resolver:

   a)   todas o parte de las demandas, de manera conjunta; o

   b)   una o más de las demandas en el entendido que ello contribuirá a la resolución de las otras.

3.   Una parte contendiente que pretenda obtener una orden de acumulación en los términos del párrafo 2, solicitará al Secretario General que instale un tribunal de acumulación y especificará en su solicitud:

   a)   el nombre de la Parte contendiente o de los inversionistas contendientes contra los cuales se pretenda obtener la orden de acumulación;

   b)   la naturaleza de la orden de acumulación solicitada; y

   c)   el fundamento en que se apoya la solicitud.

4.   En un plazo de sesenta (60) días a partir de la fecha de la recepción de la solicitud, el Secretario General instalará un tribunal de acumulación integrado por tres (3) árbitros. El Secretario General nombrará de la lista de árbitros a que se refiere el Artículo 3.27 al presidente del tribunal de acumulación, quien no será nacional de la Parte contendiente ni nacional de la Parte del inversionista contendiente. En caso que no se encuentre en la lista un árbitro disponible para presidir el tribunal de acumulación, el Secretario General designará, de la Lista de Árbitros del CIADI, al presidente de dicho tribunal, quien no será nacional de la Parte contendiente ni nacional de la Parte del inversionista contendiente. El Secretario General designará a los otros dos (2) integrantes del tribunal de acumulación de la lista de árbitros que se refiere el Artículo 3.27 y, cuando no estén disponibles en dicha lista, los seleccionará de la Lista de Árbitros del CIADI. De no haber disponibilidad de árbitros en esa Lista, el Secretario General hará discrecionalmente los nombramientos faltantes. Uno de los miembros será nacional de la Parte contendiente y el otro miembro del tribunal de acumulación será nacional de una Parte de los inversionistas contendientes.

5.   Cuando se haya establecido un tribunal de acumulación conforme a este Artículo, el inversionista contendiente que haya sometido una demanda a arbitraje conforme al Artículo 3.19, y no haya sido mencionado en la solicitud de acumulación hecha de acuerdo con el párrafo 3, podrá solicitar por escrito al tribunal de acumulación que se le incluya en una orden de acumulación formulada de acuerdo con el párrafo 2, y especificará en dicha solicitud:

   a)   el nombre y domicilio y, en su caso, la denominación o razón social y el domicilio de la empresa;

b)   la naturaleza de la orden de acumulación solicitada; y

c)   los fundamentos en que se apoya la solicitud.

6.   El tribunal de acumulación proporcionará, a costa del inversionista interesado, copia de la petición de acumulación a los inversionistas contendientes que quedarían sujetos a la resolución de acumulación.

7.   Un tribunal no tendrá jurisdicción para resolver una demanda, o parte de ella, respecto de la cual haya asumido jurisdicción un tribunal de acumulación.

8.   A solicitud de una parte contendiente, un tribunal de acumulación podrá, en espera de su decisión conforme al párrafo 2, disponer que los procedimientos de un tribunal se suspendan, hasta en tanto se resuelva sobre la procedencia de la acumulación. Lo ordenado por el tribunal de acumulación deberá ser acatado por el tribunal.

Artículo 3.30 Notificaciones

1.   Dentro del plazo de quince (15) días contado a partir de la fecha de su recepción, la Parte contendiente hará llegar al Secretariado una copia de:

a)   una solicitud de arbitraje hecha conforme al párrafo 1 del Artículo 36 del Convenio del CIADI;

b)   una notificación de arbitraje en los términos del Artículo 2 de la parte C de las Reglas del Mecanismo Complementario del CIADI; o

c)   una notificación de arbitraje en los términos previstos por las Reglas de Arbitraje de la CNUDMI.

2.   La Parte contendiente entregará al Secretariado copia de la solicitud formulada en los términos del párrafo 3 del Artículo 3.29:

a)   en un plazo de quince (15) días a partir de la recepción de la solicitud, en el caso de una petición hecha por el inversionista contendiente; o

b)   en un plazo de quince (15) días a partir de la fecha de la solicitud, en el caso de una petición hecha por la Parte contendiente.

3.   La Parte contendiente entregará al Secretariado copia de una solicitud formulada en los términos del párrafo 5 del Artículo 3.29 en un plazo de quince (15) días a partir de la fecha de recepción de la solicitud.

4.   El Secretariado conservará un registro público de los documentos a los que se refieren los párrafos 1, 2 y 3.

5.   La Parte contendiente entregará a las otras Partes:

a)   notificación escrita de una demanda que se haya sometido a arbitraje a más tardar treinta (30) días después de la fecha de sometimiento de la demanda a arbitraje; y

b)   copias de todos los escritos presentados en el procedimiento arbitral.

Artículo 3.31 Participación de una Parte

Previa notificación escrita a las partes contendientes, una Parte podrá presentar escritos a un tribunal establecido conforme a esta Sección, sobre cuestiones de interpretación de este Tratado, que se estén discutiendo ante dicho tribunal.

Artículo 3.32 Sede del procedimiento arbitral

La sede del procedimiento arbitral estará ubicada en el territorio de la Parte contendiente salvo que las partes contendientes acuerden otra cosa, en todo caso, un tribunal establecido conforme a esta Sección, llevará a cabo el procedimiento arbitral en el territorio de una Parte que sea miembro de la Convención de Nueva York, el cual será elegido de conformidad con:

a)   las Reglas del Mecanismo Complementario del CIADI, si el arbitraje se rige por esas Reglas o por el Convenio del CIADI; o

b)   las Reglas de Arbitraje de la CNUDMI, si el arbitraje se rige por esas Reglas.

Artículo 3.33 Derecho aplicable

1.   Un tribunal establecido conforme a esta Sección, decidirá las controversias que se sometan a su consideración de conformidad con este Tratado y con las disposiciones aplicables del Derecho Internacional y supletoriamente, la legislación de la Parte contendiente.

2.   La interpretación que formule el Consejo sobre una disposición de este Tratado, será obligatoria para un tribunal establecido conforme a esta Sección.

Artículo 3.34 Interpretación de los Anexos

1.   Cuando una Parte alegue como defensa que una medida presuntamente violatoria cae en el ámbito de una reserva o excepción consignada en cualquiera de los Anexos, a petición de la Parte contendiente, un tribunal establecido conforme a esta Sección, solicitará al Consejo una interpretación sobre ese asunto. El Consejo, en un plazo de sesenta (60) días a partir de la entrega de la solicitud, presentará por escrito a dicho tribunal su interpretación.

2.   La interpretación del Consejo a que se refiere el párrafo 1, será obligatoria para un tribunal establecido conforme a esta Sección. Si el Consejo no presenta su interpretación dentro del plazo señalado, dicho tribunal decidirá sobre el asunto.

Artículo 3.35 Dictámenes de expertos

Sin perjuicio de la designación de otro tipo de expertos cuando lo autoricen las reglas de arbitraje aplicables, el tribunal establecido conforme a esta Sección, a petición de una parte contendiente, o por iniciativa propia a menos que las partes contendientes no lo acepten, podrá designar uno o más expertos para dictaminar por escrito cualquier cuestión que haya planteado una parte contendiente en un procedimiento, de acuerdo a los términos y condiciones que acuerden las partes contendientes.

Artículo 3.36 Medidas provisionales o precautorias

Un tribunal establecido conforme a esta Sección, podrá solicitar a los tribunales nacionales, o dictar a las partes contendientes, medidas provisionales o precautorias para preservar los derechos de la parte contendiente o para asegurar que la jurisdicción del tribunal establecido conforme a esta Sección, surta plenos efectos. Ese tribunal no podrá ordenar el acatamiento o la suspensión de la medida presuntamente violatoria a que se refiere el Artículo 3.19.

Artículo 3.37 Laudo definitivo

1.   Cuando un tribunal establecido conforme a esta Sección dicte un laudo definitivo desfavorable a una Parte, dicho tribunal sólo podrá ordenar:

    a)   el pago de daños pecuniarios y los intereses correspondientes; o

    b)   la restitución de la propiedad, en cuyo caso el laudo dispondrá que la Parte contendiente pueda pagar daños pecuniarios, más los intereses que procedan, en lugar de la restitución.

2.   Un tribunal establecido conforme a esta Sección, podrá también ordenar el pago de costas de acuerdo con las reglas de arbitraje aplicables.

3.   Cuando la demanda la haga un inversionista en representación de una empresa con base en el Artículo 3.19:

    a)   el laudo que prevea la restitución de la propiedad dispondrá que se otorgue a la empresa; y

    b)   el laudo que conceda daños pecuniarios e intereses correspondientes dispondrá que la suma de dinero se pague a la empresa.

4.   Un tribunal establecido conforme a esta Sección, no podrá ordenar que una Parte pague daños de carácter punitivo.

5.   Para los efectos de los párrafos 1 y 2 los daños se determinarán en la moneda en que se haya realizado la inversión.

6.   El laudo se dictará sin perjuicio de los derechos que cualquier persona con interés jurídico tenga sobre la reparación de los daños que haya sufrido, conforme a la legislación aplicable.

Artículo 3.38 Definitividad y ejecución del laudo

1.   El laudo dictado por un tribunal establecido conforme a esta Sección, será obligatorio sólo para las partes contendientes y únicamente respecto del caso concreto.

2.   Conforme a lo dispuesto en el párrafo 3 y al procedimiento de revisión, aclaración o anulación aplicable a un laudo previstos bajo el mecanismo que sea procedente a juicio del Secretario General, una parte contendiente acatará y cumplirá con el laudo sin demora.

3.   Una parte contendiente podrá solicitar la ejecución de un laudo definitivo siempre que:

   a)   en el caso de un laudo definitivo dictado conforme al Convenio del CIADI:

      i)   hayan transcurrido ciento veinte (120) días desde la fecha en que se dictó el laudo sin que alguna parte contendiente haya solicitado la aclaración, revisión o anulación del mismo; o

      ii)   hayan concluido los procedimientos de aclaración, revisión y anulación; o

   b)   en el caso de un laudo definitivo conforme a las Reglas del Mecanismo Complementario del CIADI o a las Reglas de Arbitraje de la CNUDMI:

      i)   hayan transcurrido noventa (90) días desde la fecha en que se dictó el laudo sin que alguna parte contendiente haya iniciado un procedimiento de interpretación, rectificación, laudo adicional o anulación; o

      ii)   hayan concluido los procedimientos de interpretación, rectificación o laudo adicional, o haya sido resuelta por un tribunal judicial de la Parte contendiente una solicitud de anulación y esta resolución no sea susceptible de ser impugnada.

4.   Cada Parte dispondrá la debida ejecución de un laudo en su territorio.

5.   Cuando una Parte contendiente incumpla o no acate un laudo definitivo, el Consejo, a la recepción de una solicitud de una Parte cuyo inversionista fue parte en el procedimiento de arbitraje, integrará un tribunal arbitral conforme a los Artículos 3.25 a 3.28 y dentro de un plazo de treinta (30) días el tribunal dictará una resolución que contendrá:

   a)   una determinación en el sentido que el incumplimiento o desacato de los términos del laudo definitivo es contrario a las obligaciones de este Tratado; y

   b)   una recomendación en el sentido que la Parte cumpla y acate el laudo definitivo.

6.   El inversionista contendiente podrá recurrir a la ejecución de un laudo arbitral conforme al Convenio del CIADI, la Convención de Nueva York o la Convención Interamericana, independientemente que se hayan iniciado o no los procedimientos contemplados en el párrafo 5.

7.   Para efectos del Artículo I de la Convención de Nueva York y del Artículo I de la Convención Interamericana, se considerará que la demanda que se somete a arbitraje conforme a esta Sección, surge de una relación u operación comercial.

Artículo 3.39 Disposiciones generales

Momento en que la demanda se considera sometida a arbitraje

1.   Una demanda se considera sometida a arbitraje en los términos de esta Sección cuando:

   a)   la solicitud para un arbitraje conforme al párrafo 1 del Artículo 36 del Convenio del CIADI ha sido recibida por el Secretario General;

b) la notificación de arbitraje, de conformidad con el Artículo 2 de la parte C de las Reglas del Mecanismo Complementario del CIADI, ha sido recibida por el Secretario General; o

c) la notificación de arbitraje contemplada en las Reglas de Arbitraje de la CNUDMI, se ha recibido por la Parte contendiente.

Entrega de documentos

2. La entrega de la notificación y otros documentos a una Parte se hará en el lugar designado por ella en el Anexo 3.39 (2).

Pagos conforme a contratos de seguro o garantía

3. En un procedimiento arbitral conforme a lo dispuesto en esta Sección, una Parte no aducirá como defensa, contrademanda, derecho de compensación, u otros, que el inversionista contendiente recibió o recibirá, de acuerdo con un contrato de seguro o garantía, indemnización u otra compensación por todos o parte de los presuntos daños cuya restitución solicita.

Publicidad de laudos

4. La publicación de laudos se realizará de conformidad con las reglas de procedimiento correspondientes de cada Parte. Dicha publicación no incluirá los aspectos que cualquiera de las partes contendientes considere de carácter confidencial.

Artículo 3.40 Subrogación

Si una Parte o su agencia designada realiza un pago en virtud de una indemnización contra riesgos no comerciales otorgados en relación con una inversión en el territorio de otra Parte, esta última reconocerá la asignación de cualquier derecho o reclamo de dicho inversionista a la primera Parte, o su agencia designada, así como el derecho en virtud de la subrogación, para ejercer los derechos y hacer cumplir el reclamo de aquel inversionista. Los derechos de subrogación o reclamo no excederán los derechos o reclamos originales del inversionista.

ANEXO 3.11
EXPROPIACIÓN E INDEMNIZACIÓN

Para efectos del Artículo 3.11(1)(a) se entienden comprendidos en el término de utilidad pública:

a) para el caso de Costa Rica: utilidad pública o interés público.

b) para el caso de El Salvador: utilidad pública o interés social;

c) para el caso de Guatemala: utilidad colectiva, beneficio social o interés público;

d) para el caso de Honduras: necesidad o interés público; y

e) para el caso de Nicaragua: utilidad pública o interés social.

ANEXO 3.22
SOMETIMIENTO DE LA DEMANDA A ARBITRAJE

Para el caso de Honduras, se reserva en su integridad la aplicación del Artículo 3.22(1)(a), mientras persisten las causas en la declaración que hiciera al suscribir el Convenio del CIADI.

ANEXO 3.39(2)
ENTREGA DE DOCUMENTOS

Para efectos del Artículo 3.39 (2), el lugar para la entrega de notificaciones y otros documentos bajo la Sección B será:

1.   para el caso de Costa Rica: Dirección General de Comercio Exterior, Ministerio de Comercio Exterior, Centro de Comercio Exterior, Avenida 3, Calle 40, San José, Costa Rica.

2.   para el caso de El Salvador: Dirección de Política Comercial, Ministerio de Economía, Alameda Juan Pablo II y Calle Guadalupe, Plan Maestro, Edificio "C", San Salvador, El Salvador, o su sucesora;

3.   para el caso de Guatemala: Dirección de Administración del Comercio Exterior, Ministerio de Economía, 8ª Avenida 10-43 zona 1, Guatemala, Guatemala, o su sucesora;

4.   para el caso de Honduras: Dirección General de Administración de Tratados, Secretaría de Estado en los Despachos de Industria y Comercio, antiguo Edificio del Lloyds Bank, Calle Peatonal frente al almacén Salamé, Tegucigalpa, Honduras, o su sucesora; y

5.   para el caso de Nicaragua: Dirección General de Comercio Exterior, Ministerio de Fomento Industria y Comercio, Km. 6, Carretera a Masaya, Managua, Nicaragua, o su sucesora.

CAPÍTULO 4
COMERCIO TRANSFRONTERIZO DE SERVICIOS

Artículo 4.01 Definiciones

1.   Para efectos de este Capítulo, la referencia a los gobiernos centrales incluye a los organismos no gubernamentales que ejerzan facultades reglamentarias, administrativas u otras de carácter gubernamental que le hayan sido delegadas por esos gobiernos.

2.   Para efectos de este Capítulo, se entenderá por:

comercio transfronterizo de servicios: el suministro de un servicio:

   a)   del territorio de una Parte al territorio de otra Parte;

   b)   en el territorio de una Parte a un consumidor de servicios de otra Parte; y

   c)   por un nacional de una Parte en el territorio de otra Parte;

consumidor de servicios: toda persona que reciba o utilice un servicio;

empresa: una "empresa", tal como se define en el Artículo 2.01, y la sucursal de una empresa;

prestador de servicios: toda persona que pretenda prestar o preste transfronterizamente un servicio;

prestador de servicios de otra Parte: una persona de otra Parte que pretenda prestar o preste un servicio;

restricciones cuantitativas: una medida no discriminatoria que impone limitaciones sobre:

a) el número de prestadores de servicios, sea a través de una cuota, monopolio o una prueba de necesidad económica, o por cualquier otro medio cuantitativo; o

b) las operaciones de cualquier prestador de servicios, sea a través de una cuota, monopolio o una prueba de necesidad económica, o por cualquier otro medio cuantitativo;

servicio suministrado en ejercicio de facultades gubernamentales: todo servicio suministrado por una institución pública, que no se suministre en condiciones comerciales ni en competencia con uno o varios proveedores de servicios.

servicios aéreos especializados: los servicios de cartografía aérea, topografía aérea, fotografía aérea, control de incendios forestales, extinción de incendios, publicidad aérea, remolque de planeadores, servicios de paracaidismo, servicios aéreos para la construcción, transporte aéreo de madera en troncos o trozas, vuelos panorámicos, vuelos de entrenamiento, inspección y vigilancia aéreas y rociamiento aéreo;

servicios profesionales: los servicios que para su prestación requieren un título o grado académico equivalente y cuyo ejercicio es autorizado, regulado o restringido en cada caso por una Parte, pero no incluye los servicios proporcionados por personas que practican un oficio o a los tripulantes de barcos mercantes y aeronaves;

Artículo 4.02 Ámbito de aplicación y extensión de las obligaciones

1. Este Capítulo se aplica a las medidas que una Parte adopte o mantenga sobre el comercio transfronterizo de servicios que realicen los prestadores de servicios de otra Parte, incluidas las relativas a:

a) la producción, distribución, comercialización, venta y prestación de un servicio;

b) la compra, pago o utilización de un servicio;

c) el acceso a, y el uso de:

i) sistemas de distribución y transporte relacionados con la prestación de un servicio; y

ii) redes y servicios públicos de telecomunicaciones;

d) la presencia en su territorio de un prestador de servicios transfronterizos de otra Parte; y

e) el otorgamiento de una fianza u otra forma de garantía financiera, como condición para la prestación de un servicio.

2. Este Capítulo no se aplica a:

a) los servicios aéreos, incluidos los de transporte aéreo nacional e internacional, con y sin itinerario fijo, así como las actividades auxiliares de apoyo a los servicios aéreos, salvo:

i) los servicios de reparación y mantenimiento de aeronaves durante el período en que se retira una aeronave de servicio;

ii) los servicios aéreos especializados; y

iii) los sistemas computarizados de reservación;

b) los servicios financieros;

c) los subsidios o donaciones otorgados por una Parte o una empresa del Estado, incluidos los préstamos, garantías y seguros apoyados por el gobierno; ni

d) los servicios o funciones gubernamentales tales como, y no limitados a, la ejecución de las leyes, los servicios de readaptación social, la seguridad o el seguro sobre el ingreso, la seguridad o el seguro social, el bienestar social, la educación pública, la capacitación pública, la salud y la atención a la niñez.

3. Ninguna disposición de este Capítulo se interpretará en el sentido de:

a) imponer a una Parte ninguna obligación respecto a un nacional de otra Parte que pretenda ingresar a su mercado de trabajo o que tenga empleo permanente en su territorio, ni de conferir ningún derecho a ese nacional, respecto a dicho ingreso o empleo; ni

b) imponer ninguna obligación ni otorgar ningún derecho a una Parte, respecto a las compras gubernamentales que realice una Parte o una empresa del Estado.

4. Para los propósitos del presente Capítulo, se entenderá por "medidas que una Parte adopte o mantenga" a las medidas adoptadas o mantenidas por:

a) los gobiernos centrales y municipales, en su caso; y

b) los organismos no gubernamentales que ejerzan facultades reglamentarias, administrativas u otras de carácter gubernamental que le hayan sido delegadas por esos gobiernos.

Respecto de los organismos no gubernamentales citados en la literal b) que ejerzan facultades reglamentarias, administrativas u otras de carácter gubernamental que le hayan sido delegadas de conformidad con la legislación nacional, el gobierno central se asegurará de tomar las medidas razonables que estén a su alcance para lograr que dichos organismos cumplan las disposiciones de este Capítulo.

5.   Las disposiciones de este Capítulo se aplicarán a las medidas relativas a los servicios contemplados en los Anexos, únicamente en la extensión y términos estipulados en los mismos.

Artículo 4.03 Trato de nación más favorecida

1.   Cada Parte otorgará inmediata e incondicionalmente a los servicios y a los prestadores de servicios de otra Parte, un trato no menos favorable que el que conceda a los servicios similares y a los prestadores de servicios similares de cualquier otro país Parte o no Parte.

2.   Las disposiciones del presente Capítulo no se interpretarán en el sentido de impedir que una Parte confiera ventajas a países adyacentes, con el fin de facilitar intercambios, limitados a las zonas fronterizas contiguas, de servicios que se produzcan o consuman localmente.

Artículo 4.04 Trato nacional

1.   Cada Parte otorgará a los servicios y a los prestadores de servicios de otra Parte, un trato no menos favorable que el que conceda a sus propios servicios similares o prestadores de servicios similares.

2.   Cada Parte podrá cumplir lo prescrito en el párrafo 1 otorgando a los servicios y proveedores de servicios de otra Parte, un trato formalmente idéntico o formalmente diferente al que otorgue a sus propios servicios similares y prestadores de servicios similares.

3.   Se considerará que un trato formalmente idéntico o formalmente diferente es menos favorable si modifica las condiciones de competencia a favor de los servicios o proveedores de servicios de la Parte en comparación con los servicios similares o los prestadores de servicios similares de otra Parte.

Artículo 4.05 Presencia local

Ninguna Parte exigirá a un prestador de servicios de otra Parte que establezca o mantenga una oficina de representación u otro tipo de empresa, o que resida en su territorio como condición para la prestación transfronteriza de un servicio.

Artículo 4.06 Reservas

1.   Los Artículos 4.03, 4.04 y 4.05 no se aplican a:

a)   cualquier medida incompatible existente que mantenga una Parte, como se estipula en su lista del Anexo I (Medidas Incompatibles Existentes);

b)   la continuación o pronta renovación de cualquier medida incompatible a que se refiere la literal a); ni

c) la reforma a cualquier medida incompatible a que se refiere la literal a), siempre que dicha reforma no disminuya el grado de compatibilidad de la medida, tal como estaba en vigor antes de la reforma, con los Artículos 4.03, 4.04 y 4.05.

2. Las Partes no tienen la obligación de inscribir las medidas municipales.

Artículo 4.07 Restricciones cuantitativas no discriminatorias

1. Cada Parte indicará en su lista del Anexo IV (Restricciones Cuantitativas no Discriminatorias), dentro de seis (6) meses a partir de la fecha de entrada en vigor de este Tratado, cualesquiera restricciones cuantitativas que se mantengan a nivel nacional.

2. Cada Parte notificará cualquier restricción cuantitativa que adopte después de la fecha de entrada en vigor de este Tratado e indicará la restricción en su lista del Anexo IV (Restricciones Cuantitativas no Discriminatorias).

3. Las Partes se esforzarán, al menos cada dos (2) años, para negociar la liberalización de las restricciones cuantitativas indicadas en su lista del Anexo IV (Restricciones Cuantitativas no Discriminatorias), de conformidad con lo establecido en los párrafos 1 y 2.

Artículo 4.08 Liberalización futura

Con miras a lograr un nivel de liberalización progresivamente más elevado, las Partes se comprometen a realizar negociaciones futuras, por lo menos cada dos (2) años, en el seno del Consejo, tendientes a eliminar las restricciones remanentes inscritas de conformidad con el Artículo 4.06(1).

Artículo 4.09 Comité de Inversión y Comercio Transfronterizo de Servicios

1. Se establece el Comité de Inversión y Comercio Transfronterizo de Servicios, cuya composición se señala en el Anexo 4.09.

2. Sin perjuicio de lo dispuesto en el Artículo 9.04, el Comité tendrá, entre otras, las siguientes funciones:

a) facilitar el intercambio de información entre las Partes, así como también la cooperación técnica en materia de comercio de servicios e inversión; y

b) examinar temas de interés para las Partes relacionado con el comercio de servicios e inversión que se discuten en foros internacionales.

Artículo 4.10 Procedimientos

El Comité establecerá procedimientos para:

a) que cada Parte notifique a otra Parte e incluya en sus Anexos pertinentes:

i) las restricciones cuantitativas no discriminatorias, de conformidad con el Artículo 4.07; y

ii)   las modificaciones a las medidas a las cuales se hace referencia en el Artículo 4.06(1); y

b)   la celebración de negociaciones futuras tendientes a profundizar y perfeccionar la liberalización global de los servicios entre las Partes, de conformidad con el Artículo 4.08.

Artículo 4.11 Otorgamiento de permisos, autorizaciones y licencias

Con el objeto de garantizar que toda medida que una Parte adopte o mantenga en relación con los requisitos y procedimientos para el otorgamiento de permisos, autorizaciones y licencias a los nacionales de otra Parte no constituya una barrera innecesaria al comercio, cada Parte procurará garantizar que dichas medidas:

a)   se sustenten en criterios objetivos y transparentes, tales como la capacidad, la aptitud y la competencia para prestar un servicio;

b)   no sean más gravosas de lo necesario para asegurar la calidad de un servicio; y

c)   no constituyan una restricción encubierta a la prestación transfronteriza de un servicio.

Artículo 4.12 Denegación de beneficios

Una Parte podrá denegar los beneficios derivados de este Capítulo a un prestador de servicios de otra Parte, previa notificación y realización de consultas, cuando la Parte determine que el servicio está siendo suministrado por un prestador de servicios que no realiza operaciones comerciales sustantivas en territorio de otra Parte y que, de conformidad con la legislación vigente de esa Parte, es propiedad o está bajo control de personas de un país no Parte.

Artículo 4.13 Servicios profesionales

En el Anexo 4.13 sobre servicios profesionales se establecen las reglas que observarán las Partes para armonizar las medidas que normarán los servicios profesionales mediante el otorgamiento de autorizaciones para el ejercicio profesional.

Artículo 4.14 Servicios de transporte terrestre

Las Partes desarrollarán un programa de trabajo con el propósito de mejorar los flujos de transporte terrestre entre sus territorios.

Artículo 4.15 Cooperación técnica

Las Partes cooperarán entre ellas para establecer, en un plazo de un (1) año después de la entrada en vigor de este Tratado, un sistema para facilitar a los prestadores de servicios información referente a sus mercados en relación con:

a)   los aspectos comerciales y técnicos del suministro de servicios;.

b)   la posibilidad de obtener tecnología en materia de servicios; y

c)   todos aquellos aspectos que identifique el Consejo en materia de servicios.

Artículo 4.16 Relación con acuerdos multilaterales sobre servicios

1.   Las Partes se comprometen a aplicar entre ellas las disposiciones contenidas en los acuerdos multilaterales sobre servicios de los cuales sean miembros.

2.   No obstante lo dispuesto en el párrafo anterior, en caso de incompatibilidad entre esos acuerdos y el presente Tratado, éste prevalecerá sobre aquellos, en la medida de la incompatibilidad.

ANEXO 4.13
SERVICIOS PROFESIONALES

Reconocimiento de títulos

1.   Cuando una Parte reconozca de manera unilateral o por acuerdo con otro país, los títulos o grados académicos obtenidos en territorio de otra Parte o país no Parte, nada de lo dispuesto en el Artículo 4.02, se interpretará en el sentido de exigir a esa Parte que reconozca los títulos obtenidos en territorio de otra Parte.

2.   No obstante lo dispuesto en el párrafo 1:

   i)   La Parte que sea parte de un acuerdo o convenio con otro país, brindará oportunidades adecuadas a las demás Partes interesadas para que negocien su adhesión a tal acuerdo o convenio o para que negocien con ella otros comparables.

   ii)   Cuando una Parte otorgue el reconocimiento de forma autónoma, brindará a cualquier otra Parte las oportunidades adecuadas para que demuestre que la educación, la experiencia, las licencias o los certificados obtenidos o los requisitos cumplidos en el territorio de esa otra Parte deben ser objeto de reconocimiento.

3.   Las Partes reiteran lo dispuesto en el Artículo 31 del Protocolo al Tratado General de Integración Económica Centroamericana (Protocolo de Guatemala).

Bases para el reconocimiento de títulos y autorización para el ejercicio profesional

4.   Las Partes acuerdan que los procesos de mutuo reconocimiento de títulos y el otorgamiento de autorizaciones para el ejercicio profesional, se harán sobre la base de mejorar la calidad de los servicios profesionales a través del establecimiento de normas y criterios para esos procesos, protegiendo al mismo tiempo a los consumidores y salvaguardando el interés público.

5.   Las Partes alentarán a los organismos pertinentes, entre otros, a autoridades gubernamentales competentes y a las asociaciones y colegios profesionales, cuando corresponda, para:

   a)   elaborar tales criterios y normas; y

b)　　formular y presentar recomendaciones sobre el mutuo reconocimiento de títulos profesionales y el otorgamiento de licencias para el ejercicio profesional.

5.　　La elaboración de normas y criterios a que se refiere el párrafo 4, podrá considerar la legislación de cada Parte y a título indicativo los elementos siguientes: educación, exámenes, experiencia, conducta y ética, desarrollo profesional y renovación de la certificación, ámbito de acción, conocimiento local, supervisión y protección al consumidor.

Revisión

6.　　Las Partes revisarán, por lo menos una vez al año, la aplicación de las disposiciones de este Anexo.

CAPÍTULO 5
TELECOMUNICACIONES

Artículo 5.01 Exclusión

Este Capítulo no se aplica a Costa Rica.

Artículo 5.02 Definiciones

Para efectos de este Capítulo, se entenderá por:

comunicaciones internas de una empresa: las telecomunicaciones mediante las cuales una empresa se comunica:

a)　　internamente, con o entre sus subsidiarias, sucursales y filiales, según las defina cada Parte; o

b)　　de manera no comercial, con otras personas que sean fundamentales para la actividad económica de la empresa y que sostengan una relación contractual continua con ella; pero no incluye los servicios de telecomunicaciones que se suministren a personas distintas a las descritas en esta definición;

equipo autorizado: el equipo terminal o de otra clase que ha sido aprobado para conectarse a la red pública de telecomunicaciones de acuerdo con los procedimientos de evaluación de la conformidad de una Parte;

equipo terminal: cualquier dispositivo analógico o digital capaz de procesar, recibir, conmutar, señalizar o transmitir señales a través de medios electromagnéticos y que se conecta a la red pública de telecomunicaciones, mediante conexiones de radio o cable, en un punto terminal;

medida relativa a la normalización: las normas, reglamentos técnicos y los procedimientos de evaluación de la conformidad;

monopolio: una entidad, incluyendo un consorcio o agencia gubernamental, que se mantenga o sea designada según su legislación, si ésta así lo permite, como proveedora exclusiva de redes o servicios públicos de telecomunicaciones en cualquier mercado pertinente en territorio de una Parte;

procedimiento de evaluación de la conformidad: cualquier procedimiento utilizado, directa o indirectamente, para determinar si los procedimientos pertinentes establecidos por reglamentos técnicos o normas se cumplen, incluidos el muestreo, pruebas de inspección; evaluación, verificación y garantía de la conformidad; registro, acreditación y aprobación, separadamente o en distintas combinaciones, e incluye los procedimientos referidos en el Anexo 5.02;

protocolo: un conjunto de reglas y formatos que rigen el intercambio de información entre dos entidades pares, para efectos de la transferencia de información de señales y datos;

proveedor principal u operador dominante: un proveedor que tenga la capacidad de afectar de manera importante las condiciones de participación (desde el punto de vista de los precios y del suministro) en un mercado dado de servicios de telecomunicaciones como resultado del control de las instalaciones esenciales o la utilización de su posición en el mercado;

punto terminal de la red: la demarcación final de la red pública de telecomunicaciones en las instalaciones del usuario;

red privada de telecomunicaciones: la red de telecomunicaciones que se utiliza exclusivamente para comunicaciones internas de una empresa o entre personas predeterminadas;

red pública de telecomunicaciones: la red de telecomunicaciones que se utiliza para explotar comercialmente servicios de telecomunicaciones destinados a satisfacer las necesidades del público en general, sin incluir los equipos terminales de telecomunicaciones de los usuarios, ni las redes de telecomunicaciones que se encuentren más allá del punto terminal de la red;

servicio de telecomunicaciones: un servicio suministrado por vías de transmisión y recepción de señales por línea física, radioelectricidad, medios ópticos u otros sistemas electromagnéticos, pero no significa distribución por cable, radiodifusión u otro tipo de distribución electromagnética de programación de radio o televisión;

servicio público de telecomunicaciones: cualquier servicio de telecomunicaciones que una Parte obligue, explícitamente o de hecho, a que se ofrezca al público en general, incluidos el telégrafo, teléfono, télex y transmisión de datos, y que por lo general conlleva la transmisión en tiempo real de información suministrada por el usuario entre dos o más puntos, sin cambio "de punto a punto" en la forma o en el contenido de la información del usuario;

servicios de valor agregado o mejorados: los servicios de telecomunicaciones que emplean sistemas de procesamiento computarizado que:

a)   actúan sobre el formato, contenido, código, protocolo o aspectos similares de la información transmitida del usuario;

b)   proporcionan al cliente información adicional, diferente o reestructurada; o

c)   implican la interacción del usuario con información almacenada; y

telecomunicaciones: toda transmisión, emisión o recepción de signos, señales, escritos, imágenes, sonidos e informaciones de cualquier naturaleza, por línea física, radioelectricidad, medios ópticos u otros sistemas electromagnéticos.

Artículo 5.03 Ámbito de aplicación

1.   Este Capítulo se aplica a:

   a)   las medidas que adopte o mantenga una Parte, relacionadas con la prestación de servicios públicos de telecomunicaciones;

   b)   las medidas que adopte o mantenga una Parte, relacionadas con el acceso a y el uso de redes o servicios públicos de telecomunicaciones por personas de otra Parte, incluso el acceso y el uso que dichas personas hagan cuando operen redes privadas para llevar a cabo sus comunicaciones internas de las empresas;

   c)   las medidas que adopte o mantenga una Parte sobre la prestación de servicios de valor agregado o mejorados por personas de otra Parte en territorio de la primera o a través de sus fronteras; y

   d)   las medidas relativas a la normalización respecto de la conexión de equipo terminal u otro equipo a las redes públicas de telecomunicaciones.

2.   Salvo para garantizar que las personas que operen estaciones de radiodifusión y sistemas de cable tengan acceso y uso de las redes y de los servicios públicos de telecomunicaciones, este.Capítulo no se aplicará a las medidas que una Parte adopte o mantenga en relación con la radiodifusión o la distribución por cable de programación de radio o televisión.

3.   Ninguna disposición de este Capítulo se interpretará en el sentido de:

   a)   obligar a una Parte a autorizar a una persona de otra Parte a que establezca, construya, adquiera, arriende, opere o suministre redes o servicios de telecomunicaciones;

   b)   obligar a una Parte o que ésta a su vez exija a una persona a que establezca, construya, adquiera, arriende, opere o suministre redes o servicios de telecomunicaciones que no se ofrezcan al público en general;

   c)   impedir a una Parte que prohiba a las personas que operen redes privadas de telecomunicaciones el uso de sus redes para suministrar redes o servicios públicos de telecomunicaciones a terceras personas; u

   d)   obligar a una Parte a exigir a una persona involucrada en la radiodifusión o distribución por cable de programación de radio o de televisión a que proporcione su infraestructura de distribución por cable o de radiodifusión como red pública de telecomunicaciones.

Artículo 5.04 Acceso a redes y servicios públicos de telecomunicaciones y su uso

1.   Para efectos de este Artículo, se entenderá por no discriminatorio, términos y condiciones no menos favorables que aquéllos otorgados a cualquier otro cliente o usuario de redes o servicios públicos de telecomunicaciones similares en condiciones similares.

2.   Cada Parte garantizará que personas de otra Parte tengan acceso a, y puedan hacer uso de cualquier red o servicio público de telecomunicaciones ofrecidos en su territorio o de manera transfronteriza, inclusive los circuitos privados arrendados, en términos y condiciones razonables y no discriminatorias, para la conducción de sus negocios, incluyendo lo especificado en los demás párrafos de este Artículo.

3.   Sujeto a lo dispuesto en los párrafos 7 y 8, cada Parte garantizará que a las personas de otra Parte se les permita:

     a)   comprar o arrendar, y conectar equipo terminal u otro equipo que haga interfaz con la red pública de telecomunicaciones;

     b)   interconectar circuitos privados, arrendados o propios, con las redes públicas de telecomunicaciones en territorio de esa Parte o a través de sus fronteras, incluido el acceso mediante marcación directa a y desde sus usuarios o clientes, o con circuitos arrendados o propios de otra persona, en términos y condiciones mutuamente aceptadas por dichas personas, conforme a lo dispuesto en el Anexo 5.04;

     c)   realizar funciones de conmutación, señalización y procesamiento; y

     d)   utilizar los protocolos de operación que ellos elijan, de conformidad con los planes técnicos de cada Parte.

4.   Cada Parte garantizará que la fijación de precios para los servicios públicos de telecomunicaciones refleje los costos económicos directamente relacionados con la prestación de dichos servicios, sin perjuicio de lo establecido en la legislación aplicable. Ninguna disposición de este párrafo se interpretará en el sentido de impedir subsidios cruzados entre los servicios públicos de telecomunicaciones.

5.   Cada Parte garantizará que las personas de otra Parte puedan usar las redes o los servicios públicos de telecomunicaciones para transmitir la información en su territorio o a través de sus fronteras, incluso para las comunicaciones internas de las empresas, y para el acceso a la información contenida en bases de datos o almacenada en otra forma que sea legible por una máquina en territorio de otra Parte.

6.   Además de lo dispuesto en el Artículo 8.02, ninguna disposición de este Capítulo se interpretará en el sentido de impedir a una Parte que adopte o aplique cualquier medida necesaria para:

     a)   garantizar la seguridad y confidencialidad de los mensajes; o

     b)   proteger la privacidad de los suscriptores de redes o de servicios públicos de telecomunicaciones.

7.   Además de lo dispuesto en el Artículo 5.06, cada Parte garantizará que no se impongan más condiciones al acceso a redes o servicios públicos de telecomunicaciones y a su uso, que las necesarias para:

a)   salvaguardar las responsabilidades del servicio público de los prestadores de redes o servicios públicos de telecomunicaciones, en particular su capacidad para poner sus redes o servicios a disposición del público en general; o

b)   proteger la integridad técnica de las redes o los servicios públicos de telecomunicaciones.

8.   Siempre que las condiciones para el acceso a redes o servicios públicos de telecomunicaciones y su uso cumplan los criterios establecidos en el párrafo 7, dichas condiciones podrán incluir:

a)   restricciones a la reventa o al uso compartido de tales servicios;

b)   requisitos para usar interfaces técnicas específicas, inclusive protocolos de interfaz, para la interconexión con las redes o los servicios mencionados;

c)   restricciones en la interconexión de circuitos privados, arrendados o propios, con las redes o los servicios mencionados o con circuitos arrendados o propios de otra persona; y cuando éstas se utilizan para el suministro de redes o servicios públicos de telecomunicaciones; y

d)   procedimientos para otorgar licencias, permisos, concesiones, registros o notificaciones que, de adoptarse o mantenerse, sean transparentes y que el trámite de las solicitudes se resuelva de manera diligente.

Artículo 5.05 Condiciones para la prestación de servicios de valor agregado o mejorados

1.   Cada Parte garantizará que:

a)   cualquier procedimiento que adopte o mantenga para otorgar licencias, permisos, concesiones, registros o notificaciones referentes a la prestación de servicios de valor agregado o mejorados, sea transparente y no discriminatorio y que el trámite de las solicitudes se resuelva de manera diligente; y

b)   la información requerida, conforme a tales procedimientos, se limite a la necesaria para acreditar que el solicitante tenga solvencia financiera para iniciar la prestación del servicio, o que los servicios o el equipo terminal u otro equipo del solicitante.cumplen con las normas o reglamentaciones técnicas aplicables de la Parte, o los requerimientos relacionados con la constitución legal del solicitante.

2.   Sin perjuicio de lo establecido en las legislaciones de cada Parte, ninguna Parte exigirá a un prestador de servicios de valor agregado o mejorados:

a)   prestar esos servicios al público en general;

b)   justificar sus tarifas de acuerdo con sus costos;

c)   registrar una tarifa;

d)   interconectar sus redes con cualquier cliente o red en particular; ni

e)   satisfacer alguna norma o reglamentación técnica específica para una interconexión distinta a la interconexión con una red pública de telecomunicaciones.

3.   No obstante lo dispuesto en el párrafo 2(c), una Parte podrá requerir el registro de una tarifa a:

a)   un prestador de servicios, con el fin de corregir una práctica de este prestador que la Parte haya considerado en un caso particular como contraria a la competencia, de conformidad con su legislación; o

b)   un monopolio, proveedor principal u operador dominante al que se le apliquen las disposiciones del Artículo 5.07.

Artículo 5.06 Medidas relativas a la normalización

1.   Cada Parte garantizará que sus medidas relativas a la normalización que se refieren a la conexión del equipo terminal o de otro equipo a las redes públicas de telecomunicaciones, incluso aquellas medidas que se refieren al uso del equipo de prueba y medición para el procedimiento de evaluación de la conformidad, se adopten o mantengan solamente en la medida que sean necesarias para:

a)   impedir daños técnicos a las redes públicas de telecomunicaciones;

b)   impedir la interferencia técnica con los servicios públicos de telecomunicaciones, o el deterioro de éstos;

c)   impedir la interferencia electromagnética, y asegurar la compatibilidad con otros usos del espectro radioeléctrico;

d)   impedir el mal funcionamiento de los equipos de tasación, cobro y facturación;

e)   garantizar la seguridad del usuario y su acceso a las redes o servicios públicos de telecomunicaciones; o

f)   asegurar el uso eficiente del espectro radioeléctrico.

2.   Cada Parte podrá establecer el requisito de aprobación para la conexión a la red pública de telecomunicaciones de equipo terminal o de otro equipo que no esté autorizado, siempre que los criterios de aprobación sean compatibles con lo dispuesto en el párrafo 1.

3.   Cada Parte garantizará que los puntos terminales de las redes públicas de telecomunicaciones se definan sobre bases razonables y transparentes.

4.   Ninguna Parte exigirá autorización por separado del equipo que se conecte por el lado del usuario al equipo autorizado que sirve como dispositivo de protección cumpliendo con los criterios del párrafo 1.

5.   Cada Parte:

a)   asegurará que sus procedimientos de evaluación de la conformidad sean transparentes y no discriminatorios, y que las solicitudes que se presenten al efecto se tramiten de manera diligente;

b)   permitirá que cualquier entidad técnicamente calificada realice la prueba requerida al equipo terminal o a otro equipo que vaya a ser conectado a la red pública de telecomunicaciones, de acuerdo con los procedimientos de evaluación de la conformidad de esa Parte, a reserva del derecho de la misma de revisar la exactitud y la integridad de los resultados de las pruebas; y

c)   garantizará que no sean discriminatorias las medidas que adopte o mantenga para autorizar a determinadas personas como agentes de proveedores de equipo de telecomunicaciones ante los organismos competentes de esa Parte para la evaluación de la conformidad.

6.   A más tardar doce (12) meses después de la fecha de entrada en vigor de este Tratado, cada Parte adoptará, como parte de sus procedimientos de evaluación de la conformidad, las disposiciones necesarias para aceptar los resultados de las pruebas realizadas por laboratorios o instalaciones de pruebas en territorio de otra Parte, de conformidad con las medidas y procedimientos relativos a la normalización de la Parte a la que le corresponda aceptar.

Artículo 5.07 Monopolios o prácticas contrarias a la competencia

1.   Cuando una Parte mantenga o designe un monopolio, o exista un proveedor principal u operador dominante, para proveer redes y servicios públicos de telecomunicaciones y éste compita, directamente o a través de una filial, en la prestación de servicios de valor agregado o mejorados u otras mercancías o servicios vinculados con las telecomunicaciones, esa Parte procurará que el monopolio, proveedor principal u operador dominante no utilice su posición para incurrir en prácticas contrarias a la competencia en esos mercados, ya sea de manera directa o a través de los tratos con sus filiales, de modo tal que afecte desventajosamente a una persona de otra Parte. Dichas prácticas pueden incluir los subsidios cruzados, conductas predatorias y la discriminación en el acceso a las redes y los servicios públicos de telecomunicaciones.

2.   Cada Parte adoptará o mantendrá medidas eficaces para impedir la conducta contraria a la competencia, a que se refiere el párrafo 1, tales como:

a)   requisitos de contabilidad;

b)   requisitos de separación estructural;

c)   reglas para procurar que el monopolio, proveedor principal u operador dominante otorgue a sus competidores acceso a y uso de sus redes o sus servicios públicos de telecomunicaciones en términos y condiciones no menos favorables que los que se conceda a sí mismo o a sus filiales; o

d) reglas para procurar la divulgación oportuna de los cambios técnicos de las redes públicas de telecomunicaciones y sus interfaces.

Artículo 5.08 Transparencia

Además de lo dispuesto en el Artículo 10.02, cada Parte pondrá a disposición del público sus medidas relativas al acceso a las redes o los servicios públicos de telecomunicaciones y a su uso, incluyendo las medidas referentes a:

a) tarifas y otros términos y condiciones del servicio;

b) especificaciones de las interfaces técnicas con tales redes y servicios;

c) información sobre los órganos responsables de la elaboración y adopción de medidas relativas a la normalización que afecten dicho acceso y uso;

d) condiciones aplicables a la conexión de equipo terminal o de otra clase a las redes públicas de telecomunicaciones; y

e) requisitos de notificación, permiso, registro, certificado, licencia o concesión.

Artículo 5.09 Relación con otros capítulos

En caso de incompatibilidad entre una disposición de este Capítulo y una disposición de otro Capítulo, prevalecerá la del primero en la medida de la incompatibilidad.

Artículo 5.10 Relación con organizaciones y tratados internacionales

Las Partes reconocen la importancia de las normas internacionales para la compatibilidad e interoperabilidad global de las redes o servicios de telecomunicaciones, y se comprometen a promover dichas normas mediante la labor de los organismos internacionales competentes, tales como la Unión Internacional de Telecomunicaciones, la Organización Internacional de Normalización y la Comisión Interamericana de Telecomunicaciones.

Artículo 5.11 Cooperación y otras consultas técnicas

1. Con el fin de estimular el desarrollo de la infraestructura de servicios de telecomunicaciones interoperables, las Partes cooperarán en el buen funcionamiento del espectro radioeléctrico, el intercambio de información técnica, en el desarrollo de programas intergubernamentales de entrenamiento, así como en otras actividades afines. En cumplimiento de esta obligación, las Partes pondrán especial énfasis en los programas de intercambio existentes.

2. Las Partes procuraràn profundizar el comercio de todos los servicios de telecomunicaciones, incluidas las redes y los servicios públicos de telecomunicaciones.

ANEXO 5.02
PROCEDIMIENTOS DE EVALUACIÓN DE LA CONFORMIDAD

Para efectos de este Capítulo, los procedimientos de evaluación de la conformidad incluyen:

a)   Para el caso de El Salvador:

   i)   Decreto Legislativo N° 142 del 6 de noviembre de 1997, Ley de Telecomunicaciones; y

   ii)   Decreto Ejecutivo N° 64 del 15 de mayo de 1998, Reglamento de la Ley de Telecomunicaciones;

b)   Para el caso de Guatemala:

   i)   Decreto N° 94-96 del 17 de octubre de 1996 del Congreso de la República, Ley General de Telecomunicaciones;

   ii)   Decreto N° 115-97 del 19 de noviembre de 1997 del Congreso de la República, Reformas a la Ley General de Telecomunicaciones;

   iii) Acuerdo Gubernativo N° 574-98 del 2 de septiembre de 1998, Reglamento para la Explotación de Sistemas Satelitales en Guatemala; y

   iv)   Acuerdo Gubernativo N° 408-99 del 25 de junio de 1999, Reglamento para la Prestación del Servicio Telefónico Internacional;

c)   Para el caso de Honduras:

   i)   Decreto N° 185-95, Ley Marco del Sector de Telecomunicaciones, publicado en el Diario Oficial "La Gaceta" el 31 de octubre de 1995;

   ii)   Acuerdo N° 89-97, Reglamento General de la Ley Marco del Sector de Telecomunicaciones, publicado en el Diario Oficial "La Gaceta", el 27 de mayo de 1997;

   iii) Decreto N° 244-98, publicado en el Diario Oficial "La Gaceta" el 19 septiembre de 1998;

   iv)   Decreto N° 89-99, publicado en el Diario Oficial "La Gaceta" el 25 de mayo de 1999;

   v)   Resolución OD 003/99, publicada en el Diario Oficial "La Gaceta" el 26 de febrero de 1999; y

   vi)   Resolución 105/98, publicada en el Diario Oficial "La Gaceta" el 11 de julio de 1998; y

c)   Para el caso de Nicaragua:

   i)   Ley N° 200 del 8 de agosto de 1995, Ley General de Telecomunicaciones y Servicios Postales, publicada en el Diario Oficial "La Gaceta" N° 154, del 18 de agosto de 1995;

ii)   Ley N° 210 del 30 de noviembre de 1995, Ley de Incorporación de Particulares en la Operación y Ampliación de los Servicios Públicos de las Telecomunicaciones, publicada en el Diario Oficial "La Gaceta" N° 231, del 7 de diciembre de 1995;

iii)   Decreto N° 19-96 del 12 de septiembre de 1996, Reglamento de la Ley General de Telecomunicaciones y Servicios Postales, publicado en el Diario Oficial "La Gaceta" N° 177, del 19 de septiembre de 1996;

iv)   Ley N° 293 del 1 de julio de 1998, Ley de reforma a la Ley N° 210, publicada en el Diario Oficial "La Gaceta" N° 123 del 2 de julio de 1998; y

v)   Código de Comercio de Nicaragua de 1916.

ANEXO 5.04
INTERCONEXIÓN DE CIRCUITOS PRIVADOS

Para efectos del Artículo 5.04, en el caso de El Salvador, Guatemala, Honduras y Nicaragua se entenderá que la interconexión de los circuitos privados con las redes públicas de telecomunicaciones, no dará acceso a tráfico desde dichos circuitos privados hacia las redes públicas o viceversa, sean dichos circuitos privados, arrendados o propios.

CAPÍTULO 6
SERVICIOS FINANCIEROS

Artículo 6.01 Definiciones

Para efectos de este Capítulo, se entenderá por:

autoridades reguladoras: cualquier entidad gubernamental que ejerza autoridad de supervisión

sobre prestadores de servicios financieros o instituciones financieras.

entidad pública: un banco central o autoridad monetaria o cualquier institución de naturaleza pública del sistema financiero de una Parte que sea propiedad o esté bajo su control, cuando no esté ejerciendo funciones comerciales;

institución financiera: cualquier intermediario financiero u otra empresa que esté autorizada para prestar servicios financieros y esté regulada o supervisada como una institución financiera conforme a la legislación de la Parte en cuyo territorio fue constituida;

institución financiera de otra Parte: una institución financiera, constituida en el territorio de una Parte que sea propiedad o esté controlada por personas de otra Parte;

inversión: toda clase de bienes o derechos de cualquier naturaleza, adquiridos o utilizados con el propósito de obtener un beneficio económico u otros fines empresariales, adquiridos con recursos transferidos o reinvertidos por un inversionista, y comprenderá:

a) una empresa, acciones de una empresa; participaciones en el capital social de una empresa, que le permitan al propietario participar en los ingresos o en las utilidades de la misma.

Instrumentos de deuda de una empresa y préstamos a una empresa cuando:

i) la empresa es una filial del inversionista; o

ii) la fecha de vencimiento original del instrumento de deuda o el préstamo sea por lo menos de tres (3) años;

b) una participación en una empresa que otorgue derecho al propietario para participar del haber social de esa empresa en una liquidación, siempre que éste no derive de un instrumento de deuda o un préstamo excluidos conforme al literal (a);

c) bienes raíces u otra propiedad, tangibles o intangibles, incluidos los derechos en el ámbito de la propiedad intelectual, así como cualquier otro derecho real (tales como hipotecas, derechos de prenda, usufructo y derechos similares) adquiridos con la expectativa de, o utilizados con el propósito de, obtener un beneficio económico o para otros fines empresariales;

d) la participación o beneficio que resulte de destinar capital u otros recursos comprometidos para el desarrollo de una actividad económica en territorio de una Parte, entre otros, conforme a:

i) contratos que involucran la presencia de la propiedad de un inversionista en territorio de la Parte, incluidos, las concesiones, los contratos de construcción y de llave en mano; o

ii) contratos donde la remuneración depende sustancialmente de la producción, ingresos o ganancias de una empresa; y

e) un préstamo otorgado por un prestador de servicios financieros transfronterizos o un valor de deuda propiedad del mismo, excepto un préstamo a una institución financiera o un valor de deuda emitido por la misma;

pero inversión no significa,

1. una obligación de pago de, ni el otorgamiento de un crédito a, el Estado o una empresa del Estado;

2. reclamaciones pecuniarias derivadas exclusivamente de:

i) contratos comerciales para la venta de bienes o servicios por un nacional o empresa en territorio de una Parte a una empresa en territorio de la otra Parte; o

ii) el otorgamiento de crédito en relación con una transacción comercial, cuya fecha de vencimiento sea menor a tres (3) años, como el financiamiento al comercio; salvo un préstamo cubierto por las disposiciones del literal (a);

3.   cualquier otra reclamación pecuniaria que no conlleve los tipos de interés dispuestos en los literales del (a) al (e);

4.   un préstamo otorgado a una institución financiera o un valor de deuda propiedad de una institución financiera, salvo que se trate de un préstamo a una institución financiera que sea tratado como capital para efectos regulatorios, por cualquier Parte en cuyo territorio esté ubicada la institución financiera;

inversionista de una Parte: una Parte o una empresa del Estado de la misma, o una persona de esa Parte que pretenda realizar, realice o haya realizado una inversión en el territorio de otra Parte. La intención de realizar una inversión podrá manifestarse, entre otras formas, mediante actos jurídicos tendientes a materializar la inversión, o estando en vías de comprometer los recursos económicos necesarios para realizarla.

inversionista contendiente: un inversionista de una Parte que formula una demanda en los términos de la Sección B del Capítulo 3;

inversión de un inversionista de una Parte: la inversión propiedad o bajo control directo o indirecto de un inversionista de esa Parte en el territorio de otra Parte;

En caso de una empresa, una inversión es propiedad de un inversionista de una Parte si ese inversionista tiene la titularidad de más del 50% de su capital social.

Una inversión está bajo el control de un inversionista de una Parte si ese inversionista tiene la facultad de:

    i)   designar a la mayoría de sus directores, o

    ii)   dirigir de cualquier modo sus operaciones;

inversión de un país no Parte: la inversión de un inversionista que no es inversionista de una Parte;

nuevo servicio financiero: un servicio financiero no prestado en territorio de la Parte que sea prestado en territorio de otra Parte, e incluye cualquier forma nueva de distribución de un servicio financiero, o de venta de un producto financiero que no sea vendido en territorio de la Parte;

organismos autoregulados: cualquier entidad no gubernamental, incluso cualquier bolsa de valores o de futuros, cámara de compensación o cualquier otra asociación u organización que ejerza una autoridad, propia o delegada, de regulación o de supervisión, sobre instituciones financieras o prestadores de servicios financieros transfronterizos;

persona: una "persona" tal como se define en el Artículo 2.01, pero no incluye una sucursal de una empresa de un país no Parte;

prestación de servicios financieros transfronterizos o comercio transfronterizo de servicios financieros:

a)   la prestación de un servicio financiero del territorio de una Parte hacia el territorio de otra Parte;

b)   en territorio de una Parte por una persona de esa Parte a una persona de otra Parte; o

c)   por una persona de una Parte en territorio de otra Parte;

prestador de servicios financieros transfronterizos de una Parte: una persona autorizada de una Parte que se dedica al negocio de prestar servicios financieros en su territorio y que pretenda realizar o realice la prestación de servicios financieros transfronterizos; y

servicio financiero: todo servicio de carácter financiero ofrecido por una institución financiera de una Parte. Los servicios financieros comprenden todos los servicios de seguros, reaseguros, los servicios bancarios y demás servicios que impliquen intermediación financiera, inclusive los servicios conexos y auxiliares de naturaleza financiera.

Artículo 6.02 Ámbito de aplicación y extensión de las obligaciones

1.   Este Capítulo se aplica a medidas que adopte o mantenga una Parte relativas a:

   a)   instituciones financieras de otra Parte;

   b)   el comercio transfronterizo de servicios financieros; y

   c)   inversionistas de otra Parte e inversiones de esos inversionistas en instituciones financieras en territorio de la Parte.

2.   Este Capítulo no se aplica a:

   a)   las actividades realizadas por las autoridades monetarias o por cualquier otra institución pública, dirigidas a la consecución de políticas monetarias o cambiarias;

   b)   las actividades o servicios que formen parte de planes públicos de retiro o de sistemas públicos de seguridad social;

   c)   el uso de los recursos financieros propiedad de otra Parte; o

   d)   otras actividades o servicios financieros por cuenta de la Parte o de sus entidades públicas o con su garantía.

3.   En caso de incompatibilidad entre las disposiciones de este Capítulo y cualquier otra disposición de este Tratado, prevalecerán las de este Capítulo en la medida de la incompatibilidad.

4.   El Artículo 3.11 y la Sección B del Capítulo 3 se incorporan a este Capítulo y forman parte integrante del mismo.

Artículo 6.03 Organismos autoregulados

Cuando una Parte requiera que una institución financiera o un prestador de servicios financieros transfronterizos de otra Parte sea miembro, participe, o tenga acceso a un organismo autoregulado para ofrecer un servicio financiero en su territorio o hacia él, la Parte se asegurará que dicho organismo cumpla con las obligaciones de este Capítulo.

Artículo 6.04 Derecho de establecimiento

1.   Las Partes reconocen el principio que a los inversionistas de cada Parte se les debe permitir establecer una institución financiera en territorio de otra Parte, mediante cualquiera de las modalidades de establecimiento y de operación que la legislación de ésta permita.

2.   Una Parte podrá imponer términos y condiciones relativas al establecimiento que sean compatibles con el Artículo 6.06.

Artículo 6.05 Comercio transfronterizo

1.   Cada Parte permitirá a las personas ubicadas en su territorio, donde quiera que se encuentren, adquirir servicios financieros de prestadores de servicios financieros transfronterizos de otra Parte ubicados en el territorio de esa otra Parte. Esto no obliga a una Parte a permitir que esos prestadores de servicios financieros transfronterizos se anuncien o lleven a cabo negocios por cualquier medio en su territorio. Las Partes podrán definir lo que es "anunciarse" y "hacer negocios" para efectos de esta obligación.

2.   Cuando una Parte permita la prestación de servicios financieros transfronterizos y sin perjuicio de otros medios de regulación prudencial al comercio transfronterizo de servicios financieros, una Parte podrá exigir el registro de los prestadores de servicios financieros transfronterizos de otra Parte y de los instrumentos financieros.

Artículo 6.06 Trato nacional

1.   Cada Parte otorgará a los inversionistas de otra Parte, un trato no menos favorable del que otorga a sus propios inversionistas similares respecto al establecimiento, adquisición, expansión, administración, conducción, operación y venta u otras formas de enajenación de instituciones financieras similares e inversiones en instituciones financieras similares en su territorio.

2.   Cada Parte otorgará a las instituciones financieras de otra Parte y a las inversiones de los inversionistas de otra Parte en instituciones financieras, un trato no menos favorable del que otorga a sus propias instituciones financieras similares y a las inversiones similares de sus propios inversionistas similares en instituciones financieras similares respecto al establecimiento, adquisición, expansión, administración, conducción, operación y venta u otras formas de enajenación de instituciones financieras e inversiones.

3.   Cuando una Parte permita la prestación transfronteriza de un servicio financiero conforme al Artículo 6.05, otorgará a prestadores de servicios financieros transfronterizos de otra Parte, un trato no menos favorable del que otorga a sus propios prestadores de servicios financieros similares, respecto a la prestación de tal servicio.

4.   El trato que una Parte otorgue a instituciones financieras y a prestadores de servicios financieros transfronterizos de otra Parte, ya sea idéntico o diferente al otorgado a sus propias instituciones similares o prestadores de servicios similares, es compatible con los párrafos 1 a 3 si ofrece igualdad en las oportunidades para competir..5. El trato de una Parte no ofrece igualdad en las oportunidades para competir si sitúa, en posición desventajosa, a las instituciones financieras similares y a los prestadores de servicios financieros transfronterizos similares de otra Parte, en su capacidad de prestar servicios financieros, comparada con la capacidad de las propias instituciones financieras y prestadores de servicios de la Parte para prestar esos servicios.

Artículo 6.07 Trato de nación más favorecida

Cada Parte otorgará a las instituciones financieras, a los prestadores de servicios financieros transfronterizos de otra Parte, a los inversionistas y a las inversiones de dichos inversionistas en instituciones financieras de otra Parte, un trato no menos favorable que el otorgado a las instituciones financieras similares, a los prestadores de servicios financieros transfronterizos similares, a los inversionistas similares y a las inversiones similares de dichos inversionistas en instituciones financieras similares de otra Parte o de otro país no Parte.

Artículo 6.08 Reconocimiento y armonización

1.   Al aplicar las medidas comprendidas en este Capítulo, una Parte podrá reconocer las medidas prudenciales de otra Parte o de un país no Parte. Ese reconocimiento podrá ser otorgado unilateralmente, alcanzado a través de la armonización u otros medios; o con base en un acuerdo o arreglo de otra Parte o con el país no Parte.

2.   La Parte que otorgue reconocimiento de medidas prudenciales de conformidad con el párrafo 1, brindará oportunidades apropiadas a cualquier otra Parte para demostrar que existen circunstancias por las cuales hay o habrá regulaciones equivalentes, supervisión y puesta en práctica de la regulación y, de ser conveniente, procedimientos para compartir información entre las Partes.

3.   Cuando una Parte otorgue reconocimiento a las medidas prudenciales de conformidad con el párrafo 1 y las circunstancias dispuestas en el párrafo 2 existan, esa Parte brindará oportunidades adecuadas a otra Parte para negociar la adhesión al acuerdo o arreglo, o para negociar un acuerdo o arreglo similar.

Artículo 6.09 Excepciones

1.   Nada de lo dispuesto en este Capítulo se interpretará como impedimento para que una Parte adopte o mantenga medidas prudenciales por motivos tales como:

     a)   proteger a tomadores de fondos, así como a inversionistas, depositantes u otros acreedores, tenedores o beneficiarios de pólizas o personas acreedoras de obligaciones fiduciarias a cargo de una institución financiera o de un prestador de servicios financieros transfronterizos ;

     b)   mantener la seguridad, solidez, integridad o responsabilidad financiera de instituciones financieras o de prestadores de servicios financieros transfronterizos; y

c)   asegurar la integridad y estabilidad del sistema financiero de esa Parte.

2.   Nada de lo dispuesto en este Capítulo se aplica a medidas no discriminatorias de aplicación general, adoptadas por una entidad pública en la conducción de políticas monetarias o las políticas de crédito conexas, o bien de políticas cambiarias. Este párrafo no afectará las obligaciones de cualquiera de las Partes derivadas de requisitos de desempeño en inversión respecto a las medidas cubiertas por el Capítulo 3 o del Artículo 6.18.

3.   No obstante lo dispuesto en el Artículo 6.18, una Parte podrá evitar o limitar las transferencias de una institución financiera o de un prestador de servicios financieros transfronterizos a, o en beneficio de, una filial o una persona relacionada con dicha institución o con ese prestador de servicios, por medio de la aplicación justa y no discriminatoria de medidas relacionadas con el mantenimiento de la seguridad, solidez, integridad o responsabilidad financiera de instituciones financieras o de prestadores de servicios financieros transfronterizos. Este párrafo es sin perjuicio de cualquier otra disposición de este Capítulo que permita a una Parte restringir transferencias.

4.   El Artículo 6.06, no se aplicará al otorgamiento de derechos de exclusividad que haga una Parte a una institución financiera para prestar uno de los servicios financieros a que se refiere el Artículo 6.02(2)(b).

Artículo 6.10 Transparencia

1.   Además de lo dispuesto en el Artículo 10.02, las autoridades reguladoras de cada Parte pondrán a disposición de los interesados toda información relativa sobre los requisitos para llenar y presentar una solicitud para la prestación de servicios financieros.

2.   A petición del solicitante, la autoridad reguladora le informará sobre la situación de su solicitud. Cuando esa autoridad requiera del solicitante información adicional, se lo comunicará sin demora injustificada.

3.   Las autoridades reguladoras de cada Parte dictarán, dentro de un plazo de ciento veinte (120) días, una resolución administrativa respecto a una solicitud completa relacionada con la prestación de un servicio financiero, presentada por un inversionista en una institución financiera, por una institución financiera o por un prestador de servicios financieros transfronterizos de otra Parte. La autoridad comunicará al interesado, sin demora, la resolución. No se considerará completa la solicitud hasta que se celebren todas las audiencias pertinentes y se reciba toda la información necesaria. Cuando no sea viable dictar una resolución dentro del plazo de ciento veinte (120) días, la autoridad reguladora lo comunicará al interesado sin demora injustificada y posteriormente procurará emitir la resolución en un plazo razonable.

4.   Ninguna disposición de este Capítulo obliga a una Parte ni a divulgar ni a permitir acceso a:

a)   información relativa a los asuntos financieros y cuentas de clientes individuales de instituciones financieras o de prestadores de servicios financieros transfronterizos; o

b)   cualquier información confidencial cuya divulgación pudiera dificultar la aplicación de la ley, o ser contraria de algún otro modo al interés público, o dañar intereses comerciales legítimos de alguna persona determinada.

5.   Las autoridades responsables de cada Parte de mantener o establecer uno o más centros de consulta, para responder a la brevedad posible todas las preguntas razonables de personas interesadas respecto de las medidas de aplicación general que adopte una Parte en relación con este Capítulo, son las señaladas en el Anexo 6.10.

Artículo 6.11 Comité de Servicios Financieros

1.   Se establece el Comité de Servicios Financieros, cuya composición se señala en el Anexo 6.10. Asimismo, podrán participar representantes de otras instituciones cuando las autoridades responsables lo consideren conveniente.

2.   Sin perjuicio de lo dispuesto en el Artículo 9.04, el Comité tendrá, entre otras, las siguientes funciones:

a)   considerar los aspectos relativos a servicios financieros que le sean presentados por una Parte;

b)   participar en los procedimientos de solución de controversias relativos a este Capítulo y el Artículo 6.19; y

c)   facilitar el intercambio de información entre autoridades nacionales de supervisión y cooperar, en materia de asesoría sobre regulación prudencial, procurando la armonización de los marcos normativos de regulación, así como de otras políticas, cuando se considere conveniente.

Artículo 6.12 Consultas generales

1.   Cada Parte podrá solicitar consultas con otra respecto a cualquier asunto relacionado con este Tratado que afecte los servicios financieros. La otra Parte considerará favorablemente esa solicitud. Las Partes consultantes darán a conocer al Comité los resultados de sus consultas, durante las reuniones que éste celebre.

2.   En las consultas previstas en este Artículo participarán funcionarios de las autoridades competentes de cada Parte señaladas en el Anexo 6.10.

3.   Cada Parte podrá solicitar que las autoridades reguladoras de otra Parte intervengan en las consultas realizadas de conformidad con este Artículo, para discutir las medidas de aplicación general de esa otra Parte que puedan afectar las operaciones de las instituciones financieras o de los prestadores de servicios financieros transfronterizos en el territorio de la Parte que solicitó la consulta.

4.   Nada de lo dispuesto en este Artículo será interpretado en el sentido de obligar a las autoridades reguladoras que intervengan en las consultas conforme al párrafo 3, a divulgar información o a actuar de manera que pudiera interferir en asuntos particulares en materia de regulación, supervisión, administración o aplicación de medidas.

5.   En los casos en que, para efecto de supervisión, una Parte necesite información sobre una institución financiera en territorio de otra Parte o sobre prestadores de servicios financieros transfronterizos en territorio de otra Parte, la Parte podrá acudir a la autoridad reguladora responsable en territorio de la otra Parte para solicitar la información.

Artículo 6.13 Nuevos servicios financieros y procesamiento de datos

1.   Cada Parte permitirá que una institución financiera de otra Parte preste cualquier nuevo servicio financiero de tipo similar a aquellos que esa Parte permite prestar a sus instituciones financieras, conforme a su legislación. La Parte podrá decidir la modalidad institucional y jurídica a través de la cual se ofrezca tal servicio y podrá exigir autorización para la prestación del mismo.

Cuando esa autorización se requiera, la resolución respectiva se dictará en un plazo razonable y solamente podrá ser denegada la autorización por razones prudenciales.

2.   Cada Parte permitirá a las instituciones financieras de otra Parte transferir, para su procesamiento, información hacia el interior o el exterior del territorio de la Parte, utilizando cualesquiera de los medios autorizados en ella, cuando sea necesario para llevar a cabo las actividades ordinarias de negocios de esas instituciones.

Artículo 6.14 Alta dirección empresarial y órganos de dirección

1.   Ninguna Parte podrá obligar a las instituciones financieras de otra Parte a que contrate personal de cualquier nacionalidad en particular para ocupar puestos de alta dirección empresarial u otros cargos esenciales.

2.   Ninguna Parte podrá exigir que la Junta Directiva o el Consejo de Administración de una institución financiera de otra Parte se integre por nacionales de esa Parte, residentes en su territorio o una combinación de ambos.

Artículo 6.15 Reservas

1.   Un año después de la entrada en vigor del Tratado, ninguna Parte incrementará el grado de disconformidad de sus medidas relativas a los Artículos 6.04, 6.05, 6.06, 6.07, 6.13 y 6.14, las que serán consignadas en la Sección A (Medidas Incompatibles Existentes) del Anexo V (Servicios Financieros).

2.   Los Artículos del 6.04 al 6.07, 6.13 y 6.14 no se aplicarán a ninguna medida que una Parte adopte o mantenga de acuerdo con la Sección B (Actividades Económicas Reservadas a cada Parte) de su lista del Anexo V (Servicios Financieros).

3.   Cualquier modificación a una medida incompatible a que se refiere el párrafo 1, no disminuirá el grado de conformidad de la medida tal como estaba en vigor inmediatamente antes de la reforma.

4.   Cuando una Parte haya establecido cualquier reserva a los Artículos 3.04, 3.05, 3.08, 4.03 ó 4.04, en su lista de los Anexos I (Medidas Incompatibles Existentes), II (Actividades Económicas Reservadas a cada Parte) y III (Excepciones al Trato de Nación Más Favorecida), la reserva se entenderá hecha al Artículo 6.04 al 6.07, 6.13 y 6.14 según sea el caso, en el grado que

la medida, sector, subsector o actividad especificados en la reserva, estén cubiertos por este Capítulo.

Artículo 6.16 Liberalización futura

Con miras a lograr un nivel de liberalización progresivamente más elevado, las Partes se comprometen a realizar negociaciones futuras, por lo menos cada dos (2) años, en el seno del Consejo, tendientes a eliminar las restricciones remanentes inscritas de conformidad con el Artículo 6.15.

Artículo 6.17 Denegación de beneficios

Una Parte podrá denegar, parcial o totalmente, los beneficios derivados de este Capítulo a una institución financiera de otra Parte o a un prestador de servicios financieros transfronterizos de otra Parte, previa comunicación y realización de consultas, de conformidad con los Artículos 6.10 y 6.12, cuando la Parte determine que el servicio está siendo prestado por una empresa que no realiza actividades de negocios importantes en territorio de cualquiera de las Partes y que de conformidad con la legislación vigente de esa Parte es propiedad o está bajo control de personas de un país no Parte.

Artículo 6.18 Transferencias

1.   Cada Parte permitirá que todas las transferencias relacionadas con la inversión en su territorio de un inversionista de otra Parte, se hagan libremente y sin demora. Esas transferencias incluyen:

a)   ganancias, dividendos, intereses, ganancias de capital, pagos por regalías, gastos por administración, asistencia técnica y otros cargos, ganancias en especie y otros montos derivados de la inversión;

b)   productos derivados de la venta o liquidación, total o parcial, de la inversión;

c)   pagos realizados conforme a un contrato del que sea parte un inversionista o su inversión;

d)   pagos efectuados de conformidad con el Artículo 3.11; y

e)   pagos que resulten de la solución de controversias entre una Parte y un inversionista de otra Parte.

2.   Cada Parte permitirá que las transferencias se realicen en divisa de libre convertibilidad, al tipo de cambio vigente en el mercado en la fecha de la transferencia para transacciones al contado de la divisa que vaya a transferirse, sin perjuicio de lo dispuesto en el Artículo 8.04.

3.   Ninguna Parte podrá exigir a sus inversionistas que efectúen transferencias de sus ingresos, ganancias o utilidades u otros montos derivados de inversiones llevadas a cabo en territorio de otra Parte, o atribuibles a las mismas.

4.   No obstante lo dispuesto en los párrafos 1 y 2, cada Parte podrá impedir la realización de transferencias, por medio de la aplicación equitativa, no discriminatoria de sus leyes, en los

siguientes casos:

a)   quiebra, insolvencia o protección de los derechos de los acreedores;

b)   emisión, comercio y operaciones de valores;

c)   infracciones penales o administrativas;

d)   reportes de transferencias de divisas u otros instrumentos monetarios; o

e)   garantía del cumplimiento de los fallos en un procedimiento contencioso.

5.   No obstante lo dispuesto en el párrafo 1, cada Parte podrá restringir las transferencias de ganancias en especie, en circunstancias en donde pudiera, de otra manera, restringir esas transferencias conforme a lo dispuesto en este Capítulo.

6.   Cada Parte podrá conservar leyes y reglamentos que establezcan impuestos sobre la renta y complementarios por medios tales como la retención de impuestos aplicables a los dividendos y otras transferencias, siempre y cuando no sean discriminatorios.

Artículo 6.19 Controversias entre un inversionista y una Parte

1.   Salvo lo dispuesto en este Artículo, las demandas que formule un inversionista contendiente contra una Parte en relación con las obligaciones previstas en este Capítulo, se resolverán de conformidad con lo establecido en la sección B del Capítulo 3.

2.   Cuando la Parte contra la cual se formula la demanda invoque cualquiera de las excepciones a que se refiere el Artículo 6.09, se observará el siguiente procedimiento:

a)   el tribunal remitirá el asunto al Comité de Servicios Financieros para su decisión. El tribunal no podrá proceder hasta que haya recibido una decisión de dicho Comité según los términos de este Artículo o hayan transcurrido sesenta (60) días desde la fecha de recepción del asunto por el referido Comité;

b)   una vez recibido, el Comité de Servicios Financieros decidirá acerca de sí y en qué grado la excepción del Artículo 6.09 invocada es una defensa válida contra la.demanda del inversionista y remitirá copia de su decisión al tribunal y al Consejo. Esa decisión será obligatoria para el tribunal.

Artículo 6.20 Controversias entre las Partes

1.   El Comité de Servicios Financieros integrará por consenso una lista de hasta quince (15) personas, que incluya tres (3) personas de cada Parte, que cuenten con las aptitudes y disposiciones necesarias para actuar como árbitros en controversias relacionadas con este Capítulo.

2.   Una Parte reclamante solo podrá suspender beneficios en el sector de servicios financieros cuando un tribunal arbitral encuentre que una medida es incompatible con las obligaciones de este Capítulo.

ANEXO 6.10
AUTORIDADES REGULADORAS, RESPONSABLES O COMPETENTES DE LOS SERVICIOS FINANCIEROS

1.   Para efectos de este Capítulo, las autoridades reguladoras, responsables o competentes de los servicios financieros serán:

a)   para el caso de Costa Rica, el Ministerio de Comercio Exterior, o su sucesor, en consulta con la autoridad competente que corresponda (Banco Central de Costa Rica, Superintendencia General de Entidades Financieras, Superintendencia de Pensiones y Superintendencia de Valores);

b)   para El Salvador: el Ministerio de Economía, la Superintendencia del Sistema Financiero, la Superintendencia de Valores, la Superintendencia de Pensiones y el Banco Central de Reserva, o sus sucesores;

c)   para Guatemala: el Ministerio de Economía, la Junta Monetaria, el Banco de Guatemala y la Superintendencia de Bancos, o sus sucesores;

d)   para Honduras: la Secretaria de Estado en los Despachos de Industria y Comercio, el Banco Central de Honduras y la Comisión Nacional de Banca y Seguros, o sus sucesores; y

e)   para Nicaragua: el Ministerio de Fomento, Industria y Comercio, el Ministerio de Hacienda o Crédito Público, el Banco Central y la Superintendencia de Bancos, o sus sucesores.

2.   El representante principal de cada Parte será el que la autoridad correspondiente designe para tal efecto.

CAPÍTULO 7
ENTRADA TEMPORAL DE PERSONAS DE NEGOCIOS

Artículo 7.01 Definiciones

1.   Para efectos de este Capítulo, se entenderá por:

actividades de negocios: aquellas actividades legítimas de naturaleza comercial creadas y operadas con el fin de obtener ganancias en el mercado. No incluye la posibilidad de obtener empleo, ni salario o remuneración proveniente de fuente laboral en territorio de una Parte;

certificación laboral: el procedimiento efectuado por la autoridad administrativa competente tendiente a determinar si un nacional de una Parte, que pretende ingresar temporalmente a territorio de otra Parte, desplaza mano de obra nacional en la misma rama laboral o perjudica sensiblemente las condiciones laborales de la misma;

entrada temporal: la entrada de una persona de negocios de una Parte a territorio de otra Parte, sin la intención de establecer residencia permanente o definitiva;

nacional: un "nacional", tal como se define en el artículo 2.01, pero no incluye a los residentes permanentes o definitivos;

persona de negocios: el nacional que participa en el comercio de mercancías o prestación de servicios, o en actividades de inversión; y

práctica recurrente: una práctica ejecutada por las autoridades migratorias de una Parte en forma repetitiva durante un período representativo anterior e inmediato a la ejecución de la misma.

2.   Para efectos del Anexo 7.04, se entenderá por:

funciones ejecutivas: aquellas funciones asignadas dentro de una organización, bajo la cual la persona de negocios tiene fundamentalmente las siguientes responsabilidades:

   a)   dirigir la administración de la organización o un componente o función relevante de la misma;

   b)   establecer las políticas y objetivos de la organización, componente o función; o

   c)   recibir supervisión o dirección general solamente por parte de ejecutivos de más alto nivel, la junta directiva o el consejo de administración de la organización o los accionistas de la misma;

funciones gerenciales: aquellas funciones asignadas dentro de una organización, bajo la cual la persona de negocios tiene fundamentalmente las siguientes responsabilidades:

   a)   dirigir la organización o una función esencial dentro de la misma;

   b)   supervisar y controlar el trabajo de otros empleados profesionales, supervisores o administradores;

   c)   tener la autoridad de contratar y despedir, o recomendar esas acciones, así como otras respecto del manejo del personal que está siendo directamente supervisado por esa persona y ejecutar funciones a nivel superior dentro de la jerarquía organizativa o con respecto a la función a su cargo; o

   d)   ejecutar acciones bajo su discreción respecto de la operación diaria de la función sobre la cual esa persona tiene la autoridad; y

funciones que conlleven conocimientos especializados: aquellas funciones que involucren un conocimiento especial de la mercancía, servicios, investigación, equipo, técnicas, administración de la organización o de sus intereses y su aplicación en los mercados internacionales, o un nivel avanzado de conocimientos o experiencias en los procesos y procedimientos de la organización.

Artículo 7.02 Principios generales

Este Capítulo refleja la relación comercial preferente que existe entre las Partes, la conveniencia de facilitar la entrada temporal conforme al principio de reciprocidad y de establecer criterios y procedimientos transparentes para tal efecto. Asimismo, refleja la necesidad de garantizar la seguridad de las fronteras y de proteger la fuerza de trabajo nacional y el empleo permanente en sus respectivos territorios.

Artículo 7.03 Obligaciones generales

1.   Cada Parte aplicará las medidas relativas a las disposiciones de este Capítulo de conformidad con el Artículo 7.02 y, en particular, las aplicará de manera expedita para evitar demoras o perjuicios indebidos en el comercio de mercancías y servicios, o en las actividades de inversión comprendidas en este Tratado.

2.   Las Partes procurarán desarrollar y adoptar criterios, definiciones e interpretaciones comunes para la aplicación de este Capítulo.

Artículo 7.04 Autorización de entrada temporal

1.   De acuerdo con las disposiciones de este Capítulo, incluso las contenidas en los Anexos 7.04 y 7.04(1), cada Parte autorizará la entrada temporal a personas de negocios que cumplan con las demás medidas aplicables relativas a la salud y seguridad pública, así como las relacionadas con la seguridad nacional.

2.   Una Parte podrá negar la expedición de un documento migratorio que autorice el empleo a una persona de negocios cuando su entrada temporal afecte desfavorablemente:

  a)   la solución de cualquier conflicto laboral en curso en el lugar donde esté empleada o vaya a emplearse; o

  b)   el empleo de cualquier persona que intervenga en ese conflicto.

3.   Cuando una Parte niegue la expedición de un documento migratorio que autorice el empleo, de conformidad con el párrafo 2, esa Parte:

  a)   informará por escrito las razones de la negativa a la persona de negocios afectada; y

  b)   notificará sin demora y por escrito las razones de la negativa a la Parte a cuyo nacional se niega la entrada.

4.   Cada Parte limitará el importe de los derechos por el trámite de las solicitudes de entrada temporal al costo aproximado de los servicios prestados, salvo que las Partes hayan acordado en el pasado la eliminación de esos derechos.

5.   La autorización de entrada temporal en virtud de este Capítulo, no reemplaza los requisitos requeridos para el ejercicio de una profesión o actividad de acuerdo con la normativa específica vigente en territorio de la Parte que autoriza la entrada temporal.

Artículo 7.05 Suministro de información

1.   Además de lo dispuesto por el Artículo 10.02, cada Parte deberá:

a)   proporcionar a otra Parte el material informativo que le permita conocer las medidas que adopte relativas a este Capítulo; y

b)   a más tardar seis (6) meses después de la fecha de entrada en vigor de este Tratado, preparar, publicar y poner a disposición de los interesados, tanto en su propio territorio como en el de otra Parte, un documento consolidado con material que explique los requisitos para la entrada temporal conforme a este Capítulo, de manera que puedan conocerlos las personas de negocios de otra Parte.

2.   Cada Parte recopilará, mantendrá y pondrá a disposición de otra Parte información relativa al otorgamiento de autorizaciones de entrada temporal, de acuerdo con este Capítulo, a personas de negocios de otra Parte a quienes se les haya expedido documentación migratoria. Esta recopilación incluirá información por cada categoría autorizada.

Artículo 7.06 Solución de controversias

1.   Una Parte no podrá dar inicio a un procedimiento de solución de controversias respecto a una negativa de autorización de entrada temporal conforme a este Capítulo, ni respecto de algún caso particular comprendido en el Artículo 7.03, salvo que:

a)   el asunto se refiera a una práctica recurrente; y

b)   la persona de negocios afectada haya agotado los recursos administrativos a su alcance respecto a ese asunto en particular.

2.   Los recursos mencionados en el párrafo 1(b) se considerarán agotados cuando la autoridad competente no haya emitido una resolución definitiva en seis (6) meses, contados desde el inicio del procedimiento administrativo, y la resolución no se haya demorado por causas imputables a la persona de negocios afectada.

Artículo 7.07 Relación con otros Capítulos

Salvo lo dispuesto en este Capítulo, en los Capítulos 2, 9 y 11 y en los Artículos 10.01, 10.02 y 10.03, ninguna disposición de este Tratado impondrá obligación alguna a las Partes respecto a sus medidas migratorias.

ANEXO 7.04
ENTRADA TEMPORAL DE PERSONAS DE NEGOCIOS

Sección A - Visitantes de negocios

1.   Cada Parte autorizará la entrada temporal y expedirá documentación comprobatoria a la persona de negocios que pretenda llevar a cabo alguna actividad de negocios mencionada en el Apéndice 7.04(A)(1), sin exigirle otros requisitos que los establecidos por las medidas migratorias vigentes aplicables a la entrada temporal, y que exhiba:

a)   prueba de nacionalidad de una Parte; y

b)   el propósito de su entrada.

2.   Cada Parte autorizará la entrada temporal, en términos no menos favorables que los previstos en las medidas señaladas en el Apéndice 7.04(A)(2), a las personas de negocios que pretendan llevar a cabo algunas actividades de negocios distintas a las señaladas en el Apéndice 7.04(A)(1).

3.   Ninguna Parte podrá:

   a)   exigir como condición para autorizar la entrada temporal conforme al párrafo 1 ó 2, procedimientos previos de aprobación, peticiones, pruebas de certificación laboral u otros procedimientos de efecto similar; o

   b)   imponer o mantener restricciones numéricas a la entrada temporal de conformidad con el párrafo 1 ó 2.

4.   No obstante lo dispuesto en el párrafo 3, una Parte podrá requerir de la persona de negocios que solicita entrada temporal conforme a esta Sección, que obtenga previamente a la entrada una visa o documento equivalente. Las Partes considerarán la posibilidad de evitar o eliminar los requisitos de visa o documento equivalente.

Sección B – Comerciantes e inversionistas

1.   Cada Parte autorizará la entrada temporal y expedirá documentación comprobatoria a la persona de negocios que ejerza funciones de supervisión, ejecutivas o con conocimientos especializados, siempre que la persona cumpla además con las medidas migratorias vigentes, aplicables a la entrada temporal y que pretenda:

   a)   llevar a cabo un intercambio comercial cuantioso de mercancías o servicios, principalmente entre el territorio de la Parte de la cual la persona de negocios es nacional y el territorio de otra Parte a la cual se solicita la entrada; o

   b)   establecer, desarrollar, administrar o prestar asesoría o servicios técnicos claves para administrar una inversión en la cual la persona de negocios o su empresa hayan comprometido, o estén en vías de comprometer, un monto importante de capital.

2.   Ninguna Parte podrá:

   a)   exigir pruebas de certificación laboral u otros procedimientos de efecto similar, como condición para autorizar la entrada temporal conforme al párrafo 1; o

   b)   imponer o mantener restricciones numéricas en relación con la entrada temporal conforme al párrafo 1..3. No obstante lo dispuesto en el párrafo 2, una Parte podrá requerir de la persona de negocios que solicita entrada temporal conforme a esta Sección, que obtenga previamente a la entrada una visa o documento equivalente. Las Partes considerarán la posibilidad de evitar o eliminar los requisitos de visa o documento equivalente.

Sección C - Transferencias de personal dentro de una empresa

1.   Cada Parte autorizará la entrada temporal y expedirá documentación comprobatoria a la persona de negocios, empleada por una empresa, que pretenda desempeñar funciones gerenciales, ejecutivas o que conlleven conocimientos especializados en esa empresa o en una de sus subsidiarias o filiales, siempre que cumpla con las medidas migratorias vigentes aplicables a la entrada temporal. Cada Parte podrá exigir que la persona haya sido empleada de la empresa, de manera continua, durante seis (6) meses, dentro de los tres (3) años inmediatamente anteriores a la fecha de presentación de la solicitud.

2.   Ninguna Parte podrá:

a)   exigir pruebas de certificación laboral u otros procedimientos de efecto similar como condición para autorizar la entrada temporal conforme al párrafo 1; o

b)   imponer o mantener restricciones numéricas en relación con la entrada temporal conforme al párrafo 1.

ANEXO 7.04(1)
DISPOSICIONES ESPECÍFICAS PARA LA ENTRADA TEMPORAL DE PERSONAS DE NEGOCIOS

1.   Se considerará que las personas de negocios que ingresen bajo cualquiera de las categorías establecidas en el Anexo 7.04, realizan actividades que son útiles o ventajosas para el país.

2.   Las personas de negocios que ingresen bajo cualquiera de las categorías establecidas en el Anexo 7.04, estarán sujetas a las disposiciones migratorias vigentes.

3.   Las personas de negocios que ingresen bajo cualquiera de las categorías establecidas en el Anexo 7.04, no podrán solicitar permanencia definitiva salvo que cumplan con las medidas migratorias vigentes.

APÉNDICE 7.04(A)(1)
VISITANTES DE NEGOCIOS

Investigación y diseño

- Investigadores técnicos, científicos y estadísticos que realicen investigaciones de manera independiente o para una empresa establecida en territorio de otra Parte.

Cultivo, manufactura y producción

- Personal de compras y de producción, a nivel gerencial, que lleve a cabo operaciones comerciales para una empresa establecida en territorio de otra Parte.

Comercialización

- Investigadores y analistas de mercado que efectúen investigaciones o análisis de manera independiente o para una empresa establecida en territorio de otra Parte.

- Personal de ferias y de promoción que asista a convenciones comerciales.

Ventas

- Representantes y agentes de ventas que tomen pedidos o negocien contratos sobre mercancías y servicios para una empresa establecida en territorio de otra Parte, pero que no entreguen las mercancías ni presten los servicios.

- Compradores que hagan adquisiciones para una empresa establecida en territorio de otra Parte.

Distribución

- Agentes de aduanas que presten servicios de asesoría para facilitar la importación o exportación de mercancías.

Servicios posteriores a la venta

- Personal de instalación, reparación, mantenimiento y supervisión que cuente con los conocimientos técnicos especializados esenciales para cumplir con la obligación contractual del vendedor; y que preste servicios, o capacite a trabajadores para que presten esos servicios de conformidad con una garantía u otro contrato de servicios relacionados con la venta de equipo o maquinaria comercial o industrial, incluidos los programas de computación comprados a una empresa establecida fuera de territorio de la Parte a la cual se solicita entrada temporal, durante la vigencia del contrato de garantía o de servicio.

Servicios generales

- Consultores que realicen actividades de negocios a nivel de prestación de servicios transfronterizos.

- Personal gerencial y de supervisión que intervenga en operaciones comerciales para una empresa establecida en territorio de otra Parte.

- Personal de servicios financieros que preste asesoría para una empresa establecida en territorio de otra Parte.

- Personal de relaciones públicas y de publicidad que brinde asesoría a clientes o que asista o participe en convenciones.

- Personal de turismo (agentes de excursiones y de viajes, guías de turistas u operadores de viajes) que asista o participe en convenciones o conduzca alguna excursión que se haya iniciado en territorio de otra Parte.

- Operadores de autobús turístico que entren en territorio de una Parte:

    a)   con un grupo de pasajeros en un viaje de autobús turístico que haya comenzado en territorio de otra Parte y vaya a regresar a él;

    b)   que vaya a recoger a un grupo de pasajeros en un viaje en autobús turístico que terminará, y se desarrollará en su mayor parte en territorio de otra Parte; o

c)   con un grupo de pasajeros en autobús turístico cuyo destino está en territorio de la Parte a la cual se solicita la entrada temporal, y que regrese sin pasajeros o con el grupo para transportarlo a territorio de otra Parte.

- Traductores o intérpretes que presten servicios como empleados de una empresa establecida en territorio de otra Parte.

APÉNDICE 7.04(A)(2)
MEDIDAS MIGRATORIAS VIGENTES

Para el caso de Costa Rica:

La Ley General de Migración y Extranjería, Ley número 7033 del 4 de agosto de 1986 Títulos II, III, IV, V, VII, VIII y X y el Reglamento a la Ley General de Migración y Extranjería, Decreto Ejecutivo número 19010 del 31 de mayo de 1989.

Para el caso de El Salvador:

a)   Ley de Migración, Decreto Legislativo N° 2772 de fecha 19 de diciembre de 1958, publicado en el Diario Oficial N° 240, tomo 181, de fecha 23 de diciembre de 1958;

b)   Reglamento de la Ley de Migración, Decreto Ejecutivo N° 33 de fecha 9 de marzo de 1959, publicado en el Diario Oficial N° 56, tomo 182, de fecha 31 de marzo de 1959;

c)   Ley de Extranjería, Decreto Legislativo N° 299 de fecha 18 de febrero de 1986, publicado en el Diario Oficial N° 34, tomo 290, de fecha 20 de febrero de 1986; y

d)   El Acuerdo de Managua, suscrito en Managua, Nicaragua, el 22 de abril de 1993 (Acuerdos del CA-4) en materia de facilitación migratoria y libre tránsito de personas.

Para el caso de Guatemala:

a)   Decreto N° 95-98 del Congreso de la República, Ley de Migración, publicado en el Diario Oficial de Centroamérica el 23 de diciembre de 1998;

b)   Acuerdo Gubernativo N° 529-99, Reglamento de Migración, publicado en el Diario Oficial de Centroamérica el 29 de julio de 1999; y

c)   El Acuerdo de Managua, suscrito en Managua, Nicaragua, el 22 de abril de 1993 (Acuerdos del CA-4) en materia de facilitación migratoria y libre tránsito de personas.

Para el caso de Honduras:

a)   Ley de Población y Política Migratoria, Decreto N° 34, publicado en el Diario Oficial "La Gaceta" el 25 de septiembre de 1970;

b)   Acuerdo N° 8 Procedimientos sobre Facilidades Migratorias a Inversionistas y Comerciantes Extranjeros, publicado en el Diario Oficial "La Gaceta" el 19 de agosto de 1998; y

c)   El Acuerdo de Managua, suscrito en Managua, Nicaragua, el 22 de abril de 1993 (Acuerdos del CA-4) en materia de facilitación migratoria y libre tránsito de personas.

Para el caso de Nicaragua:

a)   Ley N° 153 del 24 de febrero de 1993, publicada en el Diario Oficial "La Gaceta" N° 80 del 30 de abril de 1993, Capítulo II, Artículos 7 al 40;

b)   Ley N° 154 del 10 de marzo de 1993, publicada en el Diario Oficial "La Gaceta" N° 81 del 3 de mayo de 1993, artículo 13;

c)   Decreto N° 628, Ley de Residentes Pensionados o Rentistas de Nicaragua, publicado en el Diario Oficial "La Gaceta" N°264 del 19 de noviembre de 1974; y

d)   El Acuerdo de Managua, suscrito en Managua, Nicaragua, el 22 de abril de 1993 (Acuerdos del CA-4) en materia de facilitación migratoria y libre tránsito de personas.

PARTE III - EXCEPCIONES GENERALES

Capítulo 8

Excepciones

Artículo 8.01 Definiciones

Para efectos de este Capítulo, se entenderá por:

convenio tributario: un convenio para evitar la doble tributación u otro convenio o arreglo internacional en materia tributaria;

Fondo: el Fondo Monetario Internacional;

pagos por transacciones internacionales corrientes: los "pagos por transacciones internacionales corrientes", tal como se define en el Convenio Constitutivo del Fondo;

transacciones internacionales de capital: las "transacciones internacionales de capital", tal como se define en el Convenio Constitutivo del Fondo; y

transferencias: las transacciones internacionales y transferencias internacionales y pagos conexos.

Artículo 8.02 Excepciones generales

Se incorporan a este Tratado y forman parte integrante del mismo, los apartados a), b) y c) del Artículo XIV del AGCS y sus modificaciones.

Artículo 8.03 Seguridad nacional

Ninguna disposición de este Tratado se interpretará en el sentido de:

a)   obligar a una Parte a proporcionar ni a dar acceso a información cuya divulgación considere contraria a los intereses esenciales de su seguridad;

b)   impedir a una Parte que adopte cualquier medida que considere necesaria para proteger los intereses esenciales de su seguridad:

   i)   relativa al comercio de armamento, municiones y pertrechos de guerra y al comercio y las operaciones sobre mercancías, materiales, servicios y tecnología que se lleven a cabo con la finalidad directa o indirecta de proporcionar suministros a una institución militar o a otro establecimiento de defensa;

   ii)   aplicadas en tiempos de guerra o en otros casos de grave tensión internacional; o

   iii)   referente a la aplicación de políticas nacionales o de acuerdos internacionales en materia de no proliferación de armas nucleares o de otros dispositivos explosivos nucleares; ni

c)   impedir a cualquier Parte adoptar medidas en cumplimiento de sus obligaciones derivadas de la Carta de las Naciones Unidas para el mantenimiento de la paz y la seguridad internacionales.

Artículo 8.04 Balanza de pagos

1.   Ninguna disposición de este Tratado se interpretará en el sentido de impedir que una Parte adopte o mantenga medidas que restrinjan las transferencias cuando la Parte afronte dificultades serias en su balanza de pagos, o amenaza de las mismas, siempre que las restricciones sean compatibles con este Artículo.

2.   Tan pronto sea factible después de que una Parte aplique una medida conforme a este Artículo, de acuerdo con lo que establecen sus obligaciones internacionales, la Parte:

   a)   someterá a revisión del Fondo todas las restricciones a las operaciones de cuenta corriente de conformidad con el Artículo VIII del Convenio Constitutivo del Fondo;

   b)   iniciará consultas de buena fe con el Fondo respecto a las medidas de ajuste económico encaminadas a afrontar los problemas económicos fundamentales que subyacen en las dificultades; y

   c)   procurará adoptar o mantener políticas económicas compatibles con dichas consultas.

3.   Las medidas que se apliquen o mantengan de conformidad con este Artículo deberán:

   a)   evitar daños innecesarios a los intereses comerciales, económicos o financieros de otra Parte;

b) no ser más onerosas de lo necesario para afrontar las dificultades en la balanza de pagos, o la amenaza de las mismas;

c) ser temporales y eliminarse progresivamente a medida que mejore la situación de la balanza de pagos;

d) ser compatibles con las del párrafo 2(c), así como con el Convenio Constitutivo del Fondo; y

e) aplicarse de acuerdo con el más favorable, entre los principios de trato nacional y de nación más favorecida.

4. Una Parte podrá adoptar o mantener una medida conforme a este Artículo que otorgue prioridad a los servicios esenciales para su programa económico, siempre que la Parte no aplique la medida con el fin de proteger a una industria o sector en particular, salvo que la medida sea compatible con el párrafo 2(c) y con el Artículo VIII(3) del Convenio Constitutivo del Fondo.

5. Las restricciones impuestas a transferencias:

a) deberán ser compatibles con el Artículo VIII(3) del Convenio Constitutivo del Fondo, cuando se apliquen a los pagos por transacciones internacionales corrientes;

b) deberán ser compatibles con el Artículo VI del Convenio Constitutivo del Fondo y aplicarse sólo en conjunción con medidas sobre los pagos por transacciones internacionales corrientes de conformidad con el párrafo 2(a), cuando se apliquen a las transacciones internacionales de capital; y

c) no podrán tomar la forma de sobretasas arancelarias, cuotas, licencias o medidas similares.

Artículo 8.05 Excepciones a la divulgación de información

Ninguna disposición de este Tratado se interpretará en el sentido de obligar a una Parte a proporcionar o a dar acceso a información, cuya divulgación pueda impedir el cumplimiento o ser contraria a su Constitución Política, al interés público o a sus leyes en lo que se refiere a la protección de la intimidad de las personas, los asuntos financieros y las cuentas bancarias de clientes individuales de las instituciones financieras.

Artículo 8.06 Tributación

1. Salvo lo dispuesto en este Artículo, ninguna disposición de este Tratado se aplicará a medidas tributarias.

2. Ninguna disposición de este Tratado afectará los derechos y las obligaciones de cualquiera de las Partes que se deriven de cualquier convenio tributario. En caso de incompatibilidad entre cualquiera de estos convenios y este Tratado, aquéllos prevalecerán en la medida de la incompatibilidad.

3.   Las Partes procurarán celebrar un tratado para evitar la doble tributación dentro de un plazo razonable después de la fecha de entrada en vigor de este Tratado.

4.   Las Partes acuerdan que, junto con la celebración de un tratado para evitar la doble tributación, intercambiarán cartas en que se establezca la relación entre el tratado para evitar la doble tributación y este Artículo.

PARTE IV - DISPOSICIONES INSTITUCIONALES

CAPÍTULO 9

ADMINISTRACIÓN DEL TRATADO

Artículo 9.01 Administración

La administración del presente Tratado estará a cargo del Consejo.

Artículo 9.02 Comisión

1.   Las Partes establecen la Comisión, integrada por los funcionarios a que se refiere el Anexo 9.02(1) o por las personas a las que éstas designen.

2.   La Comisión tendrá las siguientes funciones:

   a)   preparar y revisar los expedientes técnicos necesarios para la toma de decisiones en el marco del Tratado;

   b)   dar seguimiento a las decisiones tomadas por el Consejo;

   c)   supervisar la labor de los Comités;

   d)   establecer grupos de trabajo y grupos de expertos ad hoc o permanentes, así como asignarles atribuciones;

   e)   conocer de cualquier otro asunto que pudiese afectar el funcionamiento de este Tratado que le sea encomendado por el Consejo;

3.   La Comisión se reunirá en cualquier tiempo a solicitud de cualquiera de las Partes o las veces que el Consejo lo considere necesario y reportará sus informes al Consejo.

Artículo 9.03 Comités o Subcomités

1.   Los Comités estarán integrados por representantes de cada Parte y podrán autorizar la participación de representantes de otras instituciones.

2.   Los Comités se reunirán en cualquier tiempo a solicitud de cualquiera de las Partes, o de la Comisión y adoptarán sus recomendaciones de conformidad con los instrumentos de la integración económica centroamericana.

3.   La Comisión podrá establecer Comités, distintos de los establecidos en el Anexo 9.03, o Subcomités que sean necesarios para atender los diversos aspectos relacionados con este Tratado.

Artículo 9.04 Funciones de los Comités

Los Comités tendrán, entre otras, las siguientes funciones:

a)   vigilar la implementación de los capítulos de este Tratado que sean de su competencia;

b)   solicitar informes técnicos a las autoridades competentes a fin de contribuir a resolver el asunto;

c)   evaluar y recomendar a la Comisión, para que ésta eleve al Consejo, las propuestas de modificación a las disposiciones de los Capítulos de este Tratado que sean de su competencia;

d)   proponer a la Comisión la revisión de medidas en vigor o en proyecto de una Parte que estime puedan ser incompatibles con las obligaciones de este Tratado; y

e)   cumplir con las demás tareas que le sean encomendadas por la Comisión y el Consejo.

ANEXO 9.02
FUNCIONARIOS DE LA COMISIÓN

Para efectos del Artículo 9.02, los funcionarios de la Comisión son:

a)   para el caso de Costa Rica, un representante del Ministro de Comercio Exterior, o su sucesor;

b)   para el caso de El Salvador, un representante del Ministerio de Economía, o su sucesor;

c)   para el caso de Guatemala, un representante del Ministerio de Economía, o su sucesor;

d)   para el caso de Honduras, un Representante de la Secretaría de Estado en los Despachos de Industria y Comercio, o su sucesora; y

e)   para el caso de Nicaragua, un representante del Ministerio de Fomento, Industria y Comercio, o su sucesor.

ANEXO 9.03
COMITÉS

Comité de Inversión y Servicios Transfronterizos (artículo 4.09).

Comité de Servicios Financieros (artículo 6.11).

CAPÍTULO 10

TRANSPARENCIA

Artículo 10.01 Definiciones

Para efectos de este Capítulo, se entenderá por "resolución administrativa de aplicación general", una resolución o interpretación administrativa que se aplica a todas las personas y situaciones de hecho que generalmente entren en su ámbito, y que establece una norma de conducta, pero no incluye:

a)   resoluciones o fallos en procedimientos administrativos que se aplican a una persona, mercancía o servicio en particular de otra Parte en un caso específico; o

b)   un fallo que resuelva respecto de un acto o práctica en particular.

Artículo 10.02 Centro de Información

1.   Cada Parte designará una dependencia u oficina como Centro de Información para facilitar la comunicación entre las Partes sobre cualquier asunto comprendido en este Tratado.

2.   Cuando una Parte lo solicite, el Centro de Información de otra Parte indicará la dependencia o funcionario responsable del asunto y prestará el apoyo que se requiera para facilitar la comunicación con la Parte solicitante.

Artículo 10.03 Publicación

1.   Cada Parte se asegurará que sus leyes, reglamentos, procedimientos y resoluciones administrativas de aplicación general que se refieran a cualquier asunto comprendido en este Tratado, se publiquen a la brevedad o se pongan a disposición para conocimiento de las Partes y de cualquier interesado.

2.   En la medida de lo posible, cada Parte:

   a)   hará pública por adelantado cualquier medida que se proponga adoptar; y

   b)   brindará a las personas y a otra Parte oportunidad razonable para formular observaciones sobre la(s) medida(s) propuesta(s).

Artículo 10.04 Suministro de información

1.   Cada Parte notificará a otra Parte, en la medida de lo posible, toda medida vigente o en proyecto que considere que pudiera afectar o afecte sustancialmente los intereses de esa otra Parte en los términos de este Tratado.

2.   Cada Parte, a solicitud de otra Parte, proporcionará información y dará respuesta pronta a sus preguntas relativas a cualquier medida vigente o en proyecto.

3.   La notificación o suministro de información a que se refiere este Artículo se realizará sin que ello prejuzgue si la medida es o no compatible con este Tratado.

Artículo 10.05 Garantías de audiencia, legalidad y debido proceso

1.   Las Partes reafirman las garantías de audiencia, de legalidad y del debido proceso consagrados en sus respectivas legislaciones en el sentido de los artículos 10.06 y 10.07;

2.   Cada Parte se asegurará que en sus procedimientos judiciales y administrativos relativos a la aplicación de cualquier medida de las mencionadas en el artículo 10.03 (1), que afecte la normativa de este Tratado, se observen las formalidades esenciales del procedimiento, y se fundamente y motive la causa legal del mismo.

Artículo 10.06 Procedimientos administrativos para la adopción de medidas de aplicación general

Con el fin de administrar en forma compatible, imparcial y razonable todas las medidas de aplicación general que afecten los aspectos que cubre este Tratado, cada Parte se asegurará de que, en sus procedimientos administrativos en que se apliquen las medidas mencionadas en el artículo 10.03(1) respecto a personas, mercancías o servicios en particular de otra Parte en casos específicos:

a)   siempre que sea posible, las personas de esa otra Parte que se vean directamente afectadas por un procedimiento, reciban conforme a las disposiciones internas, aviso razonable del inicio del mismo, incluidas una descripción de su naturaleza, la declaración de la autoridad a la que legalmente le corresponda iniciarlo y una descripción general de todas las cuestiones controvertidas;

b)   cuando el tiempo, la naturaleza del procedimiento y el interés público lo permitan, dichas personas reciban una oportunidad razonable para presentar hechos y argumentos en apoyo de sus pretensiones, previamente a cualquier acción administrativa definitiva; y

c)   sus procedimientos se ajusten a su legislación.

Artículo 10.07 Revisión e impugnación

1.   Cada Parte mantendrá tribunales o procedimientos judiciales o de naturaleza administrativa para efectos de la pronta revisión y, cuando se justifique, la corrección de las acciones administrativas definitivas relacionadas con los asuntos comprendidos en este Tratado. Estos tribunales serán imparciales y no estarán vinculados con la dependencia ni con la autoridad encargada de la aplicación administrativa de la ley, y no tendrán interés sustancial en el resultado del asunto.

2.   Cada Parte se asegurará que, ante dichos tribunales o en esos procedimientos, las partes tengan derecho a:

a)   una oportunidad razonable para apoyar o defender sus respectivas posturas; y

b)   una resolución fundada en las pruebas y argumentaciones presentadas por las mismas.

3.   Cada Parte se asegurará que, con apego a los medios de impugnación o revisión ulterior a que se pudiese acudir de conformidad con su legislación, dichas resoluciones sean implementadas por las dependencias o autoridades.

Artículo 10.08 Comunicaciones y notificaciones

1.   Para efectos de este Tratado, toda comunicación o notificación dirigida a una Parte o enviada por una Parte, deberá realizarse a través de su sección nacional del Secretariado, informando sucintamente de tal hecho a las secciones nacionales de las demás Partes.

2.   No obstante lo dispuesto en el párrafo 1, en el caso de una comunicación o notificación realizada conforme a la normativa aplicable al tema de solución de controversias de conformidad con este Tratado, una copia de ésta deberá enviarse a la Secretaría de Integración Económica Centroamericana (SIECA), para efecto de su archivo.

3.   Salvo disposición en contrario, se entenderá entregada una comunicación o notificación a una Parte a partir de su recepción en la sección nacional del Secretariado de esa Parte.

PARTE V - DISPOSICIONES FINALES

CAPÍTULO 11

DISPOSICIONES FINALES

Artículo 11.01 Evaluación del Tratado

Las Partes evaluarán periódicamente el desarrollo de este Tratado con objeto de buscar su perfeccionamiento y consolidar el proceso de integración en la región, promoviendo una activa participación de los sectores productivos.

Artículo 11.02 Modificaciones

1.   Sin perjuicio de lo dispuesto en los artículos 9.02 y 11.04 cualquier modificación a este Tratado requerirá el acuerdo de todas las partes.

2.   Las modificaciones acordadas entrarán en vigor una vez que se aprueben según los procedimientos jurídicos correspondientes de las Partes y constituirán parte integral de este Tratado.

Artículo 11.03 Reservas

Este Tratado no podrá ser objeto de reservas ni declaraciones interpretativas unilaterales.

Artículo 11.04 Vigencia

Este Tratado tendrá duración indefinida y entrará en vigor treinta (30) días después de la fecha en que se deposite el segundo instrumento de ratificación, para los primeros dos (2) depositantes, y para los demás, ocho (8) días después de la fecha de depósito de su respectivo instrumento.

Artículo 11.05 Denuncia

1.   El presente instrumento podrá ser denunciado por cualquiera de las Partes y la denuncia producirá efectos ciento ochenta (180) días después de su presentación a la SG-SICA, sin perjuicio de que las Partes puedan pactar un plazo distinto.

2.   El Tratado quedará en vigor entre las demás Partes, en tanto permanezcan adheridos a él, por lo menos dos de ellos.

Artículo 11.06 Depósito

La SG-SICA será depositaria del presente Tratado, del cual enviará copias certificadas a las Cancillerías de cada Estado Contratante, al Ministerio de Comercio Exterior de Costa Rica y a la.Secretaría de Integración Económica Centroamericana (SIECA). Asimismo, les notificará inmediatamente del depósito de cada uno de los instrumentos de ratificación. A la entrada en vigor de este Tratado, la SG-SICA procederá a enviar copia certificada del mismo a la Secretaria General de la Organización de las Naciones Unidas, para los fines del registro que señala el Artículo 102 de la Carta de dicha Organización.

Artículo 11.07 Anexos

Los Anexos de este Tratado constituyen parte integral del mismo.

Artículo 11.08 Intercambio de reservas

1.   Las Partes acordarán sus listas de reservas, del Anexo I, II, III contempladas en los Artículos 3.09 y 4.06 de los Capítulos 3 y 4, y se comprometen a intercambiarlas a más tardar en seis (6) meses a partir de la fecha de suscripción del Tratado.

2.   Con el propósito de avanzar en el cumplimiento del compromiso establecido en el párrafo 1, las Partes presentarán un listado preliminar de medidas disconformes existentes, a más tardar dentro de un plazo de cuatro (4) meses contado desde la fecha de suscripción de este Tratado.

3.   Las listas de reservas entrarán en vigencia, para cada Parte, ocho (8) días después de su respectivo depósito en la SG-SICA.

Artículo 11.09 Sustitución

El presente Tratado sustituye en todas sus partes al Tratado sobre Inversión y Comercio de Servicios entre las Repúblicas de El Salvador y Guatemala, suscrito en la Ciudad de Guatemala, República de Guatemala, el 13 de enero del año 2000.

*

PART TWO

BILATERAL INSTRUMENTS

AGREEMENT ON TRADE AND COMMERCIAL RELATIONS BETWEEN THE GOVERNMENT OF AUSTRALIA AND THE GOVERNMENT OF PAPUA NEW GUINEA [PATCRA II]*
[excerpts]

The Agreement on Trade and Commercial Relations between the Government of Australia and the Government of Papua New Guinea [PATCRA II] was signed at Canberra on 21 February 1991. It entered into force on 20 September 1991.

THE GOVERNMENT OF AUSTRALIA AND THE GOVERNMENT OF PAPUA NEW GUINEA,

RECOGNISING the importance of measures to strengthen their relationship in accordance with the Joint Declaration of Principles Guiding Relations between Papua New Guinea and Australia, including the principle that co-operation and exchange between the two countries shall be mutually beneficial and based on full participation by both countries, with due regard to the capacity, resources and development needs of both countries, and on mutual respect;

BEARING in mind the close trading and commercial relations existing between their two countries;

ACKNOWLEDGING their respective international rights and obligations;

RE-AFFIRMING their desire to maintain and strengthen trade, investment and private sector co-operation between the two countries;

HAVING resolved to establish between their two countries a Free Trade Area with a view to achieving sustained development of their economies through expansion of trade and investment in accordance with their respective objectives and priorities for economic development and social progress;

HAVE AGREED as follows:

Article 1

Definitions

In this Agreement, which may be referred to as PATCRA II, unless the contrary intention appears:

* Source: The Government of Australia and the Government of Papua New Guinea (1991). "Agreement on Trade and Commercial Relations between the Government of Australia and the Government of Papua New Guinea [PATCRA II]", *Australian Treaty Series 1991 No 37* Australian Government (Publishing Service: Canberra); also available on the Internet (http://www.austlii.edu.au/au/other/dfat/treaties/1991/37.html). [Note added by the editor.]

"free goods" means goods which when the subject of trade between the Member States are free of duties and other restrictive regulations of commerce pursuant to Article 3 of this Agreement;

"law" and "laws" includes "regulations";

"Member States" means Papua New Guinea and Australia or, as the context requires, the Government of Papua New Guinea and the Government of Australia;

"primary industry" means any industry producing, processing or marketing agricultural, livestock, fisheries or forestry products;

"the Area" means the Free Trade Area established under Article 3 of this Agreement.

Article 2
Objectives

The objectives of this Agreement are:

(a)   to further the development of the Area through the expansion and diversification of trade in goods and services between the Member States;

(b)   to further the development and use of the resources of the Area in accordance with the respective social and economic objectives of the Member States;

(c)   to further promote the development of the trade and industrial capacity of the Member States;

(d)   to further the development of the Area by the promotion of direct investment which is consistent with foreign investment policies and priorities of the recipient Member States;

(e)   to promote and facilitate commercial, industrial, administrative and technical co-operation between the Member States; and

(f)   to contribute to the harmonious development and expansion of world trade and to the progressive removal of barriers to it.

Article 3
Free trade

1.   A Free Trade Area is hereby established. The Area consists of Papua New Guinea and Australia.

2.   Subject to the provisions of this Agreement, trade between the Member States shall be free of duties and other restrictive regulations of commerce.

3.   This Article applies only to trade in goods which originate in a Member State.

Article 4
Rules of origin of goods

1.   Goods shall be treated as originating in a Member State if those goods are:

    (a)   the unmanufactured raw products of that Member State; or

    (b)   manufactured goods in relation to which:

        (i)   the process last performed in the manufacture was performed in that Member State, and

        (ii)   the expenditure

            (A)   on material that is of Member State origin,

            (B)   on labour, factory overheads and inner containers that are of Member State origin, or

            (C)   partly on such material and partly on such other items of factory cost,

is not less than one-half of the factory or works costs at the time of exportation.

2.   Notwithstanding the provisions of paragraph 1 of this Article, the Government of Australia shall also treat goods as originating in Papua New Guinea if:

    (a)   they comply with applicable provisions of the South Pacific Regional Trade and Economic Co-operation Agreement done at Tarawa on 14 July 1980, as amended, and

    (b)   the Member States agree, as signified by an exchange of letters, to treat particular goods or classes of goods as originating in a Member State, provided that, in the case of manufactured goods, the process last performed in the manufacture was performed in the territory of the exporting Member State.

Article 5
Excepted goods

1.   Notwithstanding the provisions of Article 3 of this Agreement:

    (a)   the goods specified in Schedule A to this Agreement, when imported into Australia from Papua New Guinea, shall be subject to the rate of import duty specified from time to time in the Australian Customs Tariff as being applicable to Papua New Guinea goods;

    (b)   the goods specified in Schedule B to this Agreement, when imported into Australia from Papua New Guinea, shall be subject to the rate of import duty and to the other regulations, if any, specified in Schedule B as being applicable to those goods;

(c)   the goods specified in Schedule C to this Agreement, when imported into Papua New Guinea from Australia, shall be subject to the rate of import duty specified from time to time in the Papua New Guinea Customs Tariff as being applicable to Australian goods; and

(d)   the goods specified in Schedule D to this Agreement, when imported into Papua New Guinea from Australia, shall be subject to the rate of import duty and to the other regulations, if any, specified in Schedule D as being applicable to those goods.

2.   (a)   A Member State shall not increase the rate of import duty on goods specified in Schedules A or C to this Agreement unless:

(i)   sixty days have passed since that Member State gave written notice to the other Member State of its intention to make such an increase, and

(ii)   if requested in writing it has entered into consultations with the affected State. Such consultations shall begin within thirty days of the receipt of such a request;

(b)   A Member State shall not increase the rate of import duty or apply more restrictive regulations of trade to the goods specified in Schedules B or D to this Agreement without the written consent of the relevant authorities of the other Member State. Such consent shall not normally be withheld provided the same notice is given and the same opportunity for consultations provided as is specified in paragraph 2(a) of this Article in relation to Schedules A or C;

(c)   The relevant authorities of the Member States may, by mutual consent, vary the requirements for notification and consultation provided for in paragraph 2(a) of this Article.

3.   The relevant authorities of Australia may at any time, following written notice to the relevant authorities of Papua New Guinea, remove goods from Schedules A or B to this Agreement or reduce the rates of import duty or make less restrictive the regulations of trade specified as being applicable to goods in those Schedules.

4.   The relevant authorities of Papua New Guinea may at any time, following written notice to the relevant authorities of Australia, remove goods from Schedules C or D to this Agreement or reduce the rates of import duty or make less restrictive the regulations of trade specified as being applicable to goods in those Schedules.

Article 6
Revenue duties

Nothing in this Agreement shall preclude the imposition by either Member State of sales taxes or other revenue duties which are levied equally on both imports and domestic products.

Article 7
Most favoured nation treatment

1.   Each Member State shall accord to the other Member State treatment no less favourable than that accorded to any third country in respect of all matters concerning:

(a)   customs duties and charges of any kind imposed on, or in connection with, the importation or exportation of any goods, or imposed on the international transfer of payments for imports or exports;

(b)   the method of levying such duties and charges;

(c)   the rules and formalities connected with the importation or exportation of goods;

(d)   all internal taxes or other internal charges of any kind imposed on, or in connection with, imported goods;

(e)   internal sale, offering for sale, purchase, distribution or use of imported goods within its territory;

(f)   restrictions or prohibitions on the importation or exportation of any goods;

(g)   the allocation of foreign exchange; and

(h)   the administration of foreign exchange restrictions affecting transactions involving the importation or exportation of any goods.

2.   The provision of paragraph 1 of this Article shall not apply to:

(a)   advantages accorded by either Member State to adjacent countries to facilitate frontier traffic;

(b)   tariff preferences or other advantages granted by either Member State consequent on the membership of that Member State in another free trade area or a customs union, or on an interim agreement leading to the formation of another free trade area or a customs union;

(c)   tariff preferences accorded by either Member State to a third country in view of that country's status as a developing country; or

(d)   such measures as either Member State may take pursuant to a multilateral international commodity agreement or arrangement.

Article 8
Other exceptions

Provided that such measures are not used as a means of arbitrary or unjustifiable discrimination, or as a disguised restriction on trade between the Member States, nothing in this Agreement shall prevent the adoption or enforcement by a Member State of measures:

(a)   necessary for the protection of its essential security interests;

(b)   necessary to protect public morals;

(c)   necessary for the prevention of disorder or crime;

(d)   imposed for the protection of its national treasures of artistic, historical, anthropological, palaeontological, archaeological or other cultural or scientific value;

(e)   necessary to reserve for approved purposes the use of Royal Arms or national, state, provincial and territorial arms, flags, crests and seals;

(f)   necessary to protect human, animal or plant life or health;

(g)   necessary to protect its indigenous flora and fauna;

(h)   undertaken in pursuance of its rights and obligations under a multilateral international commodity agreement or arrangement;

(i)   necessary to prevent or relieve shortages of foodstuffs or other essential goods;

(j)   related to the conservation of limited natural resources;

(k)   necessary to protect industrial property rights or copyright, or to prevent unfair, deceptive or misleading practices;

(l)   necessary to secure compliance with laws relating to customs enforcement, or to tax avoidance or evasion, or to the classification, grading or marketing of goods, or to the operation of recognised commodity marketing boards;

(m)   relating to products of prison labour;

(n)   relating to trade in gold or silver; or

(o)   necessary to safeguard its external financial position and balance of payments.

Article 9
Suspension of obligations: protection of threatened or developing industries

1.   If in the opinion of a Member State (in this Article called "the importing Member State") goods are, as a result of the operation of Article 3 of this Agreement, being imported into it from the other Member State in such quantities or under such conditions as to cause or threaten serious injury to an industry in the importing Member State producing like or directly competitive goods, or to retard materially the establishment of an industry in the importing Member State to produce like or directly competitive goods, the importing Member State may request the other Member State to consult with it on measures to reduce or prevent such injury or retardation.

2.   If a mutually acceptable solution is not reached within sixty days of the date of the request referred to in paragraph 1 of this Article, the importing Member State may, after giving

notice to the other Member State, suspend to such extent and for so long as necessary the application of the provisions of Article 3 of this Agreement to the goods concerned.

Article 10
Suspension of obligations: protection of Papua New Guinea primary industry

1.   In order to protect an existing primary industry or to foster the development of a new primary industry, the Government of Papua New Guinea may suspend its obligations under Article 3 of this Agreement in respect of the products of a like or directly competitive industry.

2.   Unless critical circumstances prevail in which delay would cause damage which would be difficult to repair, the Government of Papua New Guinea shall give sixty days notice to the Australian Government prior to taking action under paragraph 1 of this Article.

3.   As soon as practicable after the need arises to take action under paragraph 1 of this Article, the Papua New Guinea Government shall enter into consultations with the Australian Government with a view to finding a mutually satisfactory solution to the problem.

Article 11
Suspension of obligations: deflection of trade

1.   If the importation into a Member State (in this Article called "the importing Member State") of free goods from the other Member State:

(a)   causes or threatens serious injury to an industry in the importing Member State producing like or directly competitive goods because:

(i)   the duties or taxes levied by the other Member State on raw materials or intermediate products imported from outside the Area and used in the production of those goods are significantly lower than the duties or taxes levied by the importing Member State on imports of similar raw materials or intermediate products imported from outside the Area, or

(ii)   the prices of raw materials or intermediate products used in the production of those goods are unduly low by reason of dumping into the Area or subsidisation, or

(iii)   drawback, exemption or remission of import duties is allowed by the other Member State on raw materials or intermediate products imported from outside the Area and used in the production of goods; and

(b)   the other Member State is deriving advantage from the circumstances, the importing Member State, if it considers that action is necessary to offset that advantage, may request consultations with the other Member State on the situation which has developed. Such consultations shall be as full as circumstances permit, and the importing Member State shall consider any measures taken or proposed by the other Member State to offset the advantage.

2.   If a mutually acceptable solution is not reached within sixty days of the date of the request referred to in paragraph 1 of this Article, the importing Member State may, after giving

notice to the other Member State, suspend to such extent and for so long as necessary the application of the provisions of Article 3 of this Agreement to the goods concerned.

Article 12
Suspension of obligations: exceptional circumstances

Member States may agree to the suspension of any obligation under this Agreement on the ground that there exist exceptional or emergency circumstances creating severe difficulties for one or both Member States.

Article 13
Suspension of obligations: dumped or subsidised imports

1.   If in the opinion of a Member State goods being imported into it from the other Member State are being dumped or are being subsidised by the other Member State so as to cause or threaten material injury to an industry producing like or directly competitive goods or to materially retard the establishment of an industry to produce like or directly competitive goods, it may request the other Member State to consult with it on measures to reduce or prevent such injury or retardation.

2.   If a mutually acceptable solution is not reached within sixty days of the date of the request referred to in paragraph 1 of this Article, the importing Member State may, after giving notice to the other Member State, suspend the application of Article 3 of this Agreement to the extent necessary to enable it to levy dumping or countervailing duties on the goods concerned.

Article 14
Investment

1.   The Member States, bearing in mind that Australian investment in Papua New Guinea and the conditions attaching to that investment will have a bearing on the long term trade and commercial relationship between the Member States, shall consult, at the request of either Member State, on the most appropriate ways in which future Australian direct investment, particularly by way of joint venture, can contribute to the social and economic development of Papua New Guinea in accordance with its foreign investment policies and priorities.

2.   The Papua New Guinea Government will draw to the attention of the Australian Government those specific fields of development in which it would particularly welcome Australian investment including through the provision of private venture capital. The Australian Government will endeavour to interest and encourage Australian enterprises, including those in the financial sector, to participate in those specific fields except where such investment would not be in the interests of both countries.

3.   In relation to a proposed investment in Papua New Guinea which might result in the export of free goods to Australia, the Member States recognise the need for prior consultations on any matter which might affect the export to Australia of those goods. It shall be a matter for the Papua New Guinea Government to determine whether or not such consultation should take place.

4.   Papua New Guinea will accord to Australian investment, in accordance with Papua New Guinea laws and related policies, treatment no less favourable than that accorded to the investment of any third country.

5.   The Member States may agree to more comprehensive provisions relating to the reciprocal promotion and protection of investments by nationals and residents of one Member State in the territory of the other Member State.

Article 15
Industry co-operation

1.   In order to further the objectives of this Agreement, the Member States shall, as appropriate, use their best endeavours to encourage co-operation between, and co-ordination of activities of, their respective firms and industries. To this end, the Member States shall exchange information and consult together on developments in industry within the Area, and may agree on, and implement, if consistent with their international obligations, special measures beneficial to the trade and development of a Member State.

2.   The Australian Government shall assist the Government of Papua New Guinea in the promotion and development of the small business sector in Papua New Guinea. Such assistance may include the provision of initial professional and technical staff and various forms of training.

Article 16
Scientific and technical co-operation

In order to further the objectives of this Agreement, the Member States shall encourage and facilitate the interchange of applied scientific and technical knowledge between their respective countries, including the supply of information, where practicable, on new issues and from international meetings at which Papua New Guinea is not represented.

Article 17
Administrative co-operation

To promote the effective and harmonious application of the provisions of this Agreement, the Member States shall take steps to facilitate administrative co-operation and to reduce, as far as practicable, formalities affecting trade within the Area.

Article 18
Promotion of trade

1.   For the purpose of promoting trade (including investment and investment in tourism) between the Member States, each Member State shall, within its competence and subject to its laws, encourage and facilitate:

(a)   the interchange of commercial and technical representatives, groups and delegations; and

(b)   the holding of, and participation in, trade fairs, trade exhibitions and other promotional activities in the fields of trade and technology in its territory by enterprises and organisations from the other Member State.

2.   In particular, each Member State shall exempt from import duties and other taxes, and from any other prohibitions and restrictions (other than those provided for under Article 8 of this Agreement) articles for display or for use in connection with fairs, exhibitions or similar events, as well as samples of goods for advertising purposes imported on a temporary basis from the other Member State. Articles and samples so exempted shall not be disposed of otherwise than by re-exportation, except with the prior approval of the competent authorities of the importing Member State and on payment of any applicable import duties and taxes.

3.   The importance of the role of the Member States' respective trade representatives in the promotion of trade and investment is recognised. The services of Australia's overseas trade representatives may be made available for the promotion of Papua New Guinea's exports. Those representatives shall not charge the Papua New Guinea Government for these services at a rate higher than the rate at which they charge the Australian Government for similar services.

4.   In recognition of the role of business visitors in the promotion of trade investment, each Member State shall accord business visitors who are nationals of the other Member State, fair and equitable treatment with respect to their entry into, stay and travel within and departure from its territory, provided that such treatment shall be in accordance with the Member State's laws and shall not be discriminatory between nationals of the other Member State and nationals of any third country.

Article 19
Commodity production and trade

1.   The Member States, recognising the importance of commodity production and trade to their economies and particularly to the development prospects of Papua New Guinea, shall consult together on commodity trade. As appropriate and consistent with its international obligations, the Australian Government shall assist the Government of Papua New Guinea in primary industry development, export expansion and diversification.

2.   To advance the objectives of this Agreement, the Member States shall:

(a)   encourage and, where practicable, facilitate the negotiation of commercial contracts between appropriate organisations or enterprises, of their two countries; and

(b)   declare their support in principle for the conclusion of long-term commercial contracts relating to the supply and purchase of goods, and encourage the relevant organisations or enterprises of their two countries to explore the scope for such commercial contracts and, where appropriate, to conclude such contracts.

3.   The organisations or enterprises referred to in this article may be either Government or private bodies.

Article 20
Scarce commodities

If a Member State has difficulty in obtaining supplies of essential commodities from the other Member State or from third countries, the other Member State shall, on request, enter into consultations on the matter.

Article 21
Payments

All commercial payments between the Member States shall be made through the banks of the two countries authorised to buy and sell foreign currency, and in any mutually acceptable freely convertible currency, in accordance with the foreign exchange regulations in force in the two countries and with general customary practice.

Article 22
Consultation and review

1.   There shall be periodic consultations between the Member States for the purpose of reviewing the operation of this Agreement. Such consultations shall be held annually or at the request of either Member State. In such consultations a Member State may raise any matters related to the implementation of this Agreement or bearing on trade (including investment and investment in tourism) or commercial relations between the Member States.

2.   Should either Member State consider that an obligation under this Agreement has not been fulfilled, or that any benefit conferred upon it by this Agreement is being or might be frustrated, or that any case of special difficulty has arisen, or that a change in circumstances necessitates or might necessitate a variation in the terms of this Agreement, the other Member State shall, on request, enter into consultations as soon as practicable with a view to reaching a mutually satisfactory solution.

3.   This Agreement may be amended by the Member States at any time in accordance with their respective constitutional requirements. The Schedules to this Agreement may be varied at any time by mutual consent of the relevant authorities of each Member State except as otherwise provided in Article 5.

Article 23
Association with the Agreement

1.   The Member States may agree to the association of any other State with this Agreement.

2.   The terms of such association shall be negotiated between the Member States and the other State.

Article 24
Entry into force and duration

1.   This Agreement shall come into force on the date on which the Member States exchange notes notifying each other that their respective constitutional and other requirements necessary to give effect to the Agreement have been complied with.

2.   A Member State may terminate this Agreement by giving notice to that effect to the other Member State. If that other Member State so requests, consultations shall take place between the Member States as soon as practicable. The notice of termination shall take effect on the one hundred and eightieth day after the day on which it was given unless earlier withdrawn.

IN WITNESS WHEREOF the undersigned, duly authorised by their respective Governments, have signed this Agreement.

DONE in two originals at Canberra this twenty-first day of February, One thousand nine hundred and ninety-one.

AGREED MINUTES

1.   The revision of PATCRA has been undertaken in the context of the Joint Declaration of Principles guiding relations between Papua New Guinea and Australia, reflecting their sovereign equality; the interdependence of all elements of the bilateral relationship and its further development on the basis of mutual benefit; and taking appropriate account of levels of economic and social development, the following understandings regarding the interpretation and operation of PATCRA II were reached.

2.   Nothing in Article 3 precludes import and export duties currently imposed by the Papua New Guinea Government solely for revenue purposes. Increases in the rates of import duties specified in Schedules C and D resulting from revenue changes announced in the Papua New Guinea budget are exempt from the provisions of Article 5(2). The Papua New Guinea Government shall, however, give written notice to the Australian Government of any increase in the rates of import duty announced in the Papua New Guinea budget within thirty days from the date upon which the increased rates are announced. The Australian Government may request consultations on such increases under Article 22.

3.   In respect of Article 4 Australia noted Papua New Guinea's objectives of encouraging investment in specific industry sectors having a significant export orientation. Australia agreed to respond promptly to any Papua New Guinea Government requests, based on this criterion, for derogations from the generally applicable rules of origin criteria.

4.   With regard to the provisions of Article 14, the Australian Government noted the concern of the Government of Papua New Guinea to explore measures to promote the trade and industrial capacity of Papua New Guinea in order to enable it to export to Australia encouraged by the free trade provisions of the Agreement. The Australian Government will endeavour to interest and encourage Australian enterprises, including in the financial sector, to participate inspecific fields of development identified by Papua New Guinea. The objectives of this article could also be supported by the expansion of the AIDAB Joint Venture Scheme to include Papua New Guinea. The Australians also agreed to conduct, as soon as possible after receiving a formal request from the Papua New Guinea Government, a study on ways to promote joint ventures between Australia and Papua New Guinea.

5.   With respect to Article 15 the Australian Government noted the concerns of the Papua New Guinea Government over the terms and coverage of investment insurance, but both sides agreed that the provision of specific incentives was not possible. The incorporation of the Australian Export Finance and Insurance Corporation into the Australian Trade Commission was also noted.

6.   In support of the objectives of Article 15 in relation to small business development it was agreed that the Australian Government assistance would be largely funded by AIDAB and might include activities such as

- fellowship and secondments for Papua New Guinean technical and managerial counterpart staff

- preparation of appropriate information packages for small business developments

- preparation of training modules in basic accounting and other business skills

- provision of advice and training to small-scale entrepreneurs and to those training entrepreneurs.

7.   In support of the objectives of Article 18 the Australian Government agreed that a programme of specific activities will be developed each year by the Market Advisory Service of the Australian Department of Foreign Affairs and Trade in conjunction with the Papua New Guinea Department of Trade and Industry; these programmes may include the following measures:

- training activities related to the development and promotion of domestic and international trade

- activities aimed at improving the quality of Papua New Guinean products including quality control, market research, product adaptation, packaging and presentation

- direct assistance to the staging of survey and selling missions, trade displays and fairs in Australia

- development of effective marketing and trade promotional knowledge and skills based on research, market studies and advertising

- promotion of the opportunities in Papua New Guinea for investment, including investment in tourism, joint ventures and technology transfer.

8.   In respect of Article 19 the Australian Government indicated its willingness to assist, wherever possible, the efforts of the Government of Papua New Guinea to encouraging the diversification of its agricultural export sector, including the improvement of Papua New Guinea's competitiveness. They also agreed to consult together on commodity programs, including:

(a)   a long term program of Developing Countries Technical Assistance Program (DCTAP) assistance in promotion, marketing and training; and

(b)   inclusion in the project aid program of projects designed to facilitate the further processing of Papua New Guinea agricultural and other commodities.

In addition other mechanisms could include:

- training of Papua New Guinean commodity board managers on an interchange basis

- possible use of the AIDAB Joint Venture Scheme. Discussions will be held to clarify how the scheme could be applied in the specific case of Papua New Guinea

- possible use of the AIDAB Development Import Finance Facility grants in conjunction with export finance (mixed credits) through the Australian Trade Commission for capital goods and related services

- the use of the services of the South Pacific Trade Commissioner based in Sydney; and

- technical assistance in respect of small business.

9.   Both sides agree that the Schedules of Excepted Goods which are subject to the provisions of Article 5, should be reviewed and updated at the earliest opportunity.

21 February 1991 Canberra

*

EURO-MEDITERRANEAN AGREEMENT ESTABLISHING AN ASSOCIATION BETWEEN THE EUROPEAN COMMUNITIES AND THEIR MEMBER STATES, OF THE ONE PART, AND THE STATE OF ISRAEL, OF THE OTHER PART[*]
[excerpts]

The Euro-Mediterranean Agreement Establishing an Association between the European Communities and Their Member States, of the One Part, and the State of Israel, of the Other Part was signed on 20 November 1995. It entered into force on 1 June 2000. The member States of the European Communities are: Austria, Belgium, Denmark, Finland, France, Germany, Greece, Ireland, Italy, Luxembourg, the Netherlands, Portugal, Spain, Sweden and the United Kingdom.

TITLE III

RIGHT OF ESTABLISHMENT AND SUPPLY OF SERVICES

Article 29

1.   The Parties agree to widen the scope of the Agreement to cover the right of establishment of firms of one Party in the territory of another Party and the liberalisation of the provision of services by one Party's firms to consumers of services in the other.

2.   The Association Council shall make the necessary recommendations for the implementation of the objective described in paragraph 1.

In making such recommendations, the Association Council shall take account of past experience of implementation of the reciprocal most-favoured-nation treatment and of the obligations of each Party under the General Agreement on Trade in Services, hereinafter referred to as the "GATS", particularly those in Article V of the latter.

3.   The Association Council shall make a first assessment of the achievement of this objective no later than three years after the Agreement enters into force.

Article 30

1.   At the outset, each of the Parties reaffirms its obligations under the GATS, particularly the obligation to grant reciprocal most-favoured-nation treatment in the services sectors covered by that obligation.

2.   In accordance with the GATS, this treatment shall not apply to:

---

[*] *Source*: European Communities (2000). "Euro-Mediterranean Agreement Establishing an Association between the European Communities and Their Member States, of the One Part, and the State of Israel, of the Other Part", *Official Journal of the European Communities*, L 147, 21 June 2000, pp. 3 - 171; available also on the Internet (http://europa.eu.int). [Note added by the editor.]

(a)   advantages accorded by either Party under the terms of an agreement of the type defined in Article V of the GATS nor to measures taken on the basis of such an agreement;

(b)   other advantages granted in accordance with the list of most-favoured-nation exemptions annexed by either Party to the GATS.

TITLE IV
CAPITAL MOVEMENTS, PAYMENTS, PUBLIC PROCUREMENT, COMPETITION AND INTELLECTUAL PROPERTY

CHAPTER 1
CAPITAL MOVEMENTS AND PAYMENTS

Article 31

Within the framework of the provisions of this Agreement, and subject to the provisions of Articles 33 and 34, there shall be no restrictions between the Community of the one part, and Israel of the other part, on the movement of capital and no discrimination based on the nationality or on the place of residence of their nationals or on the place where such capital is invested.

Article 32

Current payments connected with the movement of goods, persons, services or capital within the framework of this Agreement shall be free of all restrictions.

Article 33

Subject to other provisions in this Agreement and other international obligations of the Community and Israel, the provisions of Articles 31 and 32 shall be without prejudice to the application of any restriction which exists between them on the date of entry into force of this Agreement, in respect of the movement of capital between them involving direct investment, including in real estate, establishment, the provision of financial services or the admission of securities to capital markets.

However, the transfer abroad of investments made in Israel by Community residents or in the Community by Israeli residents and of any profit stemming therefrom shall not be affected.

Article 34

Where, in exceptional circumstances, movements of capital between the Community and Israel cause, or threaten to cause, serious difficulties for the operation of exchange rate policy or monetary policy in the Community or Israel, the Community or Israel respectively may, in conformity within the conditions laid down within the framework of the GATS and with Articles VIII and XIV of the Articles of Agreement of the International Monetary Fund, take safeguard measures with regard to movements of capital between the Community and Israel for a period not exceeding six months if such measures are strictly necessary.

CHAPTER 2
PUBLIC PROCUREMENT

Article 35

The Parties shall take measures with a view to a mutual opening of their respective government procurement markets and the procurement markets of undertakings operating in the utilities sectors for purchase of goods, works and services beyond the scope of what has been mutually and reciprocally covered under the Government Procurement Agreement concluded in the framework of the WTO.

CHAPTER 3
COMPETITION

Article 36

1.   The following are incompatible with the proper functioning of the Agreement, in so far as they may affect trade between the Community and Israel:

   (i)   all agreements between undertakings, decisions by associations of undertakings and concerted practices between undertakings which have as their object or effect the prevention, restriction or distortion of competition;

   (ii)   abuse by one or more undertakings of a dominant position in the territories of the Community or Israel as a whole or in a substantial part thereof;

   (iii)   any public aid which distorts or threatens to distort competition by favouring certain undertakings or the production of certain goods.

2.   The Association Council shall, within three years of the entry into force of the Agreement, adopt by decision the necessary rules for the implementation of paragraph 1.

Until these rules are adopted, the provisions of the Agreement on interpretation and application of Articles VI, XVI and XXIII of the GATT shall be applied as the rules for the implementation of paragraph 1(iii).

3.   Each Party shall ensure transparency in the area of public aid, inter alia, by reporting annually to the other Party on the total amount and the distribution of the aid given and by providing, upon request, information on aid schemes. Upon request by one Party, the other Party shall provide information on particular individual cases of public aid.

4.   With regard to agricultural products referred to in Title II, Chapter 3, paragraph 1(iii) does not apply.

5.   If the Community or Israel considers that a particular practice is incompatible with the terms of paragraph 1 and:

      - is not adequately dealt with under the implementing rules referred to in paragraph 2, or

- in the absence of such rules, and if such practice causes or threatens to cause serious prejudice to the interest of the other Party or material injury to its domestic industry, including its services industry, it may take appropriate measures after consultation within the Association Committee or after 30 working days following referral for such consultation.

With reference to practices incompatible with paragraph 1(iii), such appropriate measures, when the GATT is applicable to them, may only be adopted in accordance with the procedures and under the conditions laid down by the GATT or by any other relevant instrument negotiated under its auspices and applicable to the Parties.

6. Notwithstanding any provisions to the contrary adopted in accordance with paragraph 2, the Parties shall exchange information taking into account the limitations imposed by the requirements of professional and business secrecy.

Article 37

1. The Member States and Israel shall progressively adjust any State monopolies of a commercial character, so as to ensure that, by the end of the fifth year following the entry into force of this Agreement, no discrimination regarding the conditions under which goods are procured and marketed exists between nationals of the Member States and Israel.

2. The Association Committee shall be informed about the measures adopted to implement this objective.

Article 38

With regard to public undertakings and undertakings to which special or exclusive rights have been granted, the Association Council shall ensure that as from the fifth year following the date of entry into force of this Agreement there is neither enacted nor maintained any measure distorting trade between the Community and Israel to an extent contrary to the Parties' interests. This provision should not obstruct the performance in law or in fact of the particular tasks assigned to those undertakings.

CHAPTER 4
INTELLECTUAL, INDUSTRIAL AND COMMERCIAL PROPERTY

Article 39

1. Pursuant to the provisions of this Article and of Annex VII, the Parties shall grant and ensure adequate and effective protection of intellectual, industrial and commercial property rights in accordance with the highest international standards, including effective means of enforcing such rights.

2. The implementation of this Article and of Annex VII shall be regularly reviewed by the Parties. If problems in the area of intellectual, industrial and commercial property affecting trading conditions were to occur, urgent consultation within the Association Committee shall be undertaken, at the request of either Party, with a view to reaching mutually satisfactory solutions.

ANNEX VII

INTELLECTUAL, INDUSTRIAL AND COMMERCIAL PROPERTY RIGHTS REFERRED TO IN ARTICLE 39

1.   By the end of the third year after the entry into force of the Agreement, Israel shall accede to the following multilateral conventions on intellectual, industrial and commercial property rights to which Member States are parties or which are de facto applied by Member States:

- Berne Convention for the Protection of Literary and Artistic Works (Paris Act, 1971),

- Madrid Agreement concerning the International Registration of Marks (Stockholm Act, 1967 and amended in 1979),

- Protocol relating to the Madrid Agreement concerning the International Registration of Marks (Madrid, 1989),

- Budapest Treaty on the International Recognition of the Deposit of Microorganisms for the Purposes of Patent Procedure (1977, modified in 1980),

- Patent Cooperation Treaty (Washington, 1970, amended in 1979 and modified in 1984).

The Association Council may decide that this paragraph shall apply to other multilateral conventions in this field.

2.   Israel shall ratify, by the end of the second year after the entry into force of the Agreement, the International Convention for the Protection of Performers, Producers of Phonograms and Broadcasting Organisations (Rome, 1961).

3.   The Parties confirm the importance they attach to the obligations arising from the following multilateral conventions:

- Paris Convention for the Protection of Industrial Property (Stockholm Act, 1967, and amended in 1979),

- Nice Agreement concerning the International Classification of Goods and Services for the purposes of the Registration of Marks (Geneva, 1977, and amended in 1979),

- International Convention for the Protection of New Varieties of Plants (UPOV) (Geneva Act, 1991).

*

EURO-MEDITERRANEAN AGREEMENT ESTABLISHING AN ASSOCIATION BETWEEN THE EUROPEAN COMMUNITIES AND THEIR MEMBER STATES, OF THE ONE PART, AND THE KINGDOM OF MOROCCO, OF THE OTHER PART[*]
[excerpts]

The Euro-Mediterranean Agreement Establishing an Association between the European Communities and Their Member States, of the One Part, and the Kingdom of Morocco, of the Other Part was signed on 26 February 1996. The member States of the European Communities are: Austria, Belgium, Denmark, Finland, France, Germany, Greece, Ireland, Italy, Luxembourg, the Netherlands, Portugal, Spain, Sweden and the United Kingdom.

Article 1

1.   An association is hereby established between the Community and its Member States, of the one part, and Morocco, of the other part.

2.   The aims of this Agreement are to:

- provide an appropriate framework for political dialogue between the Parties, allowing the development of close relations in all areas they consider relevant to such dialogue,

- establish the conditions for the gradual liberalisation of trade in goods, services and capital,

- promote trade and the expansion of harmonious economic and social relations between the Parties, notably through dialogue and cooperation, so as to foster the development and prosperity of Morocco and its people,

- encourage integration of the Maghreb countries by promoting trade and cooperation between Morocco and other countries of the region, - promote economic, social, cultural and financial cooperation.

---

[*] *Source*: European Communities (2000). "Euro-Mediterranean Agreement Establishing an Association between the European Communities and Their Member States, of the One Part, and the Kingdom of Morocco, of the Other Part", *Official Journal of the European Communities*, L 070, 18 March 2000, pp. 2 - 204; available also on the Internet (http://www.europa.eu.int). [Note added by the editor.]

TITLE III
RIGHT OF ESTABLISHMENT AND SERVICES

Article 31

1.   The Parties agree to widen the scope of this Agreement to cover the right of establishment of one Party's firms on the territory of the other and liberalisation of the provision of services by one Party's firms to consumers of services in the other.

2.   The Association Council will make recommendations for achieving the objective described in paragraph 1.

In making such recommendations, the Association Council will take account of past experience of implementation of reciprocal most-favoured-nation treatment and of the respective obligations of each Party under the General Agreement on Trade in Services annexed to the Agreement establishing the WTO, hereinafter referred to as the "GATS", particularly those in Article V of the latter.

3.   The Association Council will make a first assessment of the achievement of this objective no later than five years after this Agreement enters into force.

4.   Without prejudice to the provisions of paragraph 3, the Association Council shall, once this Agreement is in force, examine the international maritime transport sector with a view to making appropriate recommendations for liberalisation measures. The Association Council shall take account of the results of GATS negotiations on this matter subsequent to the end of the Uruguay Round.

Article 32

1.   At the outset, each of the Parties shall reaffirm its obligations under the GATS, particularly the obligation to grant reciprocal most-favoured-nation treatment in the service sectors covered by that obligation.

2.   In accordance with the GATS, such treatment shall not apply to:

(a)   advantages granted by either Party under the terms of an agreement of the type defined in Article V of the GATS or to measures taken on the basis of such an agreement;

(b)   other advantages granted in accordance with the list of exemptions from most-favoured-nation treatment annexed by either Party to the GATS.

TITLE IV
PAYMENTS, CAPITAL, COMPETITION AND OTHER ECONOMIC PROVISIONS

CHAPTER I
CURRENT PAYMENTS AND MOVEMENT OF CAPITAL

Article 33

Subject to the provisions of Article 35, the Parties undertake to allow all current payments for current transactions to be made in a freely convertible currency.

Article 34

1. With regard to transactions on the capital account of balance of payments, the Community and Morocco shall ensure, from the entry into force of this Agreement, that capital relating to direct investments in Morocco in companies formed in accordance with current laws can move freely and that the yield from such investments and any profit stemming therefrom can be liquidated and repatriated. 2. The Parties shall consult each other with a view to facilitating, and fully liberalising when the time is right, the movement of capital between the Community and Morocco.

Article 35

Where one or more Member States of the Community, or Morocco, is in serious balance of payments difficulties, or under threat thereof, the Community or Morocco, as the case may be, may, in accordance with the conditions established under the GATT and Articles VIII and XIV of the Articles of Agreement of the International Monetary Fund, adopt restrictions on current transactions which shall be of limited duration and may not go beyond what is strictly necessary to remedy the balance of payments situation. The Community or Morocco, as the case may be, shall inform the other Party forthwith and shall submit to it as soon as possible a timetable for the elimination of the measures concerned.

CHAPTER II
COMPETITION AND OTHER ECONOMIC PROVISIONS

Article 36

1. The following are incompatible with the proper functioning of this Agreement, in so far as they may affect trade between the Community and
Morocco:

    (a)   all agreements between undertakings, decisions by associations of undertakings and concerted practices between undertakings which have as their object or effect the prevention, restriction or distortion of competition;

    (b)   abuse by one or more undertakings of a dominant position in the territories of the Community or of Morocco as a whole or in a substantial part thereof;

(c)   any official aid which distorts or threatens to distort competition by favouring certain undertakings or the production of certain goods, with the exception of cases in which a derogation is allowed under the Treaty establishing the European Coal and Steel Community.

2.   Any practices contrary to this Article shall be assessed on the basis of criteria arising from the application of the rules of Articles 85, 86 and 92 of the Treaty establishing the European Community(1) and, in the case of products falling within the scope of the European Coal and Steel Community, the rules of Articles 65 and 66 of the Treaty establishing that Community, and the rules relating to State aid, including secondary legislation.

3.   The Association Council shall, within five years of the entry into force of this Agreement, adopt the necessary rules for the implementation of paragraphs 1 and 2.

Until these rules are adopted, the provisions of the Agreement on interpretation and application of Articles VI, XVI and XXIII of the General Agreement on Tariffs and Trade shall be applied as the rules for the implementation of paragraph 1(c) and related parts of paragraph 2.

4.   (a)   For the purposes of applying the provisions of paragraph 1(c), the Parties recognise that during the first five years after the entry into force of this Agreement, any State aid granted by Morocco shall be assessed taking into account the fact that Morocco shall be regarded as an area identical to those areas of the Community described in Article 92(3)(a) of the Treaty establishing the European Community.

During the same period of time, Morocco may exceptionally, as regards ECSC steel products, grant State aid for restructuring purposes provided that:

- it leads to the viability of the recipient firms under normal market conditions at the end of the restructuring period,

- the amount and intensity of such aid are strictly limited to what is absolutely necessary in order to restore such viability and are progressively reduced,

- the restructuring programme is linked to a comprehensive plan for rationalising capacity in Morocco.

The Association Council shall, taking into account the economic situation of Morocco, decide whether the period should be extended every five years.

b)   Each Party shall ensure transparency in the area of official aid, inter alia, by reporting annually to the other Party on the total amount and the distribution of the aid given and by providing, upon request, information on aid schemes. Upon request by one Party, the other Party shall provide information on particular individual cases of official aid.

5.   With regard to products referred to in Chapter II of Title II:

- the provisions of paragraph 1(c) do not apply,

- any practices contrary to paragraph 1(a) shall be assessed according to the criteria established by the Community on the basis of Articles 42 and 43 of the Treaty establishing the European Community, and in particular those established in Council Regulation (EEC) No 26/62.

6.   If the Community or Morocco considers that a particular practice is incompatible with the terms of paragraph 1, and:

- is not adequately dealt with under the implementing rules referred to in paragraph 3, or

- in the absence of such rules, and if such practice causes or threatens to cause serious prejudice to the interest of the other Party or material injury to its domestic industry, including its services industry, it may take appropriate measures after consultation within the Association Committee or after 30 working days following referral to that Committee.

In the case of practices incompatible with paragraph 1(c) of this Article, such appropriate measures may, where the GATT applies thereto, only be adopted in accordance with the procedures and under the conditions laid down by the General Agreement on Tariffs and Trade and any other relevant instrument negotiated under its auspices which is applicable between the Parties.

7.   Notwithstanding any provisions to the contrary adopted in accordance with paragraph 3, the Parties shall exchange information taking into account the limitations imposed by the requirements of professional and business secrecy.

Article 37

The Member States and Morocco shall progressively adjust, without affecting commitments made under the GATT, any State monopolies of a commercial character so as to ensure that, by the end of the fifth year following the entry into force of this Agreement, no discrimination regarding the conditions under which goods are procured and marketed exists between nationals of the Member States and of Morocco. The Association Committee will be informed about the measures adopted to implement this objective.

Article 38

With regard to public enterprises and enterprises which have been granted special or exclusive rights, the Association Council shall ensure, from the fifth year following the entry into force of this Agreement, that no measure which disturbs trade between the Community and Morocco in a manner which runs counter to the interests of the Parties is adopted or maintained. This provision shall not impede the performance in fact or in law of the specific functions assigned to those enterprises.

Article 39

1.   The Parties shall provide suitable and effective protection of intellectual, industrial and commercial property rights, in line with the highest international standards. This shall encompass effective means of enforcing such rights.

2.   Implementation of this Article and of Annex 7 shall be regularly assessed by the Parties. If difficulties which affect trade arise in connection with intellectual, industrial and commercial property rights, either Party may request urgent consultations to find mutually satisfactory solutions.

Article 40

1.   The Parties shall take appropriate steps to promote the use by Morocco of Community technical rules and European standards for industrial and agri-food products and certification procedures.

2.   Using the principles set out in paragraph 1 as a basis, the Parties shall, when the circumstances are right, conclude agreements for the mutual recognition of certifications.

Article 41

1.   The Parties shall set as their objective a reciprocal and gradual liberalisation of public procurement contracts.

2.   The Association Council shall take the steps necessary to implement paragraph 1.

Article 49
Industrial cooperation

The aim of cooperation shall be to:

(a)   encourage cooperation between the Parties' economic operators, including cooperation in the context of access for Morocco to Community business networks and decentralised cooperation networks;

(b)   back the effort to modernise and restructure Morocco's public and private sector industry (including the agri-food industry);

(c)   foster an environment which favours private initiative, with the aim of stimulating and diversifying output for the domestic and export markets;

(d)   make the most of Morocco's human resources and industrial potential through better use of policy in the fields of innovation and research and technological development;

(e)   facilitate access to credit to finance investment.

Article 50
Promotion and protection of investment

The aim of cooperation shall be to create a favourable climate for flows of investment, and to use the following in particular:

(a)   the establishment of harmonised and simplified procedures, co-investment machinery (especially to link small and medium-sized enterprises) and methods of identifying and providing information on investment opportunities;

(b)   the establishment, where appropriate, of a legal framework to promote investment, chiefly through the conclusion by Morocco and the Member States of investment protection agreements and agreements preventing double taxation.

ANNEX 7

relating to intellectual, industrial and commercial property

1.   By the end of the fourth year after the entry into force of the Agreement, Morocco shall accede to the following multilateral conventions on the protection of intellectual, industrial and commercial property:

- International Convention for the Protection of Performers, Producers of Phonograms and Broadcasting Organisations (Rome, 1961),

- Budapest Treaty on the International Recognition of the Deposit of Micro-Oganisms for the Purposes of Patent Procedure (1977, amended in 1980),

- Patent Cooperation Treaty (1970, amended in 1979 and modified in 1984),

- International Convention for the Protection of the New Varieties of Plants (Act of Geneva, 1991).

2.   The Association Council may decide that paragraph 1 of this Annex applies to other multilateral conventions in this field.

3.   The Contracting Parties express their attachment to observing the obligations flowing from the following multilateral conventions:

- Paris Convention for the Protection of Industrial Property in the 1967 Act of Stockholm (Paris Union),

- Madrid Agreement concerning the International Registration of Marks in the 1969 Act of Stockholm (Madrid Union),

- Berne Convention for the Protection of Literary and Artistic Works in the Act of Paris of 24 July 1971,

- Protocol relating to the Madrid Agreement concerning the International Registration of Marks (1989),

- Nice Agreement concerning the International Classification of Goods and Services for the purposes of the Registration of Marks (Geneva, 1977).

*

EUROPE AGREEMENT ESTABLISHING AN ASSOCIATION BETWEEN THE EUROPEAN COMMUNITIES AND THEIR MEMBER STATES, ACTING WITHIN THE FRAMEWORK OF THE EUROPEAN UNION, OF THE ONE PART, AND THE REPUBLIC OF SLOVENIA, OF THE OTHER PART*
[excerpts]

The Europe Agreement Establishing an Association between the European Communities and Their Member States, Acting Within the Framework of the European Union, of the One Part, and the Republic of Slovenia, of the Other Part was signed on 10 June 1996. It entered into force on 1 February 1999. The member States of the European Communities are: Austria, Belgium, Denmark, Finland, France, Germany, Greece, Ireland, Italy, Luxembourg, the Netherlands, Portugal, Spain, Sweden and the United Kingdom.

TITLE IV
MOVEMENT OF WORKERS, ESTABLISHMENT, SUPPLY OF SERVICES

CHAPTER I
MOVEMENT OF WORKERS

Article 38

1.   Subject to the conditions and modalities applicable in each Member State:

- treatment accorded to workers of Slovenian nationality, legally employed in the territory of a Member State shall be free from any discrimination based on nationality, as regards working conditions, remuneration or dismissal, as compared to its own nationals;

- the legally resident spouse and children of a worker legally employed in the territory of a Member State, with the exception of seasonal workers and of workers coming under bilateral agreements within the meaning of Article 42, unless otherwise provided by such agreements, shall have access to the labour market of that Member State, during the period of that worker's authorised stay of employment.

2.   Slovenia shall, subject to the conditions and modalities applicable in that country, accord the treatment referred to in paragraph 1 to workers who are nationals of a Member State and are legally employed in its territory as well as to their spouse and children who are legally resident in the said territory.

---

* *Source*: European Communities (1999). "Europe Agreement Establishing an Association between the European Communities and Their Member States, Acting Within the Framework of the European Union, of the One Part, and the Republic of Slovenia, of the Other Part", *Official Journal of the European Communities*, L 051, 26 February 1999, pp. 3 - 206; available also on the Internet (http://www.europa.eu.int). [Note added by the editor.]

Article 39

1.   With a view to coordinating social security systems for workers of Slovenian nationality legally employed in the territory of a Member State and for the members of their family, legally resident there, and subject to the conditions and modalities applicable in each Member State:

- all periods of insurance, employment or residence completed by such workers in the various Member States shall be added together for the purpose of pensions and annuities in respect of old age, invalidity and death and for the purpose of medical care for such workers and such family members;

- any pensions or annuities in respect of old age, death, industrial accident or occupational disease, or of invalidity resulting therefrom, with the exception of non-contributory benefits, shall be freely transferable at the rate applied by virtue of the law of the debtor Member State or States;

- the workers in question shall receive family allowances for the members of their family as defined above.

2.   Slovenia shall accord to workers who are nationals of a Member State and legally employed in its territory, and to members of their families legally resident there, treatment similar to that specified in the second and third indents of paragraph 1.

Article 40

1.   The Association Council shall by decision adopt the appropriate provisions to give effect to the objectives set out in Article 39.

2.   The Association Council shall by decision adopt detailed rules for administrative cooperation providing the necessary management and control guarantees for the application of the provisions referred to in paragraph 1.

Article 41

The provisions adopted by the Association Council in accordance with Article 40 shall not affect any rights or obligations arising from bilateral agreements linking Slovenia and the Member States where those agreements provide for more favourable treatment of nationals of Slovenia or of the Member States.

Article 42

1.   Taking into account the labour market situation in the Member States, subject to their legislation and to compliance with rules in force in those Member States in the area of mobility of workers:

- the existing facilities for access to employment for Slovenian workers accorded by Member States under bilateral agreements should be preserved and if possible improved;

- the other Member States shall consider the possibility of concluding similar agreements.

2.   The Association Council shall examine the granting of other improvements, including facilities for access to vocational training, in accordance with rules and procedures in force in the Member States, and taking account of the labour market situation in the Member States and in the Community.

Article 43

During the second stage referred to in Article 3, or earlier if so decided, the Association Council shall examine further ways of improving the movement of workers, taking into account inter alia the social and economic situation in Slovenia and the employment situation in the Community. The Association Council shall make appropriate recommendations.

Article 44

In the interest of facilitating the redeployment of labour resources resulting from economic restructuring in Slovenia, the Community shall provide technical assistance for the establishment of a suitable social security system in Slovenia as set out in Article 89.

CHAPTER II
ESTABLISHMENT

Article 45

1.   Slovenia shall, during the transitional period referred to in Article 3, facilitate the setting-up of operations on its territory by Community companies and nationals. To that end, it shall grant, from the entry into force of this Agreement:

   (i)   as regards the establishment of Community companies treatment no less favourable than that accorded to its own companies or to any third country company, whichever is the better, save for the sectors referred to in Annex IX(a), where such treatment shall be granted at the latest by the end of the transitional period referred to in Article 3 and;

   (ii)   as regards the operation of subsidiaries and branches of Community companies in Slovenia, once established, treatment no less favourable than that accorded to its own companies and branches or to any Slovenian subsidiary and branch of any third country company, whichever is the better.

2.   Slovenia shall not, during the transitional periods referred to in paragraph 1, adopt any new regulations or measures which introduce discrimination as regards the establishment of Community companies or nationals on its territory or in respect of their operation, once established, by comparison with its own companies and nationals.

3.   The Community and its Member States shall grant, from the entry into force of this Agreement:

   - as regards the establishment of Slovenian companies, treatment no less favourable than that accorded by Member States to their own companies or to any company of any third country, whichever is the better;

- as regards the operation of subsidiaries and branches of Slovenian companies, established in their territory, treatment no less favourable than that accorded by Member States to their own companies and branches, or to any subsidiary and branch of any third country company, established in their territory, whichever is the better.

4.   The treatment described in paragraphs 1 and 3 shall be applicable for the establishment and operation of nationals as from the end of the transitional period referred to in Article 3.

5.   The provisions concerning national treatment for the establishment and operation of Community companies and nationals contained in paragraph 1 of this Article shall not apply to the areas or matters listed in Annex IX(b).

6.   The Association Council shall during the transitional period referred to in paragraph 1 (i) examine regularly the possibility of accelerating the granting of national treatment in the sectors referred to in Annex IX(a) and the inclusion of areas or matters listed in Annex IX(b) within the scope of the provisions of paragraphs 1 and 3 of this Article. Amendments may be made to these Annexes by decision of the Association Council.

Following the expiry of the transitional period referred to in paragraph 1(i), the Association Council may exceptionally, at the request of Slovenia, and if the necessity arises, decide to prolong the duration of exclusion of certain areas or matters listed in Annex IX(a) for a limited period of time.

7.   Notwithstanding the provisions of this Article:

   (a)   Community nationals and subsidiaries and branches of Community companies shall have, from the entry into force of this Agreement, the right to use and rent real property in Slovenia;

   (b)   subsidiaries of Community companies shall also have the right to acquire and sell real property and, as regards natural resources, agricultural land and forestry, the same rights as enjoyed by Slovenian nationals and companies, where these rights are necessary for the conduct of the economic activities for which they are established;

   (c)   Slovenia shall grant the rights under (b) to Community nationals and branches of Community companies by the end of the first stage of the transitional period.

Article 46

1.   The provisions of this Chapter shall not apply to air transport services, inland waterway transport services and maritime cabotage transport services.

2.   The Association Council may make recommendations for improving establishment and operations in the areas covered by paragraph 1.

Article 47

For the purposes of this Agreement:

(a)   a 'Community company` or a 'Slovenian company` respectively shall mean a company set up in accordance with the laws of a Member State or of Slovenia respectively and having its registered office or central administration or principal place of business in the territory of the Community or Slovenia respectively.

However, should the company, set up in accordance with the laws of a Member State or Slovenia respectively, have only its registered office in the territory of the Community or Slovenia respectively, the company shall be considered a Community or a Slovenian company respectively if its operations possess a real and continuous link with the economy of one of the Member States or Slovenia respectively;

(b)   'Subsidiary` of a company shall mean a company which is effectively controlled by the first company;

(c)   'Branch` of a company shall mean a place of business not having legal personality which has the appearance of permanency, such as the extension of a parent body, has a management and is materially equipped to negotiate business with third parties so that the latter, although knowing that there will if necessary be a legal link with the parent body, the head office of which is abroad, do not have to deal directly with such parent body but may transact business at the place of business constituting the extension;

(d)   'Establishment` shall mean:

(i)   as regards nationals, the right to take up economic activities as self-employed persons, and to set up undertakings, in particular companies, which they effectively control. Self-employment and business undertakings by nationals shall not extend to seeking or taking employment in the labour market or confer a right of access to the labour market of another party. The provisions of this Chapter do not apply to those who are not exclusively self-employed;

(ii)   as regards Community or Slovenian companies, the right to take up economic activities by means of the setting up of subsidiaries and branches in Slovenia or in the Community respectively;

(e)   'Operations` shall mean the pursuit of economic activities;

(f)   'Economic activities` shall in principle include activities of an industrial, commercial and professional character and activities of craftsmen;

(g)   'Community national` and 'Slovenian national` shall mean respectively a natural person who is a national of one of the Member States or of Slovenia;

(h)   with regard to international maritime transport, including intermodal operations involving a sea leg, nationals of the Member States or of Slovenia established outside the Community or Slovenia respectively, and shipping companies established outside the Community or Slovenia and controlled by nationals of a Member State or Slovenian nationals respectively, shall also be beneficiaries of the provisions of this Chapter and Chapter III, if their vessels are registered in that Member State or in Slovenia respectively, in accordance with their respective legislation;

(i)   'Financial services` shall mean those activities described in Annex IX(c). The Association Council may extend or modify the scope of that Annex.

Article 48

1.   Subject to the provisions of Article 45, with the exception of financial services described in Annex IX(c), each party may regulate the establishment and operation of companies and nationals on its territory, in so far as these regulations do not discriminate against companies and nationals of the other party in comparison with its own companies and nationals.

2.   In respect of financial services, notwithstanding any other provisions of this Agreement, a party shall not be prevented from taking measures for prudential reasons, including for the protection of investors, depositors, policy holders or persons to whom a fiduciary duty is owned by a financial service supplier, or to ensure the integrity and stability of the financial system. Such measures shall not be used as a means of avoiding the party's obligations under the Agreement.

3.   Nothing in the Agreement shall be construed to require a party to disclose information relating to the affairs and accounts of individual customers or any confidential or proprietary information in the possession of public entities.

Article 49

1.   The provisions of Articles 45 and 48 do not preclude the application by a party of particular rules concerning the establishment and operation in its territory of branches of companies of another party not incorporated in the territory of the first party, which are justified by legal or technical differences between such branches as compared to branches of companies incorporated in its territory or, as regards financial services, for prudential reasons.

2.   The difference in treatment shall not go beyond what is strictly necessary as a result of such legal or technical differences or, as regards financial services, for prudential reasons.

Article 50

1.   A Community company or a Slovenian company established in the territory of Slovenia or the Community respectively shall be entitled to employ, or have employed by one of its subsidiaries or branches, in accordance with the legislation in force in the host country of establishment, in the territory of Slovenia and the Community respectively, employees who are nationals of the Community Member States and Slovenia respectively, provided that such employees are key personnel as defined in paragraph 2 and that they are employed exclusively by companies, subsidiaries or branches.

The residence and work permits of such employees shall only cover the period of such employment.

2.   Key personnel of the abovementioned companies herein referred to as 'organisations` are 'intra-corporate transferees` as defined in (c) of this paragraph in the following categories, provided that the organisation is a legal person and that the persons concerned have been employed by it or have been partners in it (other than as majority shareholders), for at least the year immediately preceding such movement:

(a)   Persons working in a senior position with an organisation, who primarily direct the management of the establishment, receiving general supervision or direction principally from the board of directors or stockholders of the business or their equivalent including:

- directing the establishment of a department or sub-division of the establishment;

- supervising and controlling the work of other supervisory, professional or managerial employees;

- having the authority personally to recruit and dismiss or recommend recruiting, dismissing or other personnel actions;

(b)   Persons working within an organisation who possess uncommon knowledge essential to the establishment's service, research equipment, techniques or management. The assessment of such knowledge may reflect, apart from knowledge specific to the establishment, a high level of qualification referring to a type of work or trade requiring specific technical knowledge, including membership of an accredited profession;

(c)   An 'intra-corporate transferee` is defined as a natural person working within an organisation in the territory of a party, and being temporarily transferred in the context of pursuit of economic activities in the territory of the other party; the organisation concerned must have its principal place of business in the territory of a party and the transfer be to an establishment (branch, subsidiary) of that organisation, effectively pursuing like economic activities in the territory of the other party.

3.   The entry into and the temporary presence within the territory if the Community or Slovenia of Slovenian and Community nationals respectively shall be permitted, when these representatives of companies are persons working in a senior position, as defined in paragraph 2(a) above, within a company, and are responsible for the setting up of a Community subsidiary or branch of a Slovenian company or of a Slovenian subsidiary or branch of a Community company in a Community Member State or Slovenia respectively, when:

- those representatives are not engaged in making direct sales or supplying services, and

- the company has its principal place of business outside the Community or Slovenia, respectively, and has no other representative, office, branch or subsidiary in that Community Member State or Slovenia respectively.

Article 51

In order to make it easier for Community nationals and Slovenian nationals to take up and pursue regulated professional activities in Slovenia and the Community respectively, the Association Council shall examine which steps are necessary for the mutual recognition of qualifications. It may take all necessary measures to that end.

Article 52

During the first four years following the date of entry into force of this Agreement, or for the sectors referred to in Annex IX(a), during the transitional period referred to in Article 3, Slovenia may introduce measures which derogate from the provisions of this Chapter as regards the establishment of Community companies and nationals of certain industries:

- are undergoing restructuring, or

- are facing serious difficulties, particularly where these entail serious social problems in Slovenia, or

- face the elimination or a drastic reduction of the total market share held by Slovenian companies or nationals in a given sector or industry in Slovenia, or
- are newly emerging industries in Slovenia.

Such measures:

(i)   shall cease to apply at the latest two years after the expiry of the fourth year following the date of entry into force of this Agreement or, for the sectors included in Annex IX(a), upon the expiry of the transitional period referred to in Article 3, and

(ii)   shall be reasonable and necessary in order to remedy the situation, and

(iii)   shall relate only to establishments in Slovenia to be set up after the entry into force of such measures and shall not introduce discrimination concerning the activities of Community companies or nationals already established in Slovenia at the time of introduction of a given measure, by comparison with Slovenian companies or nationals.

The Association Council may exceptionally, at the request of Slovenia, and if the necessity arises, decide to prolong the periods referred to in (i) above for a given sector for a limited period of time.

While devising and applying such measures, Slovenia shall grant preferential treatment wherever possible to Community companies and nationals, and in no case treatment less favourable than that accorded to companies or nationals from any third country.

Prior to the adoption of these measures, Slovenia shall consult the Association Council and shall not put them into effect before a one month period has elapsed following the notification to the Association Council of the concrete measures to be introduced by Slovenia, except where the threat of irreparable damage requires the taking of urgent measures, in which case Slovenia shall consult the Association Council immediately after their adoption.

Upon the expiry of the fourth year following the entry into force of this Agreement or, for the sectors included in Annex IX(a), upon the expiry of the transitional period referred to in Article 3, Slovenia may introduce such measures only with the authorisation of the Association Council and under conditions determined by the latter.

CHAPTER III
SUPPLY OF SERVICES BETWEEN THE COMMUNITY AND SLOVENIA

Article 53

1.   The parties undertake in accordance with the following provisions to take the necessary steps to allow progressively the supply of services by Community or Slovenian companies or nationals which are established in a party other than that of the person for whom the services are intended.

2.   In step with the liberalization process mentioned in paragraph 1, and subject to the provisions of Article 57(1), the parties shall permit the temporary movement of natural persons providing the service or who are employed by the service provider as key personnel as defined in Article 50(2), including natural persons who are representatives of a Community or Slovenian company or national and are seeking temporary entry for the purpose of negotiating for the sale of services or entering into agreements to sell services for that service provider, where those representatives will not be engaged in making direct sales to the general public or in supplying services themselves.

3.   At the latest eight years after the entry into force of this Agreement, the Association Council shall take the measures necessary to implement progressively the provisions of paragraph 1. Account shall be taken of the progress achieved by the parties in the approximation of their laws.

Article 54

1.   The parties shall not take any measures or actions which render the conditions for the supply of services by Community and Slovenian nationals or companies which are established in a party other than that of the person for whom the services are intended significantly more restrictive as compared to the situation existing on the day preceding the day of entry into force of the Agreement.

2.   If one party is the view that measures introduced by the other party since the signature of the Agreement result in a situation which is significantly more restrictive in respect of supply of services as compared with the situation existing at the date of signature of the Agreement, such first party may request the other party to enter into consultations.

Article 55

With regard to supply of transport services between the Community and Slovenia, the following shall apply without prejudice to the provisions of Article 53:

1.   With regard to inland transport, the relationship between the parties is governed by the Agreement between the European Economic Community and the Republic of Slovenia in the field of transport, signed on 5 April 1993. The parties confirm the importance they attach to the correct application of this Agreement, and underline the particular importance of the freedom of road transit traffic, as defined in the Agreement, without prejudice to the conditions regulating transit through Austria following Austria's accession to the European Union, of non-discrimination and of harmonisation of the Slovenian transport legislation with that of the Community.

2.   With regard to international maritime transport the parties undertake to apply effectively the principle of unrestricted access to the market and traffic on a commercial basis.

> (a)   The above provision does not prejudice the rights and obligations under the United Nations Code of Conduct for Liner Conferences, as applied by one or the other party to this Agreement. Non-conference liners will be free to operate in competition with a conference as long as they adhere to the principle of fair competition on a commercial basis.

> (b)   The parties affirm their commitment to a freely competitive environment as being an essential feature of the dry and liquid bulk trade.

3.   In applying the principles of point 2, the parties shall:

> (a)   not introduce cargo-sharing clauses in future bilateral agreements with third countries, other than in those exceptional circumstances where liner shipping companies from one or other party to this Agreement would not otherwise have an effective opportunity to ply for trade to and from the third country concerned;

> (b)   prohibit cargo-sharing arrangements in future bilateral agreements concerning dry and liquid bulk trade;

> (c)   abolish, upon the entry into force of this Agreement, all unilateral measures and administrative, technical and other obstacles which could have restrictive or discriminatory effects on the free supply of services in international maritime transport.

4.   With a view to ensuring a coordinated development and progressive liberalization of transport between the parties adapted to their reciprocal commercial needs, the conditions of mutual market access in air transport shall be dealt with by special agreement to be negotiated between the parties after the entry into force of this Agreement.

5.   Prior to the conclusion of the agreement referred to in point 4, the parties shall not take any measures or actions which are more restrictive or discriminatory as compared with the situation existing prior to the entry into force of this Agreement.

6.   During the transitional period, Slovenia shall progressively adapt its legislation, including administrative, technical and other rules, to that of the Community existing at any time in the field of air and inland transport in so far as it serves liberalization purposes and mutual access to markets of the parties and facilitates the movement of passengers and of goods.

7.   In step with the common progress in the achievement of the objectives of this Chapter, the Association Council shall examine ways of creating the conditions necessary for improving freedom to provide air and inland transport services.

CHAPTER IV
GENERAL PROVISIONS

Article 56

1.   The provisions of this Title shall be applied subject to limitations justified on grounds of public policy, public security or public health.

2.   They shall not apply to activities which in the territory of either party are connected, even occasionally, with the exercise of official authority.

Article 57

1.   For the purpose of this Title, nothing in this Agreement shall prevent the parties from applying their laws and regulations regarding entry and stay, employment, working conditions, establishment of natural persons and supply of services, provided that, in so doing, they do not apply them in such a manner as to nullify or impair the benefits accruing to any party under the terms of a specific provision of this Agreement. This provision shall be without prejudice to the application of Article 56.

2.   The exclusion of Community companies and nationals established in Slovenia in accordance with the provisions of Chapter II from public aid granted by Slovenia in the areas of public education services, health-related and social services and cultural services shall, for the duration of the transitional period referred to in Article 3, be deemed compatible with the provisions of this title and with the competition rules referred to in Title V.

Article 58

Companies which are controlled and exclusively owned jointly by Slovenian companies or nationals and Community companies or nationals shall also be covered by the provisions of this Title.

Article 59

1.   The Most-Favoured-Nation treatment granted in accordance with the provisions of this Title shall not apply to the tax advantages which the parties are providing or will provide in the future on the basis of agreements designed to avoid double taxation or other tax arrangements.

2.   None of the provisions of this Title shall be construed to prevent the adoption or enforcement by the parties of any measure aimed at preventing the avoidance or evasion of taxes pursuant to the tax provisions of agreements to avoid double taxation and other tax arrangements or domestic fiscal legislation.

3.   None of the provisions of this Title shall be construed to prevent Member States or Slovenia in applying the relevant provisions of their fiscal legislation, from distinguishing between taxpayers who are not in identical situations, in particular as regards their place of residence.

Article 60

The provisions of this Title shall be progressively adjusted, notably in the light of requirements arising from Article V of the General Agreement on Trade in Services (GATS).

Article 61

The provisions of this Agreement shall not prejudice the application by each party of any measure necessary to prevent the circumvention of its measures concerning third-country access to its market through the provisions of this Agreement.

TITLE V
PAYMENTS, CAPITAL, COMPETITION AND OTHER
ECONOMIC PROVISIONS, APPROXIMATION OF LAWS

CHAPTER I
CURRENT PAYMENTS AND MOVEMENT OF CAPITAL

Article 62

The parties undertake to authorise, in freely convertible currency, any payments on the current account of balance of payments to the extent that the transactions underlying the payments concern movements of goods, services or persons between the parties which have been liberalised pursuant to this Agreement.

Article 63

1.   With regard to transactions on the capital account of balance of payments from the entry into force of this Agreement, the Member States and Slovenia respectively shall ensure the free movement of capital relating to direct investments made in companies formed in accordance with the laws of the host country and investments made in accordance with the provisions of Chapter II of Title IV, and the liquidation or repatriation of the product of those investments and of any profit stemming therefrom.

Notwithstanding the above provision, such free movement, liquidation and repatriation shall be ensured by the end of the fourth year following the entry into force of this Agreement for all investments linked to establishment of Community nationals pursuing an activity in Slovenia as self-employed persons pursuant to Chapter II of Title IV.

With regard to acquisition of more than 25 % of shares providing voting rights issued under the Law on the Ownership Transformation of Enterprises in a company with a nominal share capital exceeding ECU 5 million, Slovenian government authorisation is required for a period of three years after the entry into force of this Agreement. Thereafter this restriction will be removed.

2.   With regard to transactions on the capital account of balance of payments, from entry into force of this Agreement, the Member States and Slovenia respectively shall ensure free movement of capital relating to credits related to commercial transactions or to the provision of services in which a resident of one of the parties is participating, and to financial loans.

They shall also ensure from the fourth year after the entry into force of this Agreement free movement of capital relating to portfolio investment.

Without prejudice to Articles 62 and 63, where, in exceptional circumstances, movements of capital between the residents of the Community and Slovenia cause, or threaten to cause, serious difficulties for the operation of exchange rate policy or monetary policy in the Community or Slovenia, the Community and Slovenia, respectively, may take safeguard measures with regard to movements of capital between the Community and Slovenia for a period not exceeding six months if such measures are strictly necessary.

3.   Without prejudice to paragraph 1, the Member States and Slovenia, as from the entry into force of this Agreement, shall not introduce any new foreign exchange restrictions on the movement of capital and current payments connected therewith between residents of the Community and Slovenia and shall not make the existing arrangements more restrictive.

4.   The parties shall consult each other with a view to facilitating the movement of capital between the Community and Slovenia in order to promote the objectives of this Agreement.

Article 64

1.   During the four years following the date of entry into force of this Agreement, the parties shall take measures permitting the creation of the necessary conditions for the further gradual application of Community rules on the free movement of capital.

2.   By the end of the fourth year from the entry into force of this Agreement, the Association Council shall examine ways of enabling Community rules on the movement of capital to be applied in full.

CHAPTER II
COMPETITION AND OTHER ECONOMIC PROVISIONS

Article 65

1.   The following are incompatible with the proper functioning of the Agreement, in so far as they may affect trade between the Community and Slovenia:

(i)   all agreements between undertakings, decisions by associations of undertakings and concerted practices between undertakings which have as their object or effect the prevention, restriction or distortion of competition;

(ii)   abuse by one or more undertakings of a dominant position in the territories of the Community or of Slovenia as a whole or in a substantial part thereof;

(iii)   any public aid which distorts or threatens to distort competition by favouring certain undertakings or certain products.

2.   Any practices contrary to this Article shall be assessed on the basis of criteria arising from the application of the rules of Articles 85, 86 and 92 of the Treaty establishing the European Community.

3.   The Association Council shall, within three years of the entry into force of this Agreement, adopt the necessary rules for the implementation of paragraphs 1 and 2. Until the implementing rules are adopted, practices incompatible with paragraph 1 shall be dealt with by the parties on their respective territories according to their respective legislation. This shall be without prejudice to paragraph 6.

4.   (a)   For the purposes of applying the provisions of paragraph 1(iii), the parties recognise that during the first four years after the entry into force of this Agreement, any public aid granted by Slovenia shall be assessed taking into account the fact that Slovenia shall be regarded as an area identical to those areas of the Community described in Article 92(3)(a) of the Treaty establishing the European Community. The Association Council shall, taking into account the economic situation of Slovenia, decide whether that period should be extended by further periods of four years.

        (b)   Each party shall ensure transparency in the area of public aid, inter alia by reporting annually to the other party on the total amount and the distribution of the aid given and by providing, upon request, information on aid schemes. Upon request by one party, the other party shall provide information on particular individual cases of public aid.

5.   With regard to products referred to in Chapters II and III of Title III:

        - paragraph 1(iii) shall not apply;

        - any practices contrary to paragraph 1(i) shall be assessed according to the criteria established by the Community on the basis of Articles 42 and 43 of the Treaty establishing the European Community and in particular of those established in Council Regulation No 26/1962.

6.   If the Community or Slovenia considers that a particular practice is incompatible with the terms of paragraph 1, and:

        - is not adequately dealt with under the implementing rules referred to in paragraph 3, or

        - in the absence of such rules, and if such practice causes or threatens to cause serious injury to the interests of the other party or material injury to its domestic industry, including its services industry, it may take appropriate measures after consultation within the Association Council or after thirty working days following referral for such consultation.

In the case of practices incompatible with paragraph 1(iii), such appropriate measures may, where the WTO Agreement applies thereto, only be adopted in accordance with the procedures and under the conditions laid down thereby and any other relevant instrument negotiated under its auspices which are applicable between the parties.

7.   Notwithstanding any provisions to the contrary adopted in accordance with paragraph 3, the parties shall exchange information taking into account the limitations imposed by the requirements of professional and business confidentiality.

8.   This Article shall not apply to the products covered by the Treaty establishing the European Coal and Steel Community which are the subject of Protocol 2.

Article 66

1.   The parties shall endeavour wherever possible to avoid the imposition of restrictive measures, including measures relating to imports, for balance of payments purposes. A party adopting such measures shall present as soon as possible to the other party a timetable for their removal.

2.   Where one or more Member States or Slovenia is in serious balance of payments difficulties, or under imminent threat thereof, the Community or Slovenia, as the case may be, may, in accordance with the conditions established under the WTO Agreement, adopt restrictive measures, including measures relating to imports, which shall be of limited duration and may not go beyond what is strictly necessary to remedy the balance of payments situation. The Community or Slovenia, as the case may be, shall inform the other party forthwith.

3.   Any restrictive measures shall not apply to transfers related to investment and in particular to the repatriation of amounts invested or reinvested or any kind of revenues stemming therefrom.

Article 67

With regard to public undertakings, and undertakings to which special or exclusive rights have been granted, the Association Council shall ensure that as from the third year following the date of entry into force of this Agreement, the principles of the Treaty establishing the European Community, in particular Article 90 thereof, are upheld.

Article 68

1.   Pursuant to the provisions of this Article and Annex X, the parties confirm the importance that they attach to ensure adequate and effective protection and enforcement of intellectual, industrial and commercial property rights.

2.   From the entry into force of the Agreement, Slovenia shall protect intellectual, industrial and commercial property rights at a level of protection similar to that existing in the Community, including effective means of enforcing such rights.

3.   Before the entry into force of the Agreement, Slovenia shall accede to the multilateral conventions on intellectual, industrial and commercial property rights referred to in paragraph 1 of Annex X.

4.   If problems in the area of intellectual, industrial and commercial property affecting trading conditions were to occur, they shall be referred urgently to the Association Council, at the request of either party, with a view to reaching mutually satisfactory solutions.

Article 69

1.   The parties consider the opening-up of the award of public contracts on the basis of non-discrimination and reciprocity, in particular in the WTO context, to be a desirable objective.

2.   Slovenian companies, shall be granted access to contract award procedures in the Community pursuant to Community procurement rules under treatment no less favourable than that accorded to Community companies as from the entry into force of this Agreement, except for contracts covered by Directive 93/38/EEC.

The above provisions would also apply to contracts covered by Directive 93/38/EEC immediately the Slovenian government introduced the appropriate legislation. The Community shall examine periodically whether Slovenia has indeed introduced such legislation.

Community companies shall be granted access to contract award procedures in Slovenia under treatment no less favourable than that accorded to Slovenian companies at the latest by the end of the transitional period referred to in Article 3.

Community companies established in Slovenia under the provisions of Chapter II of Title IV shall have upon entry into force of this Agreement access to contract award procedures under treatment no less favourable than that accorded to Slovenian companies.

The Association Council shall periodically examine the possibility for Slovenia to introduce access to award procedures in Slovenia for all Community companies prior to the end of the transitional period.

3.   As regards establishment, operations, supply of services between the Community and Slovenia, and also employment and movement of labour linked to the fulfilment of public contracts, the provisions of Articles 38 to 61 are applicable.

TITLE VI
ECONOMIC COOPERATION

Article 74 Industrial cooperation

1.   Cooperation shall be aimed at promoting the modernisation and restructuring of Slovenian industry in both public and private sectors as well as industrial cooperation between economic operators of both sides, with the particular objective of strengthening the private sector, while respecting the environment.

2.   In particular cooperation shall promote:

   - the restructuring of individual sectors; in this context, the Association Council will examine in particular the problems affecting the coal and steel sectors;

   - the establishment of new undertakings in areas offering potential for growth.

3.   Industrial cooperation initiatives shall take into account priorities determined by Slovenia. The initiatives should seek in particular to establish a suitable framework for undertakings, to improve management know-how, to promote markets, market transparency and the business environment, and will include technical assistance where appropriate.

Article 75 Investment promotion and protection

1.   Cooperation between the parties shall be aimed at establishing a favourable climate for private investment, both domestic and foreign, which is essential to economic and industrial reconstruction in Slovenia.

2.   The particular aims of cooperation shall be:

- for Slovenia to establish a legal framework which favours and protects investment;

- the conclusion, where appropriate, with Member States of bilateral agreements for the promotion and protection of investment;

- to conclude, where appropriate, agreements between Member States and Slovenia to avoid double taxation;

- to implement suitable arrangements for the transfer of capital;

- to proceed with deregulation;

- to improve economic infrastructure;

- to exchange information on investment opportunities through trade fairs, exhibitions, trade weeks and other events.

ANNEX IX (c)

ESTABLISHMENT: FINANCIAL SERVICES REFERRED TO IN TITLE IV, CHAPTER II

Financial Services: Definitions

A financial service is any service of a financial nature offered by a financial service provider of a party.

Financial services include the following activities:

A.   All Insurance and insurance-related services:

      1.   direct insurance (including co-insurance):

            (i)   life;

            (ii)   non-life;

      2.   reinsurance and retrocession;

      3.   insurance inter mediation, such as brokerage and agency;

4.   services auxiliary to insurance, such as consultancy, actuarial, risk assessment and claim settlement services;

B.   Banking and other financial services (excluding insurance):

     1.   acceptance of deposits and other repayable funds from the public;

     2.   lending of all types, including, inter alia, consumer-credit, mortgage credit, factoring and financing of commercial transaction;

     3.   financial leasing;

     4.   all payment and money transmission services, including credit charge and debit cards, travellers cheques and bankers draft;

     5.   guarantees and commitments;

     6.   trading for own account of customers, whether on an exchange, in an over the counter market or otherwise, the following:

         (a)   money market instruments (cheques, bills, certificates of deposits, etc.),

         (b)   foreign exchange,

         (c)   derivative products including, but not limited to, futures and options,

         (d)   exchange rates and interest rate instruments, including products such as swaps, forward rate agreements, etc.,

         (e)   transferable securities,

         (f)   other negotiable instruments and financial assets, including bullion;

     7.   participation in issues of all kinds of securities, including underwriting and placement as agent (whether publicly or privately) and provision of services related to such issues;

     8.   money broking;

     9.   asset management, such as cash or portfolio management, all forms of collective investment management, pension-fund management, custodial depository and trust services;

     10.   settlement and clearing services for financial assets, including securities, derivative products, and other negotiable instruments;

     11.   advisory intermediation and other auxiliary financial services on all the activities listed in points 1 to 10 above, including credit reference and analysis, investment and portfolio research and advice, advice on acquisitions and on corporate restructuring and strategy;

12.   provision and transfer of financial information, and financial data processing and related software by providers of other financial services.

The following activities are excluded from the definition of financial services:

(a)   activities carried out by central banks or by any other public institution in pursuit of monetary and exchange rate policies;

(b)   activities conducted by central banks, government agencies or departments, or public institutions, for the account or with the guarantee of the government, except when those activities may be carried out by financial service providers in competition with such public entities;

(c)   activities forming part of a statutory system of social security or public retirement plans, except when those activities may be carried by financial service providers in competition with public entities or private institutions.

ANNEX X

INTELLECTUAL, INDUSTRIAL AND COMMERCIAL PROPERTY RIGHTS REFERRED TO IN ARTICLE 68

1.   Paragraph 3 of Article 68 concerns the following multilateral conventions:

- International Convention for the Protection of Performers, Producers of Phonograms and Broadcasting Organizations (Rome, 1961);

- Protocol relating to the Madrid Agreement concerning the International Registration of Marks (Madrid, 1989);

- Budapest Treaty on the international Recognition of the Deposit of Micro-organisms for the purposes of Patent Procedures (1977, modified in 1980);

- International Convention for the Protection of New Varieties of Plants (UPOV Geneva Act, 1991).

The Association Council may decide that paragraph 3 of Article 68 shall apply to other multilateral conventions.

2.   The parties confirm the importance they attach to the obligations arising from the following multilateral conventions:

- Paris Convention for the Protection of Industrial Property (Stockholm Act, 1967 and amended in 1979);

- Madrid Agreement concerning the International Registration of Marks (Stockholm Act, 1967 and amended in 1979);

- Nice Agreement concerning the International Classification of Goods and Services for the purposes of the Registration of Marks (Geneva, 1977 and amended in 1979);

- Patent Cooperation Treaty (Washington, 1970, amended in 1979 and modified in 1984);

- Berne Convention for the Protection of Literary and Artistic Works (Paris Act, 1971).

3.   From entry into force of this Agreement, Slovenia shall grant to Community companies and nationals, in respect of the recognition and protection of intellectual, industrial and commercial property, treatment no less favourable than that granted by it to any third country under bilateral agreements.

*

PARTNERSHIP AND COOPERATION AGREEMENT ESTABLISHING A PARTNERSHIP BETWEEN THE EUROPEAN COMMUNITIES AND THEIR MEMBER STATES, OF THE ONE PART, AND THE REPUBLIC OF UZBEKISTAN, OF THE OTHER PART[*]
[excerpts]

The Partnership and Cooperation Agreement Establishing a Partnership between the European Communities and Their Member States, of the One Part, and the Republic of Uzbekistan, of the Other Part was signed on 21 June 1996. The member States of the European Communities are: Austria, Belgium, Denmark, Finland, France, Germany, Greece, Ireland, Italy, Luxembourg, the Netherlands, Portugal, Spain, Sweden and the United Kingdom.

TITLE IV

PROVISIONS AFFECTING BUSINESS AND INVESTMENT

CHAPTER I
LABOUR CONDITIONS

Article 19

1.   Subject to the laws, conditions and procedures applicable in each Member State, the Community and the Member States shall endeavour to ensure that the treatment accorded to nationals of the Republic of Uzbekistan legally employed in the territory of a Member State shall be free from any discrimination based on nationality, as regards working conditions, remuneration or dismissal, as compared to its own nationals.

2.   Subject to the laws, conditions and procedures applicable in the Republic of Uzbekistan, the Republic of Uzbekistan shall ensure that the treatment accorded to nationals of a Member State legally employed in the territory of the Republic of Uzbekistan shall be free from any discrimination based on nationality, as regards working conditions, remuneration or dismissal, as compared to its own nationals.

Article 20

The Cooperation Council shall examine which improvements can be made in working conditions for business people consistent with the international commitments of the Parties, including those set out in the document of the CSCE Bonn Conference.

---

[*]   *Source*: European Communities (1999). "Partnership and Cooperation Agreement Establishing a Partnership between the European Communities and Their Member States, of the One Part, and the Republic of Uzbekistan, of the Other Part", *Official Journal of the European Communities*, L 229, 31 August 1999, pp. 3 - 52; available also on the Internet (http://www.europa.eu.int). [Note added by the editor.]

Article 21

The Cooperation Council shall make recommendations for the implementation of Articles 19 and 20.

CHAPTER II
CONDITIONS AFFECTING THE ESTABLISHMENT AND OPERATION OF COMPANIES

Article 22

1.   The Community and its Member States shall grant, for the establishment of Uzbek companies as defined in Article 24(d), treatment no less favourable than that accorded to any third country companies.

2.   Without prejudice to the reservations listed in Annex II, the Community and its Member States shall grant to subsidiaries of Uzbek companies established in their territories a treatment no less favourable than that granted to any Community companies, in respect of their operation.

3.   The Community and its Member States shall grant to branches of Uzbek companies established in their territories treatment no less favourable than that accorded to branches of companies of any third country, in respect of their operations.

4.   Without prejudice to the reservations listed in Annex III, the Republic of Uzbekistan shall grant, for the establishment of Community companies as defined in Article 24(d), treatment no less favourable than that accorded to Uzbek companies or to any third country companies, whichever is the better.

5.   The Republic of Uzbekistan shall grant to subsidiaries and branches of Community companies established in its territory treatment no less favourable than that accorded to its own companies or branches or to any third country company or branch, whichever is the better, in respect of their operations.

Article 23

1.   The provisions of Article 22 shall not apply to air transport, inland waterways transport and maritime transport.

2.   However, in respect of activities, as indicated below, undertaken by shipping agencies for the provision of services to international maritime transport, including intermodal transport operations involving a sea-leg, each Party shall permit the companies of the other Party to have a commercial presence in its territory in the form of subsidiaries or branches, under conditions of establishment and operation no less favourable than those accorded to its own companies or to subsidiaries or branches of companies of any third country, whichever are the better.

3.   Such activities include but are not limited to:

(a)   marketing and sales of maritime transport and related services through direct contact with customers, from quotation to invoicing, whether these services are operated or offered by the service supplier itself or by service suppliers with which the service seller has established standing business arrangements;

(b)   purchase and use, on their own account or on behalf of their customers (and the resale to their customers) of any transport and related services, including inward transport services by any mode, particularly inland waterways, road and rail, necessary for the supply of an integrated service;

(c)   preparation of documentation concerning transport documents, customs documents, or other documents related to the origin and character of the goods transported;

(d)   provision of business information by any means, including computerised information systems and electronic data interchange (subject to any non-discriminatory restrictions concerning telecommunications);

(e)   setting up of any business arrangement, including participation in the company's stock and the appointment of personnel recruited locally (or, in the case of foreign personnel, subject to the relevant provisions of this Agreement), with any locally established shipping agency;

(f)   acting on behalf of the companies, inter alia, in organising the call of the vessel or taking over cargoes when required.

Article 24
For the purpose of this Agreement:

(a)   a "Community company" or an "Uzbek company" respectively shall mean a company set up in accordance with the laws of a Member State or of the Republic of Uzbekistan respectively and having its registered office or central administration, or principal place of business in the territory of the Community or the Republic of Uzbekistan respectively. However, should the company, set up in accordance with the laws of a Member State or the Republic of Uzbekistan respectively, have only its registered office in the territory of the Community or the Republic of Uzbekistan respectively, the company shall be considered a Community or Uzbek company respectively if its operations possess a real and continuous link with the economy of one of the Member States or the Republic of Uzbekistan respectively.

(b)   "subsidiary" of a company shall mean a company which is effectively controlled by the first company.

(c)   "branch" of a company shall mean a place of business not having legal personality which has the appearance of permanency, such as the extension of a parent body, has a management and is materially equipped to negotiate business with third parties so that the latter, although knowing that there will if necessary be a legal link with the parent body, the head office of which is abroad, do not have to deal directly with such parent body but may transact business at the place of business constituting the extension.

(d)   "establishment" shall mean the right of Community or Uzbek companies as referred to in point (a), to take up economic activities by means of the setting up of subsidiaries and branches in the Republic of Uzbekistan or in the Community respectively.

(e)   "operation" shall mean the pursuit of economic activities.

(f)   "economic activities" shall mean activities of an industrial, commercial and professional character.

With regard to international maritime transport, including inter modal operations involving a sea-leg, nationals of the Member States or the Republic of Uzbekistan established outside the Community or the Republic of Uzbekistan respectively, and shipping companies established outside the Community or the Republic of Uzbekistan and controlled by nationals of a Member State or nationals of the Republic of Uzbekistan respectively, shall also be beneficiaries of the provisions of this Chapter and Chapter III if their vessels are registered in that Member State or in the Republic of Uzbekistan respectively in accordance with their respective legislation.

Article 25

1.   Notwithstanding any other provisions of this Agreement, a Party shall not be prevented from taking measures for prudential reasons, including for the protection of investors, depositors, policy holders or persons to whom a fiduciary duty is owed by a financial service supplier, or to ensure the integrity and stability of the financial system. Where such measures do not conform with the provisions of this Agreement, they shall not be used as a means of avoiding the obligations of a Party under this Agreement.

2.   Nothing in this Agreement shall be construed as requiring a Party to disclose information relating to the affairs and accounts of individual customers or any confidential or proprietary information in the possession of public entities.

3.   For the purpose of this Agreement, "financial services" shall mean those activities described in Annex IV.

Article 26

The provisions of this Agreement shall not prejudice the application by each Party of any measure necessary to prevent the circumvention of its measures concerning third country access to its market, through the provisions of this Agreement.

Article 27

1.   Notwithstanding the provisions of Chapter I of this Title, a Community company or an Uzbek company established in the territory of the Republic of Uzbekistan or the Community respectively shall be entitled to employ, or have employed by one of its subsidiaries or branches, in accordance with the legislation in force in the host country of establishment, in the territory of the Republic of Uzbekistan and the Community respectively, employees who are nationals of Community Member States and the Republic of Uzbekistan respectively, provided that such

employees are key personnel as defined in paragraph 2, and that they are employed exclusively by companies, or branches. The residence and work permits of such employees shall only cover the period of such employment.

2.   Key personnel of the abovementioned companies herein referred to as "organisations" are "intra-corporate transferees" as defined in (c) in the following categories, provided that the organisation is a legal person and that the persons concerned have been employed by it or have been partners in it (other than majority shareholders), for at least the year immediately preceding such movement:

(a)   Persons working in a senior position with an organisation, who primarily direct the management of the establishment, receiving general supervision or direction principally from the board of directors or stockholders of the business or their equivalent, including:

- directing the establishment or a department or subdivision of the establishment,

- supervising and controlling the work of other supervisory, professional or managerial employees,

- having the authority personally to hire and fire or recommend hiring, firing or other personnel actions;

(b)   Persons working within an organisation who possess uncommon knowledge essential to the establishment's service, research equipment, techniques or management. The assessment of such knowledge may reflect, apart from knowledge specific to the establishment, a high level of qualification referring to a type of work or trade requiring specific technical knowledge, including membership of an accredited profession;

(c)   An "intra-corporate transferee" is defined as a natural person working within an organisation in the territory of a Party, and being temporarily transferred in the context of pursuit of economic activities in the territory of the other Party; the organisation concerned must have its principal place of business in the territory of a Party and the transfer be to an establishment (branch, subsidiary) of that organisation, effectively pursuing like economic activities in the territory of the other Party.

Article 28

1.   The Parties shall use their best endeavours to avoid taking any measures or actions which render the conditions for the establishment and operation of each other's companies more restrictive than the situation existing on the day preceding the date of signature of this Agreement.

2.   The provisions of this Article are without prejudice to those of Article 36: the situations covered by such Article 36 shall be solely governed by its provisions to the exclusion of any other.

3.   Acting in the spirit of partnership and cooperation and in the light of the provisions of Article 42, the Government of the Republic of Uzbekistan shall inform the Community of its intentions to submit new legislation or adopt new regulations which may render the conditions for the establishment or operation in the Republic of Uzbekistan of subsidiaries and branches of Community companies more restrictive than the situation existing on the day preceding the date of signature of this Agreement. The Community may request the Republic of Uzbekistan to communicate the drafts of such legislation or regulations and to enter into consultations about those drafts.

4.   Where new legislation or regulations introduced in the Republic of Uzbekistan would result in rendering the conditions for operation of subsidiaries and branches of Community companies established in the Republic of Uzbekistan more restrictive than the situation existing on the day of signature of this Agreement, such respective legislation or regulations shall not apply during three years following the entry into force of the relevant act to those subsidiaries and branches already established in the Republic of Uzbekistan at the time of entry into force of the relevant act.

CHAPTER III
CROSS BORDER SUPPLY OF SERVICES BETWEEN THE COMMUNITY AND THE REPUBLIC OF UZBEKISTAN

Article 29

1.   The Parties undertake in accordance with the provisions of this Chapter to take the necessary steps to allow progressively the supply of services by Community or Uzbek companies which are established in a Party other than that of the person for whom the services are intended taking into account the development of the service sectors in the Parties.

2.   The Cooperation Council shall make recommendations for the implementation of paragraph 1.

Article 30

The Parties shall cooperate with the aim of developing a market oriented service sector in the Republic of Uzbekistan.

Article 31

1.   The Parties undertake to apply effectively the principle of unrestricted access to the international maritime market and traffic on a commercial basis:

   (a)   the above provision does not prejudice the rights and obligations arising from the United Nations Convention on a Code of Conduct for Liner Conferences, as applicable to one or other Party to this Agreement. Non-conference lines will be free to operate in competition with a conference as long as they adhere to the principle of fair competition on a commercial basis;

   (b)   the Parties affirm their commitment to a freely competitive environment as being an essential feature of the dry and liquid bulk trade.

2.   In applying the principles of paragraph 1, the Parties shall:

(a)   not apply, as from the entry into force of this Agreement, any cargo sharing provisions of bilateral agreements between any Member States of the Community and the former Soviet Union;

(b)   not introduce cargo sharing clauses into future bilateral agreements with third countries, other than in those exceptional circumstances where liner shipping companies from one or other Party to this Agreement would not otherwise have an effective opportunity to ply for trade to and from the third country concerned;

(c)   prohibit cargo sharing arrangements in future bilateral agreements concerning dry and liquid bulk trade;

(d)   abolish upon entry into force of this Agreement, all unilateral measures, administrative, technical and other obstacles which could have restrictive or discriminatory effects on the free supply of services in international maritime transport.

Article 32

With a view to assuring a coordinated development of transport between the Parties, adapted to their commercial needs, the conditions of mutual market access and provision of services in transport by road, rail and inland waterways and, if applicable, in air transport may be dealt with by specific agreements where appropriate negotiated between the Parties after entry into force of this Agreement.

CHAPTER IV
GENERAL PROVISIONS

Article 33

1.   The provisions of this Title shall be applied subject to limitations justified on grounds of public policy, public security or public health.

2.   They shall not apply to activities which in the territory of either Party are connected, even occasionally, with the exercise of official authority.

Article 34

For the purpose of this Title, nothing in this Agreement shall prevent the Parties from applying their laws and regulations regarding entry and stay, work, labour conditions and establishment of natural persons and supply of services, provided that, in so doing, they do not apply them in a manner as to nullify or impair the benefits accruing to any Party under the terms of a specific provision of this Agreement. The above provision does not prejudice the application of Article 33.

Article 35

Companies which are controlled and exclusively owned by Uzbek companies and Community companies jointly shall also be beneficiaries of the provisions of Chapters II, III and IV.

Article 36

Treatment granted by either Party to the other thereunder shall, as from the day one month prior to the date of entry into force of the relevant obligations of the General Agreement on Trade in Services (GATS), in respect of sectors or measures covered by the GATS, in no case be more favourable than that accorded by such first Party under the provisions of GATS and this in respect of each service sector, sub-sector and mode of supply.

Article 37

For the purposes of Chapters II, III and IV, no account shall be taken of treatment accorded by the Community, its Member States or the Republic of Uzbekistan pursuant to commitments entered into in economic integration agreements in accordance with the principles of Article V of GATS.

Article 38

1.   The most-favoured-nation treatment granted in accordance with the provisions of this Title shall not apply to the tax advantages which the Parties are providing or will provide in the future on the basis of agreements to avoid double taxation, or other tax arrangements.

2.   Nothing in this Title shall be construed to prevent the adoption or enforcement by the Parties of any measure aimed at preventing the avoidance or evasion of taxes pursuant to the tax provisions of agreements to avoid double taxation and other tax arrangements, or domestic fiscal legislation.

3.   Nothing in this Title shall be construed to prevent Member States or the Republic of Uzbekistan from distinguishing, in the application of the relevant provisions of their fiscal legislation, between tax payers who are not in identical situations, in particular as regards their place of residence.

Article 39

Without prejudice to Article 27, no provision of Chapters II, III and IV shall be interpreted as giving the right to:

- nationals of the Member States or of the Republic of Uzbekistan respectively to enter, or stay in, the territory of the Republic of Uzbekistan or the Community respectively in any capacity whatsoever, and in particular as a shareholder or partner in a company or manager or employee thereof or supplier or recipient of services,

- Community subsidiaries or branches of Uzbek companies to employ or have employed in the territory of the Community nationals of the Republic of Uzbekistan,

- Uzbek subsidiaries or branches of Community companies to employ or have employed in the territory of the Republic of Uzbekistan nationals of the Member States,

- Uzbek companies or Community subsidiaries or branches of Uzbek companies to supply Uzbek persons to act for and under the control of other persons by temporary employment contracts,

- Community companies or Uzbek subsidiaries or branches of Community companies to supply workers who are nationals of the Member States by temporary employment contracts.

CHAPTER V
CURRENT PAYMENTS AND CAPITAL

Article 40

1.   The Parties undertake to authorise in freely convertible currency, any current payments between residents of the Community and of the Republic of Uzbekistan connected with the movement of goods, services or persons made in accordance with the provisions of this Agreement.

2.   With regard to transactions on the capital account of balance of payments, from entry into force of this Agreement, the free movement of capital relating to direct investments made in companies formed in accordance with the laws of the host country and investments made in accordance with the provisions of Chapter II, and the liquidation or repatriation of these investments and of any profit stemming therefrom shall be ensured.

3.   Without prejudice to paragraph 2 or to paragraph 5, as from the entry into force of this Agreement, no new foreign exchange restrictions on the movement of capital and current payments connected therewith between residents of the Community and the Republic of Uzbekistan shall be introduced and the existing arrangements shall not become more restrictive.

4.   The Parties shall consult each other with a view to facilitating the movements of forms of capital other than those referred to in paragraph 2 above between the Community and the Republic of Uzbekistan in order to promote the objectives of this Agreement.

5.   With reference to the provisions of this Article, until a full convertibility of the Uzbek currency within the meaning of Article VIII of the Articles of Agreement of the International Monetary Fund (IMF) is introduced, the Republic of Uzbekistan may in exceptional circumstances apply exchange restrictions connected with the granting or taking up of short and medium-term financial credits to the extent that such restrictions are imposed on the Republic of Uzbekistan for the granting of such credits and are permitted according to the Republic of Uzbekistan's status under the IMF. The Republic of Uzbekistan shall apply these restrictions in a non-discriminatory manner. They shall be applied in such a manner as to cause the least possible disruption to this Agreement. The Republic of Uzbekistan shall inform the Cooperation Council promptly of the introduction of such measures and of any changes therein.

6.   Without prejudice to paragraphs 1 and 2, where, in exceptional circumstances, movement of capital between the Community and the Republic of Uzbekistan cause, or threaten to cause,

serious difficulties for the operation of exchange rate policy or monetary policy in the Community or the Republic of Uzbekistan, the Community and the Republic of Uzbekistan, respectively, may take safeguard measures with regard to movements of capital between the Community and the Republic of Uzbekistan for a period not exceeding six months if such measures are strictly necessary.

CHAPTER VI
INTELLECTUAL, INDUSTRIAL AND COMMERCIAL PROPERTY PROTECTION

Article 41

1.   Pursuant to the provisions of this Article and of Annex V, the Republic of Uzbekistan shall continue to improve the protection of intellectual, industrial and commercial property rights in order to provide, by the end of the fifth year after the entry into force of this Agreement, for a level of protection similar to that existing in the Community, including effective means of enforcing such rights.

2.   By the end of the fifth year after entry into force of this Agreement, the Republic of Uzbekistan shall accede to the multilateral conventions on intellectual, industrial and commercial property rights referred to in paragraph 1 of Annex V to which Member States are parties or which are de facto applied by Member States, according to the relevant provisions contained in these conventions.

TITLE V
LEGISLATIVE COOPERATION

Article 42

1.   The Parties recognise that an important condition for strengthening the economic links between the Republic of Uzbekistan and the Community is the approximation of the Republic of Uzbekistan's existing and future legislation to that of the Community. The Republic of Uzbekistan shall endeavour to ensure that its legislation will be gradually made compatible with that of the Community.

2.   The approximation of laws shall extend to the following areas in particular: customs law, company law, laws on banking and other financial services, company accounts and taxes, intellectual property, protection of workers at the workplace, rules on competition including any related issues and practices affecting trade, public procurement, protection of health and life of humans, animals and plants, the environment, consumer protection, indirect taxation, technical rules and standards, nuclear laws and regulations, transport and telecommunications.

3.   The Community shall provide the Republic of Uzbekistan with technical assistance for the implementation of these measures, which may include, inter alia:

   - the exchange of experts,
   - the provision of early information especially on relevant legislation,
   - organisation of seminars,
   - training of personnel involved in the drafting and implementation of legislation,

- aid for translation of Community legislation in the relevant sectors.

4.   The Parties agree to examine ways to apply their respective competition laws on a concerted basis in such cases where trade between them is affected.

TITLE VI

ECONOMIC COOPERATION

Article 43

1.   The Community and the Republic of Uzbekistan shall establish economic cooperation aimed at contributing to the process of economic reform and recovery and sustainable development of the Republic of Uzbekistan. Such cooperation shall strengthen existing economic links, to the benefit of both parties.

2.   Policies and other measures will be designed to bring about economic and social reforms and restructuring of the economic and trading systems in the Republic of Uzbekistan and will be guided by the requirements of sustainability and harmonious social development; they will also fully incorporate environmental considerations.

3.   To this end, cooperation will concentrate, in particular, on economic and social development, human resources development, support for enterprises (including privatisation, investment and development of financial services, agriculture and food, energy and civil nuclear safety, transport, tourism, postal services and telecommunications, environmental protection and regional cooperation.

4.   Special attention shall be devoted to measures capable of fostering regional cooperation.

5.   Where appropriate, economic cooperation and other forms of cooperation provided for in this Agreement may be supported by technical assistance from the Community, taking into account the Community's relevant Council regulation applicable to technical assistance in the Independent States, the priorities agreed upon in the indicative programme related to Community technical assistance to the Republic of Uzbekistan and its established coordination and implementation procedures.

Article 44
Cooperation in the field of trade in goods and services

The Parties will cooperate with a view to ensuring that the Republic of Uzbekistan's international trade is conducted in conformity with the rules of the WTO.

Such cooperation shall include specific issues directly relevant to trade facilitation, in particular with a view to assisting the Republic of Uzbekistan to harmonise its legislation and regulations with WTO rules and so to fulfil as soon as possible the conditions of accession to that Organisation. These include:

- formulation of policy on trade and trade-related questions, including payments and clearing mechanisms,

- drafting of relevant legislation.

Article 45
Industrial cooperation

1.   Cooperation shall aim at promoting the following in particular:

- the development of business links between economic operators of both sides,

- Community participation in the Republic of Uzbekistan's efforts to restructure its industry,

- the improvement of management,

- the development of the quality of industrial products,

- the development of efficient production and processing capacity in the raw materials sector,

- the development of appropriate commercial rules and practices, including product marketing,

- environmental protection,

- defence conversion,

- training of management personnel.

2.   The provisions of this Article shall not affect the enforcement of Community competition rules applicable to undertakings.

Article 46
Investment promotion and protection

1.   Bearing in mind the respective powers and competences of the Community and the Member States, cooperation shall aim to establish a favourable climate for private investment, both domestic and foreign, especially through better conditions for investment protection, the transfer of capital and the exchange of information on investment opportunities.

2.   The aims of cooperation shall be in particular:

- the conclusion, where appropriate, between the Member States and the Republic of Uzbekistan of agreements for the promotion and protection of investment,

- the conclusion, where appropriate, between the Member States and the Republic of Uzbekistan of agreements to avoid double taxation,

- the creation of favourable conditions for attracting foreign investments into the Uzbek economy,

- to establish stable and adequate business law and conditions, and to exchange information on laws, regulations and administrative practices in the field of investment,

- to exchange information on investment opportunities in the form of, inter alia, trade fairs, exhibitions, trade weeks and other events.

Article 47
Public procurement

The Parties shall cooperate to develop conditions for open and competitive award of contracts for goods and services in particular through calls for tenders.

Article 48
Cooperation in the field of standards and conformity assessment

1.   Cooperation between the Parties shall promote alignment with internationally agreed criteria, principles and guidelines followed in the field of quality. The required actions will facilitate progress towards mutual recognition in the field of conformity assessment, as well as the improvement of Uzbek product quality.

2.   To this end the Parties shall seek to cooperate in technical assistance projects which will:

- promote appropriate cooperation with organisations and institutions specialised in these fields,

- promote the use of Community technical regulations and the application of European standards and conformity assessment procedures,

- permit the sharing of experience and technical information in the field of quality management.

Article 49
Mining and raw materials

1.   The Parties shall aim at increasing investment and trade in mining and raw materials.

2.   The cooperation shall focus in particular on the following areas:

- exchange of information on the prospects of the mining and non-ferrous metals sectors;
- the establishment of a legal framework for cooperation;
- trade matters;
- the adoption and implementation of environmental legislation;
- training;
- safety in the mining industry.

Article 53
Energy

1.   Cooperation shall take place within the principles of the market economy and the European Energy Charter, against a background of the progressive integration of the energy markets in Europe.

2.   Cooperation shall concentrate, inter alia, upon the formulation and development of energy policy. It shall include among others the following areas:

- improvement in management and regulation of the energy sector in line with a market economy;

- improvement of energy supply, including security of supply, in an economic and environmentally sound manner;

- promotion of energy saving and energy efficiency and implementation of the Energy Charter Protocol on Energy Efficiency and related environmental aspects;

- modernisation of energy infrastructures;

- improvement of energy technologies in supply and end use across the range of energy types;

- management and technical training in the energy sector;

- transportation and transit of energy materials and products;

- the introduction of the range of institutional, legal, fiscal and other conditions necessary to encourage increased energy trade and investment;

- development of hydro-electric and other renewable energy resources.

3.   The Parties shall exchange relevant information relating to investment projects in the energy sector, in particular concerning the production of energy resources and the construction and refurbishing of oil and gas pipelines or other means of transporting energy products. The Parties attach particular importance to cooperation regarding investments in the energy sector and the manner in which these are regulated. They shall cooperate with a view to implementing as efficaciously as possible the provisions of Title IV and of Article 46, in respect of investments in the energy sector.

Article 56
Postal services and telecommunications

Within their respective powers and competences the Parties shall expand and strengthen cooperation in the following areas:

- the establishment of policies and guidelines for the development of the telecommunications sector and postal services;

- development of principles of a tariff policy and marketing in telecommunications and postal services;

- transferring technology and know how, including on European Technical standards and certification systems;

- encouraging the development of projects for telecommunications and postal services and attracting investment;

- enhancing efficiency and quality of the provision of telecommunications and postal services, amongst others through liberalisation of activities of sub-sectors;

- advanced application of telecommunications, notably in the area of electronic funds transfer;

- management of telecommunications networks and their "optimisation";

- an appropriate regulatory basis for the provision of telecommunications and postal services and for the use of the radio frequency spectrum;

- training in the field of telecommunications and postal services for operations in market conditions.

Article 57
Financial services and fiscal institutions

1.   Cooperation shall in particular aim at facilitating the involvement of the Republic of Uzbekistan in universally accepted systems of mutual settlements. Technical assistance shall focus on:

- the development of a stock market and a securities market,

- the development of banking services, the development of a common market of credit resources, the involvement of the Republic of Uzbekistan in a universally accepted system of mutual settlements,

- the development of insurance services, which would, inter alia, create a favourable framework for Community companies' participation in the establishment of joint ventures in the insurance sector in the Republic of Uzbekistan, as well as the development of export credit insurance.

This cooperation shall in particular contribute to foster the development of relations between the Parties in the financial services sector.

2.   The Parties shall cooperate in developing the fiscal system and fiscal institutions in the Republic of Uzbekistan. This cooperation shall include the exchange of information and experience on fiscal matters and the training of personnel involved in the formulation and implementation of fiscal policy.

Article 58
Enterprise restructuring and privatisation

Recognising that privatisation is of fundamental importance to a sustainable economic recovery, the Parties agree to cooperate in the development of the necessary institutional, legal and methodological framework. Particular attention will be paid to the orderly and transparent nature of the privatisation process.

Technical assistance shall focus on, inter alia:

- the further development of an institutional base within the Government of the Republic of Uzbekistan to assist with defining and managing the privatisation process;

- the further development of the privatisation strategy of the Government of the Republic of Uzbekistan, including the legislative framework, and implementation mechanisms;

- furthering market approaches to land use and ownership, and the privatisation of land;

- the restructuring of those enterprises not yet ready for privatisation;

- the development of private enterprise, particularly in the small and medium enterprise sector;

- the development of investment privatisation funds systems.

The objective of this cooperation is also to contribute to the promotion of Community investment in the Republic of Uzbekistan.

Article 62
Small and medium-sized enterprises

1.   The Parties shall aim to develop and strengthen small and medium-sized enterprises (SMEs) and their associations and cooperation between SMEs in the Community and the Republic of Uzbekistan.

2.   Cooperation shall include technical assistance, in particular in the following areas:

- the development of a legislative framework for SMEs;

- the development of an appropriate infrastructure to support SMEs; to promote communication between SMEs both within Uzbekistan and further afield; and to train SMEs in the skills necessary to access funding;

- training in the areas of marketing, accounting and control of the quality of products.

ANNEX III

UZBEKISTAN'S RESERVATIONS IN ACCORDANCE WITH ARTICLE 22(4)

Under current Uzbek investment law, foreign companies wishing to establish in Uzbekistan are required to register at the Ministry of Justice and to provide documentation demonstrating that they have been duly registered in their home country and are financially solvent.

This registration procedure may not be used in order to nullify the benefits accorded to Community companies pursuant to Article 22 of this Agreement, nor to circumvent any other provisions of this Agreement.

ANNEX IV
FINANCIAL SERVICES REFERRED TO IN ARTICLE 25(3)

A financial service is any service of a financial nature offered by a financial service provider of a Party. Financial services include the following activities:

A.   All insurance and insurance-related services;

     1.   Direct insurance (including co-insurance).

         (i)   life

         (ii)   non-life

     2.   Reinsurance and retrocession.

     3.   Insurance intermediation, such as brokerage and agency.

     4.   Services auxiliary to insurance, such as consultancy, actuarial, risk assessment and claim settlement services.

B.   Banking and other financial services (excluding insurance).

     1.   Acceptance of deposits and other repayable funds from the public.

     2.   Lending of all types, including, inter alia, consumer credit, mortgage credit, factoring and financing of commercial transactions.

     3.   Financial leasing.

     4.   All payment and money transmission services, including credit charge and debit cards, travellers cheques and bankers drafts.

5.   Guarantees and commitments.

6.   Trading for own account or for the account of customers, whether on an exchange, in an over the counter market or otherwise, the following:

(a) money market instruments (cheques, bills, certificates of deposits, etc.)

(b) foreign exchange

(c) derivative products including, but not limited to, futures and options

(d) exchange rates and interest rate instruments, including products such as swaps, forward rate agreements, etc.

(e) transferable securities

(f) other negotiable instruments and financial assets, including bullion.

7. Participation in issues of all kinds of securities, including under-writing and placement as agent (whether publicly or privately) and provision of services related to such issues.

8. Money brokering.

9. Asset management, such as cash or portfolio management, all forms of collective investment management, pension fund management, custodial depository and trust services.

10. Settlement and clearing services for financial assets, including securities, derivative products, and other negotiable instruments.

11. Advisory intermediation and other auxiliary financial services on all the activities listed in points 1 to 10 above, including credit reference and analysis, investment and portfolio research and advice, advice on acquisitions and on corporate restructuring and strategy.

12. Provision and transfer of financial information, and financial data processing and related software by providers of other financial services.
The following activities are excluded from the definition of financial services:

(a) Activities carried out by central banks or by any other public institution in pursuit of monetary and exchange rate policies.

(b) Activities conducted by central banks, government agencies or departments, or public institutions, for the account or with the guarantee of the government, except when those activities may be carried out by financial service providers in competition with such public entities.

(c) Activities forming part of a statutory system of social security or public retirement plans, except when those activities may be carried out by financial service providers in competition with public entities or private institutions.

ANNEX V
INTELLECTUAL, INDUSTRIAL AND COMMERCIAL PROPERTY CONVENTIONS REFERRED TO IN ARTICLE 41

1. Article 41(2) concerns the following multilateral conventions:

- Berne Convention for the Protection of Literary and Artistic Works (Paris Act, 1971);

- International Convention for the Protection of Performers, Producers of Phonograms and Broadcasting Organizations (Rome, 1961);

- Protocol relating to the Madrid Agreement concerning the International Registration of Marks (Madrid, 1989);

- Nice Agreement concerning the International Classification of Goods and Services for the purposes of the Registration of Marks (Geneva 1977 and amended in 1979);

- Budapest Treaty on the International Recognition of the Deposit of Micro-organisms for the purposes of Patent Procedures (1977, modified in 1980);

- International Convention for the Protection of New Varieties of Plants (UPOV) (Geneva Act, 1991).

2.   The Cooperation Council may recommend that Article 41(2) shall apply to other multilateral conventions. If problems in the area of intellectual, industrial and commercial property affecting trading conditions were to occur, urgent consultations will be undertaken, at the request of either party, with a view to reaching mutually satisfactory solutions.

3.   The Parties confirm the importance they attach to the obligations arising from the following multilateral conventions:

- Paris Convention for the Protection of Industrial Property (Stockholm Act, 1967 and amended in 1979);

- Madrid Agreement concerning the International Registration of Marks (Stockholm Act, 1967 and amended in 1979);

- Patent Cooperation Treaty (Washington, 1970, amended in 1979 and modified in 1984).

4.   From the entry into force of this Agreement, the Republic of Uzbekistan shall grant to Community companies and nationals, in respect of the recognition and protection of intellectual, industrial and commercial property, treatment no less favourable than that granted by it to any third country under bilateral agreements.

5.   The provisions of paragraph 4 shall not apply to advantages granted by the Republic of Uzbekistan to any third country on an effective reciprocal basis and to advantages granted by the Republic of Uzbekistan to another country of the former USSR.

*

ARRANGEMENT ON TRADE AND ECONOMIC COOPERATION BETWEEN THE GOVERNMENT OF CANADA AND THE GOVERNMENT OF THE SWISS CONFEDERATION [*]

> The Arrangement on Trade and Economic Cooperation between the Government of Canada and the Government of the Swiss Confederation was signed at Bern, Switzerland on 9 December 1997. It took effect on the date of signature.

THE GOVERNMENT OF CANADA AND THE GOVERNMENT OF THE SWISS CONFEDERATION hereinafter referred to as "the Parties");

DESIRING to enhance the traditional bonds of friendship and cooperation between the two countries acknowledged in the Treaty of Friendship, Commerce, and Reciprocal Establishment Between Great Britain and Switzerland, signed at Berne on September 6, 1855; the Convention Additional to the Treaty of Friendship, Commerce, and Reciprocal Establishment Between Great Britain and the Swiss Confederation of September 6, 1855, signed at London on March 30, 1914; and the Convention for the Avoidance of Double Taxation with respect to Taxes on Income and on Capital between the Government of Canada and the Government of the Swiss Confederation done at Berne on May 5, 1997;

REAFFIRMING their respective rights and obligations under the Marrakesh Agreement establishing the World Trade Organization, (hereinafter the "WTO Agreement") and other multilateral instruments, in particular of the Organization for Economic Cooperation and Development (OECD), as well as under bilateral instruments of trade and economic cooperation;

ACKNOWLEDGING their mutual commitment toward the effective implementation of the WTO Agreement;

NOTING the importance they attach to the development of transatlantic relations;

ASPIRING to strengthen through continued and institutionalized dialogue, framework conditions favourable to the expansion and diversification of bilateral trade and investments;

WISHING to explore opportunities to strengthen bilateral cooperation in other areas and activities;

HAVE REACHED the following understanding:

---

[*]   *Source*: The Government of Canada and the Government of Switzerland (1997). "Arrangement on Trade and Economic Cooperation between the Government of Canada and the Government of the Swiss Confederation", available on the Internet (http://www.dfait-maeci.gc.ca/tna-nac/swiss-e.asp). [Note added by the editor.]

I. OBJECTIVES

The Parties will seek to:

a.   enhance economic relations between the two countries, in particular trade in goods and services as well as investment;

b.   strengthen their cooperation with a view to liberalizing trade between them by identifying and working toward the removal of measures that impede or distort bilateral trade and investment flows; and

c.   increase the participation of the private sector in both countries, in particular of the smaller and medium-sized enterprises, in bilateral economic cooperation.

II. LIBERALIZATION OF TRADE AND INVESTMENT

1.   In conformity with their international commitments, especially within the context of the WTO Agreement and the Organization for Economic Cooperation and Development (OECD), the Parties will endeavour to create the most favourable conditions for a liberalization of trade in goods and services as well as of investment between them in accordance with the enclosed Joint Work Program.

2.   The Parties will collaborate on investment issues, with a particular focus on cooperating in the development of a Multilateral Agreement on Investment and in an effective work program in the WTO.

3.   The Parties will examine all questions defined in the Joint Work Program influencing bilateral economic relations or their respective interests in respect of trade and investment in third countries, including multilateral and plurilateral questions of common interest arising in appropriate fora.

III. PROMOTION OF TRADE AND INVESTMENT

1.   The Parties will encourage the expansion of trade and investment between the private sectors of both countries.

2.   To this end they will, in particular, foster regular exchanges of information on opportunities for trade and investment and for other promotional initiatives, including contacts on the business level, in accordance with the Joint Work Program attached to this Arrangement.

IV. CONSULTATIVE GROUP

1.   The Parties hereby establish a Consultative Group to ensure the implementation of this Arrangement and the fulfilment of its objectives. The Government of Canada will be represented by the Minister for International Trade and the Government of the Swiss Confederation will be represented by the Minister for Economic Affairs, or their designees.

Private sector representatives may participate in the Consultative Group, with the consent of both Parties.

2.   The Consultative Group will convene periodically, ordinarily every eighteen months, alternatively in Canada and Switzerland, as may be arranged by the Parties. Sessions of the Consultative Group will be chaired by the host Party.

V. CONSULTATIONS

Either Party may request consultations with the other Party regarding any question relative to bilateral economic relations, trade and investment. Such consultations will take place promptly.

VI. FINAL CLAUSES

1.   Nothing in this Arrangement affects the respective rights and obligations of either Party to the other Party under Agreements, Conventions or other instruments to which they are both Parties.

2.   This Arrangement may be amended by the written concurrence of both Parties.

3.   The Arrangement comes into effect on signature and will remain in effect unless terminated by either Party on 180 days notice to the other Party.

ANNEX

JOINT WORK PROGRAM

- This Joint Work Program constitutes an integral part of the Arrangement on Trade and Economic Cooperation between the Government of Canada and the Government of the Swiss Confederation signed at Berne on December 9th 1997.

- The Joint Work Program, in conformity with the objectives of the said Arrangement, will include the following areas of priority interest:

a.   Liberalization of trade and strengthening of economic cooperation:

- identification and analysis of factors and measures, including those of third countries, influencing bilateral trade and investment;

- Definition of options and appropriate actions in order to promote market access for goods and services;

- negotiation of a Customs Cooperation and Mutual Assistance Agreement;

- mutual recognition of conformity assessment procedures in specific sectors; and cooperation in the WTO to bring about the progressive liberalization of public procurement, trade and competition, trade-related intellectual property measures and investment.

b.   Promotion of trade and investment:

- by exchanging information on international trade and on business opportunities in all economic sectors;

- by encouraging small and medium-sized enterprises to participate in bilateral trade and economic cooperation;

- by promoting economic missions, trade fairs and industrial expositions, symposia, conferences and technical presentations; and

- by encouraging joint efforts of the private sector in third country markets.

- The present Joint Work Program may be reviewed and revised periodically by the Consultative Group.

*

ARRANGEMENT ON TRADE AND ECONOMIC COOPERATION BETWEEN THE GOVERNMENT OF CANADA AND THE GOVERNMENT OF THE KINGDOM OF NORWAY[*]

The Arrangement on Trade and Economic Cooperation between the Government of Canada and the Government of the Kingdom of Norway was signed at Ottawa, Canada on 3 December 1997. It took effect on the date of signature.

THE GOVERNMENT OF CANADA AND THE GOVERNMENT OF THE KINGDOM OF NORWAY (hereinafter referred to as "Canada" and "Norway"),

DESIRING to enhance the traditional bonds of friendship and cooperation between the two countries acknowledged in the Convention of Commerce and Navigation between the United Kingdom and Sweden and Norway (with additional Article), done at London on March 18, 1826 and extended to Canada by the Convention signed at Kristiania., May 16, 1913,

BUILDING on their respective rights and obligations under the Agreement establishing the WTO, other multilateral instruments, in particular of the Organization for Economic Cooperation and Development (OECD), as well as under bilateral instruments of trade and economic cooperation,

REAFFIRMING their mutual commitment to effective implementation of the Marrakesh Agreement Establishing the World Trade Organization (WTO),

NOTING the importance they attach to the development of transatlantic relations,

ACKNOWLEDGING that nothing in this Arrangement affects the rights and obligations of either Party to the other Party under Agreements to which they are both Parties,

DECLARING their intention to strengthen, through continued and institutionalized dialogue, conditions favourable to the expansion and diversification of bilateral trade and investment,

WISHING to explore opportunities to strengthen bilateral cooperation in other areas and activities,

HAVE REACHED the following understanding:

---

[*] *Source*: The Government of Canada and the Government of Norway (1997). "Arrangement on Trade and Economic Cooperation between the Government of Canada and the Government of the Kingdom of Norway", available on the Internet (http://www.dfait-maeci.gc.ca/tna-nac/Norway-e.asp). [Note added by the editor.]

I. Objectives

Canada and Norway will seek to:

a.   enhance economic relations between the two countries, in particular trade in goods and services as well as investment;

b.   strengthen their cooperation with a view to liberalizing trade between them by identifying and working toward the removal of measures that impede or distort bilateral trade and investment flows; and

c.   increase the participation of the private sector in both countries, in particular of smaller and medium-sized enterprises, in bilateral economic cooperation.

II. Liberalization of Trade and Investment

1.   In conformity with their international commitments, especially within the context of the Marrakesh Agreement Establishing the World Trade Organization (WTO) and the Organization of Economic Cooperation and Development (OECD), Canada and Norway will endeavour to create the most favourable conditions for liberalization of trade in goods and services as well as of investment between them in accordance with the attached Joint Work Program.

2.   Canada and Norway will collaborate on investment issues, with a particular focus on cooperating in the development of a Multilateral Agreement on Investment (MAI) and in an effective work program in the WTO.

3.   Canada and Norway will examine all questions defined in the Joint Work Program influencing bilateral economic relations or their respective interests respecting trade and investment in third countries, including multilateral and plurilateral questions of common interest arising in appropriate fora.

III. Promotion of Trade and Investment

1.   C anada and Norway will encourage the expansion of trade and investment between the private sectors of both countries.

2.   To this end they will, in particular, foster regular exchanges of information on opportunities for trade and investment and for other promotional initiatives, including contacts on the business level, in accordance with the Joint Work Program, set out in the Annex to this Arrangement.

IV. Consultative Group

1.   Canada and Norway hereby establish a Consultative Group to ensure the implementation of this Arrangement and the fulfilment of its objectives. The Government of Canada will be represented by the Minister for International Trade, or designee, and the Government of the Kingdom of Norway will be represented at ministerial level or by designated representative.

Private sector representatives may participate in the Consultative Group, with the consent of both Canada and Norway.

2.   The Consultative Group will convene periodically, ordinarily every eighteen months, alternatively in Canada and Norway, as may be arranged by Canada and Norway. Sessions of the Consultative Group will be chaired by the host country.

V. Consultations

Canada and Norway declare their readiness, on request, to promptly enter into consultations on any question relating to bilateral economic relations, trade or investment.

VI. Other Provisions

1.   This Arrangement may be amended by the written concurrence of both Canada and Norway.

2.   The Arrangement comes into effect on signature and will remain in effect unless terminated by either Party on 180 days notice to the other Party.

Done in duplicate at Ottawa, this 3rd day of December 1997, in the English, French and Norwegian languages, each language version being equally valid.

ANNEX

JOINT WORK PROGRAM

1.   This Joint Work Program constitutes an integral part of the Arrangement on Trade and Economic Cooperation between the Government of Canada and the Government of the Kingdom of Norway signed on December 3, 1997.

2.   The Joint Work Program includes the following areas of priority interest:

   a.   Liberalization of trade and strengthening of economic cooperation

   •   identification and analysis of factors and measures, including those of third countries, influencing bilateral trade and investment;

   •   definition of options and appropriate actions in order to promote market access for goods and services; and

   •   cooperation in the WTO, inter alia, on public procurement, trade and environment, trade and competition, trade-related intellectual property measures, investment, and technical barriers to trade.

   b.   Promotion of trade and investment

- by exchanging information on technology, international trade and business opportunities in all economic sectors;

- by encouraging small and medium-sized enterprises to participate in trade and economic cooperation;

- by promoting economic missions, trade fairs and industrial expositions, symposia, conferences and technical presentations;

- by encouraging joint efforts of the private sector in third country markets; and by promoting cooperation between the petroleum sectors of Canada and Norway.

3.   This Joint Work Program may be reviewed and revised periodically by the Consultative

*

ARRANGEMENT ON TRADE AND ECONOMIC COOPERATION BETWEEN THE GOVERNMENT OF CANADA AND THE GOVERNMENT OF THE REPUBLIC OF ICELAND[*]

The Arrangement on Trade and Economic Cooperation between the Government of Canada and the Government of the Republic of Iceland was signed at Reykjavik, Iceland on 24 March 1998. It took effect on the date of signature.

Preamble

The Government of Canada and the Government of the Republic of Iceland (hereinafter referred to as "the Parties"),

Desiring to enhance the traditional bonds of friendship and cooperation between the two countries,

Reaffirming their respective rights and obligations under the Marrakesh Agreement establishing the World Trade Organization, (hereinafter the "WTO Agreement") and other multilateral instruments, in particular of the Organization for Economic Cooperation and Development (OECD), as well as under bilateral instruments of trade and economic cooperation,

Acknowledging their mutual commitment toward the effective implementation of the WTO Agreement,

Noting the importance they attach to the development of transatlantic relations,

Aspiring to strengthen through continued and institutionalized dialogue, framework conditions favourable to the expansion and diversification of bilateral trade and investment,

Wishing to explore opportunities to strengthen bilateral cooperation in other areas and activities,

Have reached the following understanding:

I Objectives

The Parties will seek to:

a.   enhance economic relations between the two countries, in particular trade in goods and services as well as investment;

---

[*]   *Source*: The Government of Canada and the Government of Iceland (1998). "Arrangement on Trade and Economic Cooperation between the Government of Canada and the Government of the Republic of Iceland", available on the Internet (http://www.dfait-maeci.gc.ca/tna-nac/iceland-e.asp). [Note added by the editor.]

b.   strengthen their cooperation with a view to liberalizing trade between them by identifying and working toward the removal of measures that impede or distort bilateral trade and investment flows; and

c.   increase the participation of the private sector in both countries, in particular smaller and medium-sized enterprises, in bilateral cooperation.

II Liberalization of trade and investment

1.   In conformity with their international commitments, especially within the context of the WTO Agreement and the Organization for Economic Cooperation and Development (OECD), the Parties will endeavour to create the most favourable conditions for the liberalization of trade in goods and services as well as of investment between them in accordance with the enclosed Joint Work Program.

2.   The Parties will collaborate on investment issues, with a particular focus on cooperating in the development of a Multilateral Agreement on Investment and an effective work program in the WTO.

3.   The Parties will examine all questions defined in the Joint Work Program influencing bilateral economic relations or their respective interests in respect of trade and investment in third countries, including multilateral and plurilateral questions of common interest arising in appropriate fora.

III Promotion of trade and investment

1.   The Parties will encourage the expansion of trade and investment between the private sectors of both countries.

2.   To this end they will, in particular, foster regular exchanges of information on opportunities for trade and investment and for other promotional initiatives, including contacts at the business level, in accordance with the Joint Work Program attached to this Arrangement.

IV Consultative Group

1.   The Parties hereby establish a Consultative Group to ensure the implementation of this Arrangement and the fulfillment of its objectives. The Government of Canada will be represented by the Minister for International Trade and the Government of the Republic of Iceland will be represented by the Minister for Foreign Affairs and External Trade, or their designees. Private sector representatives may participate in the Consultative Group, with the consent of both Parties.

2.   The Consultative Group will convene periodically, ordinarily every eighteen. months, alternatively in Canada and Iceland, as may be arranged by the Parties. Sessions of the Consultative Group will be chaired by the host Party.

V Consultations

Either Party may request consultations with the other Party regarding any question relative to bilateral economic relations, trade and investment. Such consultations will take place promptly.

VI Final Clauses

1.   Nothing in this Arrangement affects the respective rights and obligations of either Party to the other Party under Agreements, Conventions or other instruments to which they are both Parties.

2.   This Arrangement may be amended by the written concurrence of both Parties.

3.   The Arrangement comes into effect on signature and will remain in effect unless terminated by either Party on 180 days notice to the other Party.

Done in duplicate at Reykjavik, on March 24th, 1998, in the French, English and Icelandic languages, each language version being equally valid.

ANNEX

Joint Work Program

1.   This Joint Work Program constitutes an integral part of the Arrangement on Trade and Economic Cooperation between the Government of Canada and the Government of the Republic of Iceland signed at Reykjavik on March 24th 1998.

2.   The Joint Work Program, in conformity with the objectives of the said Arrangement, will include the following areas of priority interest:

   a.   *Liberalization of trade and strengthening of economic cooperation*

   - identification and analysis of factors and measures, including those of third countries, influencing bilateral trade and investment;

   - definition of options and appropriate actions in order to promote market access for goods and services; and

   - cooperation in the WTO inter alia in trade and environment, trade and competition, trade-related intellectual property measures and technical barriers to trade, as well as the progressive liberalization of public procurement and investment.

   b.   *Promotion of trade and investment*

   - the exchange of information on technology, international trade and on business opportunities in all economic sectors;

- the encouragement of small and medium-sized enterprises to participate in trade and economic cooperation;

- the promotion of economic missions, trade fairs and industrial expositions, symposia, conferences and technical presentations;

- the encouragement of joint efforts of the private sector in third country markets; and the promotion of cooperation in the fisheries sector.

3.   The present Joint Work Program may be reviewed and revised periodically by the Consultative Group.

*

TRADE AND INVESTMENT COOPERATION ARRANGEMENT AND ACTION PLAN BETWEEN CANADA AND THE MERCOSUR[*]

The Trade and Investment Cooperation Arrangement and Action Plan between Canada and the MERCOSUR was signed in Buenos Aires, Argentina on 16 June 1998. It took effect on the date of signature.

Canada and the Southern Common Market (MERCOSUR), hereinafter referred to as "the Parties";

Desiring to enhance the long-standing bonds of friendship and cooperation between Canada and MERCOSUR;

Noting the importance they attach to the strengthening of trade and economic relations in the Western Hemisphere;

Reaffirming their resolution to conclude the negotiation of Free Trade Area of the Americas no later than 2005;

Building on their mutual commitment to the World Trade Organization and their cooperation in the Cairns Group;

Declaring their intention to establish a bilateral framework for the expansion and diversification of Canada-MERCOSUR trade and investment;

Wishing to explore opportunities to strengthen bilateral cooperation in other areas and activities;

Have reached the following understanding:

1. Objectives

The Parties will seek to:

a.   enhance economic relations between Canada and the MERCOSUR, in particular concerning trade in goods and services, as well as investment;

b.   strengthen their cooperation with a view to liberalizing trade and investment between them by identifying those measures that impede or distort trade and investment flows between Canada and the MERCOSUR;

---

[*]   *Source*: The Government of Canada and MERCOSUR (1998). "Trade and Investment Cooperation Arrangement and Action Plan between Canada and the MERCOSUR", available on the Internet (http://www.dfait-maeci.gc.ca/tna-nac/Mercosur-e.asp). [Note added by the editor.]

c.   facilitate the increased involvement of the private sector, in particular of the smaller and medium-sized enterprises, in trade and commercial cooperation between Canada and the MERCOSUR;

d.   increase mutual understanding of their respective positions in the negotiations of the Free Trade Area of the Americas; and,

e.   develop greater co-ordination and consultation in the World Trade Organization and in the Cairns Group.

2. Expansion of trade and investment

1.   The Parties will endeavour to create the most favourable conditions for expanding trade in goods and services, and the expansion of investment between them in accordance with the annexed Action Plan.

2.   The Parties will examine all questions set out in the Action Plan influencing bilateral economic relations or their respective interests in respect of trade and investment in third countries, including multilateral and plurilateral questions of common interest arising in appropriate fora.

3.   In enhancing the expansion of trade and investment between the private sectors in Canada and the MERCOSUR, the Parties will, in particular, foster regular exchanges of information on opportunities for trade and investment and for other promotional initiatives, including contacts at the business level, in accordance with the annexed Action Plan.

3. Consultative Group and Advisory Council

1.   The Parties establish the Consultative Group on Trade and Investment Cooperation (hereinafter referred to as the Consultative Group) chaired by high-level officials of the Parties responsible for international trade, or their designated alternate. In the case of the MERCOSUR, the responsible representatives are the Coordinators of the Common Market Group. The Consultative Group may comprise other high-level officials or their designated alternate as may be mutually decided from time to time.

2.   The Consultative Group will convene periodically, ordinarily once every twelve months, to review and direct progress on the Action Plan. Special meetings will be held at the request of either Party. The meetings of the Consultative Group will alternate between Canada and MERCOSUR or another agreed location at the request of either Party. Sessions of the Consultative Group will be chaired by the host Party.

3.   The Parties will establish an Advisory Council of business representatives to advise them on areas of particular concern to the private sector.

4. Final Clauses

1.   Nothing in this Arrangement affects the respective rights and obligations of either Party to the other Party under Agreements, Conventions or other instruments to which they are both Parties, either individually or collectively.

2.   This Arrangement may be amended by the written concurrence of both Parties.

3.   The Arrangement comes into effect on signature and will remain in effect unless terminated by either Party on 180 days notice to the other Party.

Done at Buenos Aires, on June 16, 1998, in two originals in the English, French, Portuguese and Spanish languages, being all equally valid.

Trade and Investment Cooperation Arrangement between Canada and the Mercosur Action Plan

1.   This Action Plan constitutes an integral part of the Trade and Investment Cooperation Arrangement between Canada and the MERCOSUR signed at Buenos Aires on June 16, 1998.

2.   The Action Plan, in conformity with the objectives of the said Arrangement, will include the following areas of priority interest:

   a.   Expansion of trade and strengthening of economic cooperation

   - identification and analysis of factors and measures, including those of third countries, influencing bilateral trade and investment;

   - definition of options and appropriate actions in order to promote market access for goods and services;

   - negotiation of Foreign Investment Protection Agreements between Canada and individual MERCOSUR countries;

   - development of Customs Cooperation and Mutual Assistance Arrangements;

   - development of cooperative arrangements in the areas of labour and environment, taking into account related discussions at the World Trade Organization and International Labour Organization, with a view to fostering the participation of civil society of both Parties in bilateral trade and investment relations;

   - dialogue on regulatory reform and development of mutual recognition of conformity assessment procedures in specific sectors to be identified;

- consultations and, as appropriate, coordination in the negotiation and implementation of the Free Trade Area of the Americas;

- consultations on areas of mutual interest in the Cairns Group; and

- cooperation in the World Trade Organization and other appropriate fora regarding any issue of common interest.

b.   Promotion of trade and investment

- exchange of information on international trade and on business opportunities in all economic sectors;

- encouragement of small and medium-sized enterprises to participate in bilateral trade and economic cooperation;

- promotion of business missions, trade fairs, strategic venturing initiatives, symposia, conferences and technical presentations;

- promotion of efforts of the private sector of both Parties in third country markets;

- fostering of joint partnerships in the area of environmental technologies; and,

- cooperation between official institutions responsible for trade and investment promotion.

3.   The present Action Plan will be reviewed periodically and revised as appropriate by the Consultative Group.

*

TRADE AND INVESTMENT COOPERATION ARRANGEMENT BETWEEN THE GOVERNMENT OF CANADA ANDTHE GOVERNMENT OF THE REPUBLIC OF SOUTH AFRICA [*]

The Trade and Investment Cooperation Arrangement between the Government of Canada and the Government of the Republic of South Africa was signed at Ottawa, Canada on 24 September 1998. It took effect on the date of signature.

PREAMBLE

THE GOVERNMENT OF CANADA AND THE GOVERNMENT OF THE REPUBLIC OF SOUTH AFRICA, hereinafter jointly referred to as 'the Parties"; and in the singular as "a party";

INSPIRED by the strong desire to strengthen the traditional ties of fiimLship and cooperation existing between them;

DETERMINED to contribute, through bade and investment, to achieving greater well-being for their peoples;

BUILDING on their mutual commitment to the World Trade

CONVINCED of the importance of reinforcing the flow of trade in goods and services;

NOTING the value of promoting a havourable environment for trade and investment;

RECOGNIZING that direct foreign investment provides benefits to both countries;

RECOGNIZING their commitment to respect, promote and realize fundamental labour rights based on the core conventions of the International Labour Organization;

REAFFIRMING their commitment to achieving economic development and greater integration of developing countries into the global economy;

HAVE REACHED the following understanding:

---

[*] *Source*: The Government of Canada and the Government of South Africa (1998). "Trade and Investment Cooperation Arrangement between the Government of Canada and the Government of the Republic of South Africa", available on the Internet (http://www.dfait-maeci.gc.ca/tna-nac/south-africa-e.asp). [Note added by the editor.]

ARTICLE I
Objectives

The Parties will seek to:

1.   enhance economic relations between the two countries, in particular in trade in goods and services and in investment;

2.   strengthen cooperation with a view to liberalizing trade between them in accordance with the principles of the World Trade Organization,

3.   promote a favourable environment and complementary, activities to encourage private sector investment between the countries;

4.   highlight the importance of private sector trade and investment initiatives as sources of prosperity and means of promoting economic development.

ARTICLE II
Trade and Investment Cooperation

To encourage the expansion of bilateral trade and investment relations, the Parties will undertake initiatives in areas such as the following, as specified in the Action Plan attached to, this Arrangement:

1.   Promotion of expanded business contacts as the means of encouraging broader trade and investment links between the private sectors of the two countries;

2.   Support for trade promotion activities;

3.   Exchange of views and information on bilateral and multilateral trade in goods' and services and investment;

4.   Identification of measures that impede or distort bilateral trade and investment flows and work toward the removal of such measures;

5.   Finalization and implementation of a bilateral foreign investment promotion and protection agreement;

6.   Development of training in trade-related areas;

7.   Identification of possible area of trade and investment that offer potential for increasing trade flows between the countries and to third markets.

ARTICLE III
Consultative Group

1.   The Parties establish a Consultative Group on Trade and Investment Cooperation, hereinafter referred to as "the Consultative Group" to ensure the implementation of this

Arrangement and the fulfilment of its objectives, in particular, progress in implementing the Action Plan attached to this Arrangement. The Consultative Group may periodically revise the attached Action Plan.

2.   In the Consultative Group, the Government of Canada will be represented by the Minister for International Trade and the Government of South Africa will be represented by the Minister of Trade and Industry, or their designees. Each Party will determine the composition of its own delegations to meetings of the Consultative Group.

3.   The Consultative Group will convene periodically, ordinarily once every 18 months. The meetings of the Consultative Group will alternate between Canada and South Africa, as may be arranged by the Parties. Sessions of the Consultative Group will be chaired by the host Party.

ARTICLE IV
Consultations

Either Party may request consultations with the other Party regarding any questions relative to bilateral trade and investment relations. Such consultations win take place promptly.

ARTICLE V
Final Clauses

1.   Nothing in this Arrangement affects the respective rights and obligations of either Party to the other Party under Agreements, Conventions or other instruments to which they are both Parties.

2.   This Arrangement may be amended by the written concurrence of both Parties.

3.   The Arrangement comes into effect upon signature and will remain in effect unless terminated by either Party on 180 days notice to the other Party.

Done in duplicate at Ottawa, on Speptember 24, 1998, in the English and languages, each language version being equally valid.

Action Plan

1.   This Action Plan constitutes an integral part of the Trade and Investment Cooperation Arrangement between the Government of Canada and the Government of the Republic of South Africa, signed at Ottawa on September 24, 1998.

2.   The Action Plan, in conformity with the objectives of thist Arrangement, comprises the following:

   a.   Expansion of trade and investment dialogue and strengthening of economic cooperation:

- cooperation in the World Trade Organization and other appropriate for a regarding issues of common interest;

- consultations on area of mutual interest in the Cairns Group;

- support for trade policy capacity building, in areas such as bade negotiations, through activities including visits by specialists, workshops and officer exchanges;

- identification of options and appropriate actions in order to facilitate trade and to improve market access for goods and services;

- finalization and implementation of the Foreign Investment Promotion and Protection Agreement between the Parties;

- ongoing cooperation in the context of international labour standards, with particular reference to the promotion of the Declaration on Fundamental Principles and Rights at Work of the International Labour Organization;

- establishment of a dialogue on a possible General Security of Information Agreement between the Parties.

b.   Promotion of trade and investment:

- fostering of business links in key sectors, including communications,

- transportation, mining and other resource sectors, education, information technology, and engineering services, including environmental goods and services;

- encouragement of small and medium-sized enterprises' participation in bilateral trade;

- promotion of trade by means of business missions, trade fairs, strategic

- venturing initiatives, symposia, conferences and technical presentations;

- encouragement of joint efforts by the private sectors of both Parties in third country markets;

- encouragement of business links being developed through the twinning efforts of Canadian and South African provinces; .

- pursuit of a collaborative Centre of Excellence in the area of advanced tele-learning in the Republic of South Africa, for eventual export to other markets in Africa.

*

TRADE AND INVESTMENT COOPERATION ARRANGEMENT BETWEEN THE GOVERNMENT OF CANADA AND THE GOVERNMENTS OF THE ANDEAN COMMUNITY *

The Trade and Investment Cooperation Arrangement between the Government of Canada and the Governments of the Andean Community was signed at Ottawa, Canada on May 31, 1999. It took effect on the date of signature.

THE GOVERNMENT OF CANADA AND THE GOVERNMENTS OF BOLIVIA, COLOMBIA, ECUADOR, PERU AND VENEZUELA, member countries of the Andean Community, hereinafter called Athe Parties;

Inspired by the firm desire to strengthen the ties of friendship and cooperation between Canada and the Andean Community;

Determined to cooperatively promote trade and investment, for the greater welfare of their peoples;

Building on their mutual commitment to the World Trade Organization (WTO);

Reaffirming their intention to conclude the negotiation of the Free Trade Area of the Americas no later than 2005;

Noting the importance they attach to strengthening trade relations and to investments in the Western Hemisphere;

Recognizing the importance of promoting a suitable environment for trade and investment between Canada and the Andean Community;

Desiring to ensure that the goals of trade liberalization and the principles of sustainable development are mutually supportive and consistent with World Trade Organization (WTO) and other international obligations;

Recognizing the significance of the promotion the International Labour Organization (ILO) Declaration of Fundamental Principles and Rights at Work to the economic welfare of all parties;

Wishing to foster the engagement of citizens in the process of trade liberalization;

Wishing to explore opportunities to strengthen bilateral and multilateral cooperation in areas of mutual interest, such as health, culture, indigenous communities and the environment;

Have reached the following understanding:

---

* *Source*: The Government of Canada and the Governments of the Andean Community (1999). "Trade and Investment Cooperation Arrangement between the Government of Canada and the Governments of the Andean Community", available on the Internet (http://www.dfait-maeci.gc.ca/tna-nac/andean-e.asp). [Note added by the editor.]

ARTICLE I
OBJECTIVES

The Parties will seek to:

a.   Intensify and strengthen economic relations between them, in particular, concerning trade in goods and services, investment and technology transfer;

b.   Promote the liberalization of trade and investment by identifying those measures that impede or distort trade and investment flows and by seeking their elimination;

c.   Promote and maintain an environment favourable to the development of trade and investment;

d.   Facilitate the greater participation and involvement of the private sectors of the Parties in strengthening trade and commercial cooperation;

e.   Promote the coordination of their respective positions in negotiations on the Free Trade Area of the Americas;

f.   Promote greater coordination in the World Trade Organization; and

g.   Promote regular sharing of information on trade and investment opportunities and other promotional initiatives.

ARTICLE II
PRINCIPLES

In carrying out the activities specified in this Arrangement, the Parties reaffirm that the promotion of trade and investment between them will be in conformity with the principles and obligations of the World Trade Organization and in accordance with the principles and objectives underlying the FTAA negotiations as stipulated in the Ministerial Declaration of San José and the Declaration of Santiago.

The Parties shall also consider the differences in degree of economic development and the size of their respective economies.

ARTICLE III
CONSULTATIVE GROUP

1.   The Parties establish a trade and investment consultative group, hereinafter called "the Consultative Group", consisting of the ministers responsible for international trade or their representatives, in order to ensure compliance with this Arrangement and its objectives, in particular, the implementation of the Action Plan attached hereto. The Consultative Group may periodically modify the Action Plan.

To support their participation, the member countries of the Andean Community may call on the Office of the Secretary General of the Andean Community for assistance.

2.   The Consultative Group shall meet periodically, with regular meetings every 18 months. The meetings of the Consultative Group will alternate between members of the Andean Community and Canada or may be held in any other agreed-upon location. Special meetings may be called at the request of any of the Parties.

3.   The Parties may consult, using their own internal mechanisms, the private sector in their respective countries on matters related to the work of the Consultative Group. The Consultative Group may invite representatives of the private sector of the Parties to express their opinions on subjects of interest to them. The Parties shall notify each other of the participation of private-sector representatives before the meetings of the Consultative Group take place.

4.   The Parties may hold consultations on any matter related to trade relations and investments. These consultations shall take place promptly.

ARTICLE IV
EXPANSION OF TRADE AND INVESTMENT

1.   The Parties shall promote the expansion of trade in goods and services between them, as well as investments, in accordance with the annexed Action Plan.

2.   The Parties shall examine all questions set out in the Action Plan influencing economic relations between the Parties, including multilateral and plurilateral questions of common interest arising in appropriate fora.

3.   In order to stimulate expansion of trade and investment, the Parties shall promote regular sharing of information on trade and investment opportunities and other promotional initiatives, including, where possible, business contacts, in accordance with the annexed Action Plan.

ARTICLE V
FINAL CLAUSES

1.   Nothing in this Arrangement affects the respective rights and obligations of either Party to the other Party under Agreements, Conventions or other instruments to which they are both Parties, either individually or collectively.

2.   This Arrangement may be amended by the written concurrence of both Parties.

3.   This Arrangement shall take effect on signature and shall remain in force unless terminated by mutual consent of the Parties or by either of the Parties on 180 days written notice to the other Party.

Done in six original copies at Ottawa on this 31st day of May, 1999, in English, French and Spanish, the version in each language being equally valid.

ACTION PLAN

1.   This Action Plan constitutes an integral part of the Trade and Investment Cooperation Arrangement between the Government of Canada and the Andean Community signed in Ottawa

on the 31stday of May 1999, and comprises the following priorities. This Action Plan will be reviewed periodically and revised, as appropriate, by the Consultative Group.

a.   Expansion of trade and strengthening of economic cooperation:

- define options and appropriate actions to promote greater market access for goods and services;

- explore opportunities to review market access under existing tariff programs;

- continue negotiations on Foreign Investment Protection Agreements and Double Taxation Agreements between Canada and the countries of the Andean Community;

- identify opportunities for technical cooperation on customs and taxation;

- consult and, as appropriate, coordinate activities related to the negotiation and implementation of the Free Trade Area of the Americas;

- coordinate, as appropriate, activities related to the World Trade Organization and other appropriate fora on any issue of common interest

b.   Promotion of trade and investment:

- exchange information on international trade and on business and investment opportunities in all economic sectors;

- promote participation of small and medium-sized businesses in bilateral trade and economic cooperation;

- promote business missions, trade fairs, strategic alliances, symposia, conferences and technical presentations;

- promote efforts of the private sector of both Parties in third-country markets;

- promote joint ventures in the field of environmental technologies.

c.   Cooperation:

- Cooperation between the public bodies responsible for trade and the agencies of the Parties that promote foreign trade, so as to make greater use of the General Preferential Tariff (GPT).

- Technical assistance and training of experts, officials, students and technicians, as appropriate, in order to meet the requirements of the markets of the Parties.

*

FREE TRADE AGREEMENT BETWEEN THE EFTA STATES AND THE UNITED MEXICAN STATES[*]
[excerpts]

> The Free Trade Agreement between the EFTA States and the United Mexican States was signed on 27 November 2000. It entered into force on 1 July 2001 for Mexico, Norway and Switzerland. For Iceland it entered into force on 1 October 2001. For Liechtenstein it entered into force on 1 November 2001.

PREAMBLE

The Republic of Iceland, the Principality of Liechtenstein, the Kingdom of Norway and the Swiss Confederation (hereinafter referred to collectively as the EFTA States) and The United Mexican States, (hereinafter referred to as Mexico) hereinafter referred to as the Parties,

CONSIDERING the important links existing between Mexico and the EFTA States, and recognizing the common wish to strengthen these links, thus establishing close and lasting relations;

DESIROUS to contribute to the harmonious development and expansion of world trade and provide a catalyst to broader international and transatlantic co-operation;

DETERMINED to create an expanded and secure market for goods and services in their territories;

RESOLVED to ensure a stable and predictable environment for investment;

INTENDING to enhance the competitiveness of their firms in global markets;

AIMING to create new employment opportunities and improve working conditions and living standards in their respective territories;

DETERMINED to ensure that the gains from trade liberalisation are not offset by the erection of private, anti-competitive barriers;

WISHING to establish a free trade area through the removal of trade barriers;

CONVINCED that this Agreement will create conditions encouraging economic, trade and investment relations between them;

BUILDING on their respective rights and obligations under the Marrakesh Agreement Establishing the World Trade Organization (hereinafter referred to as "the WTO") and other multilateral and bilateral instruments of co-operation;

---

[*] *Source*: European Free Trade Association Secretariat (2000). "Free Trade Agreement between the EFTA States and the United Mexican States", available on the Internet (http://secretariat.efta.int). [Note added by the editor.]

RESOLVED to foster environmental protection and conservation, and to promote sustainable development,

HAVE AGREED, in pursuit of the above, to conclude this Free Trade Agreement:

GENERAL PROVISIONS

ARTICLE 1
Objectives

1   The EFTA States and Mexico hereby establish a Free Trade Area in accordance with the provisions of this Agreement.

2.   The objectives of this Agreement are:

   (a)   the progressive and reciprocal liberalisation of trade in goods, in conformity with Article XXIV of the General Agreement on Tariffs and Trade (hereinafter referred to as "the GATT 1994');

   (b)   to provide fair conditions of competition affecting trade between the Parties;

   (c)   to open the government procurement markets of the Parties;

   (d)   the liberalisation of trade in services, in conformity with Article V of the General Agreement on Trade in Services (hereinafter referred to as "the GATS');

   (e)   the progressive liberalisation of investment;

   (f)   to ensure an adequate and effective protection of intellectual property rights, in accordance with the highest international standards; and

   (g)   to contribute in this way, by the removal of barriers to trade, to the harmonious development and expansion of world trade.

III SERVICES AND INVESTMENT

SECTION 1 - TRADE IN SERVICES

ARTICLE 19
Coverage

1.   For the purposes of this Section, trade in services is defined as the supply of a service:

   (a)   from the territory of a Party into the territory of another Party;

   (b)   in the territory of a Party to the service consumer of another Party;

     (c)   by a service supplier of a Party, through commercial presence in the territory of another Party;

     (d)   by a service supplier of a Party, through presence of natural persons in the territory of another Party.

2.   This Section applies to trade in all services sectors with the exception of:

     (a)   air services, including domestic and international air transportation services, whether scheduled or non-scheduled, and related services in support of air services, other than:

          (i)   aircraft repair and maintenance services during which an aircraft is withdrawn from servic e;

          (ii)   the selling and marketing of air transport services;

          (iii)   computer reservation system (CRS) services.

3.   Maritime transport and financial services shall be governed by the provisions of Sections II and III, respectively, unless otherwise specified.

4.   Nothing in this Section shall be construed to impose any obligation with respect to government procurement.

5.   Subsidies related to trade in services shall not be covered under this Section. The Parties shall pay particular attention to any disciplines agreed under the negotiations mandated by Article XV of the GATS with a view to their incorporation into this Agreement.

6.   This Section applies to measures taken by central, regional or local governments and authorities as well as by non-governmental bodies in the exercise of powers delegated by central, regional or local governments or authorities.

ARTICLE 20
Definitions

For purposes of this Section:

"commercial presence" means:

(i)   as regards nationals, the right to set up and manage undertakings, which they effectively control. This shall not extend to seeking or taking employment in the labour market or confer a right of access to the labour market of another Party; [2]

(ii)   as regards juridical persons, the right to take up and pursue the economic activities covered by this Section by means of the setting up and management of subsidiaries, branches or any other form of secondary establishment; [3]

---

[2] The right to set up undertakings which they effectively control includes the right to acquire controlling stakes in a company of a Party

"EFTA State juridical person" or "Mexican juridical person" means a juridical person set up in accordance with the laws of an EFTA State or of Mexico, respectively, and having its registered office, central administration, or principal place of business in the territory of an EFTA State or of Mexico, respectively;

Should the juridical person have only its registered office or central administration in the territory of an EFTA State or Mexico, respectively, it shall not be considered as an EFTA State or a Mexican juridical person, respectively, unless its operations possess a real and continuous link with the economy of an EFTA State or Mexico, respectively;

"national" means a natural person who is a national of one of the EFTA States or Mexico in accordance with their respective legislations;[4]

"service supplier" of a Party means any person of a Party that seeks to provide or provides a service;

"subsidiary" means a juridical person that is effectively controlled by another juridical person.

"territory" means the geographical area referred to in paragraph 1 of Article 2.

ARTICLE 21
Market access

In those sectors and modes of supply which shall be liberalised pursuant to the decision provided for in paragraph 3 of Article 24, no Party shall adopt or maintain:

(a) limitations on the number of service suppliers whether in the form of numerical quotas, monopolies, exclusive service suppliers or the requirements of an economic needs test;

(b) limitations on the total value of service transactions or assets in the form of numerical quotas or the requirement of an economic needs test;

(c) limitations on the total number of service operations or on the total quantity of service output expressed in the terms of designated numerical units in the form of quotas or the requirement of an economic needs test;

(d) limitations on the total number of natural persons that may be employed in a particular service sector or that a service supplier may employ and who are necessary for, and directly related to, the supply of a specific service in the form of numerical quotas or a requirement of an economic needs test;

(e) limitations on the participation of foreign capital in terms of maximum percentage limit on foreign shareholding or the total value of individual or aggregate foreign investment; and

---

[3] The setting up of secondary establishments includes the right to acquire controlling stakes in a company of a Party.

[4] National includes a permanent resident if he or she is treated as a national in accordance with the legislation of such Party.

(f)   measures which require specific types of legal entities or joint ventures through which a service supplier of another Party may supply a service.

ARTICLE 22
Most favoured nation treatment

1.   Subject to exceptions that may derive from harmonisation of regulations based on agreements concluded by a Party with a third country providing for mutual recognition in accordance with Article VII of the GATS, the EFTA States and Mexico shall accord to service suppliers of another Party treatment no less favourable than that they accord to like service suppliers of any other country.

2.   Treatment granted under other agreements concluded by one of the Parties with a third country which have been notified under Article V of the GATS shall be excluded from this provision.

3.   If a Party enters into an agreement of the type referred to in paragraph 2, it shall afford adequate opportunity to the other Parties to negotiate the benefits granted therein. 4. The Parties agree to review the exclusion provided for in paragraph 2 with a view to its deletion not later than three years after the entry into force of this Agreement.

ARTICLE 23
National treatment

1.   Each Party shall, in accordance with Article 24, grant to service suppliers of another Party, in respect of all measures affecting the supply of services, treatment no less favourable than that it accords to its own like service suppliers.

2.   A Party may meet the requirement of paragraph 1 by according to service suppliers of another Party, either formally identical treatment or formally different treatment to that it accords to its own like service suppliers.

3.   Formally identical or formally different treatment shall be considered to be less favourable if it modifies the conditions of competition in favour of service suppliers of a Party compared to like service suppliers of the other Party.

ARTICLE 24
Trade liberalisation

1.   As provided for in paragraphs 2 to 4, the Parties shall liberalise trade in services between themselves, in conformity with Article V of the GATS.

2.   From the entry into force of this Agreement, neither Party shall adopt new, or more, discriminatory measures as regards services or service suppliers of another Party, in comparison with the treatment accorded to its own like services or service suppliers.

3.   No later than three years following the entry into force of this Agreement, the Joint Committee shall adopt a decision providing for the elimination of substantially all remaining discrimination between the Parties in the sectors and modes of supply covered by this Section. That decision shall contain:

(a)   a list of commitments establishing the level of liberalisation which the Parties agree to grant each other at the end of a transitional period of ten years from the entry into force of this Agreement;

(b)   a liberalisation calendar for each Party in order to reach, at the end of the ten-year transitional period, the level of liberalisation described in paragraph a).

4.   Except as provided for in paragraph 2, Articles 21, 22 and 23 shall become applicable in accordance with the calendar and subject to any reservations stipulated in the Parties' lists of commitments provided for in paragraph 3.

5.   The Joint Committee may amend the liberalisation calendar and the list of commitments established in accordance with paragraph 3, with a view to removing or adding exceptions.

ARTICLE 25
Right to regulate

1.   Each Party may regulate, and introduce new regulations, on the supply of services within its territory in order to meet national policy objectives, in so far as regulations do not impair on any rights and obligations arising under this Agreement.

2.   Each Party shall ensure that all measures of general application affecting trade in services are administered in a reasonable, objective and impartial manner.

ARTICLE 26
Mutual recognition

1.   In principle no later than three years following the entry into force of this Agreement, the Joint Committee shall establish the necessary steps for the negotiation of agreements providing for the mutual recognition of requirements, qualifications, licenses and other regulations, for the purpose of the fulfilment, in whole or in part, by service suppliers of the criteria applied by each Party for the authorisation, licensing, operation and certification of service suppliers and, in particular, professional services.

2.   Any such agreement shall be in conformity with the relevant provisions of the WTO and, in particular, Article VII of the GATS.

SECTION II - MARITIME TRANSPORT

ARTICLE 27
International maritime transport

1.   This Section applies to international maritime transport, including door-to-door and intermodal transport operations involving a sea- leg.

2.   The definitions contained in Article 20 apply to this Section. 5

3.   In view of the existing levels of liberalisation between the Parties in international maritime transport:

(a)   the Parties shall continue to effectively apply the principle of unrestricted access to the international maritime market and traffic on a commercial and non-discriminatory basis;

(b)   each Party shall continue to grant to ships operated by service suppliers of another Party treatment no less favourable than that accorded to its own ships with regard to, inter alia, access to ports, use of infrastructure and auxiliary maritime services of the ports, as well as related fees and charges, customs facilities and the assignment of berths and facilities for loading and unloading.

5   Notwithstanding Article 20, shipping companies established outside the EFTA States or Mexico and controlled by nationals of an EFTA State or Mexico, respectively, shall also be beneficiaries of the provisions of this Chapter, if their vessels are registered in accordance with their respective legislation, in that EFTA State or in Mexico and carry the flag of an EFTA State or Mexico.

4.   Each Party shall permit to service suppliers of another Party to have a commercial presence in its territory under conditions of establishment and operation no less favourable than those accorded to its own service suppliers or those of any third country, whichever are the better, in conformity with the applicable legislation and regulations in each Party.

5.   Paragraph 4 shall become applicable in accordance with the calendar and subject to any reservation stipulated in the Parties' list of commitments provided for in paragraph 3 of Article 24.

SECTION III - FINANCIAL SERVICES

ARTICLE 28
Definitions

In accordance with the terms of the Annex on Financial Services to the GATS and the GATS Understanding on Commitments in Financial Services, for the purposes of this Section:

"commercial presence" means a juridical entity within a Party's territory that supplies financial services and includes wholly or partly owned subsidiaries, joint ventures, partnerships, branches, agencies, representative offices or other organisations through franchising operations.

"financial service" means any service of a financial nature offered by a financial service supplier of a Party. Financial services comprise the following activities:

A.   Insurance and insurance-related services:

1.   direct insurance (including co-insurance):

(a) life;
(b) non- life;

2.   reinsurance and retrocession;

3.   insurance inter-mediation, such as brokerage and agency; and

4.   services auxiliary to insurance, such as consultancy, actuarial, risk assessment and claim settlement services.

B.   Banking and other financial services (excluding insurance):

1.   acceptance of deposits and other repayable funds from the public;

2.   lending of all types, including consumer credit, mortgage credit, factoring and financing of commercial transaction;

3.   financial leasing;

4.   all payment and money transmission services, including credit, charge and debit cards, travellers cheques and bankers drafts;

5.   guarantees and commitments;

6.   trading for own account or for account of customers, whether on an exchange, in an over-the-counter market or otherwise, the following:

   (a)   money market instruments (including cheques, bills, certificates of deposits);

   (b)   foreign exchange;

   (c)   derivative products including, but not limited to, futures and options;

   (d)   exchange rate and interest rate instruments, including products such as swaps, forward rate agreements;

   (e)   transferable securities;

   (f)   other negotiable instruments and financial assets, including bullion;

7.   participation in issues of all kinds of securities, including underwriting and placement as agent (whether publicly or privately) and provision of services related to such issues;

8.   money broking;

9.   asset management, such as cash or portfolio management, all forms of collective investment management, pension fund management, custodial, depository and trust services;

10.   settlement and clearing services for financial assets, including securities, derivative products, and other negotiable instruments;

11.   provision and transfer of financial information, and financial data processing and related software by suppliers of other financial services;

12.   advisory, intermediation and other auxiliary financial services on all the activities listed in subparagraphs (1) through (11), including credit reference and analysis, investment and portfolio research and advice, advice on acquisitions and on corporate restructuring and strategy;

"financial service supplier" means any natural or juridical person of a Party authorised to supply financial services. The term "financial service supplier" does not include a public entity;

"new financial service" means a service of a financial nature, including services related to existing and new products or the manner in which a product is delivered, that is not supplied by any financial service supplier in the territory of a Party but which is supplied in the territory of another Party;

"public entity" means:

1.   a government, a central bank or a monetary authority, of a Party, or an entity owned or controlled by a Party, that is principally engaged in carrying out governmental functions or activities for governmental purposes, not including an entity principally engaged in supplying financial services on commercial terms; or

2.   a private entity, performing functions normally performed by a central bank or monetary authority, when exercising those functions.

ARTICLE 29
Establishment of financial service suppliers

1.   Each Party shall allow the financial service suppliers of another Party to establish, including through the acquisition of existing enterprises, a commercial presence in its territory.

2.   Each Party may require a financial service supplier of another Party to incorporate under its own law or impose terms and conditions on establishment that are consistent with the other provisions of this Section.

3.   No Party may adopt new measures as regards to the establishment and operation of financial service suppliers of another Party, which are more discriminatory than those applied on the date of entry into force of this Agreement.

4.   No Party shall maintain or adopt the following measures:

(a)   limitations on the number of financial service suppliers whether in the form of numerical quotas, monopolies, exclusive financial service suppliers or the requirements of an economic needs test;

(b)   limitations on the total value of financial service transactions or assets in the form of numerical quotas or the requirement of an economic test;

(c)   limitations on the total number of service operations or on the total quantity of service output expressed in the terms of designated numerical units in the form of quotas or the requirement of an economic needs test;

(d)   limitations on the total number of natural persons that may be employed in a particular financial service sector or that a financial service supplier may employ and who are necessary for, and directly related to, the supply of a specific financial service in the form of numerical quotas or a requirement of an economic needs test; and

(e)   limitations on the participation of foreign capital in the terms of maximum percentage limit on foreign shareholding or the total value of individual or aggregate foreign investment.

ARTICLE 30
Cross-border provision of financial services

1.   Each party shall allow the cross-border provision of financial services.

2.   No Party may adopt new measures as regards the cross-border provision of financial services by financial service suppliers of another Party, which are more discriminatory as compared to those applied on the date of entry into force of this Agreement.

3.   Without prejudice to other means of prudential regulation of the cross-border provision of financial services, a Party may require the registration of cross-border financial service suppliers of another Party.

4.   Each Party shall permit persons located in its territory to purchase financial services from financial service suppliers of another Party located in the territory of that other Party. This obligation does not require a Party to permit such suppliers to do business or carry on commercial operations, or to solicit, market or advertise their activities in its territory. Each Party may define the meaning of "doing business", "carry on commercial operations", "solicit", "market" and "advertise" for purposes of this obligation.

ARTICLE 31
National treatment

1.   Each Party shall grant to financial service suppliers of the other Parties, including those already established in its territory on the date of entry into force of this Agreement, treatment no less favourable than that it accords to its own like financial service suppliers with respect to the establishment, acquisition, expansion, management, conduct, operation and sale or other disposition of commercial operations of financial service suppliers in its territory.

2.   Where a Party permits the cross-border provision of a financial service it shall accord to the financial service suppliers of the other Party treatment no less favourable than that it accords to its own like financial service suppliers with respect to the provision of such a service.

3.   A Party's treatment of financial service suppliers of another Party, whether different or identical to that accorded to its own like financial service suppliers, is consistent with paragraph 1 if the treatment affords equal competitive opportunities.

4.   A Party's treatment affords equal competitive opportunities if it does not modify the conditions of competition in favour of its own financial service suppliers as compared to like financial service suppliers of any other Party.

5.   Differences in market share, profitability or size do not in themselves establish a denial regarding equal competitive opportunities, but such differences may be used as evidence regarding whether a Party's treatment affords equal competitive opportunities.

ARTICLE 32
Most favoured nation treatment

1.   Each Party shall accord to financial service suppliers of another Party treatment no less favourable than it accords to the like financial service suppliers of another Party or a non-Party.

2.   Treatment granted under other agreements concluded by one of the Parties with a third country which have been notified under Article V of the GATS shall be excluded from this provision.

3.   If a Party enters into an agreement of the type referred to in paragraph 2, it shall afford adequate opportunity to the other Parties to negotiate the benefits granted therein.

4.   The Parties agree to review the exclusion provided for in paragraph 2 with a view to its deletion not later than three years after the entry into force of this Agreement.

ARTICLE 33
Key personnel

1.   No Party may require a financial service supplier of another Party to engage individuals of any particular nationality as senior managerial or other key personnel.

2.   No Party may require that more than a simple majority of the board of directors of a financial service supplier of another Party be composed of nationals of the Party, persons residing in the territory of the Party, or a combination thereof.

ARTICLE 34
Commitments

1.   Nothing in this Section shall be construed to prevent a Party from applying:

   (a)   any existing measure inconsistent with Articles 29 to 33 which is listed in Annex VIII; or

   (b)   an amendment to any discriminatory measure referred to in Annex VIII in subparagraph (a) to the extent that the amendment does not increase the inconsistency of the measure with Article 29 to 33, as it existed immediately before the amendment.

2.   The measures listed in Annex VIII as well as in paragraph 2 of Article 29 shall be reviewed by the Sub-Committee on Financial Services established under Article 40, with a view to proposing to the Joint Committee their modification, suspension or elimination.

3.   No later than three years following the entry into force of this Agreement, the Joint Committee shall adopt a decision providing for the elimination of substantially all remaining discrimination. That decision shall contain a list of commitments establishing the level of liberalisation which the Parties agree to grant each other.

ARTICLE 35
Right to regulate

1.   Each Party may regulate, and introduce new regulations, on the supply of financial services within their territory in order to meet national policy objectives, in so far as regulations do not impair on any rights and obligations arising under this Agreement.

2.   Each Party shall ensure that all measures of general application affecting trade in services are administered in a reasonable, objective and impartial manner.

ARTICLE 36
Prudential carve-out

1.   Nothing in this Section shall be construed to prevent a Party from adopting or maintaining reasonable measures for prudential reasons, such as:

   (a)   the protection of investors, depositors, policy- holders, policy-claimants, persons to whom a fiduciary duty is owed by a financial service supplier, or any similar financial market participants; or

   (b)   the maintenance of the safety, soundness, integrity or financial responsibility of financial service suppliers; or

   (c)   ensuring the integrity and stability of a Party's financial system.

2.   These measures shall not be more burdensome than necessary to achieve their aim, and shall not discriminate against financial service suppliers of another Party in comparison to its own like financial service suppliers.

3.   Nothing in this Section shall be construed to require a Party to disclose information relating to the affairs and accounts of individual consumers or any confidential or proprietary information in the possession of public entities.

ARTICLE 37
Effective and transparent regulation

1.   Each Party shall make its best endeavours to provide in advance to all interested persons any measure of general application that the Party proposes to adopt in order to allow an opportunity for such persons to comment on the measure. Such measure shall be provided:

   (a)   by means of an official publication; or

   (b)   in other written or electronic form.

2.   Each Party's appropriate financial authorities shall make available to interested persons its requirements for completing applications relating to the supply of financial services.

3.   On the request of an applicant, the appropriate financial authorities shall inform the applicant of the status of its application. If such authorities require additional information from the applicant, they shall notify the applicant without undue delay.

4.   Each Party shall make its best endeavours to ensure that the Basle Committee's "Core Principles for Effective Banking Supervision", the standards and principles of the International Association of Insurance Supervisors and the International Organisation of Securities Commissions' "Objectives and Principles of Securities Regulation" are implemented and applied in its territory.

ARTICLE 38
New financial services

Each Party shall permit a financial service supplier of another Party to provide any new financial service of a type similar to those services that the Party permits its own financial service suppliers to provide under its domestic law in like circumstances.

A Party may determine the juridical form through which the service may be provided and may require authorisation for the provision of the service. Where such authorisation is required, a decision shall be made within a reasonable time and the authorisation may only be refused for prudential reasons.

ARTICLE 39
Data processing

1.   Each Party shall permit a financial service supplier of another Party to transfer information in electronic or other form, into and out of its territory, for data processing where such processing is required in the ordinary course of business of such financial service supplier.

2.   As far as the transfer of personal data is concerned, each Party shall adopt adequate safeguards to the protection of privacy and fundamental rights, and freedom of individuals. To that end, the Parties agree to co-operate in order to improve the level of protection, in accordance with standards adopted by relevant international organisations.

3.   Nothing in this Article restricts the right of a Party to protect personal data, personal privacy and the confidentiality of individual records and accounts so long as such right is not used to circumvent the provisions of this Agreement.

ARTICLE 40
Sub-Committee on financial services

1.   A Sub-Committee on Financial Services is hereby established. The Sub-Committee shall comprise representatives of the Parties. The principal representative of each Party shall be an official of the Party's authorities responsible for financial services set out in Annex IX.

2.   The functions of the Sub-Committee are set out at Annex X to this Agreement.

ARTICLE 41
Consultations

1.   A Party may request consultations with another Party regarding any matter arising under this Section. The other Party shall give sympathetic consideration to the request. The Parties shall report the results of their consultations to the Sub-Committee on Financial Services at its annual meeting.

2.   Consultations under this Article shall include officials of the authorities specified in Annex IX.

3.   Nothing in this Article shall be construed to require financial authorities participating in consultations to disclose information or take any action that would interfere with individual regulatory, supervisory, administrative or enforcement matters.

4.   Where a competent authority of a Party requires information for supervisory purposes concerning a financial service supplier in another Party's territory, it may approach the competent authorities in the other Party's territory to seek the information.

ARTICLE 42
Dispute settlement

Arbitrators appointed in accordance with Chapter VIII for disputes on prudential issues and other financial matters shall have the necessary expertise relevant to the specific financial service under dispute, as well as expertise or experience in financial services law or practice, which may include the regulation of financial institutions.

ARTICLE 43
Specific exceptions

1.   Nothing in Sections I, II and III of this Chapter shall be construed to prevent a Party, including its public entities, from exclusively conducting or providing in its territory activities or services forming part of a public retirement plan or statutory system of social security, except when those activities may be carried out on a commercial basis.

2.   Nothing in this Section applies to activities conducted by a central bank or monetary authority or by any other public entity in pursuit of monetary or exchange rate policies.

3.   Nothing in this Section shall be construed to prevent a Party, including its public entities, from exclusively conducting or providing in its territory activities or services for the account or with the guarantee or using the financial resources of the Party, or its public entities.

SECTION IV - GENERAL EXCEPTIONS

ARTICLE 44
Exceptions

1   The provisions of Sections I, II and III are subject to the exceptions contained in this Article.

2.   Subject to the requirement that such measures are not applied in a manner which would constitute a means of arbitrary or unjustifiable discrimination between countries where like conditions prevail, or a disguised restriction on trade in services, nothing in Sections I, II and III shall be construed to prevent the adoption or enforcement by any Party of measures:

    (a)   necessary to protect public morals or to maintain public order and public security;

    (b)   necessary to protect human, animal or plant life or health;

    (c)   necessary to secure compliance with laws or regulations which are not inconsistent with the provisions of Sections I, II and III including those relating to:

        (i)   the prevention of deceptive and fraudulent practices or to deal with the effects of a default on services contracts;

        (ii)   the protection of the privacy of individuals in relation to the processing and dissemination of personal data and the protection of confidentiality of individual records and accounts;

        (iii)   safety.

    (d)   inconsistent with Articles 22 and 32 provided that the difference in treatment is the result of an agreement on the avoidance of double taxation or provisions on the avoidance on double taxation in any other international agreement or arrangement by which a Party is bound, or domestic fiscal legislation;[6]

    (e)   aimed at preventing the avoidance or evasion of taxes pursuant to the tax provisions of the agreements to avoid double taxation or other tax arrangements, or domestic fiscal legislation;

    (f)   distinguishing, in the application of the relevant provisions of their fiscal legislation, between taxpayers who are not in the same situation, in particular with regard to their place of residence, or with regard to the place where their capital is invested.[7]

3.   The provisions of Sections I, II and III shall not apply to the Parties' respective social security systems or to activities in the territory of each Party, which are connected, even occasionally, with the exercise of official authority, except when those activities may be carried out on a commercial basis.

4.   Nothing in Sections I, II and III shall prevent a Party from applying its laws, regulations and requirements regarding entry and stay, work, labour conditions, and establishment of natural

---

[6] The provision is without prejudice to rights and obligations arising under any double taxation agreements between the Parties

[7] The provision is without prejudice to rights and obligations arising under any double taxation agreements between the Parties.

persons[8] provided that, in so doing, it does not apply them in a manner as to nullify or impair the benefits accruing to another Party under the terms of a specific provision of Sections I, II and III.

SECTION V - INVESTMENT

ARTICLE 45
Definitions

For the purpose of this Section, investment made in accordance with the laws and regulations of the Parties means direct investment, which is defined as investment for the purpose of establishing lasting economic relations with an undertaking such as, in particular, investments which give the possibility of exercising an effective influence on the management thereof.[9]

ARTICLE 46
Transfers

1.   The EFTA States and Mexico shall with respect to investments in their territories by investors of another Party guarantee the right of free transfer, into and out of their territories, including initial plus any additional capital, returns, payments under contract, royalties and fees, proceeds from the sale or liquidation of all or any part of an investment.

2.   Transfers shall be made at the market rate of exchange prevailing on the date of transfer.

3.   Notwithstanding paragraphs 1 and 2, a Party may delay or prevent a transfer through the equitable, non-discriminatory and good faith application of measures:

   (a)   taken to protect the rights of creditors in case of bankruptcy, insolvency or other legal actions;

   (b)   relating to or ensuring compliance with the laws and regulations:

      (i)   on the issuing, trading and dealing in securities, futures and derivatives,

      (ii)   concerning reports or records of transfers, or

   (c)   in connection with criminal offences and orders or judgements in administrative and adjudicatory proceedings.

---

[8] In particular, a Party may require that natural persons must possess the necessary academic qualifications and/or professional experience specified in the territory where the service is supplied, for the sector of activity concerned.
[9] Direct Investment embraces operations carried out in the country concerned by non-residents and operations abroad by residents by means of: 1) creation or extension of a wholly-owned enterprise, subsidiary or branch, acquisition of full ownership of an existing enterprise; 2) participation in a new or existing enterprise; 3) a loan of five years or longer.

ARTICLE 47
Investment promotion between the Parties

The EFTA States and Mexico shall aim to promote an attractive and stable environment for reciprocal investment. Such promotion should take the form, in particular, of:

(a)   mechanisms for information about and identification and dissemination of investment legislation and opportunities;

(b)   development of a legal framework favourable to investment on both sides, particularly through the conclusion by the EFTA States and Mexico of bilateral agreements promoting and protecting investment and preventing double taxation;

(c)   development of uniform and simplified administrative procedures; and

(d)   development of mechanisms for joint investments, in particular with the small and medium enterprises of both Parties.

ARTICLE 48
International commitments on investment

1.   The EFTA States and Mexico recall their international commitments with regard to investment, and especially, where applicable, the OECD Codes of Liberalisation and OECD National Treatment Instrument.

2.   The provisions of this Agreement shall be without prejudice to the rights and obligations under any bilateral investment treaty concluded by the Parties to this Agreement.

ARTICLE 49
Review clause

With the objective of progressively liberalising investment, the EFTA States and Mexico affirm their commitment to review, not later than three years after the entry into force of this Agreement, the investment legal framework, the investment climate and the flow of investment between their territories, consistent with their commitments in international investment agreements.

SECTION VI - BALANCE OF PAYMENTS DIFFICULTIES

ARTICLE 50
Balance of payments difficulties

1.   Where an EFTA State or Mexico is in serious balance of payments difficulties, or under imminent threat thereof, the EFTA State concerned, or Mexico, as the case may be, may adopt restrictive measures with regard to transfers and payments relating to services and investment. Such measures shall be equitable, non-discriminatory, in good faith, of limited duration and may not go beyond what is necessary to remedy the balance of payments situation.

2.   The EFTA State concerned, or Mexico, as the case may be, shall inform the other Party forthwith and present, as soon as possible, a timetable for their removal. Such measures shall be taken in accordance with other international obligations of the Party concerned, including those under the WTO Agreement and the Articles of the Agreement of the International Monetary Fund.

IV COMPETITION

ARTICLE 51
Objective and general principles

1.   The Parties agree that anticompetitive business conduct can hinder the fulfilment of the objectives of this Agreement. Accordingly, each Party shall adopt or maintain measures to proscribe such conduct and take appropriate action with respect thereto.

2.   The Parties undertake to apply their respective competition laws so as to avoid that the benefits of this Agreement may be undermined or nullified by anticompetitive business conduct. The Parties shall give particular attention to anticompetitive agreements, abuse of market power and anticompetitive mergers and acquisitions in accordance with their respective competition laws.

3.   The competition laws for each Party are listed in Annex XI.

ARTICLE 52
Co-operation

1.   The Parties recognise the importance of co-operation on issues concerning competition law enforcement policy, such as notification, consultation and exchange of information related to the enforcement of their competition laws and policies.

2.   A Party shall notify the other Party of competition enforcement activities that may affect important interests of that other Party. Such activities may include investigations that involve: anticompetitive business conduct, remedies and seeking of information in the territory of the other Party, as well as mergers and acquisitions in which a party to the transaction is a company of a Party controlling a company established in the territory of the other Party. Notifications shall be sufficiently detailed to enable the notified Party to make an initial evaluation of the effect of the enforcement activity within its territory.

3.   If a Party considers that an anticompetitive business conduct carried out within the territory of the other Party has an appreciable adverse effect within its territory, it may request that the other Party initiate appropriate enforcement activities. The request shall be as specific as possible about the nature of the anticompetitive business conduct and its effect within the territory of the requesting Party, and shall include an offer of such further information and other cooperation as the requesting Party is able to provide.

4.   The requested Party shall carefully consider whether to initiate enforcement activities, or to expand ongoing enforcement activities, with respect to the anticompetitive business conduct identified in the request. The requested Party shall advise the requesting Party of the outcome of the enforcement activities and, to the extent possible, of significant interim developments.

ARTICLE 53
Confidentiality

Nothing in this Chapter shall require a Party to provide information when this is contrary to its laws, including those regarding disclosure of information, confidentiality or business secrecy.

ARTICLE 54
Sub-Committee on competition

The Joint Committee may, if the need arises, establish a Sub-Committee on competition.

ARTICLE 55
Consultations

A Party may request consultations regarding any matter related to this Chapter.

The request for consultations shall indicate the reasons for the request and whether any procedural time limit or other constraints require that consultations be expedited. Upon request of a Party, consultations shall promptly be held with a view to reaching a conclusion consistent with the objectives set forth in this Chapter. Any Party may request that consultations continue within the Joint Committee in order to obtain its recommendations in relation thereto.

V GOVERNMENT PROCUREMENT

ARTICLE 56
Coverage

1.   This Chapter applies to any law, regulation, procedure or practice regarding any procurement:

   (a)   by entities set out in Annex XII;

   (b)   of goods in accordance with Annex XIII, services in accordance with Annex XIV, or construction services in accordance with Annex XV; and

   (c)   where the value of the contract to be awarded is estimated to be equal to or greater than a threshold as set out in Annex XVI.

2.   Paragraph 1 is subject to the provisions set out in Annex XVII.

3.   Subject to paragraph 4, where a contract to be awarded by an entity is not covered by this Chapter, this Chapter shall not be construed to cover any good or service component of that contract.

4.   No Party may prepare, design or otherwise structure any procurement contract in order to avoid the obligations of this Chapter.

5. Procurement includes procurement by such methods as purchase, lease or rental, with or without an option to buy.[10]

ARTICLE 57
National treatment and non-discrimination

1. With respect to all laws, regulations, procedures and practices regarding government procurement covered by this Chapter, each Party shall provide immediately and unconditionally to the products, services and suppliers of the other Party treatment no less favourable than that accorded to domestic products, services and suppliers.

2. With respect to all laws, regulations, procedures and practices regarding government procurement covered by this Chapter, each Party shall ensure:

    (a) that its entities do not treat a locally-established supplier less favourably than another locally-established supplier on the basis of the degree of foreign affiliation to, or ownership by, a person of the other Party; and

    (b) that its entities do not discriminate against locally- established suppliers on the basis of the country of production of the good or service being supplied, provided that the country of production is the other Party.

3. The provisions of paragraphs 1 and 2 shall not apply to customs duties and charges of any kind imposed on, or in connection with, importation, the method of levying such duties and charges, other import regulations and formalities, and measures affecting trade in services other than laws, regulations, procedures and practices regarding government procurement covered by this Chapter.

ARTICLE 58
Rules of origin

No Party may apply rules of origin to goods imported from the other Party for purposes of government procurement covered by this Chapter that are different from, or inconsistent with, the rules of origin which that Party applies in the normal course of trade.

ARTICLE 59
Denial of benefits

Subject to prior notification and consultation, a Party may deny the benefits of this Chapter to a service supplier of the other Party, where the Party establishes that the service is being provided by an enterprise that is owned or controlled by persons of a non-Party and that has no substantial business activities in the territory of either Party.

---

[10]Procurement does not include:

    (a) non-contractual agreements or any form of government assistance, including cooperative agreements, grants, loans, equity infusions, guarantees, fiscal incentives, and government provision of goods and services to persons or states and municipal governments; and

    (b) the acquisition of fiscal agency or depository services, liquidation and management services for regulated financial institutions and sale and distribution services for government debt.

ARTICLE 60
Prohibition of offsets

Each Party shall ensure that its entities do not, in the qualification and selection of suppliers, goods or services, or in the evaluation of bids or the award of contracts, consider, seek or impose offsets. For purposes of this Article, offsets means conditions imposed or considered by an entity prior to, or in the course of, its procurement process that encourage local development or improve its Party's balance of payments accounts, by means of requirements of local content, licensing of technology, investment, counter-trade or similar requirements.

ARTICLE 61
Procurement procedures and other provisions

1.	Mexico shall apply the rules and procedures specified in Part A of Annex XVIII and the EFTA States shall apply the rules and procedures specified in Part B of Annex XVIII. Both sets of rules and procedures are considered to provide equivalent treatment.

2.	The rules and procedures specified in Anne x XVIII may only be modified by the Party concerned in order to reflect amendments to the corresponding provisions of the North American Free Trade Agreement (hereinafter NAFTA) and the WTO Agreement on Government Procurement (hereinafter GPA), respectively, provided that the rules and procedures applied by that Party, as modified, continue to afford equivalent treatment.

3.	The Party concerned shall notify the other Party of any modification to the rules and procedures specified in Annex XVIII no later than 30 days prior to their date of entry into force, and shall bear the burden of proving that the rules and procedures, as modified, continue to afford equivalent treatment.

4.	Where a Party considers that such a modification affects access to the other Party's procurement market considerably, it can request consultations. If no satisfactory solution can be found the Party may have recourse to dispute settlement procedures under Chapter VIII, with a view to maintaining an equivalent level of access to the other Party's procurement market.

5.	No entity of a Party may make it a condition for the qualification of suppliers and for the awarding of a contract that the supplier has previously been awarded one or more contracts by an entity of that Party or that the supplier has prior work experience in the territory of that Party.

ARTICLE 62
Bid challenge

1.	In the event of a complaint by a supplier that there has been a breach of this Chapter in the context of a procurement, each Party shall encourage the supplier to seek resolution of its complaint in consultation with the procuring entity. In such instances the procuring entity shall accord impartial and timely consideration to any such complaint, in a manner that is not prejudicial to obtaining corrective measures under the challenge system.

2.	Each Party shall provide non-discriminatory, timely, transparent and effective procedures enabling suppliers to challenge alleged breaches of this Chapter arising in the context of procurements in which they have, or have had, an interest.

3.   Each Party shall provide its challenge procedures in writing and make them generally available.

4.   Each Party shall ensure that documentation relating to all aspects of the process concerning procurements covered by this Chapter shall be retained for three years.

5.   The interested supplier may be required to initiate a challenge procedure and notify the procuring entity within specified time- limits from the time when the basis of the complaint is known or reasonably should have been known, but in no case within a period of less than 10 days from that time.

6.   A Party may require under its legislation that a challenge procedure be initiated only after the notice of procurement has been published or, where a notice is not published, after tender documentation has been made available. Where a Party imposes such a requirement, the 10-day period described in paragraph 5 shall begin no earlier than the date that the notice is published or the tender documentation is made available.

Nothing in this provision precludes the right of interested suppliers to judicial review.

7.   Challenges shall be heard by an impartial and independent reviewing authority with no interest in the outcome of the procurement and the members of which are secure from external influence during the term of appointment. A reviewing authority which is not a court shall either be subject to judicial review or shall have procedures which provide that:

(a)   participants can be heard before an opinion is given or a decision is reached;

(b)   participants can be represented and accompanied;

(c)   participants shall have access to all proceedings;

(d)   proceedings can take place in public;

(e)   opinions or decisions are given in writing with a statement describing the basis for the opinions or decisions;

(f)   witnesses can be presented; and

(g)   documents are disclosed to the reviewing authority.

8.   Challenge procedures shall provide for:

(a)   rapid interim measures to correct breaches of this Chapter and to preserve commercial opportunities. Such action may result in suspension of the procurement process. However, procedures may provide that overriding adverse consequences for the interests concerned, including the public interest, may be taken into account in deciding whether such measures should be applied. In such circumstances, just cause for not acting shall be provided in writing;

(b)   where appropriate, correction of the breach of this Chapter or compensation for the loss or damages suffered, which may be limited to costs for tender preparation or protest.

9.   With a view to the preservation of the commercial and other interests involved, the challenge procedure shall normally be completed in a timely fashion.

ARTICLE 63
Provision of information

1.   Each Party shall promptly publish any law, regulation, precedential judicial decision, administrative ruling of general application and any procedure regarding government procurement covered by this Chapter in the appropriate publications referred to in Annex XIX.

2.   Each Party shall designate upon entry into force of this Agreement one or more contact points to:

(a)   facilitate communication between the Parties;

(b)   answer all reasonable inquiries from the other Party to provide relevant information on matters covered by this Chapter; and

(c)   on request of a supplier of a Party, provide in writing within a reasonable time period a reasoned answer to the supplier and the other Party as to whether a specific entity is covered by this Chapter.

3.   A Party may seek such additional information on the award of the contract as may be necessary to determine whether the procurement was made fairly and impartially, in particular with respect to unsuccessful tenders. To this end, the Party of the procuring entity shall provide information on the characteristics and relative advantages of the winning tender and the contract price. Where release of this information would prejudice competition in future tenders, the information shall not be released by the requesting Party, except after consultation with, and agreement of, the Party that provided the information.

4.   Upon request, each Party shall provide to the other Party information available to that Party and its entities concerning covered procurement of its entities and the individual contracts awarded by its entities.

5.   No Party may disclose confidential information the disclosure of which would prejudice the legitimate commercial interests of a particular person or might prejudice fair competition between suppliers, without the formal authorisation of the person that provided the information to that Party.

6.   Nothing in this Chapter shall be construed as requiring any Party to disclose confidential information, the disclosure of which would impede law enforcement or otherwise be contrary to the public interest.

7.   Each Party shall collect and exchange on an annual basis statistics on its procurements covered by this Chapter[11]. Such reports shall comply with the requirements of Annex XX.

ARTICLE 64
Technical co-operation

1.   The Parties shall co-operate to increase the understanding of their respective government procurement systems, with a view to maximising the access to government procurement opportunities for the suppliers of both Parties.

2.   Each Party shall take reasonable measures to provide to the other Party and to the suppliers of the other Party, on a cost recovery basis, information concerning training and orientation programs regarding its government procurement system.

ARTICLE 65
Exceptions

1.   Nothing in this Chapter shall be construed to prevent any Party from taking any action or not disclosing any information which it considers necessary for the protection of its essential security interests relating to the procurement of arms, ammunition or war materials, or to procurement indispensable for national security or for national defense purposes.

2.   Provided that such measures are not applied in a manner that would constitute a means of arbitrary or unjustifiable discrimination between Parties where the same conditions prevail or a disguised restriction on trade between the Parties, nothing in this Chapter shall be construed to prevent any Party from adopting or maintaining measures:

(a)   necessary to protect public morals, order or safety;

(b)   necessary to protect human, animal or plant life or health;

(c)   necessary to protect intellectual property; or

(d)   relating to goods or services of handicapped persons, of philanthropic institutions or of prison labor.

ARTICLE 66
Privatisation of entities

1.   Where a Party wishes to withdraw an entity from Section 2 of Annex XII.A or XII.B, as appropriate, on the grounds that government control over it has been effectively eliminated, that Party shall notify the other Party.[12]

---

[11] The first exchange of information under paragraph 7 of Article 63 (Provision of Information) will take place two years after the entry into force of this Agreement. In the meantime, the Parties will communicate to each other all available and comparable relevant data on a reciprocal basis.

[12] Where both Parties have adopted rules that allow a covered entity to derogate from procurement procedures if such entity intends to purchase exclusively to enable it to provide goods or services where other market participants are free to offer the same goods or services in the same geographical area and under substantially the same conditions, the Parties shall review the wording of this provision accordingly.

2.   Where a Party objects to the withdrawal on the grounds that the entity remains subject to government control, the Parties will enter into consultations to restore the balance of their offers. If no satisfactory solution can be reached, the claiming Party may have recourse to dispute settlement procedures under Chapter VIII.

ARTICLE 67
Further negotiations

In the case that the EFTA States or Mexico offer, after the entry into force of this Agreement, a GPA or NAFTA Party, respectively, additional advantages with regard to the access to their respective procurement markets beyond what has been agreed under this Chapter, they shall agree to enter into negotiations with the other Party with a view to extending these advantages to the other Party on a reciprocal basis.

ARTICLE 68
Other provisions

1.   The Joint Committee may adopt appropriate measures to enhance the conditions for effective access to a Party's covered procurement or, as the case may be, adjust a Party's coverage so that such conditions for effective access are maintained on an equitable basis.

2.   The EFTA States shall provide to Mexico, at the entry into force of this Agreement, an indicative list of 40 public authorities or public undertakings covered by Annex XII.B.2. The entities contained in this list shall be representative of the coverage offered under that Section in terms of geographical location and sectorial distribution.

VI INTELLECTUAL PROPERTY

ARTICLE 69
Protection of intellectual property

1.   The Parties shall grant and ensure adequate, effective and non-discriminatory protection of intellectual property rights, and provide for measures for the enforcement of such rights against infringement, counterfeiting and piracy, in accordance with the provisions of this Article and Annex XXI.

2.   The Parties shall accord to each others' nationals treatment not less favourable than that they accord to their own nationals. Exemptions from this obligation shall be in accordance with the substantive provisions of Article 3 of the Agreement on Trade- Related Aspects of Intellectual Property Rights (hereinafter referred to as the TRIPS Agreement).

3.   The Parties shall grant to each others' nationals treatment not less favourable than that accorded to nationals of any other State. Exemptions from this obligation shall be in accordance with the substantive provisions of the TRIPS Agreement, in particular Articles 4 and 5 thereof.

In case Article XXIV:6(b) of the GPA or Article 1023 of NAFTA is amended, the Parties shall review the wording of this provision accordingly. The amended provision of the GPA or NAFTA shall not apply between the Parties until it has been incorporated in accordance with this paragraph.

---

4.   Upon request of any Party, the Joint Committee shall hold consultations on issues concerning the protection of intellectual property rights, with a view to reaching mutually satisfactory solutions to difficulties that may arise in this context. For the purposes of this paragraph, "protection" shall include matters affecting the availability, acquisition, scope, maintenance and enforcement of intellectual property rights as well as those matters affecting the use of intellectual property rights.

VII INSTITUTIONAL PROVISIONS

ARTICLE 70
The Joint Committee

1.   The Parties hereby establish the EFTA-Mexico Joint Committee comprising of representatives of each Party.

2.   The Joint Committee shall:

(a)   supervise the implementation of this Agreement;

(b)   keep under review the possibility of further removal of barriers to trade and other restrictive regulations of commerce between the EFTA States and Mexico;

(c)   oversee the further elaboration of this Agreement;

(d)   supervise the work of all sub-committees and working groups established under this Agreement;

(e)   endeavour to resolve disputes that may arise regarding the interpretation or application of this Agreement, and

(f)   consider any other matter that may affect the operation of this Agreement.

3.   The Joint Committee may decide to set up such sub-committees and working groups as it considers necessary to assist it in accomplishing its tasks. Except where specifically provided for in this Agreement, the sub-committees and working groups shall work under a mandate established by the Joint Committee.

4.   The Joint Committee may take decisions as provided in this Agreement. On other matters the Joint Committee may make recommendations.

5.   The Joint Committee shall take decisions by consensus.

6.   The Joint Committee shall normally convene once a year in a regular meeting.

The regular meetings of the Joint Committee shall be chaired jointly by one of the EFTA Parties and Mexico. The Joint Committee shall establish its rules of procedure.

7.   Each Party may request at any time, through a notice in writing to the other Parties, that a special meeting of the Joint Committee be held. Such a meeting shall take place within 30 days of receipt of the request, unless the Parties agree otherwise.

8.   The Joint Committee may decide to amend the Annexes and the Appendices to this Agreement. Subject to paragraph 9, it may set a date for the entry into force of such decisions.

9.   If a representative of a Party in the Joint Committee has accepted a decision subject to the fulfilment of constitutional requirements, the decision shall enter into force on the date that the last Party notifies that its internal requirements have been fulfilled, unless the decision itself specifies a later date. The Joint Committee may decide that the decision shall enter into force for those Parties that have fulfilled their internal requirements, provided that Mexico is one of those Parties. A Party may apply a decision of the Joint Committee provisionally until such decision enters into force, subject to its constitutional requirements.

ANNEX XXI

PROTECTION OF INTELLECTUAL PROPERTY
Referred to in Article 69

ARTICLE 1
Definition and scope of protection

"Intellectual property protection" comprises, in particular, protection of copyright, including computer programmes and compilations of data, as well as of neighbouring rights, trademarks for goods and services, geographical indications, including appellations of origin, industrial designs, patents, plant varieties, topographies of integrated circuits, as well as of undisclosed information.

ARTICLE 2
International conventions

1.   The Parties to this Agreement reaffirm their commitment to comply with the obligations set out in the following multilateral agreements:

- WTO Agreement of 15 April 1994 on Trade-Related Aspects of Intellectual Property Rights (TRIPS Agreement);

- Paris Convention of 20 March 1883 for the Protection of Industrial Property (Stockholm Act, 1967);

- Bern Convention of 9 September 1886 for the Protection of Literary and Artistic Works (Paris Act, 1971);

- International Convention of 26 October 1961 for the Protection of Performers, Producers of Phonograms and Broadcasting Organisations (Rome Convention).

2.   The Parties confirm the importance they attach to their obligations arising from the Patent Co-operation Treaty of 19 June 1970 (Washington Act, amended in 1979 and modified in 1984).

3.   The Parties which are not parties to one or more of the agreements listed below shall undertake to obtain the ir adherence thereto before 1 January 2002 or at the date of entry into force of this Agreement, if this date is later:

- Nice Agreement of 15 June 1957 Concerning the International Classification of Goods and Services for the Purposes of the Registration Marks (Geneva Act 1977, as amended in 1979);

- Budapest Treaty of 28 April 1977 on the International Recognition of the Deposit of Micro-organisms for the Purposes of Patent Procedure;

- International Convention of 2 December 1961 for the Protection of New Varieties of Plants (UPOV Convention).

4.   The Parties shall make every effort to complete the necessary procedures for their accession to the following multilateral conventions at the earliest possible opportunity:

a)   the WIPO Copyright Treaty (Geneva 1996); and

b)   the WIPO Performances and Phonogram Treaty (Geneva 1996).

5.   With a view to strengthening co-operation links, the Parties shall hold expert consultations, upon request of a Party, on international activities, relations and developments in the field of intellectual property.

ARTICLE 3
Additional substantive standards

The Parties shall ensure in their respective laws at least the following:

- adequate and effective protection of copyright, including computer programmes and compilations of data, as well as of neighbouring rights;

- adequate and effective protection of trademarks, including collective marks, for goods and services, in particular of well-known trademarks;

- adequate and effective means to protect geographical indications with regard to all products, including appellations of origin, in accordance with the TRIPS Agreement. A Party shall, ex officio, if its legislation so permits, or at the request of an interested party, refuse or invalidate the registration of a trademark which contains or consists of a geographical indication with respect to services not originating in or connected to the territory indicated, if use of the indication in the trademark for such services in that Party is of such a nature so as to mislead the public as to the true place of origin;

- adequate and effective protection of industrial designs by providing in particular a period of protection of 15 years in total;

- adequate and effective patent protection for technological inventions; in Iceland, Liechtenstein and Switzerland this means a level of protection corresponding to the one in the European Patent Convention; and in Mexico and Norway this means protection in accordance with their national laws;

- adequate and effective protection of undisclosed information consistent with the level provided for in the TRIPS Agreement, in particular Article 39;

- adequate and effective protection of topographies of integrated circuits consistent with the level provided for in the TRIPS Agreement, in particular Articles 35 - 38;

- compulsory licensing of patents shall only be granted under the conditions established in Article 31 of the TRIPS Agreement.

ARTICLE 4
Acquisition and maintenance of intellectual property rights

Where the acquisition of an intellectual property right is subject to the right being granted or registered, the Parties shall ensure that the procedures for granting or registration are consistent with the level provided for in the TRIPS Agreement, in particular Article 62.

ARTICLE 5
Enforcement of intellectual property rights

The Parties shall provide in their respective laws for enforcement of IPR consistent with the level provided for in the TRIPS Agreement, in particular Articles 41 to 61.

*

FREE TRADE AGREEMENT BETWEEN THE EFTA STATES AND THE REPUBLIC OF MACEDONIA[*]
[excerpts]

The Free Trade Agreement between the EFTA States and the Republic of Macedonia was signed on 19 June 2000. It entered into force between Macedonia, Liechtenstein, Norway and Switzerland on 1 May 2002.

ARTICLE 14
Payments and Transfers

1.   Payments relating to trade between an EFTA State and Macedonia and the transfer of such payments to the territory of the Party where the creditor resides, shall be free from any restrictions.

2.   The Parties shall refrain from any currency exchange or administrative restrictions on the grant, repayment or acceptance of short and medium-term credits covering commercial transactions in which a resident participates.

3.   No restrictive measures shall apply to transfers related to investments and in particular to the repatriation of amounts invested or reinvested and of any kind of revenues stemming therefrom.

ARTICLE 15
Public procurement

1.   The Parties consider the effective liberalisation of their respective public procurement markets on the basis of non-discrimination and reciprocity, as an integral objective of this Agreement.

2.   To this effect, the Parties shall elaborate rules within the framework of the Joint Committee. The rules shall in particular be based on the WTO Agreement on Government Procurement.

3.   The Parties concerned shall endeavour to accede to the WTO Agreement of Government Procurement and to further liberalise access to their respective public procurement markets.

ARTICLE 16
Protection of intellectual property

1.   The Parties shall grant and ensure adequate, effective and non-discriminatory protection of intellectual property rights, and provide for measures for the enforcement of such rights

---

[*]   *Source*: European Free Trade Association Secretariat (2000). "Free Trade Agreement between the EFTA States and the Republic of Macedonia", available on the Internet (http://secretariat.efta.int). [Note added by the editor.]

against infringement thereof, counterfeiting and piracy, in accordance with the provisions of this Article, Annex V to this Agreement and the international agreements referred to therein.

2.   The Parties shall accord to each others' nationals treatment no less favourable than that they accord to their own nationals. Exemptions from this obligation must be in accordance with the substantive provisions of Article 3 of the WTO TRIPS Agreement.

3.   The Parties shall grant to each others' nationals treatment no less favourable than that accorded to nationals of any other State. In accordance with Article 4, paragraph (d) of the TRIPS Agreement, any advantage, favour, privilege or immunity deriving from international agreements in force before this Agreement and notified to the other Parties at the latest six months after the entry into force of this Agreement, shall be exempted from this obligation, provided that it does not constitute an arbitrary or unjustifiable discrimination of nationals of the other Parties. The Parties shall be exempted from the notification if they have already made such notification to the TRIPS Council. Exemptions from this obligation must be in accordance with the substantive provisions of the TRIPS Agreement, in particular Articles 4 and 5 thereof.

4.   The Parties agree, upon request of any Party, to review the provisions on the protection of intellectual property rights contained in the present Article and in Annex V, with a view to further improving the levels of protection and to avoid or remedy trade distortions caused by actual levels of protection of intellectual property rights.

ARTICLE 17
Rules of competition concerning undertakings

1.   The following are incompatible with the proper functioning of this Agreement in so far as they may affect trade between an EFTA State and Macedonia:

(a)   all agreements between undertakings, decisions by associations of undertakings and concerted practices between undertakings which have as their object or effect the prevention, restriction or distortion of competition;

(b)   abuse by one or more undertakings of a dominant position in the territories of the Parties as a whole or in a substantial part thereof.

2.   The provisions of paragraph 1 shall also apply to the activities of public undertakings, and undertakings for which the Parties grant special or exclusive rights, in so far as the application of these provisions does not obstruct the performance, in law or in fact, of the particular public tasks assigned to them.

3.   If a Party considers that a given practice is incompatible with the provisions of paragraphs 1 and 2, it may take appropriate measures under the conditions and in accordance with the procedures laid down in Article 24 (Procedure for the application of safeguard measures).

ARTICLE 18
Subsidies
1.   The rights and obligations of the Parties relating to subsidies and countervailing measures shall be governed by Article XVI of the GATT 1994 and the WTO Agreement on Subsidies and Countervailing Measures, except as otherwise provided for in this Article.

2.   The extent of the Parties' obligations to ensure transparency of subsidy measures shall be governed by the criteria set out in Article XVI:1 of the GATT 1994 and Article 25 of the Agreement on Subsidies and Countervailing Measures. The EFTA States will make their notifications on subsidies to the WTO available to Macedonia. Macedonia shall notify its subsidies to the EFTA Secretariat, which shall distribute them to the other Parties.

3.   Before an EFTA State or Macedonia, as the case may be, initiates an investigation to determine the existence, degree and effect of any alleged subsidy in Macedonia, or in an EFTA State, as provided for in Article 11 of the Agreement on Subsidies and Countervailing Measures, the Party considering initiating an investigation shall notify in writing the Party whose goods are subject to investigation and allow for a 30 day period with a view to finding a mutually acceptable solution. The consultations shall take place in the Joint Committee if any Party so requests within 10 days from the receipt of the notification.

ARTICLE 27
Services and Investments

1.   The Parties recognise the growing importance of services and investments. In their efforts to gradually develop and broaden their co-operation, in particular in the context of European integration, they will co-operate with the aim of further promoting investments and achieving a gradual liberalisation and mutual opening of markets for trade in services, taking into account on-going work under the auspices of the WTO.

2.   The EFTA States and Macedonia shall review developments in the services sectors with a view to considering liberalisation measures between the Parties.

3.   The EFTA States and Macedonia will discuss this co-operation in the Joint Committee with the aim of developing and deepening their relations under this Agreement.

ANNEX V

REFERRED TO IN ARTICLE 16
PROTECTION OF INTELLECTUAL PROPERTY

Article 1
Definition and scope of protection

"Intellectual property protection" comprises in particular protection of copyright, including computer programmes and databases, as well as of neighbouring rights, trademarks for goods and services, geographical indications, including appellations of origin, industrial designs, patents, plant varieties, topographies of integrated circuits, as well as of undisclosed information.

Article 2
International conventions

1.   The Parties to this Agreement shall comply with the obligations set out in the following multilateral agreements:

- WTO Agreement of 15 April 1994 on Trade-Related Aspects of Intellectual Property Rights (TRIPS Agreement);

- Paris Convention of 20 March 1883 for the Protection of Industrial Property (Stockholm Act, 1967);

- Bern Convention of 9 September 1886 for the Protection of Literary and Artistic Works (Paris Act, 1971).

2.   The Parties to this Agreement which are not Parties to one or more of the agreements listed below shall undertake to obtain their adherence to the following multilateral agreements before 1 January 2001:

- Protocol of 27 June 1989 relating to the Madrid Agreement concerning the International Registration of Marks;

- Budapest Treaty of 28 April 1977 on the International Recognition of the Deposit of Micro-organisms for the Purposes of Patent Procedure;

3.   The Parties to this Agreement which are not Parties to the International Convention of 2 December 1961 for the Protection of New Varieties of Plants (UPOV Convention), shall undertake to obtain their adherence thereto before 1 January 2002.

4.   The Parties to this Agreement agree to promptly hold expert consultations, upon request of any Party, on activities relating to the identified or to future international conventions on harmonization, administration and enforcement of intellectual property rights and on activities in international organizations, such as the WTO and the World Intellectual Property Organization (WIPO), as well as relations of the Parties with third countries on matters concerning intellectual property.

Article 3
Additional substantive standards

The Parties to this Agreement shall ensure in their national laws at least the following:

- adequate and effective protection of copyright, including computer programmes and compilations of data, as well as of neighbouring rights;

- adequate and effective protection of trademarks, including collective marks, for goods and services, in particular of well-known trademarks;

- adequate and effective protection of industrial designs by providing in particular a period of protection of five years from the date of application with a possibility of renewal for two consecutive periods of five years each;

- adequate and effective patent protection for inventions in all fields of technology on a level similar to that prevailing in the European Patent Convention of 5 October 1973, as well as, before 1 January 2002, additional protection of up to five years for pharmaceutical and plant protection products;

- adequate and effective protection of undisclosed information;

- compulsory licensing of patents shall only be granted under the conditions of Article 31 of the TRIPS Agreement. Licences granted on the grounds of nonworking shall be used only to the extent necessary to satisfy the domestic market on reasonable commercial terms;

- adequate and effective means to protect geographical indications, including appellations of origin, with regard to all products and services;

- adequate and effective protection of topographies of integrated circuits.

Article 4
Acquisition and maintenance of intellectual property rights

Where the acquisition of an intellectual property right is subject to the right being granted or registered, the Parties to this Agreement shall ensure that the procedures for grant or registration are of the same level as that provided in the TRIPS Agreement, in particular Article 62.

Article 5
Enforcement of intellectual property rights

The Parties to this Agreement shall provide for enforcement provisions under their national laws of the same level as that provided in the TRIPS Agreement, in particular Articles 41 to 61.

*

AGREEMENT BETWEEN THE GOVERNMENT OF THE UNITED STATES OF AMERICA AND THE GOVERNMENT OF THE UNITED MEXICAN STATES REGARDING THE APPLICATION OF THEIR COMPETITION LAWS[*]

> The Agreement between the Government of the United States of America and the Government of the United Mexican States Regarding the Application of Their Competition Laws was signed on 11 July 2000.

The Government of the United States of America and the Government of the United Mexican States (hereinafter referred to as "Parties");

Having regard to their close economic relations and cooperation within the framework of the North American Free Trade Agreement ("NAFTA");

Noting that the sound and effective enforcement of their competition laws is a matter of importance to the efficient operation of markets within the free trade area and to the economic welfare of the Parties' citizens;

Having regard to their commitment in Chapter 15 of NAFTA to the importance of cooperation and coordination among their competition authorities to further effective competition law enforcement in the free trade area;

Recognizing that coordination of enforcement activities under the Parties' competition laws may, in appropriate cases, result in a more effective resolution of the Parties' respective concerns than would be attained through independent action;

Further recognizing that technical cooperation between the Parties' competition authorities will contribute to improving and strengthening their relationship;

Noting that from time to time differences may arise between the Parties concerning the application of their competition laws to conduct or transactions that implicate the important interests of both Parties;

Noting further their commitment to give careful consideration to each other's important interests in the application of their competition laws; and

Having regard to the growing cooperation between the Parties in matters relating to competition law, including the 1995 Recommendation of the Council of the OECD Concerning Cooperation Between Member Countries on Anticompetitive Practices Affecting International Trade, the 1998 Recommendation of the Council of the OECD Concerning Effective Action Against Hard

---

[*] *Source*: Government of the United States and Government of Mexico (2000). "Agreement between the Government of the United States of America and the Government of the United Mexican States Regarding the Application of Their Competition Laws", available on the Internet (http://www.usdoj.gov/atr/icpac/5145.htm). [Note added by the editor.]

Core Cartels, and the Communiqué issued at the Panama Antitrust Summit Meeting in October 1998;

Have agreed as follows:

Article I
PURPOSE AND DEFINITIONS

1.   The purposes of this Agreement are to promote cooperation, including both enforcement and technical cooperation, and coordination between the competition authorities of the Parties, to avoid conflicts arising from the application of the Parties' competition laws, and to minimize the impact on their respective important interests of any differences that may arise.

2.   For the purposes of this Agreement, the following terms shall have the following definitions:

  a.   "Anticompetitive activity (ies)" means any conduct or transaction that may be subject to penalties or relief under the competition laws of a Party;

  b.   "Competition authority(ies)" means

    i.   for the United Mexican States, the Federal Competition Commission;

    ii.   for the United States of America, the United States Department of Justice and the Federal Trade Commission;

  c.   "Competition law(s)" means

    i.   for the United Mexican States, the Federal Law of Economic Competition of December 24, 1992, except for Articles 14 and 15, and the Regulations of the Federal Law of Economic Competition of March 4, 1998, except for article 8;

    ii.   for the United States of America, the Sherman Act (15 U.S.C. §§ 1-7), the Clayton Act (15 U.S.C. §§ 12-27), the Wilson Tariff Act (15 U.S.C. §§ 8-11) and the Federal Trade Commission Act (15 U.S.C. §§ 41-58), to the extent that it applies to unfair methods of competition, as well as any amendments thereto, and such other laws or regulations as the Parties may from time to time agree in writing to be a "competition law" for the purposes of this Agreement; and

    iii.   "Enforcement activity(ies)" means any investigation or proceeding conducted by a Party in relation to its competition laws.

3.   Any reference in this Agreement to a specific provision in either Party's competition law shall be interpreted as referring to that provision as amended from time to time and to any successor provision thereof. Each Party shall promptly notify the other of any amendments to its competition laws.

Article II
NOTIFICATION

1.   Each Party shall, subject to Article X(1), notify the other Party in the manner provided by this Article and Article XII with respect to its enforcement activities that may affect important interests of the other Party.

2.   Enforcement activities that may affect the important interests of the other Party and therefore ordinarily require notification include those that:

     a.   are relevant to enforcement activities of the other Party;

     b.   involve anticompetitive activities, other than mergers or acquisitions, carried out in whole or in substantial part in the territory of the other Party;

     c.   involve mergers or acquisitions in which one or more of the parties to the transaction, or

          a   company controlling one or more of the parties to the transaction, is a company incorporated or organized under the laws of the other Party or of one of its States;

     d.   involve conduct believed to have been required, encouraged or approved by the other Party;

     e.   involve remedies that expressly require or prohibit conduct in the territory of the other Party or are otherwise directed at conduct in the territory of the other Party; or

     f.   involve the seeking of information located in the territory of the other Party.

3.   Notification pursuant to this Article shall ordinarily be given as soon as a Party's competition authorities become aware that notifiable circumstances are present, and in any event in sufficient time to permit the views of the other Party to be taken into account.

4.   When the competition authorities of a Party request that a person provide information, documents or other records located in the territory of the notified Party, or request oral testimony in a proceeding or participation in a personal interview by a person located in the territory of the notified Party, notification shall be given:

     a.   if compliance with a request for written information, documents or other records is voluntary, at or before the time that the request is made;

     b.   if compliance with a request for written information, documents or other records is compulsory, at least seven (7) days prior to the request, (or, when seven (7) days' notice cannot be given, as promptly as circumstances permit); and

     c.   in the case of oral testimony or personal interviews, at or before the time arrangements for the interview or testimony are made.

5.   Notification that would otherwise be required by this Article is not required with respect to telephone contacts with a person where:

> a.   that person is not the subject of an investigation,

> b.   the contact seeks only an oral response on a voluntary basis (although the availability and possible voluntary provision of documents may be discussed), and

> c.   the other Party's important interests do not appear to be otherwise implicated, unless the other Party requests such notification in relation to a particular matter.

6.   Notification is not required for each subsequent request for information in relation to the same matter unless the Party seeking information becomes aware of new issues bearing on the important interests of the other Party, or the other Party requests otherwise in relation to a particular matter.

7.   The Parties acknowledge that officials of either Party may visit the territory of the other Party in the course of conducting investigations pursuant to their respective competition laws. Such visits shall be subject to notification pursuant to this Article and the consent of the notified Party.

8.   Notifications shall be sufficiently detailed to enable the notified Party to make an initial evaluation of the effect of the enforcement activity on its own important interests, and shall include the nature of the activities under investigation and the legal provisions concerned. Where possible, notifications shall include the names and locations of the persons involved. Notifications concerning a proposed conditioned approval, consent order or decree shall either include or, as soon as practicable be followed by, copies of the proposed conditioned approval, order or decree and any competitive impact statement relating to the matter.

9.   Each Party shall also notify the other whenever its competition authorities intervene or otherwise publicly participate in a regulatory or judicial proceeding that is not an enforcement activity if the issue addressed in the intervention or participation may affect the other Party's important interests. Such notification shall be made at the time of the intervention or participation or as soon thereafter as possible.

Article III
ENFORCEMENT COOPERATION

1.   a.   The Parties acknowledge that it is in their common interest to cooperate in the detection of anticompetitive activities and the enforcement of their competition laws to the extent compatible with their respective laws and important interests, and within their reasonably available resources.

>   b.   The Parties further acknowledge that it is in their common interest to share information which will facilitate the effective application of their competition laws and promote better understanding of each other's enforcement policies and activities.

2.   The Parties will consider adopting such further arrangements as may be feasible and desirable to enhance cooperation in the enforcement of their competition laws.

3.   Each Party's competition authorities will, to the extent compatible with that Party's laws, enforcement policies and other important interests:

    a.   assist the other Party's competition authorities, upon request, in locating and obtaining evidence and witnesses, and in obtaining voluntary compliance with requests for information, in the requested Party's territory;

    b.   inform the other Party's competition authorities with respect to enforcement activities involving conduct that may also have an adverse effect on competition within the territory of the other Party;

    c.   provide to the other Party's competition authorities, upon request, such information within its possession as the requesting Party's competition authorities may specify that is relevant to the requesting Party's enforcement activities; and

    d.   provide the other Party's competition authorities with any significant information that comes to their attention about anticompetitive activities that may be relevant to, or may warrant, enforcement activity by the other Party's competition authorities.

4.   Nothing in this Agreement shall prevent the Parties from seeking or providing assistance to one another pursuant to other agreements, treaties, arrangements or practices between them.

Article IV
COORDINATION WITH REGARD TO RELATED MATTERS

1.   Where both Parties' competition authorities are pursuing enforcement activities with regard to related matters, they will consider coordination of their enforcement activities. In such matters, the Parties may invoke such mutual assistance arrangements as may be in force from time to time.

2.   In considering whether particular enforcement activities should be coordinated, either in whole or in part, the Parties' competition authorities shall take into account the following factors, among others:

    a.   the effect of such coordination on the ability of both Parties to achieve their respective enforcement objectives;

    b.   the relative abilities of the Parties' competition authorities to obtain information necessary to conduct the enforcement activities;

    c.   the extent to which either Party's competition authorities can secure effective relief against the anticompetitive activities involved;

    d.   the possible reduction of cost to the Parties and to the persons subject to enforcement activities; and

e.   the potential advantages of coordinated remedies to the Parties and to the persons subject to the enforcement activities.

3.   In any coordination arrangement, each Party's competition authorities shall seek to conduct their enforcement activities consistently with the enforcement objectives of the other Party's competition authorities.

4.   In the case of concurrent or coordinated enforcement activities, the competition authorities of each Party shall consider, upon request by the competition authorities of the other Party and where consistent with the requested Party's enforcement interests, ascertaining whether persons that have provided confidential information in connection with those enforcement activities will consent to the sharing of such information between the Parties' competition authorities.

5.   Either Party's competition authorities may at any time notify the other Party's competition authorities that they intend to limit or terminate coordinated enforcement and pursue their enforcement activities independently and subject to the other provisions of this Agreement.

Article V
COOPERATION REGARDING ANTICOMPETITIVE ACTIVITIES IN THE TERRITORY OF ONE PARTY THAT ADVERSELY AFFECT THE INTERESTS OF THE OTHER PARTY

1.   The Parties note that anticompetitive activities may occur within the territory of one Party that, in addition to violating that Party's competition laws, adversely affect important interests of the other Party. The Parties agree that it is in their common interest to seek relief against anticompetitive activities of this nature.

2.   If a Party believes that anticompetitive activities carried out in the territory of the other Party adversely affect its important interests, the first Party may request that the other Party's competition authorities initiate appropriate enforcement activities. The request shall be as specific as possible about the nature of the anticompetitive activities and their effects on the interests of the Party, and shall include an offer of such further information and other cooperation as the requesting Party's competition authorities are able to provide.

3.   The requested Party's competition authorities shall carefully consider whether to initiate enforcement activities, or to expand ongoing enforcement activities, with respect to the anticompetitive activities identified in the request. The requested Party's competition authorities shall promptly inform the requesting Party of its decision. If enforcement activities are initiated, the requested Party's competition authorities shall advise the requesting Party of their outcome and, to the extent possible, of significant interim developments.

4.   Nothing in this Article limits the discretion of the requested Party's competition authorities under its competition laws and enforcement policies as to whether to undertake enforcement activities with respect to the anticompetitive activities identified in a request, or precludes the requesting Party's competition authorities from undertaking enforcement activities with respect to such anticompetitive activities.

Article VI
AVOIDANCE OF CONFLICTS

1.   Within the framework of its own laws and to the extent compatible with its important interests, each Party shall, having regard to the purpose of this Agreement as set out in Article I, give careful consideration to the other Party's important interests throughout all phases of its enforcement activities, including decisions regarding the initiation of an investigation or proceeding, the scope of an investigation or proceeding and the nature of the remedies or penalties sought in each case.

2.   When a Party informs the other that a specific enforcement activity may affect the first Party's important interests, the second Party shall provide timely notice of developments of significance to those interests.

3.   While an important interest of a Party may exist in the absence of official involvement by the Party with the activity in question, it is recognized that such interest would normally be reflected in antecedent laws, decisions or statements of policy by its competent authorities.

4.   A Party's important interests may be affected at any stage of enforcement activity by the other Party. The Parties recognize the desirability of minimizing any adverse effects of their enforcement activities on each other's important interests, particularly in the choice of remedies. Typically, the potential for adverse impact on one Party's important interests arising from enforcement activity by the other Party is less at the investigative stage and greater at the stage at which conduct is prohibited or penalized, or at which other forms of remedial orders are imposed.

5.   Where it appears that one Party's enforcement activities may adversely affect the important interests of the other Party, each Party shall, in assessing what measures it will take, consider all appropriate factors, which may include but are not limited to:

   a.   the relative significance to the anticompetitive activities involved of conduct occurring within one Party's territory as compared to conduct occurring within that of the other;

   b.   the relative significance and foreseeability of the effects of the anticompetitive activities on one Party's important interests as compared to the effects on the other Party's important interests;

   c.   the presence or absence of a purpose on the part of those engaged in the anticompetitive activities to affect consumers, suppliers or competitors within the enforcing Party's territory;

   d.   the degree of conflict or consistency between the first Party's enforcement activities (including remedies) and the other Party's laws or other important interests;

   e.   whether private persons, either natural or legal, will be placed under conflicting requirements by both Parties;

f.   the existence or absence of reasonable expectations that would be furthered or defeated by the enforcement activities;

g.   the location of relevant assets;

h.   the degree to which a remedy, in order to be effective, must be carried out within the other Party's territory; and

i.   the extent to which enforcement activities of the other Party with respect to the same persons, including judgments or conditioned approvals resulting from such activities, would be affected.

Article VII
TECHNICAL COOPERATION

The Parties agree that it is in their common interest for their competition authorities to work together in technical cooperation activities related to competition law enforcement and policy. These activities may include, within their competition agencies' reasonably available resources and to the extent authorized by their respective laws: exchanges of information pursuant to Article III of this Agreement; exchanges of competition agency personnel for training purposes at each other's competition agencies;

participation of competition agency personnel as lecturers or consultants at training courses on competition law and policy organized or sponsored by each other's competition authorities; and such other forms of technical cooperation as the Parties' competition authorities agree are appropriate for purposes of this Agreement.

Article VIII
CONSULTATIONS

1.   Either Party may request consultations regarding any matter relating to this Agreement. The request for consultations shall indicate the reasons for the request and whether any procedural time limits or other constraints require that consultations be expedited. Each Party shall consult promptly when so requested with the view to reaching a conclusion that is consistent with the principles set forth in this Agreement.

2.   Consultations under this Article shall take place at the appropriate level as determined by each Party.

3.   During consultations under this Article, each Party shall provide to the other as much information as it is able in order to facilitate the broadest possible discussion regarding the relevant aspects of the matter that is the subject of consultations. Each Party shall carefully consider the representations of the other Party in light of the principles set out in this Agreement and shall be prepared to explain the specific results of its application of those principles to the matter that is the subject of consultations.

Article IX
PERIODIC MEETINGS

Officials of the Parties' competition authorities shall meet periodically to:

a.   exchange information on their current enforcement efforts and priorities in relation to their competition laws;

b.   exchange information on economic sectors of common interest;

c.   discuss policy changes that they are considering; and

d.   discuss other matters of mutual interest relating to the application of their competition laws and the operation of this Agreement.

Article X
CONFIDENTIALITY OF INFORMATION

1.   Notwithstanding any other provision of this Agreement, neither Party is required to communicate information to the other Party if such communication is prohibited by the laws of the Party possessing the information or would be incompatible with that Party's important interests.

2.   Unless otherwise agreed by the Parties, each Party shall, to the fullest extent possible consistent with that Party's laws, (i) maintain the confidentiality of any information communicated to it in confidence by the other Party under this Agreement, and (ii) oppose any application by a third party for disclosure of such confidential information.

Article XI
EXISTING LAWS

Nothing in this Agreement shall require a Party to take any action, or to refrain from acting, in a manner that is inconsistent with its existing laws, or require any change in the laws of the Parties or of their respective States.

Article XII
COMMUNICATIONS UNDER THIS AGREEMENT

Communications under this Agreement may be carried out directly between the competition authorities of the Parties. Requests under Articles V(2) and VIII(1) shall, however, be confirmed in writing through customary diplomatic channels.

Article XIII
ENTRY INTO FORCE AND TERMINATION

1.   This Agreement shall enter into force upon signature.

2.   This Agreement shall remain in force until 60 days after the date on which either Party notifies the other Party in writing that it wishes to terminate the Agreement.

IN WITNESS WHEREOF, the undersigned, being duly authorized by their respective Governments, have signed this Agreement.

DONE at Mexico City, in duplicate, this eleventh day of July, 2000, in the English and Spanish languages, each text being equally authentic.

FREE TRADE AGREEMENT BETWEEN THE EFTA STATES AND THE REPUBLIC OF CROATIA*
[excerpts]

The Free Trade Agreement between the EFTA States and the Republic of Croatia was signed on 21 June 2001.

ARTICLE 13
Payments and Transfers

1. Payments relating to trade between an EFTA State and Croatia and the transfer of such payments to the territory of the Party where the creditor resides, shall be free from any restrictions.

2. The Parties shall refrain from any currency exchange or administrative restrictions on the grant, repayment or acceptance of short and medium-term credits covering commercial transactions in which a resident participates.

3. No restrictive measures shall apply to transfers related to investments and in particular to the repatriation of amounts invested or reinvested and of any kind of revenues stemming therefrom.

ARTICLE 14
Protection of intellectual property

1. The Parties shall grant and ensure adequate, effective and non-discriminatory protection of intellectual property rights, and provide for measures for the enforcement of such rights against infringement thereof, counterfeiting and piracy, in accordance with the provisions of this Article, Annex VII to this Agreement and the international agreements referred to therein.

2. The Parties shall accord to each others' nationals treatment no less favourable than that they accord to their own nationals. Exemptions from this obligation must be in accordance with the substantive provisions of Article 3 of the WTO Agreement on Trade-Related Aspects of Intellectual Property Rights (hereinafter referred to as "the TRIPS Agreement").

3. The Parties shall grant to each others' nationals treatment no less favourable than that accorded to nationals of any other State. In accordance with Article 4, paragraph (d) of the TRIPS Agreement, any advantage, favour, privilege or immunity deriving from international agreements in force before this Agreement and notified to the other Parties at the latest six months after the entry into force of this Agreement, shall be exempted from this obligation, provided that it does not constitute an arbitrary or unjustifiable discrimination of nationals of the other Parties. The Parties shall be exempted from the notification if they have already made such

---

* *Source*: European Free Trade Association Secretariat (2001). "Free Trade Agreement between the EFTA States and Croatia", available on the Internet (http://secretariat.efta.int). [Note added by the editor.]

notification to the TRIPS Council. Exemptions from this obligation must be in accordance with the substantive provisions of the TRIPS Agreement, in particular Articles 4 and 5 thereof.

4.   The Parties agree, upon request of any Party, to review the provisions on the protection of intellectual property rights contained in the present Article and in Annex VII, with a view to further improving the levels of protection and to avoid or remedy trade distortions caused by actual levels of protection of intellectual property rights.

ARTICLE 15
Public procurement

1.   The Parties consider the effective liberalisation of their respective public procurement markets on the basis of non-discrimination and reciprocity, as an integral objective of this Agreement.

2.   The rights and obligations of the Parties in respect of public procurement shall be governed by the WTO Agreement on Government Procurement upon all the Parties' accession. The Parties shall co-operate in the Joint Committee, with the aim of achieving liberalisation of public procurement markets beyond the level of the WTO Agreement on Public Procurement.

3.   If Croatia has not acceded to the WTO Agreement on Government Procurement by 1 January 2004, the Parties shall elaborate rules on public procurement within the framework of the Joint Committee. These rules shall be based on the WTO Agreement on Government Procurement. Croatia shall endeavour to accede to the WTO Agreement on Government Procurement as soon as possible.

ARTILE 16
Services and investments

1.   The Parties recognise the increasing importance of trade in services and investment in their economies. In their efforts to gradually develop and broaden their co-operation, they will co-operate with the aim of creating the most favourable conditions for expanding investment between them and achieving further liberalisation and additional mutual opening of markets for trade in services, taking into account on-going work under the auspices of the WTO.

2.   If, after the entry into force of this Agreement, a Party concludes a free trade agreement with any third country or group of countries that contains provisions providing for a better treatment with respect to any measure affecting trade in services or investors and their investments than the treatment granted to another Party, that Party shall, upon request by another Party, provide adequate opportunity for that Party to enter into negotiation with a view to obtaining equivalent treatment.

3.   Upon request of a Party, the requested Party shall endeavour to provide information on measures that may have an impact on trade in services or investment.

4.   The Parties shall encourage the relevant bodies in their respective territories to co-operate with a view to achieving mutual recognition for licensing and certification of professional service providers.

5.   The EFTA States and Croatia will, in the Joint Committee, review developments related to investments and trade in services with a view to developing and deepening their relations under this Agreement in these fields.

ARTICLE 19
Rules of competition concerning undertakings

1.   The following are incompatible with the proper functioning of this Agreement in so far as they may affect trade between an EFTA State and Croatia:

(a)   all agreements between undertakings, decisions by associations of undertakings and concerted practices between undertakings which have as their object or effect the prevention, restriction or distortion of competition;

(b)   abuse by one or more undertakings of a dominant position in the territories of the Parties as a whole or in a substantial part thereof.

2.   The provisions of paragraph 1 shall also apply to the activities of public undertakings, and undertakings for which the Parties grant special or exclusive rights, in so far as the application of these provisions does not obstruct the performance, in law or in fact, of the particular public tasks assigned to them.

3.   The provisions of paragraphs 1 and 2 shall not be construed such as to create any direct obligations for undertakings.

4.   If a Party considers that a given practice is incompatible with the provisions of paragraphs 1 and 2, the Parties concerned shall give to the Joint Committee all the assistance required in order to examine the case and, where appropriate, eliminate the practice objected to. If the Party in question fails to put an end to the practice objected to within the period fixed by the Joint Committee or if the Joint Committee fails to reach an agreement after consultations, or after thirty days following referral for such consultations, the Party concerned may adopt the appropriate measures to deal with the difficulties resulting from the practice in question. The application and removal of such measures shall be governed by Article 28.

ARTICLE 20
Subsidies

1.   The rights and obligations of the Parties relating to subsidies and countervailing measures shall be governed by Article XVI of the GATT 1994 and the WTO Agreement on Subsidies and Countervailing Measures, except as otherwise provided for in this Article.

2.   The Parties shall ensure transparency of subsidies by exchanging their most recent notifications to the WTO pursuant to Article XVI:1 of the GATT 1994 and the WTO Agreement on Subsidies and Countervailing Measures.

3.   Before an EFTA State or Croatia, as the case may be, initiates an investigation to determine the existence, degree and effect of any alleged subsidy in Croatia, or in an EFTA State, as provided for in Article 11 of the Agreement on Subsidies and Countervailing Measures, the Party considering initiating an investigation shall notify in writing the Party whose goods are subject to investigation and allow for a 30 day period with a view to finding a mutually

acceptable solution. The consultations shall take place in the Joint Committee if any Party so requests within 10 days from the receipt of the notification.

ANNEX VII

REFERRED TO IN ARTICLE 14
PROTECTION OF INTELLECTUAL PROPERTY

Article 1
Definition and scope of protection

"Intellectual property protection" comprises in particular protection of copyright, including computer programmes and databases, as well as of neighbouring rights, trademarks for goods and services, geographical indications, including appellations of origin, industrial designs, patents, plant varieties, topographies of integrated circuits, as well as of undisclosed information.

Article 2
International conventions

1.   The Parties to this Agreement shall comply with the obligations set out in the following multilateral agreements:

- WTO Agreement of 15 April 1994 on Trade-Related Aspects of Intellectual Property Rights (TRIPS Agreement);

- Paris Convention of 20 March 1883 for the Protection of Industrial Property (Stockholm Act, 1967);

- Bern Convention of 9 September 1886 for the Protection of Literary and Artistic Works (Paris Act, 1971);

- International Convention of 26 October 1961 for the Protection of Performers, Producers of Phonograms and Broadcasting Organisations (Rome Convention).

2.   The Parties to this Agreement which are not Parties to one or more of the agreements listed below shall undertake to obtain their adherence to the following multilateral agreements before 1 January 2003.

- Protocol of 27 June 1989 relating to the Madrid Agreement concerning the International Registration of Marks;

- International Convention of 2 December 1961 for the Protection of New Varieties of Plants (UPOV Convention);

3.   The Parties to this Agreement agree to promptly hold expert consultations, upon request of any Party, on activities relating to the identified or to future international conventions on harmonization, administration and enforcement of intellectual property rights and on activities in international organizations, such as the WTO and the World Intellectual Property Organization

(WIPO), as well as relations of the Parties with third countries on matters concerning intellectual property.

Article 3
Additional substantive standards

The Parties to this Agreement shall ensure in their national laws at least the following:

- adequate and effective protection of copyright, including computer programmes and compilations of data, as well as of neighbouring rights;

- adequate and effective protection of trademarks, including collective marks, for goods and services, in particular of well-known trademarks;

- adequate and effective protection of industrial designs by providing in particular a period of protection of five years from the date of application with a possibility of renewal for two consecutive periods of five years each;

- adequate and effective patent protection for inventions in all fields of technology on a level similar to the protection prevailing in the European Patent Convention of 5 October 1973[1], as well as additional protection of up to five years before 1 January 2004 for pharmaceutical and plant protection products;

- adequate and effective protection of undisclosed information;

- compulsory licensing of patents shall only be granted under the conditions of Article 31 of the TRIPS Agreement. Licences granted on the grounds of non-working shall be used only to the extent necessary to satisfy the domestic market on reasonable commercial terms[1];

- adequate and effective means to protect geographical indications, including appellations of origin, with regard to all products and services;

- adequate and effective protection of topographies of integrated circuits.

Article 4
Acquisition and maintenance of intellectual property rights

Where the acquisition of an intellectual property right is subject to the right being granted or registered, the Parties to this Agreement shall ensure that the procedures for grant or registration are of the same level as that provided in the TRIPS Agreement, in particular Article 62.

Article 5
Enforcement of intellectual property rights

The Parties to this Agreement shall provide for enforcement provisions under their national laws of the same level as that provided in the TRIPS Agreement, in particular Articles 41 to 61.

---

[1] A reservation for Norway is set out in an Appendix to this Annex.

FREE TRADE AGREEMENT BETWEEN THE EFTA STATES AND THE HASHIMITE KINGDOM OF JORDAN[*]
[excerpts]

> The Free Trade Agreement between the EFTA States and the Hashimite Kingdom of Jordan was signed on 21 June 2001.

ARTICLE 15
Payments and Transfers

1.   Payments relating to trade between an EFTA State and Jordan and the transfer of such payments to the territory of the Party where the creditor resides, shall be free from any restrictions.

2.   The Parties shall refrain from any currency exchange or administrative restrictions on the grant, repayment or acceptance of short and medium-term credits covering commercial transactions in which a resident participates.

3.   No restrictive measures shall apply to transfers related to investments and in particular to the repatriation of amounts invested or reinvested and of any kind of revenues stemming therefrom.

ARTICLE 16
Public procurement

1.   The Parties consider the effective liberalisation of their respective public procurement markets on the basis of non-discrimination and reciprocity, as an integral objective of this Agreement.

2.   To this effect, the Parties shall elaborate rules within the framework of the Joint Committee with a view to ensuring such liberalisation. Due account shall be given to developments under the auspices of the WTO.

3.   The Parties concerned shall endeavour to accede to the WTO Agreement on Government Procurement.

ARTICLE 17
Protection of intellectual property

1.   The Parties shall grant and ensure adequate, effective and non-discriminatory protection of intellectual property rights, and provide for measures for the enforcement of such rights

---

[*]   *Source*: European Free Trade Association Secretariat (2001). "Free Trade Agreement between the EFTA States and the Hashimite Kingdom of Jordan", available on the Internet (http://secretariat.efta.int). [Note added by the editor.]

against infringement thereof, counterfeiting and piracy, in accordance with the provisions of this Article, Annex VI to this Agreement and the international agreements referred to therein.

2.   The Parties shall accord to each others' nationals treatment no less favourable than that they accord to their own nationals. Exemptions from this obligation must be in accordance with the substantive provisions of Article 3 of the Agreement on Trade-Related Aspects of Intellectual Property Rights (hereinafter "the TRIPS Agreement").

3.   The Parties shall grant to each others' nationals treatment no less favourable than that accorded to nationals of any other State. In accordance with Article 4, paragraph (d) of the TRIPS Agreement, any advantage, favour, privilege or immunity deriving from international agreements in force before this Agreement and notified to the other Parties at the latest six months after the entry into force of this Agreement, shall be exempted from this obligation, provided that it does not constitute an arbitrary or unjustifiable discrimination of nationals of the other Parties. The Parties shall be exempted from the notification if they have already made such notification to the TRIPS Council. Exemptions from this obligation must be in accordance with the substantive provisions of the TRIPS Agreement, in particular Articles 4 and 5 thereof.

4.   The Parties agree, upon request of any Party, to review the provisions on the protection of intellectual property rights contained in the present Article and in Annex VI, with a view to further improve levels of protection and to avoid or remedy trade distortions caused by actual levels of protection of intellectual property rights.

ARTICLE 18
Rules of competition concerning undertakings

1.   The following are incompatible with the proper functioning of this Agreement in so far as they may affect trade between an EFTA State and Jordan:

(a)   all agreements between undertakings, decisions by associations of undertakings and concerted practices between undertakings which have as their object or effect the prevention, restriction or distortion of competition;

(b)   abuse by one or more undertakings of a dominant position in the territories of the Parties as a whole or in a substantial part thereof.

2.   The provisions of paragraph 1 shall also apply to the activities of public undertakings, and undertakings for which the Parties grant special or exclusive rights, in so far as the application of these provisions does not obstruct the performance, in law or in fact, of the particular tasks assigned to them.

3.   If a Party, within five years after the date of entry into force of this Agreement, considers that a given practice referred to in paragraphs 1 and 2 causes, or threatens to cause, serious prejudice to its interest or material injury to its domestic industry, it may take appropriate measures under the conditions and in accordance with the procedures laid down in Article 25.

4.   The Joint Committee shall, taking into account the economic situation of Jordan, decide whether the period referred to in paragraph 3 should be extended for further periods of five years.

5.   Without prejudice to paragraph 4, following the expiry of the period set out in paragraph 3, a Party that considers that a given practice is incompatible with the provisions of paragraphs 1 and 2 may take appropriate measures under the conditions and in accordance with the procedures laid down in Article 25.

ARTICLE 19
Subsidies

1.   The rights and obligations of the Parties' relating to subsidies and countervailing measures shall be governed by Article XVI of the GATT 1994 and the WTO Agreement on Subsidies and Countervailing Measures, except as otherwise provided in this Article.

2.   The Parties shall ensure transparency of subsidy measures by exchanging their annual notifications to the WTO pursuant to Article XVI:1 of the GATT 1994 and Article 25 of the WTO Agreement on Subsidies and Countervailing Measures.

3.   Before an EFTA State or Jordan, as the case may be, initiates an investigation to determine the existence, degree and effect of any alleged subsidy in Jordan, or in an EFTA State, as provided for in Article 11 of the Agreement on subsidies and countervailing measures, the Party considering initiating an investigation shall notify in writing the Party whose goods are subject to investigation and allow for a 45 day period of consultations from the receipt of notification with a view to finding a mutually acceptable solution. The consultations shall take place in the Joint Committee, if any Party so requests, within 20 days from the receipt of the notification.

ARTICLE 28
Services and Investments

1.   The Parties recognise the growing importance of certain areas, such as services and investments. In their efforts to gradually develop and broaden their co-operation, in particular in the context of Euro-Mediterranean integration, they will co-operate with the aim of further promoting investments and achieving a gradual liberalization and mutual opening of markets for trade in services, taking into account on-going work under the auspices of the WTO.

2.   The EFTA States and Jordan shall review developments in the services sectors with a view to considering liberalisation measures between the parties.

3.   The EFTA States and Jordan will discuss this co-operation in the Joint Committee with the aim of developing and deepening their relations under this Agreement.

ANNEX VI

REFERRED TO IN ARTICLE 17
PROTECTION OF INTELLECTUAL PROPERTY

Article 1
Definition and scope of protection

"Intellectual property protection" comprises in particular protection of copyright, including computer programmes and databases, as well as of neighbouring rights, trademarks for goods and services, geographical indications, including appellations of origin, industrial designs, patents, plant varieties, topographies of integrated circuits, as well as of undisclosed information.

Article 2
International conventions

1.   The Parties to this Agreement shall comply with the obligations set out in the following multilateral agreements:

- WTO Agreement of 15 April 1994 on Trade-Related Aspects of Intellectual Property Rights (TRIPS Agreement);

- Paris Convention of 20 March 1883 for the Protection of Industrial Property (Stockholm Act, 1967);

- Bern Convention of 9 September 1886 for the Protection of Literary and Artistic Works (Paris Act, 1971).

2.   The Parties to this Agreement which are not Parties to one or more of the agreements listed below shall undertake to obtain their adherence to the following multilateral agreements before 1 January 2006:

- Protocol of 27 June 1989 relating to the Madrid Agreement concerning the International Registration of Marks;

- Nice Agreement of 15 June 1957 Concerning the International Classification of Goods and Services for the Purposes of the Registration Marks (Geneva Act 1977, amended in 1979);

- International Convention of 2 December 1961 for the Protection of New Varieties of Plants (UPOV Convention);

- International Convention of 26 October 1961 for the Protection of Performers, Producers of Phonograms and Broadcasting Organisations (Rome Convention);

- Budapest Treaty of 28 April 1977 on the International Recognition of the Deposit of Micro-organisms for the Purposes of Patent Procedure.

The Parties to this Agreement which are not Parties to the agreement listed below shall undertake to obtain their adherence to the following multilateral agreement before 1 January 2007:

- Patent Co-operation Treaty of 19 June 1970 (PCT, Washington 1970, amended in 1979 and modified in 1984).

3.   The Parties to this Agreement agree to promptly hold expert consultations, upon request of any Party, on activities relating to the identified or to future international conventions on harmonization, administration and enforcement of intellectual property rights and on activities in international organizations, such as the WTO and the World Intellectual Property Organization (WIPO), as well as relations of the Parties with third countries on matters concerning intellectual property.

Article 3
Additional substantive standards

The Parties to this Agreement shall ensure in their national laws at least the following:

- adequate and effective protection of copyright, including computer programmes and compilations of data, as well as of neighbouring rights;

- adequate and effective protection of trademarks, including collective marks, for goods and services, in particular of well-known trademarks;

- adequate and effective protection of industrial designs by providing in particular a period of protection of five years from the date of application with a possibility of renewal for two consecutive periods of five years each;

- adequate and effective patent protection for inventions in all fields of technology on a level similar to that prevailing in the European Patent Convention of 5 October 1973, as prevailing on 2 May 1992;

- adequate and effective protection of undisclosed information;

- compulsory licensing of patents shall only be granted under the conditions of Article 31 of the TRIPS Agreement. Licences granted on the grounds of nonworking shall be used only to the extent necessary to satisfy the domestic market on reasonable commercial terms;

- adequate and effective means to protect geographical indications with regard to all products and services and appellations of origin with regard to all products;

- adequate and effective protection of topographies of integrated circuits.

Article 4
Acquisition and maintenance of intellectual property rights

Where the acquisition of an intellectual property right is subject to the right being granted or registered, the Parties to this Agreement shall ensure that the procedures for grant or registration are of the same level as that provided in the TRIPS Agreement, in particular Article 62.

Article 5
Enforcement of intellectual property rights

The Parties to this Agreement shall provide for enforcement provisions under their national laws of the same level as that provided in the TRIPS Agreement, in particular Articles 41 to 61.

*

EURO-MEDITERRANEAN AGREEMENT ESTABLISHING AN ASSOCIATION BETWEEN THE EUROPEAN ECONOMIC COMMUNITIES AND THEIR MEMBER STATES, OF THE ONE PART, AND THE ARAB REPUBLIC OF EGYPT, OF THE OTHER PART[*]
[excerpts]

The Euro-Mediterranean Agreement Establishing an Association between the European Economic Communities and Their Member States, of the One Part, and the Arab Republic of Egypt, of the Other Part was signed on 25 June 2001. The member States of the European Communities are: Austria, Belgium, Denmark, Finland, France, Germany, Greece, Ireland, Italy, Luxembourg, the Netherlands, Portugal, Spain, Sweden and the United Kingdom.

ARTICLE 1

1.   An Association is hereby established between the Community and its Member States of the one part and Egypt of the other part.

2.   The aims of this Agreement are:

– to provide an appropriate framework for political dialogue, allowing the development of close political relations between the Parties;

– to establish conditions for the progressive liberalisation of trade in goods, services and capital;

– to foster the development of balanced economic and social relations between the Parties through dialogue and cooperation;

– to contribute to the economic and social development of Egypt;

– to encourage regional cooperation with a view to the consolidation of peaceful co-existence and economic and political stability;

– to promote cooperation in other areas which are of mutual interest.

---

[*] *Source*: European Communities (2001). "Euro-Mediterranean Establishing an Association between the European Economic Communities and Their Member States, of the One Part, and the Arab Republic of Egypt, of the Other Part", available on the Internet (http://www.eu-delegation.org.eg/EUEGAg.htm). [Note added by the editor.]

TITLE III
RIGHT OF ESTABLISHMENT AND SUPPLY OF SERVICES

ARTICLE 29

1.   The Parties reaffirm their respective commitments under the terms of the General Agreement on Trade in Services (GATS) annexed to the Agreement establishing the WTO, and in particular the commitment to accord each other most-favoured-nation treatment in trade in service sectors covered by these commitments.

2.   In accordance with the GATS, this treatment shall not apply to:

(a)   advantages accorded by either Party under the provisions of an agreement as defined in Article V of the GATS or under measures adopted on the basis of such an agreement;

(b)   other advantages accorded pursuant to the list of most-favoured-nation exemptions annexed by either Party to the GATS.

ARTICLE 30

1.   The Parties will consider extending the scope of the Agreement to include the right of establishment of companies of one Party in the territory of another Party and the liberalisation of the supply of services by companies of one Party to service consumers in another Party.

2.   The Association Council shall make the necessary recommendations for the implementation of the objective set out in paragraph 1.

When formulating these recommendations, the Association Council shall take into account the experience gained by the implementation of the MFN treatment granted to each other by the Parties in accordance with their respective obligations under the GATS, and in particular Article V thereof.

3.   The objective set out in paragraph 1 of this Article shall be subject to a first examination by the Association Council at the latest five years after the entry into force of this Agreement.

TITLE IV
CAPITAL MOVEMENTS AND OTHER ECONOMIC MATTERS

CHAPTER 1
PAYMENTS AND CAPITAL MOVEMENTS

ARTICLE 31

Subject to the provisions of Article 33, the Parties undertake to authorise, in fully convertible currency, any payments to the current account.

ARTICLE 32

1.   The Community and Egypt will ensure, from the entry into force of the Agreement, the free circulation of capital for direct investments made in companies formed in accordance with the laws of the host country, and the liquidation or repatriation of these investments and of any profit stemming therefrom.

2.   The Parties will hold consultations with a view to facilitating the movement of capital between the Community and Egypt and achieve its complete liberalisation as soon as conditions are met.

ARTICLE 33

Where one or several Member States of the Community or Egypt face, or risk facing, serious difficulties concerning balance of payments, the Community or Egypt respectively may, in conformity with the conditions laid down within the framework of the GATT and Articles VIII and XIV of the Statutes of the International Monetary Fund, take restrictive measures with regard to current payments if such measures are strictly necessary. The Community or Egypt, as appropriate, shall inform the other Party immediately thereof and shall provide as soon as possible a timetable for the removal of such measures.

CHAPTER 2
COMPETITION AND OTHER ECONOMIC MATTERS

ARTICLE 34

1.   The following are incompatible with the proper functioning of the Agreement, insofar as they may affect trade between the Community and Egypt:

(i)   all agreements between undertakings, decisions by associations of undertakings and concerted practices between undertakings which have as their object or effect the prevention, restriction or distortion of competition;

(ii)   abuse by one or more undertakings of a dominant position in the territories of the Community or Egypt as a whole or in a substantial part thereof;

(iii)   any public aid which distorts, or threatens to distort, competition by favoring certain undertakings or the production of certain goods.

2.   The Association Council shall, within five years of the entry into force of the Agreement, adopt by decision the necessary rules for the implementation of paragraph 1.

Until these rules are adopted, the provisions of Article 23 shall be applied as regards the implementation of paragraph 1(iii).

3.   Each Party shall ensure transparency in the area of public aid, inter alia by reporting annually to the other Party on the total amount and the distribution of the aid given and by providing, upon request, information on aid schemes. Upon request by one Party, the other Party shall provide information on particular individual cases of public aid.

4.   With regard to agricultural products referred to in Title II, Chapter 2, paragraph 1(iii) does not apply. The WTO Agreement on Agriculture and the relevant provisions on WTO Agreement on Subsidies and Countervailing Duties shall apply with regard to these products.

5.   If the Community or Egypt considers that a particular practice is incompatible with the terms of paragraph 1, and:

   – is not adequately dealt with under the implementing rules referred to in paragraph 2, or

   – in the absence of such rules, and if such practice causes, or threatens to cause, serious prejudice to the interest of the other Party or material injury to its domestic industry, including its services industry.

it may take appropriate measures after consultation within the Association Committee or after thirty working days following referral for such consultation.

With reference to practices incompatible with paragraph 1(iii), such appropriate measures, when the WTO rules are applicable to them, may only be adopted in accordance with the procedures and under the conditions laid down by the WTO or by any other relevant instrument negotiated under its auspices and applicable to the Parties.

6.   Notwithstanding any provisions to the contrary adopted in conformity with paragraph 2, the Parties shall exchange information taking into account the limitations imposed by the requirements of professional and business secrecy.

ARTICLE 35

The Member States and Egypt shall progressively adjust, without prejudice to their commitments to the GATT, any State monopolies of a commercial character, so as to ensure that, by the end of the fifth year following the entry into force of this Agreement, no discrimination regarding the conditions under which goods are procured and marketed exists between nationals of the Member States and Egypt. The Association Committee will be informed of the measures adopted to implement this objective.

ARTICLE 36

With regard to public enterprises and enterprises to which special or exclusive rights have been granted, the Association Council shall ensure that, as from the fifth year following the date of entry into force of this Agreement, there is neither enacted nor maintained any measure distorting trade between the Community and Egypt contrary to the Parties' interests. This provision should not obstruct the performance in law or in fact of the particular tasks assigned to these enterprises.

ARTICLE 37

1.   Pursuant to the provisions of this Article and of Annex VI, the Parties shall grant and ensure adequate and effective protection of intellectual property rights in accordance with the prevailing international standards, including effective means of enforcing such rights.

2. The implementation of this Article and of Annex VI shall be regularly reviewed by the Parties. If problems in the area of intellectual property affecting trading conditions were to occur, urgent consultations shall be undertaken, at the request of either Party, with a view to reaching mutually satisfactory solutions.

ARTICLE 38

The Parties agree on the objective of a progressive liberalisation of public procurement. The Association Council will hold consultations on the implementation of this objective.

TITLE V
ECONOMIC COOPERATION

ARTICLE 39
Objectives

1. The Parties undertake to intensify economic cooperation in their mutual interest.

2. The aim of economic cooperation shall be to:

   - encourage the implementation of the overall objectives of this Agreement;

   - promote balanced economic relations between the Parties;

   - support Egypt's own efforts to achieve sustainable economic and social development.

ARTICLE 40
Scope

1. Cooperation shall focus primarily on sectors suffering from internal difficulties or affected by the overall process of liberalisation of the Egyptian economy, and in particular by the liberalisation of trade between Egypt and the Community.

2. Similarly, cooperation shall focus on areas likely to bring the economies of the Community and Egypt closer together, particularly those which will generate growth and employment.

3. Cooperation shall encourage the implementation of measures designed to develop intra-regional cooperation.

4. Conservation of the environment and ecological balance shall be taken into account in the implementation of the various sectors of economic cooperation to which it is relevant.

5. The Parties may agree to extend the economic cooperation to other sectors not covered by the provisions of this Title.

ARTICLE 41
Methods and Modalities

Economic cooperation shall be implemented in particular by:

(a)   a regular economic dialogue between the Parties, which covers all areas of macro-economic policy;

(b)   regular exchange of information and ideas in every sector of cooperation including meetings of officials and experts;

(c)   transfer of advice, expertise and training;

(d)   implementation of joint actions such as seminars and workshops;

(e)   technical, administrative and regulatory assistance.

ARTICLE 42
Education and Training

The Parties shall cooperate with the objective of identifying and employing the most effective means to improve significantly education and vocational training, in particular with regard to public and private enterprises, trade-related services, public administrations and authorities, technical agencies, standardisation and certification bodies and other relevant organisations. In this context, the access of women to higher education and training will receive special attention.

Cooperation shall also encourage the establishment of links between specialised bodies in the Community and in Egypt and shall promote the exchange of information and experience and the pooling of technical resources.

ARTICLE 43
Scientific and Technological Cooperation

Cooperation shall have the objective of:

(a)   encouraging the establishment of durable links between the scientific communities of the Parties, notably through:

-    the access of Egypt to Community R&D programmes, in conformity with existing provisions concerning the participation of third countries;

-   the participation of Egypt in networks of decentralised cooperation;

-   the promotion of synergy between training and research;

(b)   strengthening research capacity in Egypt;

(c)   stimulating technological innovation, transfer of new technologies, and dissemination of know-how.

ARTICLE 45
Industrial Cooperation

Cooperation shall promote and encourage in particular:

– the debate regarding industrial policy and competitiveness in an open economy;

– industrial cooperation between economic operators in the Community and in Egypt, including access for Egypt to the Community's networks for the rapprochement of businesses and to networks created in the context of decentralised cooperation;

– modernisation and restructuring of Egyptian industry;

– the establishment of an environment favourable to the development of private enterprise, in order to stimulate the growth and the diversification of industrial production;

– technology transfer, innovation and R&D;

– the enhancement of human resources;

– access to the capital market for the financing of productive investments.

ARTICLE 46
Investments and promotion of investments

Cooperation shall aim at increasing the flow of capital, expertise and technology to Egypt through, inter alia:

– appropriate means of identifying investment opportunities and information channels on investment regulations;

– providing information on European investment regimes (such as technical assistance, direct financial support, fiscal incentives and investment insurance) related to outward investments and enhancing the possibility for Egypt to benefit from them;

– a legal environment conducive to investment between the two Parties, where appropriate through the conclusion by the Member States and Egypt of investment protection agreements, and agreements to prevent double taxation;

– examining the creation of joint ventures, especially for SMEs and, when appropriate, the conclusion of agreements between the Member States and Egypt;

– establishing mechanisms for encouraging and promoting investments.

Cooperation may extend to the planning and implementation of projects demonstrating the effective acquisition and use of basic technologies, the use of standards, the development of human resources and the creation of jobs locally.

ARTICLE 54
Tourism

Priorities for cooperation shall be:

    – promoting investments in tourism;

    – improving the knowledge of the tourist industry and ensuring greater consistency of policies affecting tourism;

    ...

TITLE VII
FINANCIAL COOPERATION

ARTICLE 72

In order to achieve the objectives of this Agreement, a financial cooperation package shall be made available to Egypt in accordance with the appropriate procedures and the financial resources required.

Financial cooperation shall focus on:

    – promoting reforms designed to modernise the economy;

    – upgrading economic infrastructure;

    – promoting private investment and job-creating activities;

    – responding to the economic repercussions for Egypt of the gradual introduction of a free trade area, notably by upgrading and restructuring industry and enhancing Egypt's export capacity;
    – accompanying measures for policies implemented in the social sector;

    – promoting Egypt's capacity and capabilities in the field of the protection of intellectual property rights;

    – where appropriate, supplementary measures for the implementation of bilateral agreements to prevent and control illegal immigration;

    – accompanying measures for the establishment and implementation of competition legislation.

ARTICLE 73

In order to ensure that a coordinated approach is adopted to any exceptional macro-economic and financial problems that might arise as a result of the implementation of this Agreement, the Parties shall use the regular economic dialogue provided for in Title V to give particular attention to monitoring trade and financial trends in relations between the Community and Egypt.

ANNEX VI
INTELLECTUAL PROPERTY RIGHTS REFERRED TO IN ARTICLE 37

1.   By the end of the fourth year after the entry into force of the Agreement, Egypt shall accede the following multilateral conventions on intellectual property rights:

– the Convention for the Protection of Performers, Producers of Phonograms and Broadcasting Organisations (Rome, 1961);

– Budapest Treaty on the International Recognition of the Deposit of Micro-organisms or the Purposes of Patent Procedure (1977, amended 1980);

– the Patent Cooperation Treaty (Washington 1970, amended in 1979 and modified in 1984);

– the International Convention for Protection of New Varieties of Plants (UPOV) (Geneva Act 1991);

– Nice Agreement concerning the international Classification of Goods and Services for the Purpose of the Registration of Marks (Geneva Act 1977 and amended in 1979);

– Protocol relating to the Madrid Agreement concerning the international registration of Marks (Madrid 1989).

2.   The Parties confirm the importance they attach to the obligations arising from the following multilateral conventions.

– the World Trade Organisation agreement on Trade Related Aspects of Intellectual Property Rights (Marrakech, April 15, 1994), taking into consideration the transitional period provided for developing countries in Article 65 of that agreement;

– the Paris Convention for the protection of industrial property (Stockholm Act 1967 amended in 1979);

- Berne Convention for the protection of literary and artistic works (Paris Act 1971);

– Madrid Agreement concerning the International Registration of Marks (Stockholm Act 1967 amended in 1979).

3.   The Association Council may decide that paragraph 1 shall apply to other multilateral conventions in this field.

EURO-MEDITERRANEAN AGREEMENT ESTABLISHING AN ASSOCIATION BETWEEN THE EUROPEAN ECONOMIC COMMUNITIES AND THEIR MEMBER STATES, OF THE ONE PART, AND THE PEOPLE'S DEMOCRATIC REPUBLIC OF ALGERIA, OF THE OTHER PART[*]
[excerpts]

The Euro-Mediterranean Agreement Establishing an Association between the European Economic Communities and Their Member States, of the One Part, and the People's Democratic Republic of Algeria, of the Other Part was signed on 22 April 2002. The member States of the European Communities are: Austria, Belgium, Denmark, Finland, France, Germany, Greece, Ireland, Italy, Luxembourg, the Netherlands, Portugal, Spain, Sweden and the United Kingdom.

TITLE II

TRADE IN SERVICES

ARTICLE 30
Reciprocal commitments

1.   The European Community and its Member States shall extend to Algeria the treatment which they are obliged to grant under Article II.I of the General Agreement on Trade in Services, hereinafter referred to as GATS.

2.   The European Community and its Member States shall grant to Algerian service suppliers no less favourable treatment than that accorded to like service suppliers as specified in the schedule of specific commitments taken by the European Community and its Member States under the GATS to which it is annexed.

3.   This treatment shall not apply to advantages accorded by either Party under the terms of an agreement of the type defined in Article V of the GATS or to measures taken on the basis of such an agreement and to other advantages granted in accordance with the list of most-favoured-nation exemptions annexed by the European Community and its Member States to the GATS.

4.   Algeria shall grant no less favourable treatment to service suppliers of the European Community and its Member States than that specified in Articles 31 to 33.

---

[*]   *Source*: European Communities (2002). "Euro-Mediterranean Establishing an Association between the European Economic Communities and Their Member States, of the One Part, and the People's Democratic Republic of Algeria, of the Other Part", *Council of the European Union: Brussels,* 12 April 2002 *(OR. fr) 6786/02AL 1*; available also on the Internet (http://europa.eu.int/comm/external_relations/algeria/docs/assoc_art.pdf). [Note added by the editor.]

ARTICLE 31
Cross-border supply of services

With regard to the supply of services by Community service suppliers into the territory of Algeria, other than through a commercial presence or the presence of natural persons, as referred to in Articles 32 and 33, Algeria shall grant treatment to Community service suppliers no less favourable than that accorded to companies of any third country.

ARTICLE 32
Commercial presence

1.   (a)   Algeria shall grant for the establishment of Community companies in its territory treatment no less favourable than that accorded to companies of any third country;

     (b)   Algeria shall grant to subsidiaries and branches of Community companies, established in its territory in accordance with its legislation, in respect of their operations, treatment no less favourable than that accorded to its own companies or branches, or to Algerian subsidiaries or branches of companies of any third country, whichever is the better.

2.   The treatment referred to in paragraph 1(a) and (b) shall be granted to companies, subsidiaries and branches established in Algeria on the date of entry into force of this Agreement and to companies, subsidiaries and branches established there after that date.

ARTICLE 33
Temporary presence of natural persons

1.   A Community company or Algerian company established in the territory of Algeria or the Community respectively shall be entitled to temporarily employ, or have temporarily employed by one of its subsidiaries or branches, in accordance with the legislation in force in the host country of establishment, employees who are nationals of Community Member States and Algeria respectively, provided that such employees are key personnel as defined in paragraph 2, and that they are employed exclusively by such companies, subsidiaries or branches. The residence and work permits of such employees shall only cover the period of such employment.

2.   Key personnel of the abovementioned companies herein referred to as "organisations" are "intra-corporate transferees" as defined in (c) in the following categories, provided that the organisation is a legal person and that the persons concerned have been employed by it or have been partners in it (other than as majority shareholders), for at least the twelve months immediately preceding such movement:

     (a)   persons working in a senior position with an organisation, who primarily direct the anagement of the establishment, receiving general supervision or direction principally from he board of directors or stockholders of the business or their equivalent, including:

          – directing the establishment or a department or sub-division of the establishment;

          – supervising and controlling the work of other supervisory, professional or managerial mployees;

– having the authority personally to recruit and dismiss or recommend recruiting, dismissing or other personnel actions;

(b)   persons working within an organisation who possess uncommon knowledge essential to the establishment's service, research equipment, techniques or management. The assessment of such knowledge may reflect, apart from knowledge specific to the establishment, a high level of qualification referring to a type of work or trade requiring specific technical knowledge, including membership of an accredited profession;

(c)   an "intra-corporate transferee" is defined as a natural person working within an organization in the territory of a Party, and being temporarily transferred in the context of pursuit of economic activities in the territory of the other Party; the organisation concerned must have its principal place of business in the territory of a Party and the transfer be to an establishment (branch, subsidiary) of that organisation, effectively pursuing like economic activities in the territory of the other Party.

3.   The entry into and the temporary presence within the respective territories of Algeria and the Community of nationals of the Member States or of Algeria respectively, shall be permitted, when these representatives of companies are persons working in a senior position, as defined in paragraph 2(a), within a company, and are responsible for the establishment of an Algerian or a Community company, in the Community or Algeria respectively, when:

– those representatives are not engaged in making direct sales or supplying services, and

– the company has no other representative, office, branch or subsidiary in a Community Member State or Algeria respectively.

ARTICLE 34
Transport

1.   Articles 30 to 33 shall not apply to air, inland waterway or land transport or to national shipping (cabotage), subject to the provisions of paragraphs 2 to 6 of this Article.

2.   In respect of activities undertaken by shipping agencies for the provision of international maritime transport services, including inter-modal activities involving a sea leg, each Party shall permit to the companies of the other Party their commercial presence in its territory in the form of subsidiaries or branches, under conditions of establishment and operation no less favourable than those accorded to its own companies or to subsidiaries or branches of companies of any third country whichever are the better. Such activities include, but are not limited to:

(a)   marketing and sales of maritime transport and related services through direct contact with customers, from quotation to invoicing, whether these services are operated or offered by the service supplier itself or by service suppliers with which the service seller has established standing business arrangements;

(b)   purchase and use, on their own account or on behalf of their customer (and the resale to their customers) of any transport and related services, including inward transport services by any mode, particularly inland waterways, road and rail, necessary for the supply of an integrated service;

(c)   preparation of transport documents, customs documents, or other documents related to the origin and character of the goods transported;

(d)   provision of business information of any means, including computerised information systems and electronic data interchange (subject to any non-discriminatory restrictions concerning telecommunications);

(e)   setting up of any business arrangement, including participation in the company's stock and the appointment of personnel recruited locally (or, in the case of foreign personnel, subject to the relevant provisions of this Agreement), with any locally established shipping agency;

(f)   acting on behalf of the companies, organising the call of the ship or taking over cargoes when required.

3.   With respect to maritime transport, the Parties undertake to apply effectively the principle of unrestricted access to the international market and traffic on a commercial basis. However, the legislation of each Party shall apply to the preferential right of the national flag for national cabotage and for salvage, towage and pilotage.

These provisions do not prejudice the rights and obligations arising under the United Nations Convention on a Code of Conduct for Liner Conferences, as applicable for either Party to this Agreement. Non-conference lines shall be free to operate in competition with a conference line as long as they adhere to the principle of fair competition on a commercial basis.

The Parties affirm their commitment to a freely competitive environment as being an essential feature of the dry and liquid bulk trade.

4.   In applying the principles of paragraph 3 above, the Parties shall:

(a)   not introduce cargo-sharing arrangements in future bilateral Agreements with third countries concerning dry and liquid bulk and liner trade. However, this does not exclude the possibility of such arrangements concerning liner cargo in those exceptional circumstances where liner shipping companies from one or other Party to this Agreement would not otherwise have an effective opportunity to ply for trade to and from the third country concerned;

(b)   abolish, upon entry into force of this Agreement, all unilateral measures, administrative, technical and other obstacles which could constitute a disguised restriction or have discriminatory effects on the free supply of services in international maritime transport.

5.   Each Party shall grant, *inter alia*, a treatment no less favourable than that accorded to its own ships, for the ships used for the transport of goods, passengers or both, sailing under the flag of the other Party or operated by its nationals or companies, with respect to access to ports, the use of infrastructure and auxiliary maritime services of those ports, as well as related fees and charges, customs facilities and the assignment of berths and facilities for loading and unloading.

6.   With a view to coordinated development of transport between the Parties, adapted to their commercial needs, the conditions of mutual market access and provision of air, road, rail and inland waterway transport services may be dealt with by specific arrangements, where appropriate, negotiated between the Parties after the entry into force of this Agreement.

ARTICLE 35
Domestic regulation

1.   The provisions of Title III shall not prejudice the application by each Party of any measures necessary to prevent the circumvention of its measures concerning third country access to its market, through the provisions of this Agreement.

2.   The provisions of this Title shall be applied subject to limitations justified on grounds of public policy, public security or public health. They shall not apply to activities which in the territory of either Party are connected, even occasionally, with the exercise of official authority.

3.   The provisions of this title do not preclude the application by a Party of particular rules concerning the establishment and operation in its territory of branches of companies of another Party not incorporated in the territory of the first Party, which are justified by legal or technical differences between such branches as compared to branches of companies incorporated in its territory or, as regards financial services, for prudential reasons. The difference in treatment shall not go beyond what is strictly necessary as a result of such legal or technical differences or, as regards financial services, for prudential reasons.

4.   Notwithstanding any other provisions of this Agreement, a Party shall not be prevented from taking measures for prudential reasons, including for the protection of investors, depositors, policy holders or persons to whom a fiduciary duty is owed by a financial service supplier, or to ensure the integrity and stability of the financial system. Where such measures do not conform with the provisions of the Agreement, they shall not be used as a means of avoiding the obligations of a Party under the Agreement.

5.   Nothing in this Agreement shall be construed to require a Party to disclose information relating to the affairs and accounts of individual customers or any confidential or proprietary information in the possession of public entities.

6.   For the purpose of the movement of natural persons supplying a service, nothing in this Agreement shall prevent the Parties from applying their laws and regulations regarding entry and stay, work, labour conditions and establishment of natural persons and supply of services, provided that, in so doing, they do not apply them in a manner as to nullify or impair the benefits accruing to any Party under the terms of a specific provision of the Agreement. The above provision does not prejudice the application of paragraph 2.

ARTICLE 36
Definitions

For the purposes of this Agreement:

(a)   A "service supplier" shall mean any natural or legal person who supplies a service from the territory of one Party into the territory of the other Party, in the territory of one Party to the service consumer of the other Party, through commercial presence (establishment) in the territory of the other Party and through the presence of a natural person of a Party in the territory of the other Party;

(b)   A "Community company" or "Algerian company" respectively shall mean a company set up in accordance with the laws of a Member State or of Algeria respectively and having its registered office or central administration or principal place of business in the territory of the Community or Algeria respectively.

However, should the company, set up in accordance with the laws of a Member State or Algeria respectively, have only its registered office in the territory of the Community or Algeria respectively, the company shall be considered a Community or Algerian company respectively if its operations possess a real and continuous link with the economy of one of the Member States or Algeria respectively;

(c)   "Subsidiary" of a company shall mean a company which is controlled by the first company;

(d)   "Branch" of a company shall mean a place of business not having legal personality which has the appearance of permanency, such as the extension of a parent body, has a management and is materially equipped to negotiate business with third parties so that the latter, although knowing that there will, if necessary, be a legal link with the parent body, the head office of which is abroad, do not have to deal directly with such parent body but may transact business at the place of business constituting the extension;

(e)   "Establishment" shall mean the right of Community or Algerian companies as referred to in subparagraph (b) to take up economic activities by means of the setting-up of subsidiaries and branches in Algeria or in the Community respectively;

(f)   "Operation" shall mean the pursuit of economic activities;

(g)   "Economic activities" shall mean activities of an industrial, commercial and professional character;

(h)   "National of a Member State or of Algeria" shall mean a natural person who is a national of one of the Member States or of Algeria respectively.

With regard to international maritime transport, including inter-modal operations involving a sea leg, nationals of the Member States or of Algeria established outside the Community or Algeria respectively, and shipping companies established outside the Community or Algeria and controlled by nationals of a Member State or Algerian nationals respectively, shall also be subject to the provisions of this Title if their vessels are registered in that Member State or in Algeria respectively in accordance with their respective legislations.

ARTICLE 37
General provisions

1.   The Parties shall avoid taking any measures or actions which render the conditions for the establishment and operation of each other's companies more restrictive than the situation existing on the day preceding the date of signature of this Agreement.

2.   The Parties undertake to consider development of this Title with a view to the establishment of an "economic integration agreement" as defined in Article V of GATS. In making such recommendations, the Association Council shall take account of past experience of implementation of the most-favoured-nation treatment and of the obligations of each Party under the GATS, and in particular Article V thereof.

The Association Council shall also, when making such examination, take into account progress made in the approximation of laws between the Parties in the relevant activities.

This objective shall be subject to a first examination by the Association Council at the latest five years after the entry into force of this Agreement.

TITLE IV

PAYMENTS, CAPITAL, COMPETITION AND OTHER ECONOMIC PROVISIONS

CHAPTER 1
CURRENT PAYMENTS AND MOVEMENT OF CAPITAL

ARTICLE 38

Subject to the provisions of Article 40, the Parties undertake to allow all current payments for current transactions to be made in a freely convertible currency.

ARTICLE 39

1.   The Community and Algeria shall ensure, from the entry into force of the Agreement, that capital relating to direct investments in Algeria in companies formed in accordance with current laws can move freely and that the yield from such investments and any profit stemming therefrom can be liquidated and repatriated.

2.   The Parties shall consult each other and cooperate with a view to establishing the necessary conditions for facilitating and fully liberalising the movement of capital between the Community and Algeria.

ARTICLE 40

Where one or more Member States of the Community, or Algeria, is in serious balance of payments difficulties, or under threat thereof, the Community or Algeria, as the case may be, may, in accordance with the conditions established under the General Agreement on Tariffs and Trade and Articles VIII and XIV of the Articles of Agreement of the International Monetary Fund, adopt restrictions on current transactions which shall be of limited duration and may not go beyond what is strictly necessary to remedy the balance of payments situation. The Community or Algeria, as the case may be, shall inform the other Party forthwith and shall submit to it as soon as possible a timetable for the abolition of the measures concerned.

CHAPTER 2

COMPETITION AND OTHER ECONOMIC MATTERS
ARTICLE 41

1. The following are incompatible with the proper functioning of the Agreement, insofar as they may affect trade between the Community and Algeria:

(a)   all agreements between undertakings, decisions by associations of undertakings and concerted practices between undertakings which have as their object or effect the prevention, restriction or distortion of competition;

(b)   abuse by one or more undertakings of a dominant position in:

* the whole of the territory of the Community or in a substantial part thereof;

* the whole of the territory of Algeria or in a substantial part thereof.

2.   The Parties shall ensure administrative cooperation in the implementation of their respective competition legislations and exchange information taking into account the limitations imposed by the requirements of professional and business secrecy in accordance with the procedures laid down in Annex 5 to this Agreement.

3.   If the Community or Algeria considers that a particular practice is incompatible with the terms of paragraph 1, and if such practice causes or threatens to cause serious prejudice to the interest of the other Party, it may take appropriate measures after consultation within the Association Committee or after 30 working days following referral for such consultation.

ARTICLE 42

The Member States and Algeria shall progressively adjust, without prejudice to their commitments to the GATT, any State monopolies of a commercial character, so as to ensure that, by the end of the fifth year following the entry into force of this Agreement, no discrimination regarding the conditions under which goods are procured and marketed exists between nationals of the Member States and Algeria. The Association Committee will be informed about the measures adopted to implement this objective.

ARTICLE 43

With regard to public enterprises and enterprises which have been granted special or exclusive rights, the Association Council shall ensure, from the fifth year following the entry into force of this Agreement, that no measure which disturbs trade between the Community and Algeria in a manner which runs counter to the interests of the Parties is adopted or maintained. This provision should not obstruct the performance in law or in fact of the particular tasks assigned to these enterprises.

ARTICLE 44

1.   The Parties shall provide suitable and effective protection of intellectual, industrial and commercial property rights, in line with the highest international standards. This shall encompass effective means of enforcing such rights.

2.   Implementation of this Article and of Annex 6 shall be regularly assessed by the Parties. If difficulties which affect trade arise in connection with intellectual, industrial and commercial property rights, either Party may request urgent consultations to find mutually satisfactory solutions.

ARTICLE 45

The Parties undertake to adopt appropriate measures to ensure the protection of personal data in order to eliminate barriers to the free movement of such data between the Parties.

ARTICLE 46

1.   The Parties shall set as their objective a reciprocal and gradual liberalisation of public procurement contracts.

2.   The Association Council shall take the steps necessary to implement paragraph 1.

TITLE V

ECONOMIC COOPERATION

ARTICLE 47
Objectives

1.   The Parties undertake to step up economic cooperation in their mutual interest and in the spirit of partnership which is at the root of this Agreement.

2.   The objective of economic cooperation shall be to support Algeria's own efforts to achieve sustainable economic and social development.

3.   Such economic cooperation is in keeping with the objectives set out in the Barcelona Declaration.

ARTICLE 48
Scope

1.   Cooperation will be targeted first and foremost at areas of activity suffering the effects of internal constraints and difficulties or affected by the process of liberalising Algeria's economy as a whole, and more particularly by the liberalisation of trade between Algeria and the Community.

2.   Similarly, cooperation shall focus on areas likely to bring the economies of the Community and Algeria closer together, particularly those which will generate growth and

employment, and foster the development of trade flows between Algeria and the Community, notably by encouraging the diversification of Algerian exports.

3.   Cooperation shall foster economic integration within the Maghreb group of countries using any measures likely to further such relations within the region.

4.   Preservation of the environment and ecological balances shall constitute a central component of the various fields of economic cooperation.

5.   The Parties may determine by agreement other fields of economic cooperation.

ARTICLE 49
Methods

Economic cooperation shall be implemented in particular by:

(a)   regular economic dialogue between the Parties covering all areas of macro-economic policy;
(b)   communication and exchanges of information;
(c)   transfer of advice, expertise and training;
(d)   implementation of joint actions;
(e)   technical, administrative and regulatory assistance;
(f)   measures to support partnerships and direct investment by operators, in particular private operators, and privatisation programmes.

ARTICLE 50
Regional Cooperation

In order to maximise the impact of this Agreement vis-à-vis the development of the Euro-Mediterranean partnership and within the countries of the Maghreb, the Parties shall foster all activities which have a regional impact or involve third countries, notably:

(a)   economic integration;
(b)   development of economic infrastructure;
(c)   environmental matters;
(d)   scientific and technological research;
(e)   education, teaching and training;
(f)   cultural matters;
(g)   customs matters.
(h)   regional institutions and the establishment of common or harmonised programmes and policies.

ARTICLE 53
Industrial cooperation

Cooperation shall be aimed at:

(a)   encouraging or supporting measures designed to promote direct investment and industrial partnership ventures in Algeria;

(b)   encouraging direct cooperation between the Parties' economic operators, including cooperation in the context of access for Algeria to Community business networks and decentralised cooperation networks;

(c)   backing the effort to modernise and restructure Algeria's public and private sector industry (including the agri-food industry);

(d)   fostering the development of small- and medium-sized enterprises;

(e)   fostering an environment which favours private initiative, with the aim of stimulating and diversifying output for the domestic and export markets;

(f)   making the most of Algeria's human resources and industrial potential through better use of policy in the fields of innovation and research and technological development;

(g)   supporting the restructuring of industry and the industrial upgrading programme with a view to the creation of the free trade area so as to make products more competitive;

(h)   contributing to the development of exports of Algerian manufactures.

ARTICLE 54
Promotion and protection of investments

The aim of cooperation shall be to create a favourable climate for investment flows, in particular by means of the following:

(a)   the establishment of harmonised and simplified procedures, co-investment machinery (especially to link small and medium-sized enterprises) and methods of identifying and providing information on investment opportunities;

(b)   a legal environment conducive to investment between the two Parties, where appropriate through the conclusion by the Member States and Algeria of investment protection agreements, and agreements to prevent double taxation;

(c)   technical assistance to schemes to promote and guarantee national and foreign investments.

ARTICLE 61
Energy and mining

The aims of cooperation in the energy and mining sectors shall be:

(a)   institutional, legislative and regulatory upgrading to ensure that activities are regulated and investment promoted;

(b)   technical and technological upgrading to prepare energy and mining companies for the requirements of the market economy and competition;

(c)   the development of partnerships between European and Algerian companies in the activities of exploration, production, processing, distribution and services in the energy and mining sectors.

The priority areas of cooperation in this respect shall be:

– adaptation of the institutional, legislative and regulatory framework of activities in the energy and mining sectors to market economy rules by means of technical, administrative and regulatory assistance;
– support for efforts to restructure public enterprises in the energy and mining sectors;
– building partnerships in the areas of:
– oil and gas exploration, production and processing
– electricity production
– distribution of petroleum products
– production of equipment and services used in the production of energy products
– developing and transforming the potential of mining;
– development of gas, oil and electricity distribution;
– support for the modernisation and development of energy networks and for their linking to European Community networks;
– the setting-up of databases on the mining and energy sectors;
– the support and promotion of private investment in energy and mining sector activities;
– the environment, the development of renewable energies and energy efficiency;
– the promotion of technology transfers in the energy and mining sectors.

TITLE VII

FINANCIAL COOPERATION

ARTICLE 79

In order to support the objectives of this Agreement, Algeria shall receive financial cooperation Algeria in accordance with the appropriate procedures and with the appropriate financial resources.

These procedures shall be adopted by mutual agreement between the Parties by means of the most suitable instruments once this Agreement enters into force.

In addition to the areas covered by Titles V and VI of this Agreement, cooperation shall apply to the following:

    – facilitating reforms designed to modernise the economy, including rural development;
    – upgrading economic infrastructure;
    – promoting private investment and job-creating activities;
    – offsetting the effects on the Algerian economy of the progressive introduction of a free trade area, in particular where the updating and restructuring of industry is concerned;
    – accompanying measures for policies implemented in the social sectors.

ARTICLE 80

Within the framework of the Community instruments designed to support structural adjustment programmes in the Mediterranean countries in order to restore key financial equilibria and create an economic environment conducive to faster growth and enhanced social welfare, the Community and Algeria, in close coordination with other contributors, in particular the international financial institutions, shall adapt the instruments intended to accompany development and liberalization policies for the Algerian economy.

ARTICLE 81

In order to ensure a coordinated approach to dealing with any exceptional macroeconomic or financial problems which might stem from the progressive implementation of the provisions of this Agreement, the Parties shall closely monitor the development of trade and financial relations between the Community and Algeria as part of the regular economic dialogue established under Title V.

ANNEX 6
INTELLECTUAL, INDUSTRIAL AND COMMERCIAL PROPERTY

1.   Before the end of the fourth year from the entry into force of this Agreement, Algeria and the European Communities and/or their Member States shall, to the extent they have not yet done so, accede to, and ensure an adequate and effective implementation of the obligations arising from, the following multilateral conventions:

- International Convention for the Protection of Performers, Producers of Phonograms and Broadcasting Organizations (Rome, 1961), known as the "Rome Convention";

- Budapest Treaty on the International Recognition of the Deposit of Micro-organisms for the Purposes of Patent Procedure (1977, amended 1980), known as the "Budapest Treaty";

- Agreement on Trade-Related Aspects of Intellectual Property Rights (Marrakech, April 15, 1994), taking into consideration the transitional period provided for developing countries in Article 65 of that Agreement;

- Protocol relating to the Madrid Agreement concerning the International Registration of Marks (1989), known as "The Protocol relating to the Madrid Agreement";

- Trademark Law Treaty (Geneva 1994);

- WIPO Copyright Treaty (Geneva, 1996);

- WIPO Performances and Phonograms Treaty (Geneva, 1996).

2.   Both Parties shall continue to ensure an adequate and effective implementation of the obligations arising from the following multilateral conventions:

• Nice Agreement concerning the International Classification of Goods and Services for the purposes of the Registration of Marks (Geneva 1977), known as the "Nice Agreement";

• Patent Cooperation Treaty (1970, amended in 1979 and modified in 1984);

• Paris Convention for the Protection of Industrial Property in the 1967 Act of Stockholm (Paris Union), hereafter referred to as the "Paris Convention";

• Berne Convention for the Protection of Literary and Artistic Works in the Act of Paris of 24 July 1971, known as the "Berne Convention";

• Madrid Agreement concerning the International Registration of Marks in the 1969 Act of Stockholm (Madrid Union), known as "Madrid Agreement"; and meanwhile, the Contacting Parties express their attachment to observing the obligations flowing from the above multilateral conventions. The Association Committee may decide that this paragraph shall apply to other multilateral conventions in this field.

*

PART THREE

PROTOTYPE INSTRUMENTS

MODEL, MAY 2002

ACCORD SUR LA PROMOTION ET LA PROTECTION DES INVESTISSEMENTS ENTRE LA REPUBLIQUE DU BENIN ET LA REPUBLIQUE DE _____ *

Le Gouvernement de la République du Bénin et le Gouvernement de la République de _____ ci-après dénommés les "Parties contractantes";

DESIREUX de renforcer les relations économiques et d'intensifier la coopération entre les deux pays, en vue de favoriser leur développement, en particulier pour l'investissement d'une Partie contractante dans le territoire de l'autre Partie contractante ;

CONVAINCUS qu'une protection réciproque des investissements en vertu d'un Accord bilatéral est susceptible de stimuler l'initiative économique privée et d'accroître la prospérité des deux pays ;

SONT CONVENUS DE CE QUI SUIT

ARTICLE 1

DEFINITIONS

Aux fins du présent Accord :

1- Le terme "investissement" désigne, conformément aux lois et règlements de la Partie contractante sur le territoire de laquelle est effectué l'investissement, toutes sortes d'avoirs investis par les personnes physiques ou morales constituées - y compris le Gouvernement - d'une Partie contractante sur le territoire de l'autre Partie contractante.

Il inclut, notamment, mais non exclusivement :

  a)- les biens meubles et immeubles ainsi que tous autres droits réels tels que les hypothèques, les privilèges, les usufruits, les cautionnements et les droits analogues ;

  b)- les actions, les valeurs, parts et obligations de sociétés, ainsi que toutes autres formes de participations dans lesdites sociétés ;

  c)- les prêts et créances et tous autres droits à prestation ayant une valeur économique ;

  d)- les droits de propriété intellectuelle et industrielle qui comprennent particulièrement les droits d'auteur, les brevets, les dessins industriels, les marques et noms déposés, les droits commerciaux et la clientèle;

---

*   *Source*: The Government of Benin, Ministry of Foreign Affairs. [Note added by the editor.]

e)- les concessions économiques accordées par la loi ou en vertu d'un contrat, notamment, les concessions relatives à la prospection, la culture, l'extraction ou l'exploitation des ressources naturelles. Toute modification de forme d'investissement des avoirs n'affecte pas leur qualification d'investissement ;

2- Le terme "investisseur" désigne : les personnes physiques ou morales y compris le Gouvernement de la Partie contractante qui investit sur le territoire de l'autre Partie contractante.

a)- Le terme "personne physique" désigne : une personne ayant la nationalité de l'une des Parties contractantes au regard de ses lois relatives à la nationalité ;

b)- Le terme "société" désigne, au regard de l'autre Partie contractante, toute personne morale constituée sur le territoire de l'une des Parties contractantes, conformément aux lois et règlements de celle-ci, comme : les institutions publiques, corporations, fondations, compagnies privées, projets, établissements et organisations, et ayant leur siège sur le territoire de l'une ou l'autre des Parties contractantes ;

3- Le terme "revenus" désigne les montants nets d'impôts rapportés par un investissement, et notamment, mais non exclusivement les bénéfices, intérêts, dividendes et redevances de licence.

4- Le terme "territoire" désigne le territoire national de chaque Partie contractante ainsi que les zones maritimes adjacentes à la limite extérieure de la mer territoriale nationale, sur lesquelles chacune des Parties contractantes peut, en conformité avec le Droit International, exercer des droits souverains ou une juridiction.

ARTICLE 2
PROMOTION ET PROTECTION DES INVESTISSEMENTS

1- Chacune des Parties contractantes s'engage à encourager sur son territoire, les investissements des investisseurs de l'autre Partie contractante et admet ces investissements en conformité avec ses lois et règlements.

2- Chacune des Parties contractantes s'engage à assurer sur son territoire, un traitement juste et équitable aux investissements des investisseurs de l'autre Partie contractante ainsi que leur protection et leur sécurité ; aucune des deux Parties ne prendra des mesures d'expropriation ou de discrimination contre les investissements de l'autre Partie contractante ;

3- Les Parties contractantes pourront échanger, en cas de besoin, des informations sur les opportunités d'investissement sur leurs territoires respectifs, afin d'aider les opérateurs à identifier les plus rentables pour les deux Parties contractantes.

ARTICLE 3
TRAITEMENT NATIONAL
ET CLAUSE DE LA NATION LA PLUS FAVORISEE

1- Les investissements consentis par les "investisseurs" d'une Partie contractante dans le territoire de l'autre Partie contractante, de même que les bénéfices générés, doivent recevoir un traitement juste et équitable et non moins favorable que celui accordé aux investissements des nationaux de cette dernière partie ou aux investisseurs d'un Etat tiers.

2- Chacune des Parties contractantes s'engage à assurer sur son territoire, un traitement juste et équitable aux investisseurs de l'autre Partie en ce qui concerne l'administration, l'emploi de leurs investissements, traitement qui ne sera pas moins favorable que celui qui est accordé à ses ressortissants ou aux investisseurs d'un Etat tiers.

3- Sans préjudice de ce qui est prévu à l'alinéa 2 ci-dessus, le traitement de la nation la plus favorisée ne s'étend pas aux avantages, préférences ou privilèges accordés aux investisseurs d'un Etat tiers en vertu:

a)- de la participation d'une Partie contractante à une zone de libre échange, union douanière, marché commun ou organisation économique similaire existante ou future ;

b)- d'un Accord international portant en partie ou en totalité sur la double imposition ;

ARTICLE 4
EXPROPRIATION

Aucune des Parties contractantes ne prendra soit directement soit indirectement des mesures de nationalisation ou d'expropriation ou autres mesures ayant le même caractère ou effet à l'encontre d'investissements sur son territoire appartenant aux investisseurs de l'autre Partie contractante, si ce n'est pour des raisons d'utilité publique, sur une base non discriminatoire et selon une procédure légale.

Les mesures doivent être assorties de dispositions prévoyant le paiement d'une indemnité prompte, adéquate et effective.

Le montant de cette indemnité devra être versé en devises librement convertibles et correspondra à la valeur réelle des investissements concernés à la veille du jour où ces mesures ont été prises ou rendues publiques.

En cas de retard de paiement, l'indemnité portera intérêt aux conditions du marché à compter de la date d'exigibilité.

ARTICLE 5
COMPENSATION DES PERTES

Les investisseurs d'une Partie contractante dont les investissements sur le territoire de l'autre Partie contractante subissent des pertes dues à une guerre ou à tout autre conflit armé, révolte, état d'urgence, insurrection ou mutinerie, bénéficieront de la part de cette dernière Partie contractante, d'un traitement non moins favorable que celui accordé à ses propres investisseurs ou aux investisseurs de tout Etat tiers. Tout paiement effectué aux termes de cet article doit être prompt, équitable, effectif et librement transférable.

ARTICLE 6
LIBERTE DES TRANSFERTS

1- Chaque Partie contractante, sur le territoire de laquelle des investissements ont été effectués par des investisseurs de l'autre Partie contractante, autorisera à ces investisseurs, le libre transfert des revenus et autres paiements inclus, en particulier :

a)- les revenus des investissements définis à l'article 1 ci-dessus ;

b)- les indemnités prévues aux articles 4 et 5 ci-dessus;

c)- le produit de la cession ou de la liquidation totale ou partielle de l'investissement ;

d)- les rémunérations des ressortissants d'une Partie contractante qui ont été autorisés à travailler, au titre d'un investissement, sur le territoire de l'autre Partie contractante.

ARTICLE 7
SUBROGATION

1- Lorsque l'une des Parties contractantes ou l'agence désignée par celle-ci effectue des paiements à ses propres investisseurs en vertu d'une garantie financière couvrant les risques non commerciaux en liaison avec un investissement sur le territoire de l'Etat de l'autre Partie contractante, cette dernière reconnaîtra, en vertu du principe de la subrogation, la cession de tout droit ou titre de cet investisseur envers la première Partie contractante ou l'agence désignée par elle. L'autre Partie contractante sera justifiée à déduire les taxes et autres obligations à caractère publique dues et payables par l'investisseur.

2- La première Partie contractante ou l'organisme désigné par ladite Partie a droit, en toutes circonstances, au même traitement, en ce qui concerne les droits et créances acquis en vertu de la cession et tous paiements reçus au titre desdits droits et créances, que celui que la partie indemnisée avait droit à recevoir en vertu du présent Accord pour l'investissement concerné et les revenus correspondants.

ARTICLE 8
REGLEMENT DES DIFFERENDS
ENTRE LES PARTIES CONTRACTANTES

1)- Tout différend entre les Parties contractantes relatif à l'interprétation ou à l'application du présent Accord sera réglé, dans la mesure du possible, par voie diplomatique.

2)- lorsqu'un différend ne peut être réglé par voie diplomatique, dans les six (6) mois qui suivent le début des négociations, il est soumis, à la requête de l'une des parties contractantes, à un tribunal arbitral ;

3)- Le tribunal arbitral est constitué ad hoc de la manière suivante : chaque Partie contractante désigne un arbitre et les deux (2) arbitres choisissent un ressortissant d'un Etat tiers comme Président du tribunal arbitral. Les arbitres seront désignés dans les trois (3) mois, le président dans les cinq (5) mois, de la réception de l'avis de l'arbitrage.

4)-   Si, dans les délais spécifiés à l'alinéa 3 du présent article, les nominations nécessaires n'ont pas été faites, l'une ou l'autre des Parties contractantes peut, en absence de tout autre accord, inviter le Président de la Cour Internationale de Justice à faire les nominations nécessaires. Si le Président est ressortissant de l'une ou l'autre des Parties contractantes ou s'il est empêché pour quelque raison que ce soit de s'acquitter lesdites fonctions, le Vice-Président est invité à faire les nominations demandées.

Si le Vice-President est ressortissant de l'une ou l'autre des Parties contractantes ou ne peut s'acquitter de ladite fonction, le membre de la Cour Internationale de Justice qui suit immédiatement dans l'ordre de préséance et qui n'est pas ressortissant de l'une ou l'autre des Parties contractantes, est invité à procéder aux nominations nécessaires.

5)-   Le tribunal arbitral décide sur la base des dispositions du présent Accord et des autres Accords en vigueur entre les Parties contractantes, selon les principes du Droit International.

6)-   Le tribunal détermine la procédure. Il statue à la majorité des voix à la demande de l'une ou l'autre Partie contractante. Cette sentence arbitrale est définitive et obligatoire pour les Parties.

7)-   Chaque Partie contractante supporte les frais afférents à son propre arbitre et à son représentant. Les frais afférents au Président ainsi que tous autres frais sont supportés à parts égales par les Parties.

ARTICLE 9
REGLEMENT DES DIFFERENDS RELATIFS AUX INVESTISSEMENTS

1)-   Tout différend relatif aux investissements au regard du présent Accord, entre l'une des Parties contractantes et un investisseur de l'autre Partie contractante est, autant que possible, réglé à l'amiable entre les deux Parties.

2)-   Si le différend n'a pu être réglé dans un délai de six (6) mois à partir du moment où il a été soulevé par l'une ou l'autre des Parties concernées, il est soumis, à la demande de l'investisseur :

    a)-   soit aux juridictions nationales de la Partie contractante impliquée dans le différend ;

    b)-   soit à l'arbitrage international, dans les conditions décrites à l'alinéa 3 ci-dessous ;

Une fois qu'un investisseur a soumis le différend soit aux juridictions de la Partie contractante concernée, soit à l'arbitrage international, le choix de l'une ou l'autre de ces procédures reste définitif.

3)-   En cas de recours à l'arbitrage international, le différend peut être porté devant l'un des organes d'arbitrage désignés ci-après, au choix de l'investisseur :

    a)-   au Centre International pour le Règlement des Différends relatifs aux Investissements (C.I.R.D.I.), créé par la "Convention pour le Règlement des

Différends relatifs aux Investissements entre Etats et ressortissants d'autres Etats" ouverte à la signature à Washington le 18 mars 1965.

b)- à un tribunal d'arbitrage ad hoc établi selon les règles d'arbitrage de la Commission des Nations Unies pour le Droit Commercial International (C.N.U.C.D.I.).

4)- L'organe d'arbitrage statuera sur la base des dispositions du présent Accord, du droit de la Partie contractante, Partie au différend, y compris des règles relatives aux conflits des lois, des termes des accords particuliers éventuels qui auraient été conclus au sujet de l'investissement ainsi que des principes de Droit International en la matière.

5)- Les sentences arbitrales sont définitives et obligatoires à l'égard des Parties au différend. Chaque Partie contractante les exécute conformément à sa législation nationale.

ARTICLE 10
CONSULTATION

Les Parties contractantes en cas de besoin devront tenir des consultations en vue de faire la revue de l'application de cet Accord. Ces consultations devront se tenir sur proposition de l'une ou l'autre des Parties contractantes, à un moment et un lieu convenus de commun accord par voie diplomatique.

ARTICLE 11
APPLICATION

Le présent Accord couvre également, en ce qui concerne son application future, les investissements effectués avant son entrée en vigueur, par les investisseurs de l'une des Parties contractantes sur le territoire de l'autre Partie contractante, conformément à ses lois et règlements. Toutefois, le présent Accord ne s'appliquera pas aux différends qui pourraient survenir avant son entrée en vigueur.

ARTICLE 12
AUTRES OBLIGATIONS

Lorsqu'une question relative aux investissements est régie à la fois par le présent Accord et par la législation nationale de l'une des Parties contractantes ou par des Conventions Internationales existantes ou souscrites par les Parties dans l'avenir, les investisseurs de l'autre Partie contractante peuvent se prévaloir des dispositions qui leur sont les plus favorables.

ARTICLE 13
ENTRÉE EN VIGUEUR

Le présent Accord entrera en vigueur à la date d'échange des Instruments de Ratification par les deux Parties contractantes.

ARTICLE 14
DUREE ET DENONCIATION

Le présent Accord est conclu pour une durée de dix (10) ans renouvelable par tacite reconduction, à moins que l'une des Parties ne le dénonce, par écrit, douze (12) mois avant son expiration.

En cas de dénonciation, le présent Accord restera applicable aux investissements effectués avant la date à laquelle prend effet l'avis de dénonciation et les articles 1 et 13 restent en vigueur pendant une période de dix (10) mois.

Chaque Partie contractante pourra demander, par écrit, l'amendement de tout ou partie du présent Accord.

Les parties amendées d'un commun accord entreront en vigueur dès la notification de leur acceptation par les deux Parties contractantes.

FAIT a COTONOU, le

En deux exemplaires originaux en langues française et anglaise, les deux textes faisant également foi.

Pour le Gouvernement de la
République du Bénin

Pour le Gouvernement
de la République de _____

*

ACCORD ENTRE LE GOUVERNEMENT DE LA REPUBLIQUE DU BURUNDI D'UNE PART, ET _____, D'AUTRE PART, CONCERNANT L'ENCOURAGEMENT ET LA PROTECTION RECIPROQUES DES INVESTISSEMENTS*

Le Gouvernement de la République du Burundi, D'une Part; et le Gouvernement de _____ D'autre Part Ci-après désignées « les Parties Contractantes »

Désireux de renforcer la coopération économique entre les deux Etats, et de créer les conditions favorables à la réalisation d'investissements par des ressortissants de l'une des parties contractantes,

Considérant qu'une telle Convention est de nature à stimuler les initiatives économiques privées et à renforcer la confiance dans le domaine des investissements,

Reconnaissant que la discrimination, exercée par l'une ou l'autre des parties contractantes, sur la base de la nationalité, à l'encontre d'investissements effectués sur son territoire par des investisseurs de l'autre partie contractante, est incompatible avec tout cadre d'investissement stable ou avec toute utilisation optimale et efficace des ressources économiques,

Sont convenues de ce qui suit:

Article 1
DEFINITIONS.

Pour l'application du présent Accord:

1.   Le terme « investisseurs » désigne:

   a)   toute personne physique qui, selon la législation _____ ou burundaise est considérée respectivement comme citoyen de _____ ou de la République du Burundi ;

   b)   toute personne morale constituée conformément à la législation _____ ou burundaise et ayant son siège social respectivement sur le territoire de _____ ou de la République du Burundi.

2.   Le terme « ressortissant » désigne les burundais au sens de la loi en vigueur en République du Burundi.

3.   Le terme « société » désigne toute personne morale ainsi que toute société commerciale, civile ou autre société, association ou coopérative, avec ou sans personnalité juridique, ayant son siège dans le champ d'application burundais du présent Accord et instituée légalement en conformité avec la loi, indépendamment de la question de savoir si la responsabilité de ses associés, participants ou membres est limitée ou illimitée, et si son activité a un but lucratif ou non.

---

*   *Source*: The Government of Burundi, Ministry of Foreign Affairs. [Note added by the editor.]

4.   Le terme « investissement » désigne tout apport direct ou indirect de capital ainsi que tout élément d'actif quelconque, investis ou réinvestis dans tout établissement de quelque secteur d'activité économique que ce soit.

Sont considérés notamment, mais pas exclusivement, comme des investissements au sens du présent Accord:

a)   les biens meubles et immeubles ainsi que tous autres droits réels tels que les hypothèques, privilèges, usufruits, gage, sûretés réelles, cautionnement et droits similaires;

b)   les actions, primes d'émission, parts sociales et autres formes de participation dans des sociétés ;

c)   les obligations émises par des entreprises, les créances et droits à toute prestation ayant une valeur économique ;

d)   les droits de propriété intellectuelle et industrielle, tels que le droit d'auteur, brevets, modèles d'utilité, dessins et modèles industriels, noms commerciaux, procédés techniques, marques de fabriques et de commerce, le savoir-faire;

e)   les concessions de Droit public ou contractuelles y compris les concessions dans le domaine de la recherche agricole, de l'extraction ou de l'exploitation de ressources naturelles.

5.   Le terme « revenus » désigne tout montant produit par un investissement c'est-à-dire notamment, mais pas exclusivement: les bénéfices, les intérêts, les accroissements de capital, les dividendes, les royalties et autres rémunérations.

Aucune modification de la forme dans laquelle les avoirs et les capitaux sont investis ou réinvestis n'affecte leur caractère d' « investissements » au sens du présent Accord.

Article 2
PROMOTION DES INVESTISSEMENTS.

1.   Chaque Partie contractante encourage et admet sur son territoire en conformité avec sa législation, les investissements effectués par des investisseurs de l'autre partie contractante ainsi que toutes les activités y afférentes.

2.   En particulier, chaque partie contractante autorise la conclusion et l'exécution de contrats de licence et de conventions d'assistance commerciale, administrative ou technique, pour autant que ces activités soient en rapport avec les investissements visés au paragraphe 1.

3.   La présent Accord s'applique aux investissements et activités y afférentes, entrepris sur le territoire de chaque partie contractante par des investisseurs de l'autre partie contractante même avant son entrée en vigueur.

Article 3
PROTECTION DES INVESTISSEMENTS.

1.   Chaque partie contractante s'engage à assurer sur son territoire un traitement juste et équitable aux investissements directs ou indirects, ainsi qu'aux activités y afférentes, entrepris par des investisseurs de l'autre partie contractante.

2.   Ces investissements et activités jouissent d'une sécurité et d'une protection constantes, excluant toute mesure injustifiée ou discriminatoire qui pourrait entraver, en droit ou en fait, leur gestion, leur entretien, leur utilisation, leur jouissance ou leur liquidation.

3.   Le traitement et la protection garantis aux paragraphes 1 et 2 ne sont pas moins favorables que ceux dont jouissent les ressortissants de l'Etat hôte de l'investissement. Ils sont en tous cas au moins égaux à ceux dont jouissent les investisseurs de la nation la plus favorisée et ne peuvent en aucun cas être moins favorables que ceux reconnus par le droit international.

Article 4
MESURES PRIVATIVES ET RESTRICTIVES DE PROPRIETE.

1.   Chaque partie contractante s'engage à ne prendre aucune mesure privative ou restrictive de propriété, ni aucune autre mesure ayant un effet similaire à l'égard des investissements situés sur son territoire, si ce n'est lorsque des impératifs d'utilité publique, de sécurité ou d'intérêt national l'exigent exceptionnellement, auquel cas les conditions suivantes doivent être remplies:

   a)   les mesures sont prises selon une procédure légale ;

   b)   elles ne sont ni discriminatoires, ni contraires à un accord particulier tel que visé à l'article 7, & 3 ;

   c)   elles sont assorties de dispositions prévoyant le paiement d'une indemnité adéquate et effective.

2.   L'indemnité visée au paragraphe 1 c) représente la valeur vénale des investissements concernés à la veille du jour où les mesures sont prises ou, le cas échéant, à la veille du jour où elles ont été rendues publiques. Toutefois, lorsqu'un investissement n'a pas de valeur vénale ou lorsque l'investisseur concerné prouve que la valeur vénale des investissements expropriés est inférieure à leur valeur réelle et objective, l'indemnité est fixée sur base de cette dernière valeur.

Toute indemnité est payée dans la monnaie de l'Etat auquel appartient l'investisseur concerné ou dans toute autre monnaie convertible.

Elle est versée sans délai, est effectivement réalisable et porte intérêt courant à partir de la date de l'expropriation, à un taux commercial raisonnable.

Elle est librement transférable.

3.   Les investisseurs de chacune des parties contractantes dont les investissements subiraient des dommages à l'occasion d'une guerre ou autre conflit armé, d'un état d'urgence national, de troubles ou d'émeutes, survenant sur le territoire de l'autre partie contactante, bénéficient de la part de cette dernière d'un traitement non discriminatoire et au moins égal à celui accordé aux

investisseurs de la nation la plus favorisée en ce qui concerne les restitutions, indemnités, compensations ou autres dédommagements.

L'indemnisation due en application du présent paragraphe sera payée conformément aux dispositions du paragraphe 2.

4.   Le traitement visé aux paragraphes 1, 2 et 3 s'applique aux investisseurs de chacune des parties contractantes titulaires de toute forme de participation, directe ou indirecte, dans quelque entreprise que ce soit sur le territoire de l'autre partie contractante.

5.   Dans tous les cas, le traitement est au moins égal à celui que l'Etat hôte de l'investissement concerné reconnaît à ses nationaux et ne peut être moins favorable que celui dont bénéficient les investisseurs de la nation la plus favorisée.

Il ne peut être inférieur au traitement accordé par le droit international.

Article 5
TRANSFERTS

1.   Eu égard aux investissements effectués sur son territoire, chaque partie contractante garantit aux investisseurs de l'autre partie contractante le libre transfert de leurs avoirs et notamment, mais pas exclusivement:

  a)   des revenus tels que visés à l'article 1, & 3 ;

  b)   des sommes nécessaires au remboursement d'emprunts régulièrement contractés ;

  c)   des produits de recouvrement de créances, de liquidation totale ou partielle des investissements ;

  d)   des indemnités payées en exécution de l'article 4.

2.   Chaque partie contractante s'engage à accorder les autorisations nécessaires pour assurer sans délai l'exécution des transferts et ce, sans autres taxes ou frais que les frais bancaires usuels. Est considéré comme effectué « sans délai » au sens du présent article, tout transfert qui a lieu dans le délai normalement nécessaire à l'accomplissement des formalités de transfert. Le délai commencera à courir à la date de l'introduction d'une demande y afférente et ne devra en aucun cas dépasser deux mois.

3.   Les transferts visés au paragraphe 1 sont effectués au taux de change applicable à la date du transfert en vertu de la réglementation de change en vigueur selon les catégories d'opérations.

4.   Le traitement visé aux paragraphes 1, 2 et 3 ne peut être moins favorable que celui accordé aux investisseurs de la nation la plus favorisée se trouvant dans des situations similaires.

Article 6
SUBROGATION

1.   Si, en vertu d'une garantie légale ou contractuelle couvrant les risques non commerciaux des investissements, des indemnités sont payées à un investisseur de l'une des parties

contractantes, l'autre partie contractante reconnaît la subrogation de l'assureur dans les droits de l'investisseur indemnisé.

2.　Conformément à la garantie accordée à l'investissement concerné, l'assureur est admis à faire valoir tous les droits que l'investisseur aurait pu exercer si l'assureur ne lui avait pas été subrogé.

3.　Tout différend entre une partie contractante et l'assureur d'un investisseur de l'autre partie contactante sera réglé conformément aux dispositions de l'article 8 du présent Accord.

Article 7
AUTRES OBLIGATIONS

1.　La présente convention ne porte pas préjudice:

    a)　aux lois, règlements, pratiques ou procédures administratives ou aux décisions administratives ou judiciaires de l'une ou l'autre des parties contractantes ;

    b)　aux obligations juridiques internationales ;

    c)　aux obligations contractées par l'une ou l'autre des parties contractantes, y compris celles figurant dans un accord particulier d'investissement ou dans une autorisation d'investissement existant, les uns ou les autres, antérieurement ou postérieurement à son entrée en vigueur.

2.　Lorsqu'une question relative à un investissement est régie à la fois par la présente Convention et par une ou plusieurs des dispositions visées au paragraphe 1, les investisseurs peuvent toujours se prévaloir des dispositions qui leur sont les plus favorables.

3.　Les investisseurs d'une partie contractante peuvent conclure avec l'autre partie contractante des accords particuliers dont les dispositions ne peuvent toutefois pas être contraires au présent Accord.

Les investissements effectués en vertu de tels accords particuliers sont, pour le surplus, régis par la présente Convention.

Article 8
DIFFERENDS RELATIFS AUX INVESTISSEMENTS

1.　Pour l'application du présent article, un différend relatif à un investissement est défini comme un différend concernant:

    a)　l'interprétation ou l'application d'un accord particulier d'investissement entre une partie contractante et un investisseur de l'autre partie contractante ;

    b)　l'interprétation ou l'application de toute autorisation d'investissement accordée par les autorités de l'Etat hôte régissant les investissements étrangers ;

    c)　l'allégation de la violation de tout droit conféré ou établi par le présent Accord en matière d'investissement.

2.	Tout différend relatif aux investissements fait l'objet d'une notification écrite, accompagnée d'un aide-mémoire suffisamment détaillé établi à l'initiative de l'investisseur de l'une des parties, à l'autre partie contractante.

Ce différend est, de préférence, réglé à l'amiable par un arrangement entre les parties au différend et, à défaut, par la conciliation entre les parties contractantes, par la voie diplomatique.

3.	Si le différend ne peut être réglé dans les trois mois à compter de la notification écrite visée au paragraphe 1, il est soumis, à la demande de l'investisseur concerné, pour conciliation ou arbitrage au Centre International pour le Règlement des Différends relatifs aux Investissements (CIRDI).

A cette fin, chaque partie contractante donne, par la présente disposition, son consentement anticipé et irrévocable à ce que tout différend de cette nature soit soumis au CIRDI.

Ce consentement implique que chaque partie contractante renonce à exiger que les recours administratifs ou judiciaires internes aient été préalablement épuisés.

4.	Aucune des parties contractantes, partie à un différend, ne peut soulever d'objection, à aucun stade de toute procédure judiciaire, arbitrale ou autre et à quelque titre que ce soit, du fait que l'investisseur, partie adverse au différend, a perçu une indemnité couvrant tout ou partie de ses dommages, en exécution d'une police d'assurance ou de la garantie prévue à l'article 6.

5.	L'organisme d'arbitrage statue sur base:

-	du droit national de la partie contractante partie au litige, sur le territoire de laquelle l'investissement est situé, y compris les règles relatives aux conflits de lois ;

-	des dispositions de la présente Convention ;

-	des termes de l'engagement particulier qui serait intervenu au sujet de l'investissement ;

-	des règles et principes de droit international généralement admis.

6.	Les sentences d'arbitrage sont définitives et exécutoires pour les parties au différend.

Article 9
DIFFERENDS S'INTERPRETATION ET D'APPLICATION ENTRE PARTIES CONTRACTANTES

1.	Tout différend entre les parties contractantes relatif à l'interprétation ou à l'application du présent Accord est, autant que possible, réglé par voie de consultations entre les deux parties, ou par toute autre voie diplomatique.

A défaut, le différend est soumis à une commission mixte composée de représentants des deux parties contractantes. Celle-ci se réunit, dans un délai de deux mois, à la demande de la partie la plus diligente.

2.   Si la commission mixte ne peut régler le différend dans un délai de six mois à compter de la date à laquelle le différend a été notifié, celui-ci est soumis à une procédure d'arbitrage, à la requête de l'une des parties contractantes.

3.   Dans chaque cas, le tribunal d'arbitrage est composé de trois arbitres: chaque partie contractante désigne un arbitre dans les deux mois suivant la notification de la requête en arbitrage. Les deux arbitres ainsi désignés choisissent de commun accord un troisième arbitre comme Président, lequel est ressortissant d'un Etat tiers. Le Président est nommé dans les deux mois suivant la désignation des deux autres arbitres.

4.   Si le tribunal n'est pas constitué endéans les délais prescrits au paragraphe 3, chaque partie contractante peut, en l'absence de tout autre arrangement, inviter le Président de la Cour Internationale de Justice à procéder aux désignations nécessaires.

Si le Président est citoyen de l'une des parties contactantes ou s'il est empêché, le Vice-Président est invité à procéder aux désignations nécessaires. Si le Vice-Président est citoyen de l'une des parties contractantes ou s'il est empêché, le Membre le plus âgé de la Cour Internationale de Justice, qui n'est pas citoyen de l'une des parties contractantes et qui peut agir, est invité à procéder aux désignations nécessaires.

5.   A moins qu'il n'en soit convenu autrement par les parties contractantes, la décision du tribunal arbitral doit être rendue au plus tard dix mois à dater de sa constitution définitive.

6.   Le tribunal fixe ses propres règles de procédure.
Ses décisions sont prises à la majorité des voix et sont définitives et exécutoires pour les parties contractantes.

7.   Chaque partie contractante supporte les frais inhérents à la désignation de son arbitre et à sa représentation dans la procédure d'arbitrage. Les frais inhérents à la désignation du Président et les autres frais de procédure sont supportés à parts égales par les parties contractantes.

Toutefois, le tribunal peut préciser dans sa décision qu'une part plus élevée des frais doit être supportée par l'une des parties contactantes et cette décision est exécutoire.

Article 10
ENTRE EN VIGUEUR ET DURE.

1.   La présente Convention entre en vigueur trente jours après la date d'échange des instruments de ratification. Elle reste en vigueur pour une période initiale de dix ans et est ensuite chaque fois tacitement reconduite pour dix ans, à moins que l'une des parties contactantes n'en notifie à l'autre partie la dénonciation par voie diplomatique au moins six mois avant la date d'expiration de la période de validité en cours.

2.   Les investissements effectués avant la date d'expiration du présent Accord lui restent soumis pendant une période supplémentaire de dix ans à dater de ladite expiration.

EN FOI DE QUOI les représentants soussignés, dûment autorisés par leurs gouvernements respectifs, ont signé la présente Convention.

FAIT à _____, le_____, en double original, en langue française.

POUR _____ :   POUR LA REPUBLIQUE DU BURUNDI :

*

POUR _____ :   POUR LA REPUBLIQUE DU BURUNDI :

ACCORD ENTRE LE GOUVERNEMENT DE LA REPUBLIQUE DE MAURICE ET LE GOUVERNEMENT DE _____ CONCERNANT LA PROMOTION ET LA PROTECTION RECIPROQUE DES INVESTISSEMENTS*

Préambule

Le Gouvernement de la République de Maurice et _____ (ci-après dénommés les « Parties Contractantes »),

Désireux de créer des conditions favorables à l'accroissement des investissements et d'intensifier la coopération économique dans l'intérêt mutuel des deux Etats,

Dans l'intention de créer et de maintenir des conditions favorables aux investissements des investisseurs d'une Partie Contractante sur le territoire de l'autre Partie Contractante,

Reconnaissant la nécessité d'encourager et de protéger les investissements étrangers en vue de promouvoir la prospérité économique des deux Etats,

Sont convenus de ce qui suit :

Article 1
Définitions

(1)   Aux fins du présent Accord :

    (A)   Le terme "investissement" désigne tout avoir et en particulier, mais non exclusivement :

        (i)   la propriété de biens meubles et immeubles, ainsi que tous les autres droits réels, tels que charges foncières, gages immobiliers et mobiliers ;

        (ii)   les actions, parts sociales et autres formes de participation dans une société ;

        (iii)   les créances monétaires et droits à toute prestation au titre d'un contrat à valeur économique ;

        (iv)   les droits de propriété industrielle et intellectuelle (tels que droits d'auteur, brevets d'invention, modèles d'utilité, dessins ou modèles industriels, marques de fabrique ou de commerce, marques de service, noms commerciaux, indications de provenance), les procédés techniques, le savoir-faire et la clientèle ;

        (v)   les concessions conférées par la loi ou par contrat, y compris les concessions de prospection, de culture, d'extraction ou d'exploitation de

---

*   *Source*: The Government of Mauritius, Ministry of Foreign Affairs. [Note added by the editor.]

ressources naturelles, ainsi que tout autre droit conféré par la loi, par contrat ou par décision de l'autorité en application de la loi.

(B) Le terme « revenus » désigne les montants issus d'un investissement et englobe notamment, mais non exclusivement, les bénéfices, les intérêts, les gains en capital, les dividendes, les redevances et les rémunérations.

(C) Le terme « investisseurs » désigne, en ce qui concerne chaque Partie Contractante :

    (i) les personnes physiques qui, d'après la législation de cette Partie Contractante, sont considérées comme ses nationaux ;

    (ii) les entités juridiques, y compris les sociétés, les sociétés enregistrées, les sociétés de personnes ou autres organisations, qui sont constituées conformément à la législation de cette Partie Contractante;

(D) Le terme "territoire" désigne,

    (i) en ce qui concerne la République de _____ ;

    (ii) en ce qui concerne la République de Maurice :

        (a) tous les territoires et îles qui, conformément à la législation de Maurice, constituent l'Etat de Maurice ;

        (b) les eaux territoriales de Maurice ; et

        (c) toute zone située au-delà des eaux territoriales de Maurice, qui, conformément au droit international, est ou sera définie par la législation de Maurice comme une zone, plateau continental inclus, sur laquelle peuvent être exercés les droits de Maurice en ce qui concerne la mer, les fonds marins et leur sous-sol, ainsi que leurs ressources naturelles.

(2) Toute modification de la forme d'investissement des avoirs n'affecte pas leur qualité d'investissement.

Article 2
Champ d'application

(1) Les dispositions du présent Accord s'appliqueront uniquement:

    (a) dans le cas des investissements dans le territoire de _____, à tous les investissements effectués par des investisseurs ou des sociétés de la République de Maurice.

    (b) dans le cas des investissements dans le territoire de Maurice, à tous les investissements effectués par des investisseurs ou des sociétés de _____.

Article 3
Encouragement et admission

(1)	Chaque Partie Contractante encouragera et facilitera, compte tenu de sa pratique générale en matière d'investissement étranger, les investissements des investisseurs de l'autre Partie Contractante sur son territoire et admettra ou approuvera ces investissements conformément à ses lois et règlements.

(2)	Chaque Partie Contractante s'efforcera de délivrer, conformément à ses lois et règlements, les autorisations nécessaires en relation avec ces investissements, y compris aux fins d'exécution de contrats de licence, d'assistance technique, commerciale ou administrative, ainsi que les autorisations requises pour les activités de consultants et d'experts.

(3)	Les investissements ayant reçu un agrément conformément à l'Article 2 ci-devant feront l'objet d'un traitement juste et équitable et d'une protection, conformément aux dispositions du présent Accord.

Article 4
Traitement des Investissements

(1)	Les investissements et les revenus des investisseurs de chaque Partie Contractante se verront accorder en tout temps un traitement juste et équitable et jouiront d'une protection et d'une sécurité pleines et entières sur le territoire de l'autre Partie Contractante. Aucune Partie Contractante n'entravera d'une quelconque manière, par des mesures injustifiées ou discriminatoires, la gestion, l'entretien, l'utilisation, la jouissance, l'accroissement ou l'aliénation de tels investissements.

(2)	Chaque Partie Contractante accordera sur son territoire aux investissements et aux revenus des investisseurs de l'autre Partie Contractante un traitement non moins favorable que celui qu'elle accorde aux investissements et aux revenus de ses propres investisseurs ou aux investissements et aux revenus des investisseurs d'un quelconque Etat tiers, le traitement le plus favorable à l'investisseur en cause étant déterminant.

(3)	Chaque Partie Contractante accordera sur son territoire aux investisseurs de l'autre Partie Contractante, en ce qui concerne la gestion, l'entretien, l'utilisation, la jouissance ou l'aliénation de leurs investissements, un traitement non moins favorable que celui qu'elle accorde à ses propres investisseurs ou aux investisseurs d'un quelconque Etat tiers, le traitement le plus favorable à l'investisseur en cause étant déterminant.

(4)	Si une Partie Contractante accorde des avantages particuliers aux investisseurs d'un quelconque Etat tiers en vertu d'un accord établissant une zone de libre-échange, une union douanière ou un marché commun, accord dont elle est déjà partie ou le deviendra, ou en vertu d'un accord pour éviter la double imposition, elle ne sera pas tenue d'accorder de tels avantages aux investisseurs de l'autre Partie Contractante.

(5)	Pour prévenir toute équivoque, il est confirmé que les principes visés aux alinéas (2) et (3) du présent article ne seront pas applicables en ce qui concerne les avantages particuliers accordés aux institutions financières de développement, par exemple en matière fiscale.

(6) Chacune des Parties Contractantes respectera tous ses engagements relatifs aux investissements ainsi que ceux pris par ses investisseurs avec les investissements de l'autre Partie Contractante, conformément aux dispositions figurant dans le présent Accord, et à ses propres lois.

Article 5
Compensation pour pertes

(1) Les investisseurs d'une Partie Contractante dont les investissements effectués sur le territoire de l'autre Partie Contractante ont subi des pertes dues à la guerre ou à tout autre conflit armé, révolution, état d'urgence national, révolte, insurrection ou émeute survenus sur le territoire de cette dernière Partie Contractante, bénéficieront, de la part de celle-ci, en ce qui concerne la restitution, l'indemnisation, la compensation ou tout autre règlement, d'un traitement non moins favorable que celui qu'elle accorde à ses propres investisseurs ou aux investisseurs d'un quelconque Etat tiers. Les paiements en résultant seront librement transférables au taux de change applicable à la date du transfert conformément aux règles de change en vigueur.

(2) Sans préjudice de l'alinéa (1) du présent article, les investisseurs d'une Partie Contractante qui, dans l'une des situations visées par ledit alinéa, ont subi des pertes sur le territoire de l'autre Partie Contractante du fait :

(a) de la réquisition de leurs avoirs par ses forces ou ses autorités, ou

(b) de la destruction de leurs avoirs par ses forces ou ses autorités, qui ne résultait pas de combats ou n'était pas requise par la situation,

se verront accorder une restitution ou une compensation adéquate. Les paiements en résultant seront librement transférables au taux de change applicable à la date du transfert conformément aux règles de change en vigueur.

Article 6
Expropriation

(1) Les investissements des investisseurs d'une Partie Contractante ne seront pas nationalisés, expropriés ou soumis à des mesures ayant des effets équivalents à une nationalisation ou à une expropriation (ci-après dénommées « expropriation ») sur le territoire de l'autre Partie Contractante, si ce n'est pour des motifs d'intérêt public et à condition que ces mesures soient conformes aux prescriptions légales, qu'elles ne soient pas discriminatoires et qu'elles donnent lieu au prompt versement d'une indemnité effective et adéquate. L'indemnité se montera à la valeur réelle de l'investissement exproprié immédiatement avant que l'expropriation ne soit entreprise ou qu'elle ne soit connue dans le public, le premier de ces faits étant déterminant. Elle inclura des intérêts calculés à un taux commercial normal jusqu'à la date du paiement, sera versée sans retard, sera pleinement réalisable et librement transférable sur la base du taux de change applicable à la date du transfert conformément aux règles de change en vigueur.

(2) L'investisseur concerné par l'expropriation aura le droit de faire procéder à un prompt réexamen, selon la législation de la Partie Contractante qui exproprie, par une autorité judiciaire ou une autre autorité indépendante de cette Partie, de son cas et de l'estimation de son investissement conformément aux principes énoncés dans le présent article.

(3)   Si une Partie Contractante exproprie les avoirs d'une société enregistrée ou constituée conformément à la législation en vigueur sur son territoire et dans laquelle des investisseurs de l'autre Partie Contractante détiennent des parts, elle fera en sorte, dans la mesure nécessaire et conformément à sa législation, que ces investisseurs soient indemnisés en conformité avec l'alinéa (1) du présent article.

Article 7
Libre transfert

(1)   Chaque Partie Contractante garantit aux investisseurs de l'autre Partie Contractante le transfert sans délai dans une monnaie librement convertible des montants afférents à un investissement conformément aux articles 5 et 6 de cet Accord.

(2)   Les transferts seront effectués au taux de change prévalant sur le marché à la date du transfert. En l'absence de marché des changes, le taux à utiliser sera le taux le plus récent appliqué aux investissements nationaux ou le taux le plus récent pour la conversion de la monnaie concernée en droits de tirage spéciaux, le taux à retenir étant celui qui est le plus favorable à l'investisseur.

Article 8
Differends relatifs à l'investissement

(1)   Sous réserve des dispositions du Paragraphe (3) ci-après, tout différend entre un investisseur d'une Partie Contractante avec un investisseur de l'autre Partie Contractante, relatif à un investissement dans l'un des deux territoires, sera dans la mesure du possible réglé à l'amiable par le biais de négociations entre les parties au différend.

(2)   Au cas où le différend ne peut être réglé par le biais de négociations dans un délai de 6 mois, l'une ou l'autre des deux parties pourra initier une procédure judiciaire auprès du tribunal compétent de la Partie Contractante qui a accueilli l'investissement.

(3)   Au cas où un différend portant sur le montant d'un indemnisation résultant d'une expropriation, d'une nationalisation, ou de toute autre mesure ayant un effet équivalent, ainsi qu'il est prévu à l'Article 6, n'a pu être réglé dans un délai de 6 mois après le recours aux tentatives amiables indiquées au Paragraph 1 du présent Article par le investisseurs, ledit différend pourra être soumis à un tribunal d'arbitrage international constitué par les deux parties. Les dispositions du présent Paragraphe ne s'appliqueront pas dans le cas où les investisseurs concernés recourent à la procédure prévue au Paragraphe (2) du présent Article.

(4)   Le tribunal d'arbitrage international auquel il est fait référence ci-devant sera constitué comme suit: chacune des parties au différend nommera un arbitre. Les 2 arbitres ainsi nommés procèderont à la nomination d'un troisième arbitre en qualité de Président du tribunal. Les arbitres seront désignés dans un délai de deux mois, et le Président du tribunal dans un délai de quatre mois, à compter de la date où l'une des deux parties aura notifié à l'autre partie son intention de soumettre le différend à l'arbitrage.

(5)   Si les désignations nécessaires ne sont pas effectuées dans le délai prescrit au Paragraphe (4) ci-devant, l'une ou l'autre des deux parties pourra, à défaut de tout autre accord, demander au Président de l'institut d'arbitrage international de la Chambre de Commerce de Stockholm de procéder aux désignations nécessaires.

(6)   Mis à part ce qui est prévu ci-après, le tribunal arbitral déterminera sa propre procédure en se référant à la "Convention sur le règlement de différends relatifs à l'investissement entre Etats et ressortissant d'autres Etats", établie à Washington le 18 mars 1965.

(7)   Le tribunal prendra sa décision à la majorité des votes.

(8)   La décision du tribunal arbitral sera définitive et obligera les parties, qui s'engageront à se conformer aux dispositions de la sentence.

(9)   Le tribunal arbitral indiquera le fondement de sa décision et en donnera les motifs sur requête de l'une ou l'autre des parties.

(10)   Chaque partie prendra à sa charge les frais de son arbitre et de ses conseillers pour la procédure arbitrale. Les frais du Président du tribunal pour sa fonction, ainsi que les autres frais du tribunal arbitral, seront pris en charge de manière égale par chacune des parties. Le tribunal pourra cependant décider dans sa sentence qu'une proportion plus importante des frais sera prise en charge par l'une des deux parties, et ladite sentence obligera les deux parties.

(11)   Les dispositions du présent Article n'affecteront pas le droit des Parties Contractantes de recourir aux procédures prévues à l'Article 9, si le différend porte sur l'interprétation ou la mise en oeuvre du présent Accord.

Article 9
Différends entre les Parties Contractantes

(1)   Tout différend entre les Parties Contractantes portant sur l'interprétation ou à la mise en oeuvre du présent Accord sera, dans la mesure du possible, réglé par voie diplomatique.

(2)   Si le différend ne peut être réglé de cette manière dans un délai de six mois, il sera soumis à l'arbitrage à la requête de l'une ou l'autre des Parties Contractantes.

(3)   Le tribunal arbitral (ci-après dénommé "le tribunal") sera composé de trois arbitres, chaque partie nommant un arbitre et le troisième, qui sera le Président du tribunal et ressortissant d'un Etat tiers, sera désigné d'un commun accord par les Parties Contractantes. Un tel tribunal sera constitué pour chaque requête. Dans un délai de deux mois après la réception de la demande d'arbitrage, chaque Partie Contractante désignera un arbitre et, dans un délai de deux mois après désignation des deux arbitres, les Parties Contractantes désigneront le troisième arbitre.

(4)   Au cas où le tribunal n'a pas été constitué dans un délai de quatre mois après la réception de la demande d'arbitrage, chacune des Parties Contractantes pourra, à défaut de tout autre accord, demander au Président de la Cour Internationale de Justice de désigner l'/les arbitre(s) non encore nommé(s). Si le Président est un ressortissant de l'une ou l'autre des Parties Contractantes ou s'il n'est pas en mesure de procéder à ladite désignation, le Vice-Président peut être appelé à le faire. Si le Vice-Président est un ressortissant de l'une ou l'autre des Parties Contractatnes ou s'il n'est pas en mesure de le faire, le membre qui, dans la hiérarchie de la Cour Internationale, vient juste après et qui n'est pas un ressortissant des Parties Contractantes, peut être appelé à procéder aux nominations nécessaires, et ainsi de suite.

(5)   Le tribunal prendra sa décision à la majorité des votes. La décision du tribunal arbitral sera définitive et obligera les parties, qui s'engageront à se conformer aux dispositions de la

sentence. Chaque Partie Contractante prendra à sa charge les frais de son arbitre et de ses conseillers pour la procédure arbitrale, ainsi que la moitié des frais du Président du tribunal et des autres frais. Le tribunal pourra cependant décider dans sa sentence qu'une proportion plus importante des frais devra être prise en charge par l'une ou l'autre des deux parties, et ladite sentence obligera les deux parties.

(6)   Excepté pour ce qui précède, le tribunal établira lui-même ses propres règles de procédure.

Article 10
Principe de subrogation

(1)   Si une Partie Contractante ou un organisme désigné par elle effectue un paiement à titre d'indemnité pour un investissement effectué sur le territoire de l'autre Partie Contractante, cette dernière Partie Contractante reconnaîtra la cession à la première Partie Contractante ou à l'organisme désigné par elle, en vertu de la loi ou d'un contrat, de tous les droits et créances de l'investisseur indemnisé et le droit pour la première Partie Contractante ou l'organisme désigné par elle d'exercer ces droits et de faire valoir ces créances par voie de subrogation, dans la même mesure que l'investisseur.

(2)   Aucune rémunération effectuée par une Partie Contractante (ou tout représentant, toute institution, tout organisme statutaire ou toute personne morale désignés par elle) à ses investisseurs ne pourra affecter le droit desdits investisseurs de procéder à des réclamations à l'encontre de l'autre Partie Contractante, conformément aux dispositions de l'Article 8, à la condition que l'exercice d'un tel droit ne fasse pas double emploi ou ne contredise pas l'exercice d'un droit en vertu de la subrogation, ainsi qu'il est prévu au Paragraphe (1) ci-devant.

Article 11
Autres règles et engagements particuliers

(1)   Si des dispositions de la législation d'une Partie Contractante ou des règles de droit international accordent aux investissements des investisseurs de l'autre Partie Contractante un traitement plus favorable que celui prévu par le présent Accord, elles prévaudront sur ce dernier dans la mesure où elles sont plus favorables.

(2)   Chaque Partie Contractante se conformera à toute obligation particulière contractée à l'égard d'un investissement effectué sur son territoire par un investisseur de l'autre Partie Contractante.

Article 12
Interdictions et Restrictions

Aucune disposition du présent Accord ne pourra être interprétée comme empêchant une Partie Contractante de prendre toute mesure nécessaire à la protection de ses intérêts essentiels en matière de sécurité, ou pour des motifs de santé publique ou de prévention des maladies affectant les animaux et les végétaux.

Article 13
Entrée en vigueur

(1)   Le présent Accord est applicable aux investissements effectués sur le territoire d'une Partie Contractante, conformément à ses lois et règlements, par des investisseurs de l'autre Partie Contractante, avant ou après son entrée en vigueur. Afin d'éviter tout doute, il est convenu que tout investissement, sous réserve des dispositions du présent Accord, sera soumis aux lois en vigueur dans le territoire de la Partie Contractante dans lequel l'investissement aura été effectué.

(2)   Chaque Partie Contractante notifiera l'autre Partie Contractante de l'accomplissement des procédures requises par sa législation pour l'entrée en vigueur du présent Accord. Celui-ci entrera en vigueur le jour suivant la réception de la dernière de ces notifications.

(3)   Le présent Accord restera valable pour une durée de dix ans. Après ce terme, il restera en vigueur jusqu'à l'expiration d'une période de douze mois à compter de la date à laquelle une Partie Contractante l'aura dénoncé par écrit à l'autre.

(4)   En ce qui concerne les investissements effectués avant l'expiration du présent accord, les dispositions de ce dernier continueront de s'appliquer pendant une période supplémentaire de dix ans à compter de ladite expiration ou pendant toute période plus longue convenue entre l'investisseur et la Partie Contractante sur le territoire de laquelle l'investissement a été effectué.

EN FOI DE QUOI, les soussignés, dûment autorisés à cet effet par leurs Gouvernements respectifs, ont signé le présent Accord.

Fait à _____, le _____, en double exemplaire, les deux textes faisant également foi.

Pour le Gouvernement de la
République de Maurice

Pour le Gouvernement
_____

*

AGREEMENT BETWEEN MONGOLIA AND _____ ON THE PROMOTION AND RECIPROCAL PROTECTION OF INVESTMENTS*

Preamble

The Government of Mongolia and the Government of _____,

Desiring to intensify economic cooperation to the mutual benefit of both States,

Intending to create and maintain favourable conditions for investments by investors of one Contracting Party in the territory of the other Contracting Party,

Recognizing the need to promote and protect foreign investments with the aim to foster the economic prosperity of both States,

Have agreed as follows:

Article 1
DEFINITIONS

For the purpose of this Agreement:

1.   The term "investor" refers with regard to either Contracting Party to

   a)   natural persons who, according to the law of that Contracting Party, are considered to be its nationals;

   b)   legal entities, including companies, corporations, business associations and other organisations, which are constituted or otherwise duly organised under the law of that Contracting Party and have their seat, together with real economic activities, in the territory of that same Contracting Party;

   c)   legal entities established under the law of any country which are, directly or indirectly, controlled by nationals of that Contracting Party or by legal entities having their seat, together with real economic activities, in the territory of that Contracting Party.

2.   The term "investments" shall include every kind of assets and particularly:

   a)   mobile and immobile property as well as any other rights in rem, such as mortgages, pledges;

   b)   shares, parts or any other kinds of participation in companies;

---

* *Source*: The Government of Mongolia, Ministry of Foreign Affairs. [Note added by the editor.]

c)   claims to money, including bonds and debentures, or to any performance having an economic value;

d)   copyrights, industrial property rights, technological processes, know-how and goodwill;

e)   business concessions and other rights to conduct economic activities conferred by law or under contract, including concessions to search for, extract or exploit natural resources.

3.   The term "return" means the amounts yielded by an investments and in particular, though not exclusively, includes profits, interests, dividends, royalties and fees.

Article 2
SCOPE OF APPLICATION

The present Agreement shall apply to investments in the territory of one Contracting Party made in accordance with its laws and regulations by investors of the other Contracting Party, whether prior to or after the entry into force of the Agreement.

Article 3
PROMOTION, ADMISSION

1.   Each Contracting Party shall in its territory promote as far as possible investments by investors of the Contracting Party and admit such investments in accordance with its laws and regulations.

2.   When a Contracting Party shall have admitted an investment on its territory it shall grant the necessary permits in connection with such an investment and with the carrying out of licensing agreements and contracts for technical, commercial or administrative assistance. Each Contracting Party shall, whenever needed, endeavour to issue the necessary authorizations concerning the activities of consultants and other qualified persons of foreign nationality.

Article 4
PROTECTION, TREATMENT

1.   Each Contracting Party shall protect within its territory investments made in accordance with its laws and regulations by investors of the other Contracting Party and shall not impair by unreasonable or discriminatory measures the management, maintenance, use, enjoyment, extension or disposal of such investments.

2.   Each Contracting Party shall ensure fair and equitable treatment within its territory of the investments of the investors of the other Contracting Party. This treatment shall not be less favourable than that granted by each Contracting Party to investments made within its territory by its own investors, or than that granted by each Contracting Party to the investments made within its territory by investors of the most favoured nation, if this latter treatment is more favourable.

3.   If a Contracting Party accords special advantages to investors of any third State by virtue of an agreement establishing a free trade area, a customs union, a common market or a similar

regional organization or by virtue of an agreement on the avoidance of double taxation, it shall not be obliged to accord such advantages to investors of the other Contracting Party.

Article 5
FREE TRANSFER

1.   Each Contracting Party in whose territory investments have been made by investors of the other Contracting Party shall guarantee those investors the unrestricted transfer of the payments relating to these investments, particularly of:

a)   returns;

b)   repayments of loans;

c)   amounts assigned to cover expenses relating to the management of the investment;

d)   royalties and other payments deriving from rights enumerated in Article 1, paragraph 2, letters c, d and e of this Agreement;

e)   additional capital necessary for the maintenance or development of the investment;

f)   the proceeds of the sale or of the partial or total liquidation of the investment, including possible increment values;

g)   earnings of natural persons.

2.   Transfers shall be effected without delay in a freely convertible currency. Such transfers shall be made at the rate of exchange applicable on the date of transfer pursuant to the exchange regulations in force.

Article 6
DISPOSSESSION, COMPENSATION

1.   Neither of the Contracting Party shall take, either directly or indirectly, measures of expropriation, nationalization or any other measures having the same nature or the same effect against investments of investors of the other Contracting Party, unless the measures are taken in the public interest, on a non discriminatory basis, and under the due process of law, and provided that provisions be made for effective and adequate compensation. The amount of compensation, interest included, shall be settled in the currency of the country of origin of the investment and paid without delay to the person entitled thereto without regard to its residence or domicile.

2.   The investors of the Contracting Party whose investments have suffered losses due too a war or any other armed conflict, revolution, state of emergency or rebellion, which took place in the territory of the other Contracting Party shall benefit, on the part of this latter, from a treatment in accordance with Article 4, paragraph 2, of this Agreement as regards restitution, indemnification, compensation or other settlement.

Article 7
PRINCIPLE OF SUBROGATION

Where one Contracting Party has granted any financial quarantee against noncommercial risks in regard to an investment by one of its investors in the territory of the other Contracting Party, the latter shall recognize the rights of the first Contracting Party by virtue of the principle of subrogation to the rights of the investor when payment has been made under this quarantee by the fist Contracting Party.

Article 8
DISPUTES BETWEEN A CONTRACTING PARTY
AND AN INVESTOR OF THE OTHER CONTRACTING PARTY

1.   With a view to an amicable solution of disputes between a Contracting Party and an investors of the other Contracting Party and without prejudice to Article 9 of this Agreement, consultations will take place between the parties concerned.

2.   If these consultations do not result in a solution within six months from the date of request for consultations, the investor may submit the dispute, at his choice, for settlement to:

   a)   the International Center for Settlement of Investment Disputes(ICSID) instituted by the Convention on the settlement of investment disputes between States and nationals of other States, opened for signature at Washington, on 18 March 1965;

   b)   an ad hoc tribunal which unless otherwise agreed upon by the parties to the dispute shall be established under the arbitration rules of the United Nations Commission on International Trade Law (UNCITRAL).

3.   Each Contracting Party hereby consents to the submission of an investment dispute to international arbitration.

4.   The Contracting Party which is a party to the dispute shall, at no time whatsoever during the settlement procedure or the execution of the sentence, raise as an objection the fact that the investor has received, by virtue of an insurance contract, a compensation covering the whole or part of the incurred damage.

5.   A company which has been incorporated or constituted according to the laws in force on the territory of the Contracting Party and which, prior to the origin of the dispute, was under the control of nationals or companies of the other Contracting Party, is considered, in the sense of the Convention of Washington and according to its Article 25 (2) (b), as a company of the latter.

6.   Neither Contracting Party shall pursue through diplomatic channels a dispute submitted to international arbitration unless the other Contracting Party does not abide by and comply with award rendered by such arbitral tribunal.

Article 9
DISPUTES BETWEEN CONTRACTING PARTY

1.   Disputes between Contracting Parties regarding the interpretation or application of the provisions of this Agreement shall be settled through diplomatic channels.

2.   If both Contracting Party cannot reach an agreement within six months after the beginning of the dispute between themselves, the latter shall, upon the request of either Contracting Party, be submitted to an arbitral tribunal of three members. Each Contracting Party shall appoint one arbitrator, and these two arbitrators shall nominate a chairman who shall be a national of a third State.

3.   If one of the Contracting Party has not appointed its arbitrator and has not followed the invitation of the other Contracting Party to make that appointment within two months, the arbitrator shall be appointed upon the request of that Contracting Party by the President of the International Court of Justice.

4.   If both arbitrators cannot reach an agreement about the choice of the chairman within two months after their appointment, the latter shall be appointed upon the request of either Contracting Party by the President of the International Court of Justice.

5.   If, in the cases specified under paragraph 3 and 4 of this Article, the President of the International Court of Justice is prevented from carrying out the said function or if he is a national of either Contracting Party, the appointment shall be made by the Vice-President, and if the latter is prevented or if he is a national of either Contracting Party, the appointment shall be made by the most senior Judge of the Court who is not a national of either Contracting Party.

6.   Subject to other provisions made by the Contracting Party, the tribunal shall determine its procedure.

7.   Each Contracting Party shall bear the cost of the arbitrator it has appointed and of its representation in the arbitral proceedings. The cost of the Chairman and the remaining costs shall be borne in equal parts by the Contracting Parties.

8.   The decisions of the tribunal are final and binding for each Contracting Party.

Article 10
OTHER COMMITMENTS

1.   If the provisions in the legislation of other Contracting Party or rules of international law entitle investments by investors of the other Contracting Party to treatment more favourable than is provided for by this Agreement, such provisions shall to the extent that they are more favourable prevail over this Agreement.

2.   Each Contracting Party shall observe any obligation it has assumed with regard to investments in its territory by investors of the other Contracting Party.

Article 11
FINAL PROVISIONS

1.   This Agreement shall enter into force on the day when both Governments have notified each other that they have complied with the constitutional requirements for the conclusion and entry into force of international agreements, and shall remain binding for a period of ten years. Unless written notice of termination is given six months before the expiration of this period, the Agreement shall be considered as renewed on the same terms for a period of two years, and so forth.

2.   In case of official notice as to the termination of the present Agreement, the provisions of Article 1 to 10 shall continue to be effective for a further period of ten years for investments made before official notice was given.

Done at_____, on _____, in duplicate, in the Mongolian, and English languages, each text being equally authentic. In case of divergence the English text shall prevail.

FOR THE GOVERNMENT _____   FOR THE GOVERNMENT
OF MONGOLIA_____   OF _____

*

AGREEMENT BETWEEN THE GOVERNMENT OF THE KINGDOM OF SWEDEN AND THE GOVERNMENT OF _____ ON THE PROMOTION AND RECIPROCAL PROTECTION OF INVESTMENTS[*]

The Government of the Kingdom of Sweden and the Government of _____

desiring to intensify economic cooperation to the mutual benefit of both countries and to maintain fair and equitable conditions for investments by investors of one Contracting Party in the territory of the other Contracting Party,

recognizing that the promotion and reciprocal protection of such investments favour the expansion of the economic relations between the two Contracting Parties and stimulate investment initiatives,

have agreed as follows:

Article 1 Definitions

For the purposes of this Agreement:

(1)   The term "investment" shall mean any kind of asset owned or controlled directly or indirectly by an investor of one Contracting Party in the territory of the other Contracting Party, provided that the investment has been made in accordance with the laws and regulations of the other Contracting Party, and shall include in particular, though not exclusively:

(a)   movable and immovable property as well as any other property rights, such as mortgage, lien, pledge, usufruct and similar rights;

(b)   a company or enterprise, or shares, stocks or other kinds of interest in a company or enterprise;

(c)   title to money or any performance having an economic value;

(d)   intellectual property rights, technical processes, trade names, know-how, goodwill and other similar rights;

(e)   business concessions conferred by law, administrative decisions or under contract, including concessions to search for, develop, extract or exploit natural resources.

Goods, that under a leasing agreement are placed at the disposal of a lessee in the territory of one Contracting Party by a lessor being an investor of the other Contracting Party shall be treated not less favourably than an investment.

---

[*]   *Source*: The Government of Sweden, Ministry of Foreign Affairs. [Note added by the editor.]

A change in the form in which assets are invested does not affect their character as investments.

(2)   The term "investor" of a Contracting Party shall mean:

(a)   any natural person who is a national of that Contracting Party in accordance with its law; and

(b)   any legal person or other organisation organized in accordance with the law applicable in that Contracting Party, and

(c)   any legal person not organized under the law of that Contracting Party but controlled by an investor as defined under (a) or (b).

(3)   The term "returns" shall mean the amounts yielded by an investment and in particular, though not exclusively, include profit, interest, capital gains, dividends, royalties or fees.

(4)   The term "territory" shall mean the territory of each Contracting Party as well as the exclusive economic zone and the seabed and subsoil, over which the Contracting Party exercises, in accordance with international law, sovereign rights and jurisdiction for the purpose of exploration, exploitation and conservation of natural resources.

Article 2 Promotion and Protection of Investments

(1)   Each Contracting Party shall, subject to its general policy in the field of foreign investment, promote in its territory investments by investors of the other Contracting Party and shall admit such investments in accordance with its legislation.

(2)   Subject to the laws and regulations relating to the entry and sojourn of aliens, individuals working for an investor of one Contracting Party, as well as members of their household, shall be permitted to enter into, remain on and leave the territory of the other Contracting Party for the purpose of carrying out activities associated with investments in the territory of the latter Contacting Party.

(3)   Each Contracting Party shall at all times ensure fair and equitable treatment of the investments by investors of the other Contracting Party and shall not impair the management, maintenance, use, enjoyment or disposal thereof nor the acquisition of goods and services or the sale of their production, through unreasonable or discriminatory measures.

(4)   The investments made in accordance with the laws and regulations of the Contracting Party in whose territory they are undertaken, shall enjoy the full protection of this Agreement and in no case shall a Contracting Party award treatment less favourable than that required by international law. Each Contracting Party shall observe any obligation it has entered into with investors of the other Contracting Party with regard to their investment.

(5)   Returns yielded from an investment shall be given the same treatment and protection as an investment.

Article 3 National and Most Favoured Nation Treatment of Investments

(1)   Each Contracting Party shall apply to investments made in its territory by investors of the other Contracting Party a treatment which is no less favourable than that accorded to investments made by its own investors or by investors of third States, whichever is the more favourable.

(2)   Notwithstanding the provisions of Paragraph (1) of this Article, a Contracting Party which has concluded or may conclude an agreement regarding the formation of a customs union, a common market or a free-trade area shall be free to grant, by virtue of such agreements, more favourable treatment to investments by investors of the State or States which are also parties to the aforesaid agreements, or by investors of some of these States.

(3)   The provisions of Paragraph (1) of this Article shall not be construed so as to oblige one Contracting Party to extend to investors of the other Contracting Party the benefit of any treatment, preference or privilege resulting from any international agreement or arrangement relating wholly or mainly to taxation or any domestic legislation relating wholly or mainly to taxation.

Article 4 Expropriation

(1)   Neither Contracting Party shall take any measures depriving, directly or indirectly, an investor of the other Contracting Party of an investment unless the following conditions are complied with:

   (a)   the measures are taken in the public interest and under due process of law;

   (b)   the measures are distinct and not discriminatory; and

   (c)   the measures are accompanied by provisions for the payment of prompt, adequate and effective compensation, which shall be transferable without delay in a freely convertible currency.

(2)   Such compensation shall amount to the fair market value of the investment expropriated at the time immediately before the expropriation or impending expropriation became known in such a way as to affect the value of the investment (hereinafter referred to as the "Valuation Date").

Such fair market value shall at the request of the investor be expressed in a freely convertible currency on the basis of the market rate of exchange existing for that currency on the Valuation Date. Compensation shall also include interest at a commercial rate established on a market basis from the date of expropriation until the date of payment.

(3)   The provisions of Paragraph (1) and (2) of this Article shall also apply to the returns from an investment as well as and, in the event of liquidation, to the proceeds from the liquidation.

(4)   Where a Contracting Party expropriates the assets of a company or an enterprise in its territory in which investors of the other Contracting Party have an investment, including through the ownership of shares, it shall ensure that the provisions of this Article are applied to the extent

311

necessary to guarantee prompt, adequate and effective compensation in respect of their investment to such investors of the other Contracting Party.

Article 5 Compensation

(1)   Investors of either Contracting Party who suffer losses of their investments in the territory of the other Contracting Party due to war or other armed conflict, a state of national emergency, revolt, insurrection or riot shall be accorded, with respect to restitution, indemnification, compensation or other settlement, a treatment which is no less favourable than that accorded to its own investors or to investors of any third State. Resulting payments shall be transferable without delay in a freely convertible currency.

(2)   Without prejudice to paragraph (1) of this Article, investors of a Contracting Party who in any of the situations referred to in that paragraph, suffer losses in the territory of the other Contracting Party resulting from

(a)   requisitioning of its investment or part thereof by the latter's forces or authorities; or

(b)   destruction of its investment or part thereof by the latter's forces or authorities, which were not required by the necessity of the situation,

shall be accorded restitution or compensation which in either case shall be prompt, adequate and effective.

Article 6 Transfers

(1)   Each Contracting Party shall allow without delay the transfer in a freely convertible currency of payments in connection with an investment, and shall include in particular though not exclusively:

(a)   the returns;

(b)   the proceeds from a total or partial sale or liquidation of any investment by an investor of the other Contracting Party;

(c)   funds in repayment of loans;

(d)   a compensation according to Article 4 or 5; and

(e)   the earnings of individuals, not being its nationals, who are allowed to work in connection with an investment in its territory and other amounts appropriated for the coverage of expenses connected with the management of the investment.

(2)   Any transfer referred to in this Agreement shall be effected at the market rate of exchange existing on the day of transfer with respect to spot transactions in the currency to be transferred. In the absence of a market for foreign exchange, the rate to be used will be the most recent rate applied to inward investments or the most recent exchange rate for conversion of currencies into Special Drawing Rights, whichever is the most favourable to the investor.

Article 7 Subrogation

If a Contracting Party or its designated agency makes a payment to any of its investors under a guarantee it has granted in respect of an investment in the territory of the other Contracting Party, the latter Contracting Party shall, without prejudice to the rights of the former Contracting Party under Article 9, recognize the transfer of any right or title of such an investor to the former Contracting Party or its designated agency and the right of the former Contracting Party or its designated agency to exercise by virtue of subrogation any such right or title to the same extent as its predecessor in title.

Article 8 Disputes between an Investor and a Contracting Party

(1)   Any dispute concerning an investment between an investor of one Contracting Party and the other Contracting Party shall, if possible, be settled amicably.

(2)   If any such dispute cannot be settled within six months following the date on which the dispute has been raised by the investor through written notification to the Contracting Party, each Contracting Party hereby consents to the submission of the dispute, at the investor's choice, for resolution by international arbitration to one of the following fora:

   i)   the International Centre for Settlement of Investment Disputes (ICSID) for settlement by arbitration under the Washington Convention of 18 March 1965 on the Settlement of Investment Disputes between States and Nationals of Other States provided both Contracting Parties have adhered to the said Convention, or

   ii)   the Additional Facility of the Centre, if the Centre is not available under the Convention, or

   iii)   an ad hoc tribunal set up under Arbitration Rules of the United Nations Commission on International Trade Law (UNCITRAL). The appointing authority under the said rules shall be the Secretary General of ICSID.

If the parties to such a dispute have different opinions as to whether conciliation or arbitration is the more appropriate method of settlement, the investor shall have the right to choose.

(3)   For the purpose of this Article and Article 25(2)(b) of the said Washington Convention, any legal person which is constituted in accordance with the legislation of one Contracting party and which, before a dispute arises, was controlled by an investor of the other Contracting Party, shall be treated as a national of the other Contracting Party.

(4)   Any arbitration under the Additional Facility Rules or under the UNCITRAL Arbitration Rules shall, at the request of either party to the dispute, be held in a state that is a party to the United Nations Convention on the Recognition and Enforcement of Foreign Arbitral Awards, done at New York, June 10, 1958 (the New York Convention).

(5)   The consent given by each Contracting Party in paragraph (2) and the submission of the dispute by an investor under the said paragraph shall constitute the written consent and written agreement of the parties to the dispute to its submission for settlement for the purposes of Chapter II of the Washington Convention (Jurisdiction of the Centre) and for the purpose of the

Additional Facility Rules, Article 1 of the UNCITRAL Arbitration Rules and Article II of the New York Convention.

6)   In any proceeding involving an investment dispute, a Contracting Party shall not assert, as a defense, counterclaim, right of set-off or for any other reason, that indemnification or other compensation for all or part of the alleged damages has been received pursuant to an insurance or guarantee contract, but the Contracting Party may require evidence that the compensating party agrees to that the investor exercises the right to claim compensation.

(7)   Any arbitral award rendered pursuant to this Article shall be final and binding on the parties to the dispute. Each Contracting Party shall carry out without delay the provisions of any such award and provide in its territory for the enforcement of such an award.

Article 9 Disputes between the Contracting Parties

(1)   Any dispute between the Contracting Parties concerning the interpretation or application of this Agreement shall, if possible, be settled by negotiations between the Governments of the two Contracting Parties.

(2)   If the dispute cannot thus be settled within six months, following the date on which such negotiations were requested by either Contracting Party, it shall at the request of either Contracting Party be submitted to an arbitration tribunal.

(3)   The arbitration tribunal shall be set up from case to case, each Contracting Party appointing one member. These two members shall then agree upon a national of a third State as their chairman, to be appointed by the Governments of the two Contracting Parties. The members shall be appointed within two months, and the chairman within four months, from the date either Contracting Party, has advised the other Contracting Party of its wish to submit the dispute to an arbitration tribunal.

(4)   If the time limits referred to in Paragraph (3) of this Article have not been complied with, either Contracting Party may, in the absence of any other relevant arrangement, invite the President of the International Court of Justice to make the necessary appointments.

(5)   If the President of the International Court of Justice is prevented from discharging the function provided for in Paragraph (4) of this Article or is a national of either Contracting Party, the Vice-President shall be invited to make the necessary appointments. If the Vice-President is prevented from discharging the said function or is a national of either Contracting Party, the most senior member of the Court who is not incapacitated or a national of either Contracting Party shall be invited to make the necessary appointments.

(6)   The arbitration tribunal shall reach its decision by a majority of votes, the decision being final and binding on the Contracting Parties. Each Contracting Party shall bear the costs of the member appointed by that Contracting Party as well as the costs for its representation in the arbitration proceedings; the cost of the chairman as well as any other costs shall be borne in equal parts by the two Contracting Parties. The arbitration tribunal may, however, in its decision direct that a higher proportion of costs shall be borne by one of the Contracting Parties. In all other respects, the procedure of the arbitration tribunal shall be determined by the tribunal itself.

Article 10 Application of the Agreement

(1)   This Agreement shall apply to all investments, whether made before or after its entry into force, but shall not apply to any dispute concerning an investment which arose, or any claim concerning an investment which was settled, before its entry into force.

(2)   This Agreement shall in no way restrict the rights and benefits which an investor of one Contracting Party enjoys under national or international law in the territory of the other Contracting Party.

Article 11 Entry into Force, Duration and Termination

(1)   This Agreement shall enter into force upon signature.

or alternatively

(1)   The Contracting Parties shall notify each other when the constitutional requirements for entry into force of this Agreement have been fulfilled. The Agreement shall enter into force on the first day of the second month following the date of receipt of the last notification.

(2)   This Agreement shall remain in force for a period of twenty years. Thereafter it shall remain in force until the expiration of twelve months from the date that either Contracting Party in writing notifies the other Contracting Party of its decision to terminate this Agreement.

(3)   In respect of investments made prior to the date when the notice of termination of this Agreement becomes effective, the provisions of Articles 1 to 10 shall remain in force for a further period of twenty years from that date.

In witness whereof the undersigned, duly authorized to this effect, have signed this Agreement.

Done at _____ on _____ in duplicate in the Swedish, the _____ and the English languages, the three texts being equally authentic. In case of divergence of interpretation the English text shall prevail.

For the Government of the
Kingdom of Sweden

For the Government of

_____

*

SELECTED UNCTAD PUBLICATIONS ON TRANSNATIONAL CORPORATIONS
AND FOREIGN DIRECT INVESTMENT
(For more information, please visit www.unctad.org/en/pub on the web.)

A. Serial publications

World Investment Report Series
http://www.unctad.org/wir

World Investment Report 2001: Promoting Linkages. 356 p. Sales No. E.01.II.D.12 $ 45.

World Investment Report 2001: Promoting Linkages: An Overview. Free of Charge
[1]Available in six UN official languages and also from the web page in electronic format.

Ten Years of World Investment Reports: The Challenges Ahead. Proceedings of an UNCTAD special event on future challenges in the area of FDI.October 2000. UNCTAD/ITE/Misc.45. Free of charge also available from the web page.

World Investment Report 2000: Cross-border Mergers and Acquisitions and Development. 368 p. Sales No. E.00.II.D.20. $45.

World Investment Report 2000: Cross-border Mergers and Acquisitions and Development. An Overview. 75 p. Free-of-charge.

World Investment Report 1999: Foreign Direct Investment and the Challenge of Development. 536 p. Sales No. E.99.II.D.3. $45.

World Investment Report 1999: Foreign Direct Investment and Challenge of Development. An Overview. 75 p. Free-of-charge.

World Investment Report 1998: Trends and Determinants. 430 p. Sales No. E.98.II.D.5. $45.

World Investment Report 1998: Trends and Determinants. An Overview. 67 p. Free-of-charge.

World Investment Report 1997: Transnational Corporations, Market Structure and Competition Policy. 420 p. Sales No. E.97.II.D.10. $45.

World Investment Report 1997: Transnational Corporations, Market Structure and Competition Policy. An Overview. 70 p. Free-of-charge.

World Investment Report 1996: Investment, Trade and International Policy Arrangements. 332 p. Sales No. E.96.II.A.14. $45.

World Investment Report 1996: Investment, Trade and International Policy Arrangements. An Overview. 51 p. Free-of-charge.

---

[1] All overviews are free of charge and are available also in electronic format on the web page of the World Investment Report http://www.unctad.org/wir

World Investment Report 1995: Transnational Corporations and Competitiveness.
491 p. Sales No. E.95.II.A.9. $45.

World Investment Report 1995: Transnational Corporations and Competitiveness. An Overview. 51 p. Free-of-charge..

World Investment Report 1994: Transnational Corporations, Employment and the Workplace. 482 p. Sales No. E.94.II.A.14. $45.

World Investment Report 1994: Transnational Corporations, Employment and the Workplace. An Executive Summary. 34 p.

World Investment Report 1993: Transnational Corporations and Integrated International Production. 290 p. Sales No. E.93.II.A.14. $45.

World Investment Report 1993: Transnational Corporations and Integrated International Production. An Executive Summary. 31 p. ST/CTC/159. Free-of-charge.

World Investment Report 1992: Transnational Corporations as Engines of Growth. 356 p. Sales No. E.92.II.A.19. $45.

World Investment Report 1992: Transnational Corporations as Engines of Growth: An Executive Summary. 30 p. Sales No. E.92.II.A.24.

World Investment Report 1991: The Triad in Foreign Direct Investment. 108 p. Sales No.E.91.II.A.12. $25. Full version at http://www.unctad.org/wir/contents/wir91content.en.htm.

World Investment Directory Series:

World Investment Directory. Vol. VII (Parts I and II): Asia and the Pacific. 646 p. Sales No. E.00.II.D.11.

World Investment Directory. Vol. VI: West Asia. 192 p. Sales No. E.97.II.A.2. $35.

World Investment Directory. Vol. V: Africa. 508 p. Sales No. E.97.II.A.1. $75.

World Investment Directory. Vol. IV: Latin America and the Caribbean. 478 p. Sales No. E.94.II.A.10. $65.

World Investment Directory 1992. Vol. III: Developed Countries. 532 p. Sales No. E.93.II.A.9. $75.

World Investment Directory 1992. Vol. II: Central and Eastern Europe. 432 p. Sales No. E.93.II.A.1. $65. (Joint publication with the United Nations Economic Commission for Europe.)

World Investment Directory 1992. Vol. I: Asia and the Pacific. 356 p. Sales No. E.92.II.A.11. $65.

Investment Policy Review Series:
http://www.unctad.org/en/pub/investpolicy.en.htm

Investment and Innovation Policy Review of Ethiopia. 115 pages.
UNCTAD/ITE/IPC/Misc.4. New York and Geneva 2002

Investment Policy Review of Ecuador. 117 pages. UNCTAD/ITE/IPC/Misc.2. Sales No.
E.01.II D.31 $ 22. New York and Geneva 2001

Investment Policy Review of Mauritius. 84 p. Sales No. E.01.II.D.11. $22. New York and
Geneva 2001

Investment Policy Review of Peru. 108 p. Sales No. E.00.II.D. 7. $22. New York and Geneva
2000 (Also available in Spanish-Tambien disponible en español)

Investment Policy Review of Uganda. 75 p. Sales No. E.99.II.D.24. $15. New York and
Geneva 1999

Investment Policy Review of Egypt. 113 p. Sales No. E.99.II.D.20. $19. New York and Geneva
1999

Investment Policy Review of Uzbekistan. 64 p. UNCTAD/ITE/IIP/Misc. 13. New York and
Geneva

International Investment Instruments: Compendia

International Investment Instruments: A Compendium Vol. VI 568 p. Sales No.
E.01.II.D.34

International Investment Instruments: A Compendium, Vol. IV, 319 p. Sales No.
E.00.II.D.13. $55, **Vol. V**, 505 p. Sales No. E.00.II.D.14. $55.

International Investment Instruments: A Compendium. Vol. I. 371 p. Sales No. E.96.II.A.9;
Vol. II. 577 p. Sales No. E.96.II.A.10; **Vol. III**. 389 p. Sales No. E.96.II.A.11; the 3-volume set,
Sales No. E.96.II.A.12. $125.

Bilateral Investment Treaties 1959-1999 143 p. UNCTAD/ITE/IIA/2, Free-of-charge.
Available only in electronic version from http://www.unctad.org/en/pub/poiteiiad2.en.htm.

Bilateral Investment Treaties in the Mid-1990s, 314 p. Sales No. E.98.II.D.8. $46.

Investment Guides for LDCs Series / UNCTAD - International Chamber of Commerce
http://www.unctad.org/en/pub/investguide.en.htm

An Investment Guide to Mozambique: Opportunities and Conditions.
72.p UNCTAD/ITE/IIA/4. Geneva and New York 2002

An Investment Guide to Uganda: Opportunities and Conditions.
76 p. UNCTAD/ITE/IIT/Misc. 30. New York and Geneva 2001

An Investment Guide to Bangladesh: Opportunities and Conditions.
66 p. UNCTAD/ITE/IIT/Misc.29. New York and Geneva 2001

Guide d'investissement au Mali. 108 p. UNCTAD/ITE/IIT/Misc.24.
http://www.unctad.org/fr/docs/poiteiitm24.fr.pdf. (Joint publication with the International
Chamber of Commerce, in association with PricewaterhouseCoopers.)

An Investment Guide to Ethiopia: Opportunities and Conditions. 69 p.
UNCTAD/ITE/IIT/Misc.19. http://www.unctad.org/en/docs/poiteiitm19.en.pdf. (Joint
publication with the International Chamber of Commerce, in association with Pricewaterhouse
Coopers.)

IIA Issues Paper Series
(http://www.unctad.org/iia.)

Transfer of Technology. p 138 $18. Sales No. E.01.II.D.33

Illicit Payments. p. 108 p. Sales No. E.01.II.D.20 $ 13

Home Country Measures. p.96. Sales No.E.01.II.D.19. $12

Host Country Operational Measures. 109 p. Sales No E.01.II.D.18. $15.

Social Responsibility. 91 p. Sales No. E.01.II.D.4. $15.

Environment. 105 p. Sales No. E.01.II.D.3. $15.

Transfer of Funds. 68 p. Sales No. E.00.II.D.27. $12.

Employment. 69 p. Sales No. E.00.II.D.15. $12.

Taxation. 111 p. Sales No. E.00.II.D.5. $12.

International Investment Agreements: Flexibility for Development. 185 p. Sales No.
E.00.II.D.6. $12.

Taking of Property. 83 p. Sales No. E.00.II.D.4. $12.

Trends in International Investment Agreements: An Overview. 112 p. Sales No.
E.99.II.D.23. $ 12.

Lessons from the MAI. 31 p. Sales No. E.99.II.D.26. $ 12.

National Treatment. 104 p. Sales No. E.99.II.D.16. $12.

Fair and Equitable Treatment. 64 p. Sales No. E.99.II.D.15. $12.

Investment-Related Trade Measures. 64 p. Sales No. E.99.II.D.12. $12.

Most-Favoured-Nation Treatment. 72p. Sales No. E.99.II.D.11. $12.

Admission and Establishment. 72p. Sales No. E.99.II.D.10. $12.

Scope and Definition. 96p. Sales No. E.99.II.D.9. $12.

Transfer Pricing. 72p. Sales No. E.99.II.D.8. $12.

Foreign Direct Investment and Development. 88p. Sales No. E.98.II.D.15. $12.

B. Current Studies

Series A

No. 30. **Incentives and Foreign Direct Investment**. 98 p. Sales No. E.96.II.A.6. $30. [Out of print.]

No. 29. **Foreign Direct Investment, Trade, Aid and Migration**. 100 p. Sales No. E.96.II.A.8. $25. (Joint publication with the International Organization for Migration.)

No. 28. **Foreign Direct Investment in Africa**. 119 p. Sales No. E.95.II.A.6. $20.

No. 27. **Tradability of Banking Services: Impact and Implications**. 195 p. Sales No. E.94.II.A.12. $50.

No. 26. **Explaining and Forecasting Regional Flows of Foreign Direct Investment**. 58 p. Sales No. E.94.II.A.5. $25.

No. 25. **International Tradability in Insurance Services**. 54 p. Sales No. E.93.II.A.11. $20.

No. 24. **Intellectual Property Rights and Foreign Direct Investment**. 108 p. Sales No. .93.II.A.10.$20.

No. 23. **The Transnationalization of Service Industries: An Empirical Analysis of the Determinants of Foreign Direct Investment by Transnational Service Corporations**. 62 p. Sales No. E.93.II.A.3. $15.

No. 22. **Transnational Banks and the External Indebtedness of Developing Countries: Impact of Regulatory Changes**. 48 p. Sales No. E.92.II.A.10. $12.

No. 20. **Foreign Direct Investment, Debt and Home Country Policies**. 50 p. Sales No. E.90.II.A.16. $12.

No. 19. **New Issues in the Uruguay Round of Multilateral Trade Negotiations**. 52 p. Sales No. E.90.II.A.15. $12.50.

No. 18. **Foreign Direct Investment and Industrial Restructuring in Mexico**. 114 p. Sales No. E.92.II.A.9. $12.

No. 17.**Government Policies and Foreign Direct Investment**. 68 p. Sales No. E.91.II.A.20. $12.50.

ASIT Advisory Studies
(Formerly Current Studies, Series B)

No. 17. **The World of Investment Promotion at a Glance: A survey of investment promotion practices.** UNCTAD/ITE/IPC/3. Free of Charge

No. 16. **Tax Incentives and Foreign Direct Investment: A Global Survey.** 180p. Sales No. E.01.II.D.5. $23. Summary available from http://www.unctad.org/asit/resumé.htm

No. 15. **Investment Regimes in the Arab World: Issues and Policies**. 232p. Sales No. E/F.00.II.D.32.

No. 14. **Handbook on Outward Investment Promotion Agencies and Institutions**. 50 p. Sales No. E.99.II.D.22. $ 15.

No. 13. **Survey of Best Practices in Investment Promotion.** 71 p., Sales No. E.97.II.D.11.$ 35.

No. 12. **Comparative Analysis of Petroleum Exploration Contracts.** 80 p. Sales No. E. 96.II.A.7. $35.

No. 11. **Administration of Fiscal Regimes for Petroleum Exploration and Development.** 45 p. Sales No. E. 95.II.A.8.

No. 10. **Formulation and Implementation of Foreign Investment Policies: Selected Key Issues.** 84 p. Sales No. E. 92.II.A.21. $12.

No. 9. **Environmental Accounting: Current Issues, Abstracts and Bibliography.** 86 p. Sales No. E.92.II.A.23.

C. Individual Studies

Compendium of International Arrangements on Transfer of Technology: Selected Instruments. 308 p. Sales No. E.01.II.D.28. $ 45

FDI in Least Developed Countries at a Glance. 150 p. UNCTAD/ITE/IIA/3. Free of charge. Full version available also from http://www.unctad.org/en/pub/poiteiiad3.en.htm.

Foreign Direct Investment in Africa: Performance and Potential. 89 p. UNCTAD/ITE/IIT/Misc. 15. Free of charge. Full version available also from http://www.unctad.org/en/docs/poiteiitm15.pdf.

TNC-SME Linkages for Development: Issues-Experiences-Best Practices. Proceedings of the Special Round Table on TNCs, SMEs and Development, UNCTAD X, 15 February 2000, Bangkok, Thailand. 113 p. UNCTAD/ITE/TEB1. Free-of-charge.

Handbook on Foreign Direct Investment by Small and Medium-sized Enterprises: Lessons from Asia. 200 p. Sales No. E.98.II.D.4. $48.

Handbook on Foreign Direct Investment by Small and Medium-sized Enterprises: Lessons from Asia. Executive Summary and Report of the Kunming Conference. 74 p. Free-of-charge.

Small and Medium-sized Transnational Corporations. Executive Summary and Report of the Osaka Conference. 60 p. Free-of-charge.

Small and Medium-sized Transnational Corporations: Role, Impact and Policy Implications. 242 p. Sales No. E.93.II.A.15. $35.

Measures of the Transnationalization of Economic Activity. 93p. Sales No. E.01.II.D.2. $20.

The Competitiveness Challenge: Transnational Corporations and Industrial Restructuring in Developing Countries. 283p. Sales No. E.00.II.D.35. $42.

Integrating International and Financial Performance at the Enterprise Level. 116 p. Sales No. E.00.II.D.28. $18.

FDI Determinants and TNCs Strategies: The Case of Brazil. 195 p. Sales No. E.00.II.D.2. $35. Summary available from http://www.unctad.org/en/pub/psiteiitd14.en.htm.

The Social Responsibility of Transnational Corporations. 75 p. UNCTAD/ITE/IIT/Misc. 21. Free of charge. Out of stock. Available on http://www.unctad.org/en/docs/poiteiitm21.en.pdf.

Conclusions on Accounting and Reporting by Transnational Corporations. 47 p. Sales No. E.94.II.A.9. $25.

Accounting, Valuation and Privatization. 190 p. Sales No. E.94.II.A.3. $25.

Environmental Management in Transnational Corporations: Report on the Benchmark Corporate Environment Survey. 278 p. Sales No. E.94.II.A.2. $29.95.

Management Consulting: A Survey of the Industry and Its Largest Firms. 100 p. Sales No. E.93.II.A.17. $25.

Transnational Corporations: A Selective Bibliography, 1991-1992. 736 p. Sales No. E.93.II.A.16. $75.

Foreign Investment and Trade Linkages in Developing Countries. 108 p. Sales No. E.93.II.A.12. $18.

Transnational Corporations from Developing Countries: Impact on Their Home Countries.116 p. Sales No. E.93.II.A.8. $15.

Debt-Equity Swaps and Development. 150 p. Sales No. E.93.II.A.7. $35.

From the Common Market to EC 92: Regional Economic Integration in the European Community and Transnational Corporations. 134 p. Sales No. E.93.II.A.2. $25.

The East-West Business Directory 1991/1992. 570 p. Sales No. E.92.II.A.20. $65.
Climate Change and Transnational Corporations: Analysis and Trends.
110 p. Sales No. E.92.II.A.7. $16.50.

Foreign Direct Investment and Transfer of Technology in India.
150 p. Sales No. E.92.II.A.3. $20.

The Determinants of Foreign Direct Investment: A Survey of the Evidence.
84 p. Sales No. E.92.II.A.2. $12.50.

Transnational Corporations and Industrial Hazards Disclosure.
98 p. Sales No. E.91.II.A.18. $17.50.

Transnational Business Information: A Manual of Needs and Sources.
216 p. Sales No. E.91.II.A.13. $45.

The Financial Crisis in Asia and Foreign Direct Investment: An Assessment.
101 p. Sales No. GV.E.98.0.29. $20.

Sharing Asia's Dynamism: Asian Direct Investment in the European Union.
192 p. Sales No. E.97.II.D.1. $26.

Investing in Asia's Dynamism: European Union Direct Investment in Asia.
124 p. ISBN 92-827-7675-1. ECU 14. (Joint publication with the European Commission.)

International Investment towards the Year 2002. 166 p. Sales No. GV.E.98.0.15. $29. (Joint publication with Invest in France Mission and Arthur Andersen, in collaboration with DATAR.)

International Investment towards the Year 2001. 81 p. Sales No. GV.E.97.0.5. $35. (Joint publication with Invest in France Mission and Arthur Andersen, in collaboration with DATAR.)

Liberalizing International Transactions in Services: A Handbook.
182 p. Sales No. E.94.II.A.11. $45. (Joint publication with the World Bank.)

The Impact of Trade-Related Investment Measures on Trade and Development: Theory, Evidence and Policy Implications. 108 p. Sales No. E.91.II.A.19. $17.50. (Joint publication with the United Nations Centre on Transnational Corporations.)

Transnational Corporations and World Development. 656 p. ISBN 0-415-08560-8 (hardback), 0-415-08561-6 (paperback). £65 (hardback), £20.00 (paperback). (Published by International Thomson Business Press on behalf of UNCTAD.)

Companies without Borders: Transnational Corporations in the 1990s. 224 p. ISBN 0-415-12526-X. £47.50. (Published by International Thomson Business Press on behalf of UNCTAD.)

The New Globalism and Developing Countries.

336 p. ISBN 92-808-0944-X. $25. (Published by United Nations University Press.)

World Economic Situation and Prospects 2002. 51 p. Sales No. E.02.II.C.2. $15. (Joint publication with the United Nations Department of Economic and Social Affairs.)

World Economic Situation and Prospects 2001. 51 p. Sales No. E.01.II.C.2. $15. (Joint publication with the United Nations Department of Economic and Social Affairs.)

D. Journals

Transnational Corporations Journal (formerly **The CTC Reporter**).
Published three times a year. Annual subscription price: $45; individual issues $20.
http://www.unctad.org/en/subsites/dite/1_itncs/1_tncs.htm

United Nations publications may be obtained from bookstores and distributors throughout the world. Please consult your bookstore or write to:

For Africa, Asia and Europe to

Sales Section
United Nations Office at Geneva
Palais des Nations
CH-1211 Geneva 10
Switzerland
Tel: (41-22) 917-1234
Fax: (41-22) 917-0123
E-mail: unpubli@unog.ch

For Latin America and U.S.A to:

Sales Section
Room DC2-0853
United Nations Secretariat
New York, NY 10017
U.S.A.
Tel: (1-212) 963-8302 or (800) 253-9646
Fax: (1-212) 963-3489
E-mail: publications@un.org

All prices are quoted in United States dollars.
For further information on the work of the Division on Investment, Technology and Enterprise Development, UNCTAD, please address inquiries to:

United Nations Conference on Trade and Development
Division on Investment, Technology and Enterprise Development
Palais des Nations, Room E-10054
CH-1211 Geneva 10, Switzerland
Telephone: (41-22) 907-5651
Telefax: (41-22) 907-0498

E-mail: natalia.guerra@unctad.org
http://www.unctad.org

QUESTIONNAIRE

International Investment Instruments: A Compendium

Volume IX

In order to improve the quality and relevance of the work of the UNCTAD Division on Investment, Technology and Enterprise Development, it would be useful to receive the views of readers on this publication. It would therefore be greatly appreciated if you could complete the following questionnaire and return it to:

Readership Survey
UNCTAD Division on Investment, Technology and Enterprise Development
United Nations Office in Geneva
Palais des Nations
Room E-9123
CH-1211 Geneva 10
Switzerland
Fax: 41-22-907-0194

1. Name and address of respondent (optional):

_____

_____

2. Which of the following best describes your area of work?

Government	○	Public enterprise	○
Private enterprise	○	Academic or research institution	○
International organization	○	Media	○
Not-for-profit organization	○	Other (specify) _____	

3. In which country do you work? _____

4. What is your assessment of the contents of this publication?

Excellent	○	Adequate	○
Good	○	Poor	○

5. How useful is this publication to your work?

Very useful ○   Of some use ○   Irrelevant ○

6. Please indicate the three things you liked best about this publication:

_____
_____
_____

7. Please indicate the three things you liked least about this publication:

_____
_____
_____

8. Are you a regular recipient of *Transnational Corporations* (formerly *The CTC Reporter*), UNCTAD-DITE's tri-annual refereed journal?

Yes   ○   No   ○

If not, please check here if you would like to receive
a sample copy sent to the name and address you have
given above   ○

*